Hallmark Keepsake Ornament Value Guide

Nicki Pierce, Editor

Bangzoom Publishers
(A Division of Bangzoom Software, Inc.)
14 Storrs Avenue
Braintree, MA 02184
www.bangzoom.com

This publication is not affiliated with Hallmark Cards, Inc. or any of its affili-ates, subsidiaries, distributors, or representatives. Product names and designs are the property of Hallmark Cards, Inc. Any opinions expressed are solely those of the authors and do not necessarily reflect those of Hallmark Cards, Inc.

MANAGING EDITOR
Nicki Pierce

SPECIAL THANKS TO CONTRIBUTORS
Jane Bigham
Nancy Copeland
Rhonda Cline
David Hamrick
Tim Kline
Sara Motsinger
Frank Williams

Jim Kelley – Publisher
Leatrice Sherry – Design Director
Sharen Forsyth – Operations Manager
Chuck Barnard – Sales and Service Manager

ISBN 0-9772927-9-7 Copyright ©2006 by Bangzoom Publishers, a division of Bangzoom Software, Inc. All rights reserved. No part of this book may be repro-duced or transmitted in any form or by any means, electronic or mechanical, includ-ing photocopying, recording, or by any information storage or retrieval system, without the written permission of the publisher.

Library of Congress Control Number: 2006927072

Printed in the United States of America

10 9 8 7 6 5 4 3 2

TABLE OF CONTENTS

Editorials

Ornaments

Other Collectibles

Indexes

Welcome to the 2nd Edition
by Nicki Pierce, Editor

Our thanks to the many collectors that showed enthusiastic support for our first edition of the Hallmark Keepsake Ornament Value Guide making it such a resounding success. With excitement, we present to you the 2nd Edition, and we hope you will be delighted with the improvements we have made.

WHAT'S NEW?

We listened to your feedback and made some changes. You've already noticed the larger size, which allowed us to increase the size of each image and to include more information. The #1 collector request was to add Merry Miniatures, which we have done, as well as Kiddie Car Classics and Legends in Flight. Many asked for artist information, and you will find that the artist abbreviations for each item (if known) are now included within the image. We found and corrected some errors and added some hard-to-find ornaments that have not been documented in any past value guide. The number of collectibles listed has increased from 6,375 last year to over 7,700 – each pictured and priced. We have done all of this, and we have not increased the retail price of our guide!

HOW DID WE GET OUR PRICES?

Collectors always raise questions about how the prices listed in any collectible value guide are determined. We are aware that there is never a single price that all collectors will agree upon. Many feel the prices are too high and others feel certain they are too low. Bangzoom does not arbitrarily decide how to price an item: we gather this information from collectors, from auction and internet web sites, and from other published pricing sources. Values are driven by two main variables: supply and demand. When demand is high and supply is low, prices go up. When demand is low and supply is high, prices go down. Currently, the overall supply of most collectibles in the marketplace, including Hallmark, is greater than the demand, hence lower values than in Hallmark guides published several years ago. One fact is true: an item is worth what someone is willing to pay for it. That amount can vary from week to week, month to month, and year to year. Some ornaments grow in popularity while others may diminish. It is not an easy process to assign values to so many items and expect they will be accurate all of the time. We must thank all of our expert contributors for their great effort in helping us set the prices in this value guide.

WHAT ELSE AFFECTS MARKET VALUE?

Other determinents influence market value. Condition certainly is an important consideration. An ornament in perfect condition, in a mint condition box, will command the highest price. The values listed in this guide are reflective of ornaments in that condition. The box condition of some of the higher value ornaments can determine up to half of the overall value. We are not suggesting that Hallmark ornament collectors become "perfect box" collectors, as love of the ornaments themselves is what creates their true value. However, just as rare books without their dust jackets are only worth a fraction of a collectible book's value with a jacket, so too are boxes in fine condition necessary in getting the highest price for an ornament.

Rare ornaments have a high value on the secondary market. We have limited the inclusion of the word "rare" in this publication to items that truly are extremely hard to find.

Limited production ornaments may also command a high secondary market value. Special color "Colorway" ornaments, for example, are produced in much smaller quantities than the regular production pieces and can increase rapidly in value in the secondary market.

The growing popularity of some ornaments also will allow the prices to climb. Mary's Angels, Puppy Love, and Mischievous Kittens series pieces, to name a few, are in high demand and have values that are on the rise.

WHAT DOES THE OVERALL MARKET LOOK LIKE?

The collectibles market overall has been hit very hard in recent years. The slowing of the economy, unemployment, military action overseas, and uncertainty on the part of consumers means fewer dollars are being spent on items that are not necessities. The number of individuals selling their collections has also increased. While making the market for collectibles more global, eBay has also increased the number of sellers who can reach buyers. Buyers are getting more conservative and more patient with the increased supply of old and rare items showing up in the secondary market. It is a great time to buy, but not necessarily a great time to sell.

SUMMING IT UP

The market is slowly improving. Bangzoom feels that the values shown in this guide are an accurate reflection of current market values and encourages you to insure your collections at these prices. We will continue to monitor values for any changes. Values should never drive a collector; rather, the love of the item collected should be the deciding factor in any purchase. This guide is a great tool to research, reference, and track what we all love…

…Hallmark Keepsake Ornaments!

How To Use This Book

We list values in this guide for items in MIB (mint in box) condition. We observe prices at auctions, the Internet, retail stores, and "buy-sell" sections in collector magazines. We list all prices gathered, then arrive at a consensus. When a sound average price could not be established, the value is designated as N/E. The word "gift" or "prize" is used to signify an ornament that was not sold by Hallmark, but rather was a club member or other type of gift or a special event prize. N/A is used to signify that there is no official style number.

All series ornaments are listed by series name and number. In cases where the ornament also has its own name, that name has been added after the series name. For instance, "A Cool Yule" is listed as "Frosty Friends 1: A Cool Yule." The series name and the word "Complement" have been added to the title of ornaments that complement a series so that the item will follow the series item.

Collection names have been put before the ornament's name so when listed alphabetically, all collection items are together. The only time the full collection name isn't used is on the "Twas the Night Before the Night Before Christmas" which is abbreviated as "Twas the Night Before..."

Colorway, Club/Event, and Series items, in this order, have been color-coded for easy reference. For example, if an item is both a Colorway and an Event piece, it has been given the Colorway color.

We urge the reader to remember that this is a guide, and the actual selling price will always depend on a number of factors, including the motivation of the buyer and seller, the location, and the economic climate. It is impossible to arrive at one definitive price. This is why we call this book a *guide*.

Series color-code — 4327. — Colorway color-code

Series name and number —
Artist abbreviation —
Mary's Angels 15: Willow
CHAD/HAMI • 795QX8013 • $22

Mary's Angels 15: Willow
CHAD/HAMI • PrizeQX8013C • $95
Edition Size -- approximately 5000.

Item name —
Value —

Retail price and item number — Notes

Artist Abbreviations

ANDR . . . . . . .Patricia Andrews	GENT . . . . .Rodney Gentry	OREA . . . . .Terry O'Reagan
AUBE . . . . .Nina Aubé	GERG . . . . .Julie Parmer George	PALM . . . . .Don Palmiter
BAST . . . . .Marjolein Bastin	GIUN . . . . .Guy Giunta	PAON . . . . .Sam Paonessa
BAUR . . . . .Tim Bauer	GOSL . . . . .Steve Goslin	PATT . . . . .Joyce Pattee
BEST . . . . .Tom Best	GRIL . . . . .Beth Grillo-Kanally	PIKE . . . . .Sharon Pike
BISH . . . . .Ron Bishop	HAAS . . . . .Robert Haas	PYDA . . . . .Michele Pyda-Sevcik
BLAC . . . . . .Thomas Blackshear	HADD . . . . .Tammy Haddix	RDON . . . . . .Ruth Donikowski
BRIC . . . . .Katrina Bricker	HAMI . . . . .Mary Hamilton	RGRS . . . . . .Anita Marra Rogers
BRWN . . . . .Andrew Brownsword	HURL . . . . .Robert Hurlbert	RHOD . . . . .Dill Rhodus
CHAD . . . . .Robert Chad	JDER . . . . . .Jusepe De Ribera	RIBE . . . . .Jusepe de Ribera
CROW . . . . .Ken Crow	JHOW . . . . .Jim Howard	SCHU . . . . .Lee Schuler
DIRH . . . . .Mike Dirham	JLEE . . . . .Julia Lee	SEAL . . . . .Ed Seale
DLEE . . . . .Donna Lee	JOGO . . . . .Joni Johnson-Godsy	SFRE . . . . .Scott Freeman
DUTK . . . . .Peter Dutkin	JOHN . . . . .Cathy Johnson	SICK . . . . .Linda Sickman
EDIS . . . . .Eric Disney	KEGR . . . . .Edythe Kegrize	SIED . . . . .Bob Siedler
ESCH . . . . . . .Joanne Eschrich	KELL . . . . .Becky Kelly	STGR . . . . .Terri Steiger
FACC . . . . .Char Faccilongo	KLIN . . . . .Kristina Kline	TAGU . . . . .Sue Tague
FALT . . . . .Mary Lou Faltico	LAPR . . . . .Rich LaPierre	UNKN . . . . .UNKNOWN
FEUR . . . . .Lane Feuer	LARS . . . . .Tracy Larsen	UNRU . . . . .Duane Unruh
FORS . . . . .Julie Forsyth	LYLE . . . . .Joyce Lyle	VARI . . . . .VARIOUS
FRAL . . . . .Tobin Fraley	MAHO . . . . .Jim Mahon	VISK . . . . .Sharon Visker
FRAN . . ."John ""Collin"" Francis"	MCGE . . . . . . .Diana McGehee	VOTR . . . . .LaDene Votruba
FREE . . . . .Scott Freeman	MMOL . . . . . . .Martha Moldaver	WAGN . . . . .John Wagner
FUNV . . . . . . .Fayrol Unverferth	MURR . . . . .Deb Murray	WEBB . . . . .Chris Webb
GARC . . . . .Rudy Garcia	NORT . . . . .Lynn Norton	WILL . . . . .Nello Williams

Hallmark Collecting 101
The Language of Hallmark Collectors
by Rhonda Cline

In the Beginning

It began simply when the first Keepsake Ornaments were produced in 1973. Over the years Hallmark collecting has grown, evolved, and without even realizing it, Hallmark collectors have developed a language all their own, full of terms and acronyms. Let's try to pin-it-all down with this Hallmark Collecting 101 lesson in understanding the language of Hallmark collectors.

Buying Ornaments

Hallmark ornaments are unveiled each year in July and are available for purchase at your local Hallmark stores through December. For some reason or another, you will eventually come across an item that you desire but are unable to purchase locally. Perhaps, it came out earlier than you expected; maybe it was only available to club members; or it was just an item that you forgot. If you can't find the item at your local Hallmark store – where do you go? Welcome to the fun and exciting world of the secondary market.

The Secondary Market

This is the source for buying and selling collectibles according to basic supply-and-demand principles. Popular pieces which have been retired can appreciate in value far above the original prices. Secondary market dealers sell past year's Hallmark collectibles at collectible shows, Hallmark Club Events, and in antique mall showcases. However, most of today's secondary market buying and selling occurs via the internet. Every internet search engine will direct you to web sites that offer large selections, on line auctions, and collector bulletin boards, all of which are very active in the Hallmark secondary market.

Box Condition

Box condition is a very important pricing factor. Unfortunately, box condition, like beauty, is in the eye of the beholder. Everyone's concept of "Mint in Box" will be similar, but never exactly the same. Often, extreme age is taken into consideration, allowing ornaments from the 1970s and 80s that have very slight box damage to be considered Mint in Box. If you are a collector who expects perfection in the box – let the dealer know. This will help you get what you expect.

All values in this guide are based on a mint ornament in a mint box. Box condition will affect the secondary market value of your collection. The degree of damage to the box will decrease the value incrementally. In general, an ornament with no box loses approximately 30-50% of it's value.

The following are the primary box conditions and their abbreviations. Note that in all instances the ornament is expected to be in mint condition:

- **Mint in Box** – (box is in undamaged condition) – MIB, MINB, MIMB, NRFB, NIB
- **Box, No Tag** – (box is undamaged, but missing price tag) – BNT
- **Slightly Damaged Box** – (slightly or very slightly damaged box) SDB, VSDB
- **Damaged Box** – DB
- **No Box** – NB

Series and Collections

Each year collectors look forward to the release of the *Dream Book*, the annual catalog unveiling the ornaments to be available for that year. The most popular aspects of Hallmark Keepsake Ornaments are the series and collections. Collectors are always excited to see the unveiling of the new series each year as well as discovering what new editions are being added and what series are ending.

Series ornaments are ornaments that are released as part of an official Hallmark series. Each year of the series, there is one edition piece released. These series edition ornaments are often marked on the bottom of the ornament with their edition number. Christmas series ornaments are identified by the edition number inside a Christmas tree, and Easter/Spring series use an Easter egg. Since 2002, the series ornaments are also specially packaged in blue boxes. Series complements are pieces that are meant to be displayed with the series, but are not edition pieces. They are as their name implies: complements to the series. Like the series edition pieces, series complements are packaged in blue boxes as well. In this guide series ornaments are tabbed in blue. Hallmark has stated that an official series will always last at least three years; beyond that, there is no way of predicting how long a series may last.

There are also a number of "unofficial" series or collections. These are groups of ornaments that are not officially recognized as a series by Hallmark, and the ornaments are not marked or packaged as series ornaments. However, each year a new ornament has been added to the line-up during the life of the "series." Some examples of "unofficial" series are Star Trek, Wizard of Oz, Feliz Navidad and Hershey's Chocolate.

Collections are different because they are not limited to one piece per year. Yearly collections such as Looney Tunes and Disney are popular with a wide range of collectors. There are also collections that focus on particular artistic styles such as Marjolein Bastin's Nature's Sketchbook, and Folk Art Americana. More recently the Frostlight Faeries have become a very popular collection.

*Merry Mayhem workshop
2005 Club Convention piece.*

More Ornament Types

• **Club Ornaments** – Each year Hallmark Keepsake Ornament Collector Club (KOCC) members receive club edition ornaments with their membership, as well as the opportunity to purchase special club edition ornaments. In this guide, club ornament pictures are tabbed in gold (see page 2).

• **Colorways** – Specially painted ornaments produced in much smaller numbers than regular issue pieces. Colorways are often awarded to club members or used as door prizes at Hallmark special events. As the popularity of Colorways has increased, Hallmark has expanded its frequency of offering them. The rarest by far are the prizes from national club events. Gold seals were added to the Colorway ornament boxes in 1999 to make them more identifiable from the regular issue ornaments. Colorway ornament pictures are tabbed in pink (see page 2).

• **Crown Reflections** – Blown glass ornaments offered from 1998 - 2001. Li'l Blown Glass were smaller versions issued in 1999.

• **Event Exclusives** – Ornaments available only during a specific Hallmark event. These ornaments may be available for purchase, awarded as prizes, or given as a participation gift. Most event items are highly sought after and higher in secondary market value because the production numbers are much lower than the regular Keepsake line of ornaments. These are also referred to as Expo or Artist on Tour (AOT) exclusives, as the different events have had different names over the years.

• **Laser Gallery** – Delicate ornaments made with archival paper, cut by a tiny, precise laser beam. The patterns were assembled by hand and most come equipped with light clips to allow the tree lights to showcase the intricate designs. Offered in 1999 and 2000.

• **Magic Ornaments** – Ornaments featuring light, sound, music and/or motion. Vastly popular with Hallmark collectors.

• **Personalized Ornaments** – Offered between 1993 and 1995, Hallmark Personalized ornaments allowed collectors to convey a personal message to someone they loved. Collectors could select an ornament and write their message on a form. The Hallmark Gold Crown store would then order the ornament directly from Hallmark imprinted with the personal message.

*Mary's Angels – Angelica
Repaint of Mary's Angels 1
2006 Ornament Premiere piece.*

• **Premier Ornaments** – As the name indicates, ornaments that are intended to be sold only during the July Hallmark Ornament Premier Weekend.

• **Reach Program** – Ran from 1989 to 2002 and consisted of several pieces that could be purchased for a special price, often with a minimum store purchase. The individual pieces made up a themed set, such as the 1989 Christmas Carrousel, 1992 Santa and His Reindeer, 2000 Snoopy Christmas, and 2002 Snow Cub Club.

• **Showcase Ornaments** – Offered from 1993 to 1996 and were a separate collection within the Keepsake line. Available only in Gold Crown Stores, these creative ornaments were distinct for their unique designs and materials.

• **Trimmers** – Holiday tree decorations and package trimmers were offered in the 1980s. They were sold without boxes and are not part of the Keepsake Ornament Collection.

• **Collector Cards** – Hallmark first included collector cards (similar to baseball cards) inside a few sports ornaments in 1995. Since 2002, the cards have been included in all ornament boxes.

Whew... we may have missed a few phrases from the Language of Hallmark (will have to catch them the next time around), but we hope this Hallmark 101 lesson will help you navigate and enjoy the Wonderful World of Hallmark Collecting!

The Ornaments That Never Were...
By Tim Kline

Each year Hallmark presents a completely new and fresh line of ornaments for faithful collectors to decorate their trees and homes. What you may not realize is that there are far more ornament ideas that never make it past the team of artists and others involved in the creative decision making process at Hallmark. Once in a while, an ornament passes beyond the concept stage to prototyping before it is cancelled. In a few cases, even packaging is developed, and limited quantities are produced before that fateful decision is made to drop the ornament. These ornaments and their associated stories add another dimension to collecting.

Although the reasons vary, most ornament cancellations are a result of production or breakage problems, a finished product that does not look quite like it was anticipated, or the combination of cost, anticipated demand, and retail price are no longer viable. In a few cases, licensing agreements were never finalized.

Production problems threading the ribbon through the doves beak may have lead to the cancellation of this 1982 ornament. A redesign was used for 1993 Baby's Christening ornament.

In an unusual case, the 1995 Jukebox Party L&M ornament was pulled after the *Dream Book* was laid out and at the printer because of a problem with licensing the music it played. Several prototypes were produced, including the one used for the catalog photo, but the caption "Not Available" was added to the booklet at the last minute. Thankfully for collectors, the problem was worked out and the popular ornament was produced in the 1996 line. In several other cases, collectors were not quite so lucky. In the late 1990s, an ornament depicting John Wayne with his rifle never made it beyond the prototype stage because the final sculpture was not approved by the licensor. In 1992 a Mary Engelbreit Santa Tin design complementing the 1991 Jolly Wolly tins was not licensed successfully in time for production. In this instance, rumor has it that the tin sheet metal had already been printed for manufac-

turing and was simply turned over and reprinted with the 1992 Stocked With Joy ornament on the other side. Supposedly, if you pry apart one of the finished ornaments you can find the Engelbreit Santa design printed on the inside.

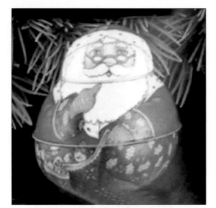

*1992 Mary Engelbreit Santa Tin 775QX5224
Estimate: 2 dozen produced.*

A cancelled ornament familiar to collectors is the 1990 Country Angel. Samples were sent to each local retailer for their store display, but no others were ever distributed. A lucky few of the most observant collectors managed to talk retailers out of their display piece, while everyone else had to search and wait for one to show up on the secondary market. Although scarce, several thousand were produced, satisfying the demand of the more serious collectors.

In a few instances, only several hundred pieces of a new ornament were produced before being dropped. Perhaps, these were given out to sales reps as samples to encourage orders, as with the homely 1986 Marionette Angel, or they were sold or given away to Hallmark employees, as with the 1980 Dove and Christmas Kitten. In this case, collectors have found the clear acetate sheets on which the ornament design was printed, the die-cut and formed shell for the Dove ornament without its white plastic-poured backing, and a few hundred completed ornaments. So the story goes that when these ornaments were cancelled, the packaging that was designed for the Doves and Kittens was ordered destroyed by warehouse employees, and the limited number of complete ornaments was to be offered in Hallmark's by-the-pound sales along with other seconds or returns. Only a handful of each managed to escape with boxes intact.

Occasionally, Hallmark will test a new product in select stores. That was the case with the 1975 Cardinal Bell, priced at $20 (when the next highest priced ornament was $5 for a set of 4 glass balls). It was never introduced to the line, and only a few were distributed. Another test which collectors are more familiar with was the 1995 NFL Sports Helmets. They were offered in markets where the 10 selected NFL teams played as part of a larger test of party ware. Collectors scoured the country, networking to complete their set. From the many sports theme ornament lines that followed, everyone can tell that the test was successful.

1979 Holiday Flight 500QX1427
Not mfg. Estimate: less than 10 produced.

Usually, an ornament is cancelled before appearing in the *Dream Book*, but sometimes not before appearing in the retailer order catalogues. The most serious collectors, who are the true ornament detectives, are thankful that these tracks have been left behind for them to search out as the starting points for a treasure hunt. Several examples include the 1979 Holiday Flight, 1983 Cloisonné Christmas Tree: Our First Christmas, and the 1989 Kringle's Karnival L&M. In the case of Kringle's Karnival, the ornament was cancelled because of difficulties in getting it to run smoothly, and only a couple of working models are known to exist at this time. Although it was pictured in the retail catalogue, no item number or price seem to have been assigned.

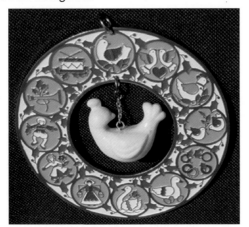

1984 12 Days of Christmas
No item# or price ever published.
Not mfg. Estimate: less than 10 produced.

Generally, the earlier in the manufacturing process that an ornament is cancelled, the fewer pieces there will be available. If a product number and price were not published, that is a good sign that there may not be many pieces. In some cases, only a few samples are known to exist, while for others there may be just a dozen or two. When collectors become aware of one of these never-issued

designs, the ornament can assume mythical proportions. For example, a 12 Days of Christmas ornament that was designed in 1984 was rumored to exist for decades among the ornament sleuths before several finally became available to collectors.

If you count yourself among the ornament detectives and remain alert, you just may be lucky enough to find one of these treasures for your own collection. Meanwhile, enjoy the short list compiled here as a starting point for your own treasure hunt. Happy Hunting!

DID YOU KNOW...

The slender design of the 1993 Toy Soldier Mayor's Ornament was the reason it was chosen because the 1992 Mayor's Christmas tree had begun to decompose before it was processed into ornaments. Very little usable wood allowed only a small number of soldiers to be produced from it, thus making it very rare.

The unsuccessful member-get-a-member promotion of the 1993 Caricature Ball (under 5,000 orders) has made it a rare sought-after ornament today.

The earliest production of the 1991 Classic American Car: Corvette was issued with a gold/brown tree. While some collectors believe the Corvette with a gold tree is more valuable, others prefer the green tree version.

Her name?...the 1993 Mary's Angel: Ivy is often called Joy, a result of the font used for the lettering on the box, making the name "Ivy" look more like "Joy."

The 2000 and 2001 Canadian Postal Exclusives were actually colorway versions of "mail"-related past issue Hallmark ornaments.

The first edition 1998 Candlelight Services Stone Church was the first regular Keepsake series ornament to be a Hallmark Gold Crown Store exclusive.

The easiest place to locate the highly sought after 1993 first edition Holiday Barbie in the fall of that year was at an Osco Drug or Walgreens Drug Store.

Many collectors consider the 1987 Bright Christmas Dreams and the 1988 Teacher ornaments to be pre-first editions of the Crayola series.

The 1995 Kansas City Joe Montana was available in dramatically larger numbers in the greater Kansas City metropolitan area.

Two of the most requested, but never produced, ornaments are the 1988 Baby's 1st Teddy Bear Years and a 1995 NFL Green Bay Packers helmet.

COLLECTING HALLMARK WITH PASSION

Hallmark collecting is a hobby enjoyed by thousands. It's always fun to hear stories of why a collector began collecting and all the sentiment each collection holds. But for some enthusiasts, Hallmark collecting is more than a casual hobby, their collections are huge and the pursuit of this hobby has changed their lives. Enjoy "meeting" the avid collectors profiled below. They certainly collect Hallmark with passion.

"THE LEE & DEAN MUSEUM"
by Nancy Copeland

For many collectors, decorating their homes with Hallmark collectibles is a seasonal treat. For Lee Schooler and Dean Oehlert, their passion for decorating with, and displaying their vast Hallmark collection, has nearly turned their Kansas City home into a year-round museum full of Hallmark treasures. Yes, they still live there, but this home is like no other, with more Hallmark items on display than anywhere else in the world.

Lee Schooler and Dean Oehlert

Lee's Hallmark collection was started in the late 1980s. The displays began to really grow in 1995 when a family member became homebound. As the displays grew, so did the number of visitors that stopped by to look and chat, making long homebound days more enjoyable. Boy Scouts, Girl Scouts, Hallmark collectors, friends and family have all visited this home, now affectionately called, "The Lee & Dean Museum." Guests are able to get ideas of what to collect and how to display their collections. They hear Lee's philosophy: "collect only what you like and display your treasures so that you can enjoy having them." From all across the U.S. and Canada, collectors have left their comments in the guest book, taken pictures, and returned home with many memories of this amazing collectible collection.

At first, Lee focused on collecting the top quality Hallmark items like Little Gallery, Victorian Memories, Majestic Wilderness, and Kiddie Car Classics. As the collection grew, it increased to "anything with Hallmark's name on it." If it's made by Hallmark, Lee wants it, collects it, displays it, and enjoys it!

Her passion for Hallmark took a new direction when Dean Oehlert, her high school sweetheart, joined her in her pursuit of new additions to the museum. The "hunt" is always part of the fun of collecting, so Lee and Dean enjoy their time together looking for new treasures and interesting things to enhance their displays. Picture frames, bookcases, Christmas trees, wreaths and banners they've found are all decorated with Hallmark items.

A friend made this display for the Clothespin Soldier ornaments allowing each design and size of the Soldiers to be displayed together.

As guests look around the museum, they see displays EVERYWERE, regardless of the season. A pair of end tables with glass sides are used to house all the mini sets of six mice ornaments that Ed Seale created in the early 1990s. They have added other props to round out the scene – a doily covers the "floor," and a small teapot fits in nicely with the Tiny Tea Party, while more items adorn the other sets to add to each scene. Small mirrors display groupings of mini ornaments. There are shelves and hanging displays on the walls of each room and door, upstairs and downstairs. Hallmark is virtually everywhere.

This 1973 Easter lapel pin store display, complete with rare 1973 pins is a favorite.

7

Their collection does not end with ornaments and lapel pins. It spans over 100 different categories of Hallmark collectibles, including: plush animals, Road Rovers, Merry Miniatures, candles, dolls, mugs, Megan and Friends figurines by Heartline, tins, puzzles, banks and stocking hangers. If you're interested in key rings, jewelry, magnets or buttons, Lee can open boxes to show you many different designs. Party favors, old and new greeting cards, package trimmers, matches, soap, cookie cutters, music boxes, mood lights, tree toppers, pencil sharpeners, sterling silver ornaments, salt and pepper shakers, stickers, plaques, wood cutouts, pop-ups, and table decorations fill their home. Hallmark books, postcards, date books, cookie jars, trays, vases, frames, sun catchers, building blocks, pincushions, candy molds, stampers, fabric, pewter plates and figurines, snow globes, windsocks, napkin rings, cookbooks, Betsey Clark, Maxine, Ice Bugs, Snortles, pencils, votives, Rondelles collector's places…the list keeps growing!

You will also find Hallmark paper goods lines. On display are 30 to 40-year-old table covers, placemats, coasters, playing cards, plates, cups, napkins, invitations, and wrapping paper. There are even fashionable paper dresses and party aprons which fit the style needs of the 1960s. And what party would have been complete without plates and a matching figurine to put on your cake (and napkins, cups and invitations too)?

The "Lee and Dean Museum" is proof that Hallmark products are meant to be enjoyed year round. It is a testimony to their belief: "Collect only what you like because you like it, and not for its monetary value. The true worth of a collection comes from the enjoyment you derive from it." To them, their collection is PRICELESS!

Editors Note: The "Lee and Dean Museum" is a private Collection which we believe to be the largest in the world. It is not connected to Hallmark Cards, Inc.

Do you remember that?…the early sell-out of the 1992 Club Edition Christmas Treasures caused a reaction similar to the 2005 club exclusive sell-outs.

Can you believe it?…many dealers in January of 1998 regarded the 1997 Lone Ranger Lunch Box and the 1997 Stock Car Champion Jeff Gordon as the top ornaments of that year.

It's true…the 1979 First Edition Bellswinger was initially a flop, and was picked up at sidewalk sales at a dollar apiece.

Can you believe?…the 1982 first edition of the 12 days of Christmas Acrylics was actually only the third best first edition as values rose that following spring.

Did you know that he's outnumbered?… there were half as many 1975 Raggedy Andy Adorables ornaments produced as the 1975 Raggedy Anns.

Surprise… no one knew at the 1998 convention that for just participating in the talent show each would receive the black colorway version of the 1998 A Pony for Christmas.

It's true…the distributed numbers of the 2001 AOT colorway prizes were reduced due to canceled convention events post September 11, 2001.

Can you believe?…the 1996 NFL Green Bay Packer ornament quickly reached values of $75 when the Packers won the following year's Super Bowl.

OOPS…the 1985 Mouse in a Wagon ornament differs from the picture on its box.

Frank's Journey into Hallmark "Illuminations": How One Collector Evolved
by Katha Decker

The Williamses were innocent enough. They had happily discovered that their newborn remained quiet for prolonged periods, if they took him for a drive. But, did they realize Frank was probably checking out all the lights overhead? Frank confesses lights were most likely a comfort to an only child, and his interest in anything lighted expanded, first to holiday items, and then, most certainly, to Christmas lights. For those with knowledge of National Lampoon's Christmas Vacation, Frank was a Clark Griswold-in-training.

Frank Williams

As a teenager, he became the designated tree decorator. Furthermore, his large, extended family afforded him opportunities to practice considerably; plus, he kept many aunts and uncles from fighting over tree light malfunctions. After-season sales found Frank at garden shops buying all red or all blue light sets. Frank even traveled with extra light sets in the trunk of his car. If he spent untold hours lighting a friend or family's tree from the bottom, only to be suddenly hundreds of lights short, he need only go to his car for more. Who could refuse a little extra investment in a now, two-thirds, stunningly-lit tree?

The first Hallmark ornaments entered the Williams' household in the late 70s, but in the fall of 1981, Frank decided to try to acquire one of every figural ornament produced that year starting with Sailing Santa. By the next holiday season, he had met Meredith DeGood of The Baggage Car and made his first trade with her for a 1979 Here Comes Santa. Their friendship grew, and Frank began attending college just an hour from The DeGoods' Hallmark secondary market store. College weekends might find Frank and friends in drug and/or office store attics, and subsequently, he would share finds to expand The Baggage Car's inventory. One particularly lucrative discovery found him writing

a large check, which Frank's father was phoned to please cover. More importantly, Frank needed to return and buy the rest of the treasures the next day, and for his dad to cover a second, much larger check! College dorm mates helped guard the boxes and boxes until Frank could get them home and to Meredith. By 1988, Frank had his figural collection needs narrowed down to eleven. Meredith called and said to bring down his many extra 1986 Dashers, as she had many people on a waiting list, and was ripe for trading. The Raggedy Andy Adorable from 1975 was Frank's final missing figural supplied by Meredith.

Frank in his 9' Sailing Santa Costume at the 1991 Keepsake Collectors first National Convention with 1991 Hallmark Keepsake Collectors Club president, Rachel Perkal.

Collecting and predicting became fun to share with others. In 1991, even a summer vacation spent with Frank's school board president and her family turned very Hallmark. From Iowa to Williamsburg, Virginia, and back, at Frank's suggestion, they bought every Corvette, Starship Enterprise, and Tiny Tea Party they could. It proved to be a wise choice; their seeking was particularly bountiful, and many boxes had to be shipped back to the Midwest from the Coast. That fall, his experience at Hallmark's first national convention was enriched as artist Linda Sickman sat at Frank's table and became a treasured ornament friend. Later that evening, she even helped him maneuver in his 9 foot costume of 1981's Sailing Santa.

Frank's love of driving has allowed him the pleasure of traveling to countless events across the country. Often accompanied by friend and co-worker,

Andrea Doubet, who also caught the Hallmark fever and became one of the select few who have one of every ornament. If they look tired on a Monday morning at school, it could be they've just driven over 1,500 miles on the two-day weekend! An elementary school teacher by day, Frank's tether stretches even further in the summer; thus, if not teaching, playing/coaching tennis, or being involved in political campaigns, Frank most likely has a route chosen to dig up an ornament treasure trove or three. While Hallmark collecting and the business of collecting changes, Frank's current interest is much the same as that in his childhood. His investment in a downtown loft has a primary consideration: choosing the perfect ornament-friendly tree to maximize a space allowing for a 14 foot spruce, and, oh yes, outlets sufficient to power 10,000 lights.

"Santa Frank" and Hallmark Artist,
Linda Sickman enjoyed every moment
of the 1991 Convention.

Frank would love to read your Hallmark histories or to help you augment your collection. He can be reached at an appropriate email address, MoreLights@aol.com.

Yarn ornaments…often show slight variations in both color and design. Rumor has it that they were manufactured in different locations and that substittions of yarn were sometimes made.

The 1979 #1 Here Comes Santa…was issued as Santa's Motor Car. It was not planned to be the first of a series. The 1980 #2 Santa's Express is printed 2nd in a Series of Santa's Travels.

1984 was magical…because that was the year Hallmark introduced the first LIGHTED ornaments.

When Artist Linda Sickman…designed the 1994 Train Engine for the Yuletide Central series, she used parts of the Tin Locomotive Trains in her design. If you look closely, you can match up the parts.

Why Not Collect Them ALL?
by Jane Bigham

If you are reading this article, we can assume that you are a Hallmark Keepsake Ornament collector. You eagerly anticipate the arrival of your *Dream Book* every year so that you can sit down and mark all the ornaments you HAVE to purchase. You begin by marking all of the ongoing series that you collect; next, you move on to the tedious task of selecting which new series you can't live without; and, finally, you study the ornaments to select the ones that have special meaning to your family and friends. Some of us are tempted more than others, but there are a few collectors that do not choose to limit the number of ornaments they purchase every year because they are collecting the ENTIRE Hallmark Keepsake collection.

Snoopy® and Friends 1: Ice-Hockey Holiday

Ann Jones in Tennessee was the first person to complete this task. Her collecting began when she purchased the 1979 first edition in the Snoopy and Friends series, "Ice-Hockey Holiday." When she noticed the detail of the design and the whimsy of the characters, she was addicted. In 1983 Ann got serious about trying to collect one of every ornament with the publication of Clara Scroggins' first collectors guide. This helped her organize her collection by enabling her to mark off the ornaments as she purchased them.

Ann and a friend started collecting together by attending secondary market shows and scouring Hallmark trade magazines. Ann was soon traveling coast to coast. She always believed that Kansas City was a treasure trove of unusual Hallmark collectibles, so one of her favorite events was a 1987 secondary market show in Kansas City. Activities were planned for the entire weekend including guest speakers from Hallmark and a tour of the Hallmark plant in Leavenworth, Kansas. At this event, Ann met Clara Scroggins, Hal and Meredith DeGood, George and Jo Wallings, and Bob Wilkes, all of whom would become her lifelong friends. They would look forward to reuniting at Hallmark events each year, coming together to share stories and discuss their recent Hallmark finds. Ann recalls the fun they all had at the 25th Anniversary Event in Kansas City when she participated in the ornament look-alike competition dressed as the Country Angel.

Ann's favorite series include the older Here Comes Santa's, Frosty Friends, and Snoopy ornaments; although she would have a difficult time choosing one favorite ornament. Her collection now includes a complete collection of Merry Miniatures combined with Little Gallery pewter, Betsey Clark, music boxes, cookie cutters, lapel pins, and just about anything with the magical name of "Hallmark" on it. Thirty years later she is still purchasing one of every ornament issued and has turned an eight room office building into "Ann's Doll House." Ann will always be adding to her collection, so she will continually have new projects to work on and new displays to enjoy. She finds great pleasure in her many Hallmark collections, but it is the friends she made along the way that she values most. Ann realizes that collectors today have the opportunity to purchase ornaments on the internet, and even though it was more challenging in the past, she enjoyed building relationships as she dealt with sellers in person.

1977 Grandson Ball

It was the elusive 1977 ball ornament, Grandson, that completed Ann's early Keepsake Ornament collection in 1990. Although "Ann's Doll House" is currently not open to the public, she is working towards that goal.

Jess Prudencio from California is a friend and fellow collector who completed his Hallmark Keepsake Collection a few months after Ann. The ornament that he had the hardest time finding was the same 1977 Grandson ball that Ann had hunted for years. Jess's entire collection is on display at the Jess Prudencio and David Hamrick Hallmark Ornament Museum inside The Party Shop, a Hallmark Gold Crown Store in Warsaw, Indiana. The

Party Shop is located at One Ornament Place, 3418 Lake City Highway. Tours are available seven days a week to groups of 1 or 100 by calling David at 574-267-8787. The Museum opened in April, 1996, and has since welcomed over 20,000 visitors. David promises this display of over 3,000 ornaments will have something that appeals to everyone.

The Hallmark Ornament Museum

Today there are less than ten complete Hallmark Keepsake Ornament collections, but there are several people working toward this goal. Will you be next? Let us know if you decide to join this exclusive group.

Look Familar???...Artist Ed Seales 1999 Grandson and Granddaughter ornament teddy bear designs were re-used in the 2002 Snow Cub Club Bears ornament promo set as Dexter Next and Wendy Whoosh.

In a last minute change... 1987 Train Station had it's perforated $14.50 tag removed, and a sticker on the back applied that read $12.75.

Only two ornaments...have white interior felt liners, the 1980 Heavenly Minstrel and 1980 Frosty Friend #1: A Cool Yule.

In 1987...the #1 Holiday Heirloom Bell was avaiable in stores, but the #2-#4 in that series were club exclusives.

Yes....all of the 1975 Adorables ornaments have a corresponding Merry Miniature except Mrs. Claus.

Christmas Wonderland...produced in 1983 is a one-of-a-kind. It is the only clear glass peek-in ball ornament, which features artwork on both the inside and outside. The inside picture can be seen by "peeking" through the glass.

In 1978...70% of the Hallmark ornament line was priced at $3.50 or less.

Keepsake Christmas Ornaments

While for some, Hallmark Ornaments may be merely Christmas decorations, Hallmark Keepsake Ornament collectors consider them little works of art that often are full of special memories and sentimental value. Clearly they are special treasures.

1973

1.
Betsey Clark
250XHD1002 • $95

2.
Betsey Clark 1: Christmas 1973
250XHD1102 • $125

3.
Christmas Is Love
250XHD1062 • $90

4.
Elves
TAGU • 250XHD1035 • $70

5.
Manger Scene
250XHD1022 • $95

6.
Santa With Elves
250XHD1015 • $70

7.
Yarn Angel
125XHD785 • $30
Re-issued in 1974 as QX1031.

8.
Yarn Blue Girl
125XHD852 • $27

9.
Yarn Boy Caroler
125XHD832 • $32

10.
Yarn Choir Boy
GERG • 125XHD805 • $28

11.
Yarn Elf
125XHD792 • $30
Re-issued in 1974 as QX1011.

12.
Yarn Green Girl
125XHD845 • $25

13.
Yarn Little Girl
125XHD825 • $35

14.
Yarn Mr. Santa
125XHD745 • $30
Re-issued in 1974 as QX1051.

15.
Yarn Mr. Snowman
125XHD765 • $30

16.
Yarn Mrs. Santa
125XHD752 • $30
Re-issued in 1974 as QX1001.

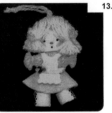

17.
Yarn Mrs. Snowman
125XHD772 • $33

18.
Yarn Soldier
100XHD812 • $28

1974

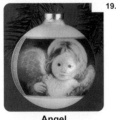

19.
Angel
250QX1101 • $70

20.
Betsey Clark 2: Musicians
250QX1081 • $70

21.
Buttons & Bo
350QX1131 • $61
Set/2

22.
Charmers
250QX1091 • $51

23.
Currier & Ives
350QX1121 • $70
Set/2

24.
Little Miracles
450QX1151 • $75
Set/4

25.
Norman Rockwell
250QX1061 • $76

26.
Norman Rockwell
250QX1111 • $74

27.
Raggedy Ann and Raggedy Andy®
450QX1141 • $95
Set/4

28.
Snowgoose
250QX1071 • $90

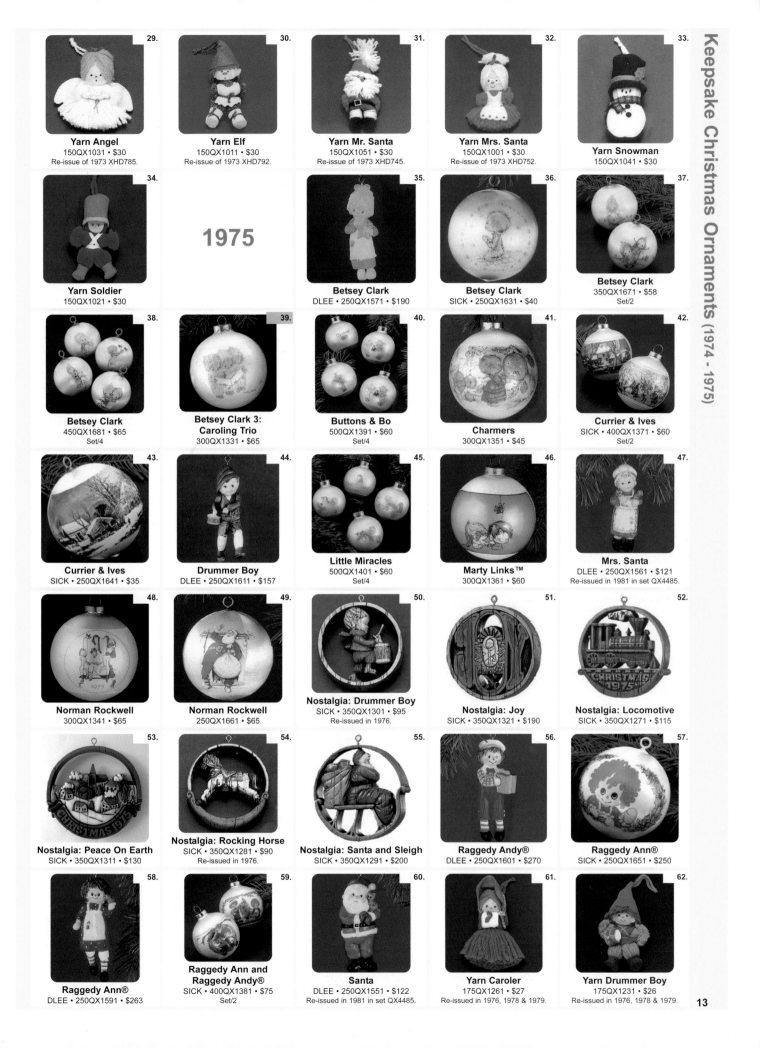

29.
Yarn Angel
150QX1031 • $30
Re-issue of 1973 XHD785.

30.
Yarn Elf
150QX1011 • $30
Re-issue of 1973 XHD792.

31.
Yarn Mr. Santa
150QX1051 • $30
Re-issue of 1973 XHD745.

32.
Yarn Mrs. Santa
150QX1001 • $30
Re-issue of 1973 XHD752.

33.
Yarn Snowman
150QX1041 • $30

34.
Yarn Soldier
150QX1021 • $30

1975

35.
Betsey Clark
DLEE • 250QX1571 • $190

36.
Betsey Clark
SICK • 250QX1631 • $40

37.
Betsey Clark
350QX1671 • $58
Set/2

38.
Betsey Clark
450QX1681 • $65
Set/4

39.
Betsey Clark 3:
Caroling Trio
300QX1331 • $65

40.
Buttons & Bo
500QX1391 • $60
Set/4

41.
Charmers
300QX1351 • $45

42.
Currier & Ives
SICK • 400QX1371 • $60
Set/2

43.
Currier & Ives
SICK • 250QX1641 • $35

44.
Drummer Boy
DLEE • 250QX1611 • $157

45.
Little Miracles
500QX1401 • $60
Set/4

46.
Marty Links™
300QX1361 • $60

47.
Mrs. Santa
DLEE • 250QX1561 • $121
Re-issued in 1981 in set QX4485.

48.
Norman Rockwell
300QX1341 • $65

49.
Norman Rockwell
250QX1661 • $65

50.
Nostalgia: Drummer Boy
SICK • 350QX1301 • $95
Re-issued in 1976.

51.
Nostalgia: Joy
SICK • 350QX1321 • $190

52.
Nostalgia: Locomotive
SICK • 350QX1271 • $115

53.
Nostalgia: Peace On Earth
SICK • 350QX1311 • $130

54.
Nostalgia: Rocking Horse
SICK • 350QX1281 • $90
Re-issued in 1976.

55.
Nostalgia: Santa and Sleigh
SICK • 350QX1291 • $200

56.
Raggedy Andy®
DLEE • 250QX1601 • $270

57.
Raggedy Ann®
SICK • 250QX1651 • $250

58.
Raggedy Ann®
DLEE • 250QX1591 • $263

59.
Raggedy Ann and
Raggedy Andy®
SICK • 400QX1381 • $75
Set/2

60.
Santa
DLEE • 250QX1551 • $122
Re-issued in 1981 in set QX4485.

61.
Yarn Caroler
175QX1261 • $27
Re-issued in 1976, 1978 & 1979.

62.
Yarn Drummer Boy
175QX1231 • $26
Re-issued in 1976, 1978 & 1979.

1976

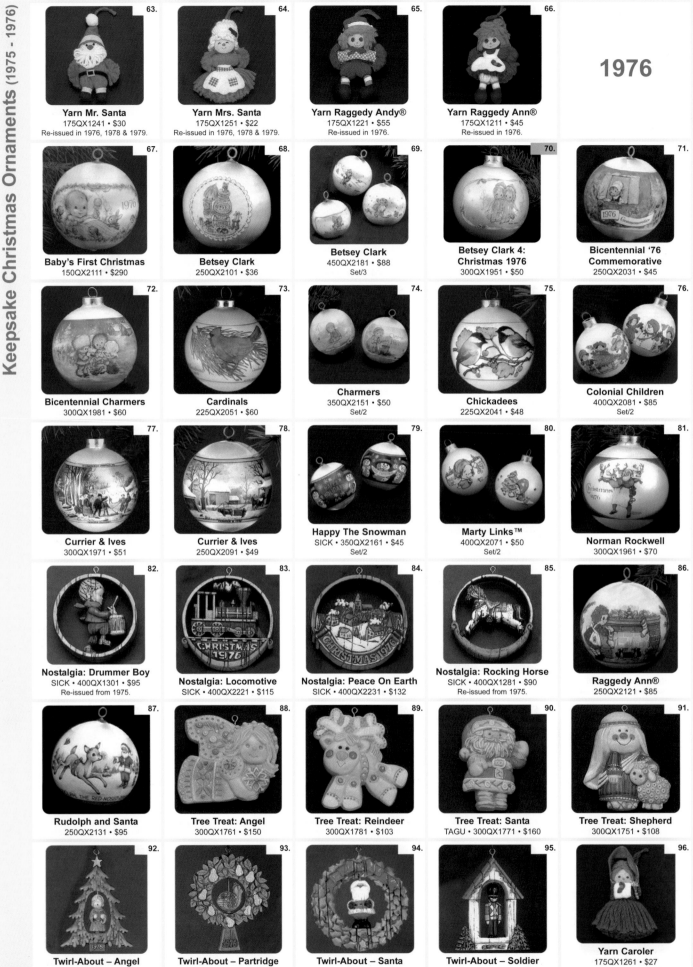

63.
Yarn Mr. Santa
175QX1241 • $30
Re-issued in 1976, 1978 & 1979.

64.
Yarn Mrs. Santa
175QX1251 • $22
Re-issued in 1976, 1978 & 1979.

65.
Yarn Raggedy Andy®
175QX1221 • $55
Re-issued in 1976.

66.
Yarn Raggedy Ann®
175QX1211 • $45
Re-issued in 1976.

67.
Baby's First Christmas
150QX2111 • $290

68.
Betsey Clark
250QX2101 • $36

69.
Betsey Clark
450QX2181 • $88
Set/3

70.
Betsey Clark 4:
Christmas 1976
300QX1951 • $50

71.
Bicentennial '76
Commemorative
250QX2031 • $45

72.
Bicentennial Charmers
300QX1981 • $60

73.
Cardinals
225QX2051 • $60

74.
Charmers
350QX2151 • $50
Set/2

75.
Chickadees
225QX2041 • $48

76.
Colonial Children
400QX2081 • $85
Set/2

77.
Currier & Ives
300QX1971 • $51

78.
Currier & Ives
250QX2091 • $49

79.
Happy The Snowman
SICK • 350QX2161 • $45
Set/2

80.
Marty Links™
400QX2071 • $50
Set/2

81.
Norman Rockwell
300QX1961 • $70

82.
Nostalgia: Drummer Boy
SICK • 400QX1301 • $95
Re-issued from 1975.

83.
Nostalgia: Locomotive
SICK • 400QX2221 • $115

84.
Nostalgia: Peace On Earth
SICK • 400QX2231 • $132

85.
Nostalgia: Rocking Horse
SICK • 400QX1281 • $90
Re-issued from 1975.

86.
Raggedy Ann®
250QX2121 • $85

87.
Rudolph and Santa
250QX2131 • $95

88.
Tree Treat: Angel
300QX1761 • $150

89.
Tree Treat: Reindeer
300QX1781 • $103

90.
Tree Treat: Santa
TAGU • 300QX1771 • $160

91.
Tree Treat: Shepherd
300QX1751 • $108

92.
Twirl-About – Angel
SICK • 450QX1711 • $110

93.
Twirl-About – Partridge
SICK • 450QX1741 • $145

94.
Twirl-About – Santa
SICK • 450QX1721 • $90

95.
Twirl-About – Soldier
SICK • 450QX1731 • $75

96.
Yarn Caroler
175QX1261 • $27
Also issued in 1975, 1978 & 1979.

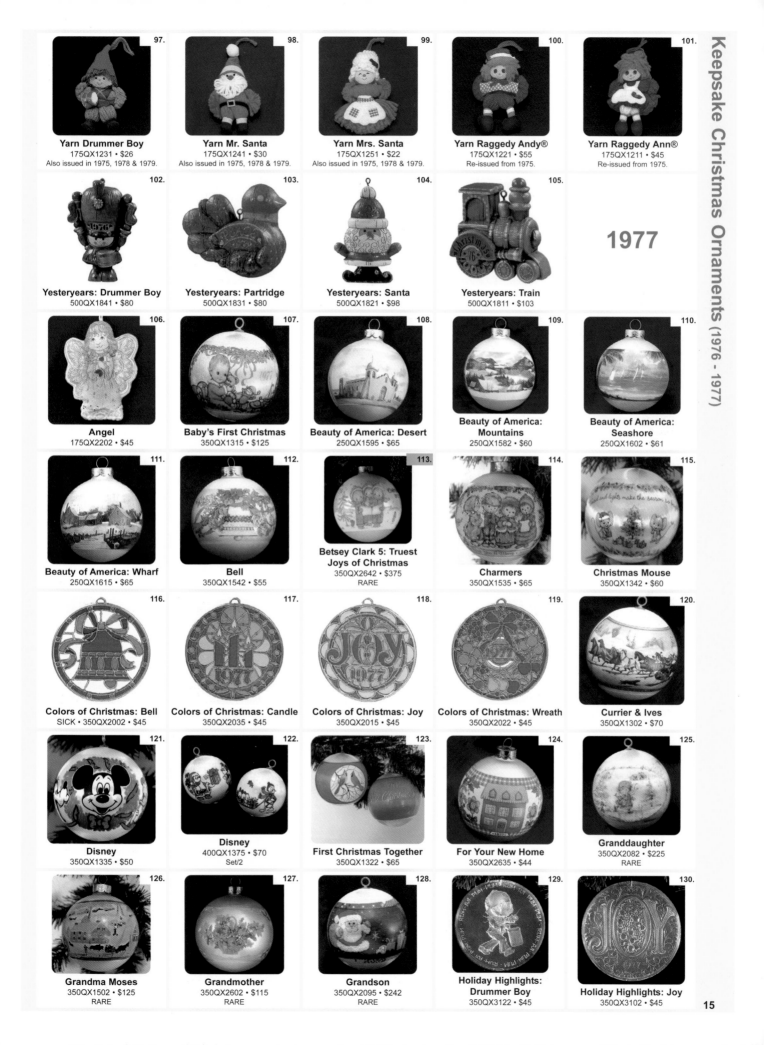

97.
Yarn Drummer Boy
175QX1231 • $26
Also issued in 1975, 1978 & 1979.

98.
Yarn Mr. Santa
175QX1241 • $30
Also issued in 1975, 1978 & 1979.

99.
Yarn Mrs. Santa
175QX1251 • $22
Also issued in 1975, 1978 & 1979.

100.
Yarn Raggedy Andy®
175QX1221 • $55
Re-issued from 1975.

101.
Yarn Raggedy Ann®
175QX1211 • $45
Re-issued from 1975.

102.
Yesteryears: Drummer Boy
500QX1841 • $80

103.
Yesteryears: Partridge
500QX1831 • $80

104.
Yesteryears: Santa
500QX1821 • $98

105.
Yesteryears: Train
500QX1811 • $103

1977

106.
Angel
175QX2202 • $45

107.
Baby's First Christmas
350QX1315 • $125

108.
Beauty of America: Desert
250QX1595 • $65

109.
Beauty of America: Mountains
250QX1582 • $60

110.
Beauty of America: Seashore
250QX1602 • $61

111.
Beauty of America: Wharf
250QX1615 • $65

112.
Bell
350QX1542 • $55

113.
Betsey Clark 5: Truest Joys of Christmas
350QX2642 • $375
RARE

114.
Charmers
350QX1535 • $65

115.
Christmas Mouse
350QX1342 • $60

116.
Colors of Christmas: Bell
SICK • 350QX2002 • $45

117.
Colors of Christmas: Candle
350QX2035 • $45

118.
Colors of Christmas: Joy
350QX2015 • $45

119.
Colors of Christmas: Wreath
350QX2022 • $45

120.
Currier & Ives
350QX1302 • $70

121.
Disney
350QX1335 • $50

122.
Disney
400QX1375 • $70
Set/2

123.
First Christmas Together
350QX1322 • $65

124.
For Your New Home
350QX2635 • $44

125.
Granddaughter
350QX2082 • $225
RARE

126.
Grandma Moses
350QX1502 • $125
RARE

127.
Grandmother
350QX2602 • $115
RARE

128.
Grandson
350QX2095 • $242
RARE

129.
Holiday Highlights: Drummer Boy
350QX3122 • $45

130.
Holiday Highlights: Joy
350QX3102 • $45

131. **Holiday Highlights: Peace On Earth**
350QX3115 • $45

132. **Holiday Highlights: Star**
350QX3135 • $45

133. **Love**
350QX2622 • $50

134. **Mandolin**
350QX1575 • $50

135. **Mother**
350QX2615 • $65

136. **Mr. and Mrs. Snowman Kissing Ball**
500QX2252 • $60

137. **Norman Rockwell**
350QX1515 • $55

138. **Nostalgia: Angel**
DLEE • 500QX1822 • $70

139. **Nostalgia: Antique Car**
SICK • 500QX1802 • $61

140. **Nostalgia: Nativity**
500QX1815 • $150

141. **Nostalgia: Toys**
SICK • 500QX1835 • $110

142. **Old Fashioned Customs Kissing Ball**
500QX2255 • $60

143. **Ornaments**
350QX1555 • $70

144. **PEANUTS®**
350QX1355 • $75

145. **PEANUTS®**
250QX1622 • $85

146. **PEANUTS®**
400QX1635 • $95

147. **Rabbit**
250QX1395 • $75

148. **Santa**
175QX2215 • $55

149. **Snowflake Collection**
SICK • 500QX2102 • $175
Set/4 • RARE

150. **Squirrel**
250QX1382 • $75

151. **Stained Glass**
350QX1522 • $50

152. **Twirl-About – Bellringer**
600QX1922 • $55

153. **Twirl-About – Della Robia Wreath**
DLEE • 450QX1935 • $67

154. **Twirl-About – Snowman**
SICK • 450QX1902 • $62

155. **Twirl-About – Weather House**
600QX1915 • $75

156. **Wreath**
350QX1562 • $60

157. **Yesteryears: Angel**
600QX1722 • $95

158. **Yesteryears: House**
600QX1702 • $95

159. **Yesteryears: Jack-in-the-Box**
600QX1715 • $95

160. **Yesteryears: Reindeer**
600QX1735 • $124

1978

161. **25th Christmas Together**
350QX2696 • $40

162. **Angel**
DLEE • 450QX1396 • $100
Re-issued in 1981.

163. **Angels**
800QX1503 • $215

164. **Animal Home**
DLEE • 600QX1496 • $83

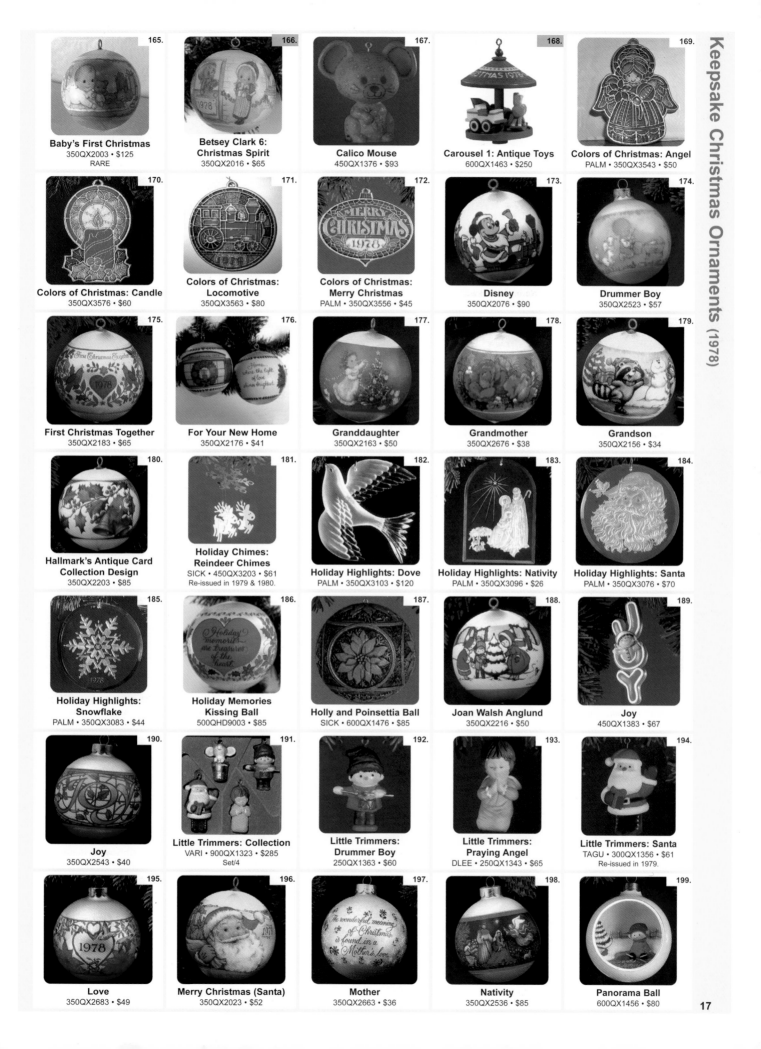

165.
Baby's First Christmas
350QX2003 • $125
RARE

166.
**Betsey Clark 6:
Christmas Spirit**
350QX2016 • $65

167.
Calico Mouse
450QX1376 • $93

168.
Carousel 1: Antique Toys
600QX1463 • $250

169.
Colors of Christmas: Angel
PALM • 350QX3543 • $50

170.
Colors of Christmas: Candle
350QX3576 • $60

171.
**Colors of Christmas:
Locomotive**
350QX3563 • $80

172.
**Colors of Christmas:
Merry Christmas**
PALM • 350QX3556 • $45

173.
Disney
350QX2076 • $90

174.
Drummer Boy
350QX2523 • $57

175.
First Christmas Together
350QX2183 • $65

176.
For Your New Home
350QX2176 • $41

177.
Granddaughter
350QX2163 • $50

178.
Grandmother
350QX2676 • $38

179.
Grandson
350QX2156 • $34

180.
**Hallmark's Antique Card
Collection Design**
350QX2203 • $85

181.
**Holiday Chimes:
Reindeer Chimes**
SICK • 450QX3203 • $61
Re-issued in 1979 & 1980.

182.
Holiday Highlights: Dove
PALM • 350QX3103 • $120

183.
Holiday Highlights: Nativity
PALM • 350QX3096 • $26

184.
Holiday Highlights: Santa
PALM • 350QX3076 • $70

185.
**Holiday Highlights:
Snowflake**
PALM • 350QX3083 • $44

186.
**Holiday Memories
Kissing Ball**
500QHD9003 • $85

187.
Holly and Poinsettia Ball
SICK • 600QX1476 • $85

188.
Joan Walsh Anglund
350QX2216 • $50

189.
Joy
450QX1383 • $67

190.
Joy
350QX2543 • $40

191.
Little Trimmers: Collection
VARI • 900QX1323 • $285
Set/4

192.
**Little Trimmers:
Drummer Boy**
250QX1363 • $60

193.
**Little Trimmers:
Praying Angel**
DLEE • 250QX1343 • $65

194.
Little Trimmers: Santa
TAGU • 300QX1356 • $61
Re-issued in 1979.

195.
Love
350QX2683 • $49

196.
Merry Christmas (Santa)
350QX2023 • $52

197.
Mother
350QX2663 • $36

198.
Nativity
350QX2536 • $85

199.
Panorama Ball
600QX1456 • $80

200.
PEANUTS®
250QX2036 • $90

201.
PEANUTS®
250QX2043 • $65

202.
PEANUTS®
350QX2056 • $80

203.
PEANUTS®
350QX2063 • $91

204.
The Quail
350QX2516 • $49

205.
Red Cardinal
UNRU • 450QX1443 • $125

206.
Rocking Horse
600QX1483 • $85

207.
Schneeberg Bell
800QX1523 • $130

208.
Skating Raccoon
DLEE • 600QX1423 • $94
Re-issued in 1979.

209.
Spencer Sparrow, Esq.
350QX2196 • $46

210.
Thimble 1:
Mouse in Thimble
TAGU • 300QX1336 • $195
Re-issued in 1979.

211.
Twirl-About – Dove
SICK • 450QX1903 • $60

212.
Yarn Caroler
200QX1261 • $27
Also issued in 1975, 1976 & 1979.

213.
Yarn Drummer Boy
200QX1231 • $26
Also issued in 1975, 1976 & 1979.

214.
Yarn Mr. Santa
200QX3403 • $30
Also issued in 1975, 1976 & 1979.

215.
Yarn Mrs. Santa
200QX1251 • $22
Also issued in 1975, 1976 & 1979.

216.
Yesterday's Toys
350QX2503 • $71

1979

217.
Angel Music
200QX3439 • $45
Re-issued in 1980.

218.
Baby's First Christmas
800QX1547 • $175
RARE

219.
Baby's First Christmas
350QX2087 • $55

220.
Behold The Star
350QX2559 • $70

221.
Bellringers 1:
The Bellswinger
TAGU • 1000QX1479 • $260

222.
Betsey Clark 7:
Holiday Fun
350QX2019 • $60

223.
Black Angel
BLAC • 350QX2079 • $65

224.
Carousel 2:
Christmas Carousel
650QX1467 • $190

225.
Christmas Chickadees
350QX2047 • $50

226.
Christmas Collage
350QX2579 • $40

227.
Christmas Eve Surprise
650QX1579 • $50

228.
Christmas Heart
SICK • 650QX1407 • $95

229.
Christmas Is for Children
500QX1359 • $65
Re-issued in 1980.

230.
Christmas Traditions
SICK • 350QX2539 • $54

231.
A Christmas Treat
500QX1347 • $66
Re-issued in 1980.

232.
Colors of Christmas:
Holiday Wreath
350QX3539 • $45

233.
Colors of Christmas:
Partridge in a Pear Tree
350QX3519 • $45

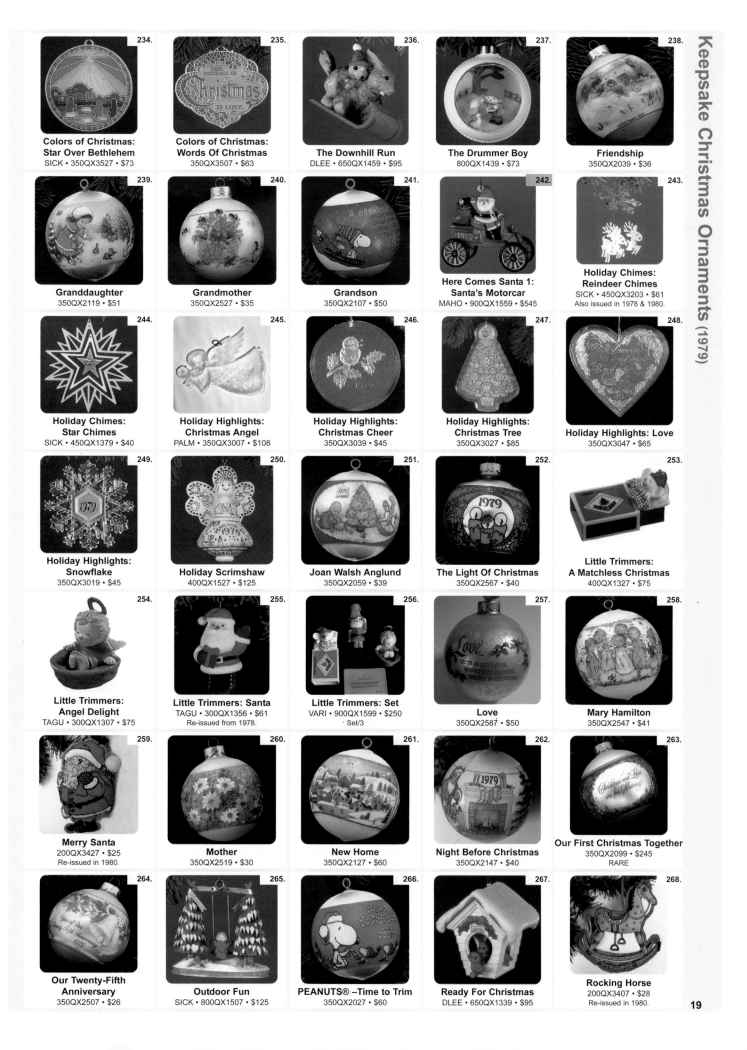

234.
Colors of Christmas:
Star Over Bethlehem
SICK • 350QX3527 • $73

235.
Colors of Christmas:
Words Of Christmas
350QX3507 • $63

236.
The Downhill Run
DLEE • 650QX1459 • $95

237.
The Drummer Boy
800QX1439 • $73

238.
Friendship
350QX2039 • $36

239.
Granddaughter
350QX2119 • $51

240.
Grandmother
350QX2527 • $35

241.
Grandson
350QX2107 • $50

242.
Here Comes Santa 1:
Santa's Motorcar
MAHO • 900QX1559 • $545

243.
Holiday Chimes:
Reindeer Chimes
SICK • 450QX3203 • $61
Also issued in 1978 & 1980.

244.
Holiday Chimes:
Star Chimes
SICK • 450QX1379 • $40

245.
Holiday Highlights:
Christmas Angel
PALM • 350QX3007 • $108

246.
Holiday Highlights:
Christmas Cheer
350QX3039 • $45

247.
Holiday Highlights:
Christmas Tree
350QX3027 • $85

248.
Holiday Highlights: Love
350QX3047 • $65

249.
Holiday Highlights:
Snowflake
350QX3019 • $45

250.
Holiday Scrimshaw
400QX1527 • $125

251.
Joan Walsh Anglund
350QX2059 • $39

252.
The Light Of Christmas
350QX2567 • $40

253.
Little Trimmers:
A Matchless Christmas
400QX1327 • $75

254.
Little Trimmers:
Angel Delight
TAGU • 300QX1307 • $75

255.
Little Trimmers: Santa
TAGU • 300QX1356 • $61
Re-issued from 1978.

256.
Little Trimmers: Set
VARI • 900QX1599 • $250
Set/3

257.
Love
350QX2587 • $50

258.
Mary Hamilton
350QX2547 • $41

259.
Merry Santa
200QX3427 • $25
Re-issued in 1980.

260.
Mother
350QX2519 • $30

261.
New Home
350QX2127 • $60

262.
Night Before Christmas
350QX2147 • $40

263.
Our First Christmas Together
350QX2099 • $245
RARE

264.
Our Twenty-Fifth
Anniversary
350QX2507 • $26

265.
Outdoor Fun
SICK • 800QX1507 • $125

266.
PEANUTS® –Time to Trim
350QX2027 • $60

267.
Ready For Christmas
DLEE • 650QX1339 • $95

268.
Rocking Horse
200QX3407 • $28
Re-issued in 1980.

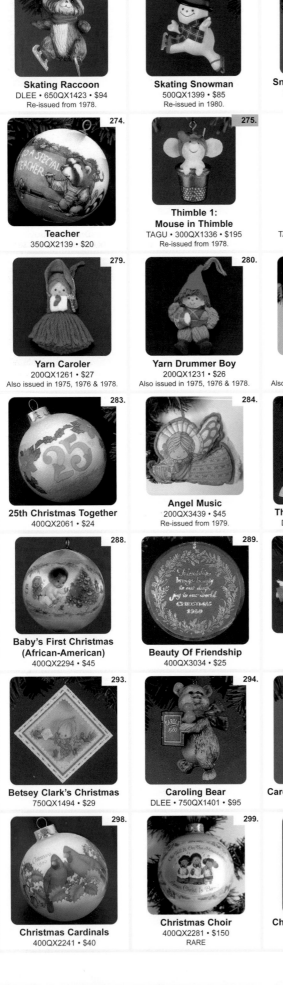

269.

Skating Raccoon
DLEE • 650QX1423 • $94
Re-issued from 1978.

270.

Skating Snowman
500QX1399 • $85
Re-issued in 1980.

271.

Snoopy® and Friends 1: Ice-Hockey Holiday
800QX1419 • $125

272.

Spencer Sparrow, Esq.
350QX2007 • $66

273.

Stuffed Full Stocking
200QX3419 • $27
Re-issued in 1980.

274.
Teacher
350QX2139 • $20

275.

Thimble 1: Mouse in Thimble
TAGU • 300QX1336 • $195
Re-issued from 1978.

276.
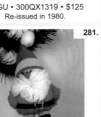
Thimble 2: A Chistmas Salute
TAGU • 300QX1319 • $125
Re-issued in 1980.

277.

Twirl-About – Santa's Here
SICK • 500QX1387 • $71

278.

Winnie the Pooh
350QX2067 • $85

279.
Yarn Caroler
200QX1261 • $27
Also issued in 1975, 1976 & 1978.

280.
Yarn Drummer Boy
200QX1231 • $26
Also issued in 1975, 1976 & 1978.

281.
Yarn Mr. Santa
200QX3403 • $30
Also issued in 1975, 1976 & 1978.

282.
Yarn Mrs. Santa
200QX1251 • $22
Also issued in 1975, 1976 & 1978.

1980

283.
25th Christmas Together
400QX2061 • $24

284.

Angel Music
200QX3439 • $45
Re-issued from 1979.

285.

The Animals' Christmas
DLEE • 800QX1501 • $55

286.
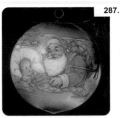
Baby's First Christmas
SICK • 1200QX1561 • $80

287.
Baby's First Christmas
400QX2001 • $45

288.
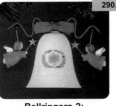
Baby's First Christmas (African-American)
400QX2294 • $45

289.
Beauty Of Friendship
400QX3034 • $25

290.

Bellringers 2: The Bellringers
1500QX1574 • $75

291.

Betsey Clark
650QX3074 • $50

292.
Betsey Clark 8: Joy-in-the-Air
400QX2154 • $32

293.
Betsey Clark's Christmas
750QX1494 • $29

294.

Caroling Bear
DLEE • 750QX1401 • $95

295.

Carousel 3: Merry Carousel
750QX1414 • $105

296.

Checking It Twice
BLAC • 2000QX1584 • $125
Re-issued in 1981.

297.
Christmas At Home
400QX2101 • $25

298.
Christmas Cardinals
400QX2241 • $40

299.

Christmas Choir
400QX2281 • $150
RARE

300.

Christmas Is for Children
550QX1359 • $65
Re-issued from 1979.

301.

Christmas Kitten Test Ornament
400QX3534 • $320
RARE

302.
Christmas Love
400QX2074 • $42

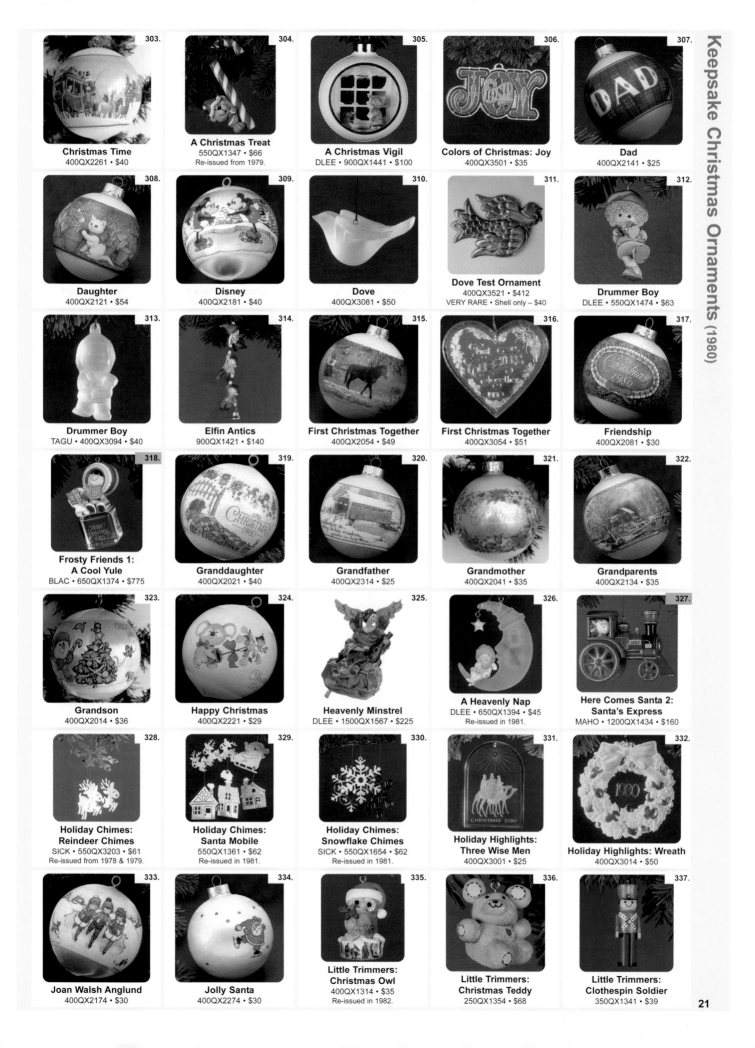

303.
Christmas Time
400QX2261 • $40

304.
A Christmas Treat
550QX1347 • $66
Re-issued from 1979.

305.
A Christmas Vigil
DLEE • 900QX1441 • $100

306.
Colors of Christmas: Joy
400QX3501 • $35

307.
Dad
400QX2141 • $25

308.
Daughter
400QX2121 • $54

309.
Disney
400QX2181 • $40

310.
Dove
400QX3081 • $50

311.
Dove Test Ornament
400QX3521 • $412
VERY RARE • Shell only – $40

312.
Drummer Boy
DLEE • 550QX1474 • $63

313.
Drummer Boy
TAGU • 400QX3094 • $40

314.
Elfin Antics
900QX1421 • $140

315.
First Christmas Together
400QX2054 • $49

316.
First Christmas Together
400QX3054 • $51

317.
Friendship
400QX2081 • $30

318.
**Frosty Friends 1:
A Cool Yule**
BLAC • 650QX1374 • $775

319.
Granddaughter
400QX2021 • $40

320.
Grandfather
400QX2314 • $25

321.
Grandmother
400QX2041 • $35

322.
Grandparents
400QX2134 • $35

323.
Grandson
400QX2014 • $36

324.
Happy Christmas
400QX2221 • $29

325.
Heavenly Minstrel
DLEE • 1500QX1567 • $225

326.
A Heavenly Nap
DLEE • 650QX1394 • $45
Re-issued in 1981.

327.
**Here Comes Santa 2:
Santa's Express**
MAHO • 1200QX1434 • $160

328.
**Holiday Chimes:
Reindeer Chimes**
SICK • 550QX3203 • $61
Re-issued from 1978 & 1979.

329.
**Holiday Chimes:
Santa Mobile**
550QX1361 • $62
Re-issued in 1981.

330.
**Holiday Chimes:
Snowflake Chimes**
SICK • 550QX1654 • $62
Re-issued in 1981.

331.
**Holiday Highlights:
Three Wise Men**
400QX3001 • $25

332.
Holiday Highlights: Wreath
400QX3014 • $50

333.
Joan Walsh Anglund
400QX2174 • $30

334.
Jolly Santa
400QX2274 • $30

335.
**Little Trimmers:
Christmas Owl**
400QX1314 • $35
Re-issued in 1982.

336.
**Little Trimmers:
Christmas Teddy**
250QX1354 • $68

337.
**Little Trimmers:
Clothespin Soldier**
350QX1341 • $39

21

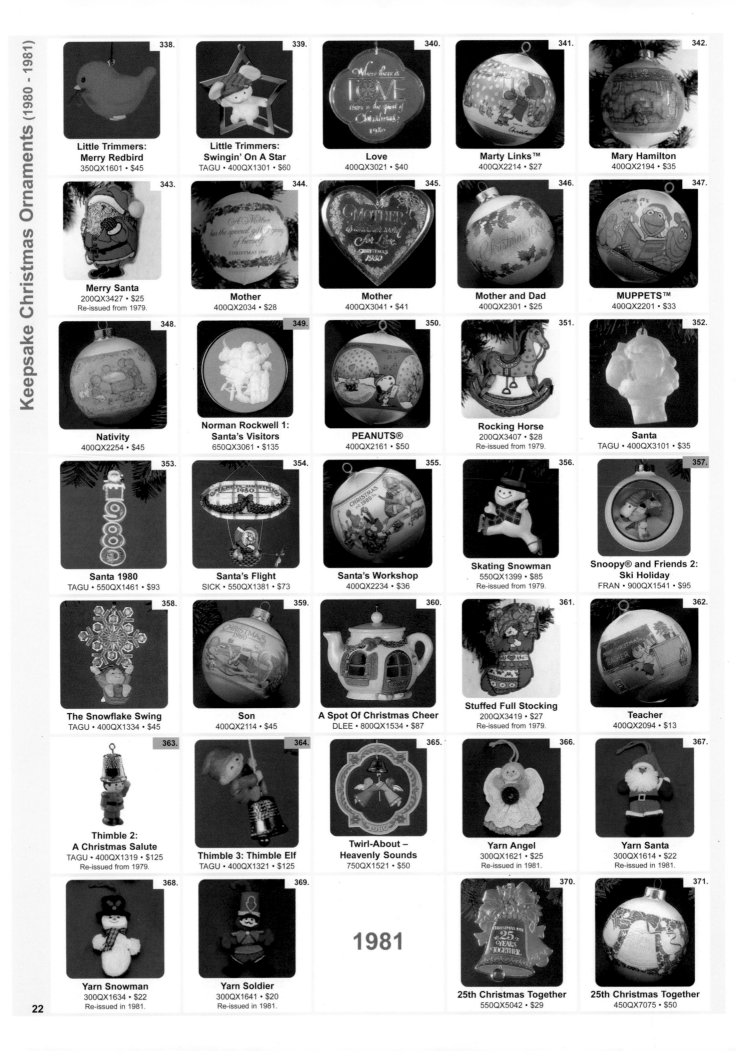

338.
Little Trimmers:
Merry Redbird
350QX1601 • $45

339.
Little Trimmers:
Swingin' On A Star
TAGU • 400QX1301 • $60

340.
Love
400QX3021 • $40

341.
Marty Links™
400QX2214 • $27

342.
Mary Hamilton
400QX2194 • $35

343.
Merry Santa
200QX3427 • $25
Re-issued from 1979.

344.
Mother
400QX2034 • $28

345.
Mother
400QX3041 • $41

346.
Mother and Dad
400QX2301 • $25

347.
MUPPETS™
400QX2201 • $33

348.
Nativity
400QX2254 • $45

349.
Norman Rockwell 1:
Santa's Visitors
650QX3061 • $135

350.
PEANUTS®
400QX2161 • $50

351.
Rocking Horse
200QX3407 • $28
Re-issued from 1979.

352.
Santa
TAGU • 400QX3101 • $35

353.
Santa 1980
TAGU • 550QX1461 • $93

354.
Santa's Flight
SICK • 550QX1381 • $73

355.
Santa's Workshop
400QX2234 • $36

356.
Skating Snowman
550QX1399 • $85
Re-issued from 1979.

357.
Snoopy® and Friends 2:
Ski Holiday
FRAN • 900QX1541 • $95

358.
The Snowflake Swing
TAGU • 400QX1334 • $45

359.
Son
400QX2114 • $45

360.
A Spot Of Christmas Cheer
DLEE • 800QX1534 • $87

361.
Stuffed Full Stocking
200QX3419 • $27
Re-issued from 1979.

362.
Teacher
400QX2094 • $13

363.
Thimble 2:
A Christmas Salute
TAGU • 400QX1319 • $125
Re-issued from 1979.

364.
Thimble 3: Thimble Elf
TAGU • 400QX1321 • $125

365.
Twirl-About –
Heavenly Sounds
750QX1521 • $50

366.
Yarn Angel
300QX1621 • $25
Re-issued in 1981.

367.
Yarn Santa
300QX1614 • $22
Re-issued in 1981.

368.
Yarn Snowman
300QX1634 • $22
Re-issued in 1981.

369.
Yarn Soldier
300QX1641 • $20
Re-issued in 1981.

1981

370.
25th Christmas Together
550QX5042 • $29

371.
25th Christmas Together
450QX7075 • $50

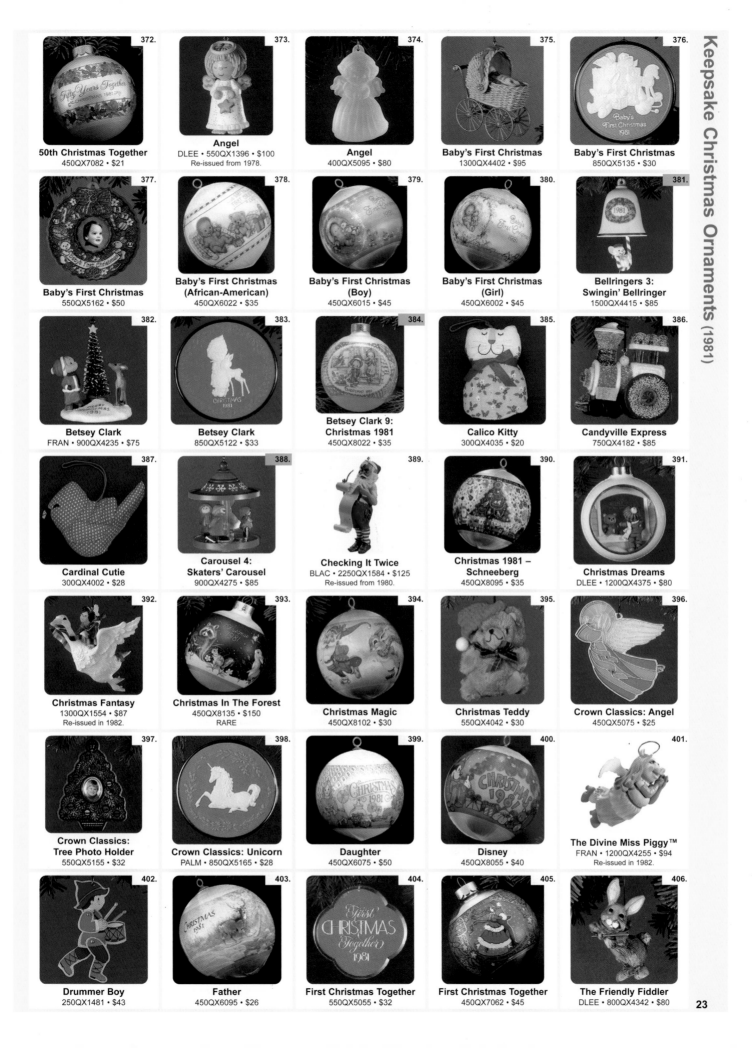

372.
50th Christmas Together
450QX7082 • $21

373.
Angel
DLEE • 550QX1396 • $100
Re-issued from 1978.

374.
Angel
400QX5095 • $80

375.
Baby's First Christmas
1300QX4402 • $95

376.
Baby's First Christmas
850QX5135 • $30

377.
Baby's First Christmas
550QX5162 • $50

378.
Baby's First Christmas
(African-American)
450QX6022 • $35

379.
Baby's First Christmas
(Boy)
450QX6015 • $45

380.
Baby's First Christmas
(Girl)
450QX6002 • $45

381.
Bellringers 3:
Swingin' Bellringer
1500QX4415 • $85

382.
Betsey Clark
FRAN • 900QX4235 • $75

383.
Betsey Clark
850QX5122 • $33

384.
Betsey Clark 9:
Christmas 1981
450QX8022 • $35

385.
Calico Kitty
300QX4035 • $20

386.
Candyville Express
750QX4182 • $85

387.
Cardinal Cutie
300QX4002 • $28

388.
Carousel 4:
Skaters' Carousel
900QX4275 • $85

389.
Checking It Twice
BLAC • 2250QX1584 • $125
Re-issued from 1980.

390.
Christmas 1981 –
Schneeberg
450QX8095 • $35

391.
Christmas Dreams
DLEE • 1200QX4375 • $80

392.
Christmas Fantasy
1300QX1554 • $87
Re-issued in 1982.

393.
Christmas In The Forest
450QX8135 • $150
RARE

394.
Christmas Magic
450QX8102 • $30

395.
Christmas Teddy
550QX4042 • $30

396.
Crown Classics: Angel
450QX5075 • $25

397.
Crown Classics:
Tree Photo Holder
550QX5155 • $32

398.
Crown Classics: Unicorn
PALM • 850QX5165 • $28

399.
Daughter
450QX6075 • $50

400.
Disney
450QX8055 • $40

401.
The Divine Miss Piggy™
FRAN • 1200QX4255 • $94
Re-issued in 1982.

402.
Drummer Boy
250QX1481 • $43

403.
Father
450QX6095 • $26

404.
First Christmas Together
550QX5055 • $32

405.
First Christmas Together
450QX7062 • $45

406.
The Friendly Fiddler
DLEE • 800QX4342 • $80

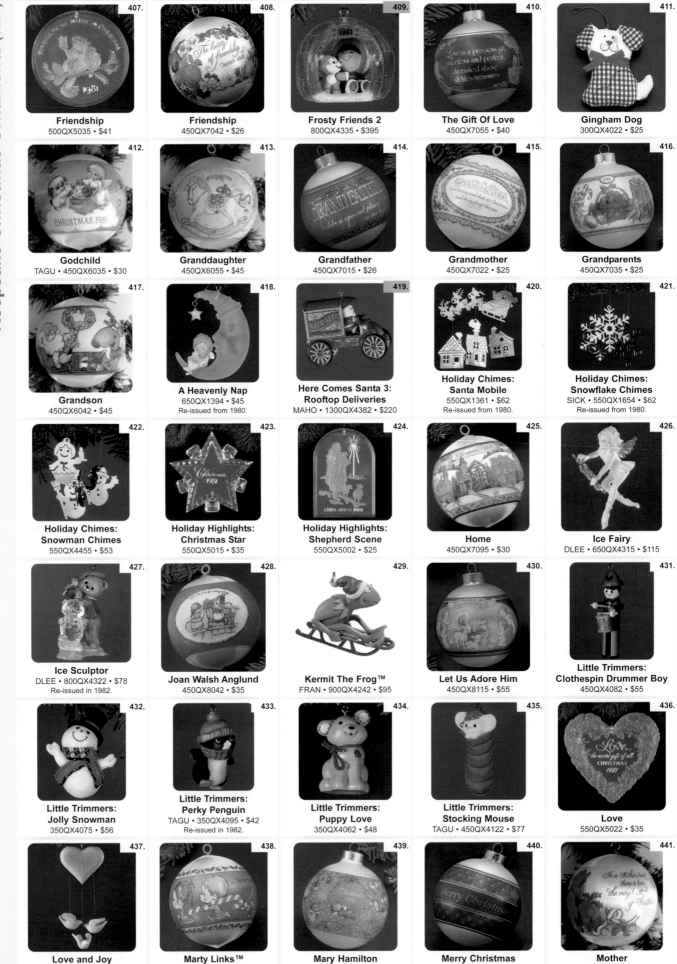

407. Friendship
500QX5035 • $41

408. Friendship
450QX7042 • $26

409. Frosty Friends 2
800QX4335 • $395

410. The Gift Of Love
450QX7055 • $40

411. Gingham Dog
300QX4022 • $25

412. Godchild
TAGU • 450QX6035 • $30

413. Granddaughter
450QX6055 • $45

414. Grandfather
450QX7015 • $26

415. Grandmother
450QX7022 • $25

416. Grandparents
450QX7035 • $25

417. Grandson
450QX6042 • $45

418. A Heavenly Nap
650QX1394 • $45
Re-issued from 1980.

419. Here Comes Santa 3: Rooftop Deliveries
MAHO • 1300QX4382 • $220

420. Holiday Chimes: Santa Mobile
550QX1361 • $62
Re-issued from 1980.

421. Holiday Chimes: Snowflake Chimes
SICK • 550QX1654 • $62
Re-issued from 1980.

422. Holiday Chimes: Snowman Chimes
550QX4455 • $53

423. Holiday Highlights: Christmas Star
550QX5015 • $35

424. Holiday Highlights: Shepherd Scene
550QX5002 • $25

425. Home
450QX7095 • $30

426. Ice Fairy
DLEE • 650QX4315 • $115

427. Ice Sculptor
DLEE • 800QX4322 • $78
Re-issued in 1982.

428. Joan Walsh Anglund
450QX8042 • $35

429. Kermit The Frog™
FRAN • 900QX4242 • $95

430. Let Us Adore Him
450QX8115 • $55

431. Little Trimmers: Clothespin Drummer Boy
450QX4082 • $55

432. Little Trimmers: Jolly Snowman
350QX4075 • $56

433. Little Trimmers: Perky Penguin
TAGU • 350QX4095 • $42
Re-issued in 1982.

434. Little Trimmers: Puppy Love
350QX4062 • $48

435. Little Trimmers: Stocking Mouse
TAGU • 450QX4122 • $77

436. Love
550QX5022 • $35

437. Love and Joy
900QX4252 • $110

438. Marty Links™
450QX8082 • $30

439. Mary Hamilton
450QX8062 • $35

440. Merry Christmas
450QX8142 • $32

441. Mother
450QX6082 • $26

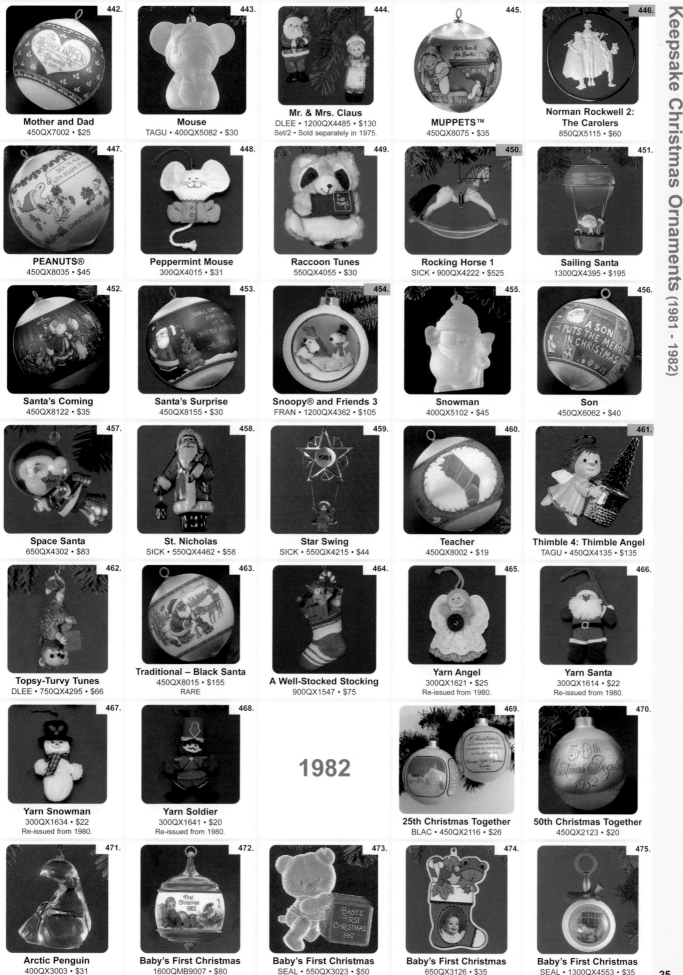

442.
Mother and Dad
450QX7002 • $25

443.
Mouse
TAGU • 400QX5082 • $30

444.
Mr. & Mrs. Claus
DLEE • 1200QX4485 • $130
Set/2 • Sold separately in 1975.

445.
MUPPETS™
450QX8075 • $35

446.
Norman Rockwell 2:
The Carolers
850QX5115 • $60

447.
PEANUTS®
450QX8035 • $45

448.
Peppermint Mouse
300QX4015 • $31

449.
Raccoon Tunes
550QX4055 • $30

450.
Rocking Horse 1
SICK • 900QX4222 • $525

451.
Sailing Santa
1300QX4395 • $195

452.
Santa's Coming
450QX8122 • $35

453.
Santa's Surprise
450QX8155 • $30

454.
Snoopy® and Friends 3
FRAN • 1200QX4362 • $105

455.
Snowman
400QX5102 • $45

456.
Son
450QX6062 • $40

457.
Space Santa
650QX4302 • $83

458.
St. Nicholas
SICK • 550QX4462 • $58

459.
Star Swing
SICK • 550QX4215 • $44

460.
Teacher
450QX8002 • $19

461.
Thimble 4: Thimble Angel
TAGU • 450QX4135 • $135

462.
Topsy-Turvy Tunes
DLEE • 750QX4295 • $66

463.
Traditional – Black Santa
450QX8015 • $155
RARE

464.
A Well-Stocked Stocking
900QX1547 • $75

465.
Yarn Angel
300QX1621 • $25
Re-issued from 1980.

466.
Yarn Santa
300QX1614 • $22
Re-issued from 1980.

467.
Yarn Snowman
300QX1634 • $22
Re-issued from 1980.

468.
Yarn Soldier
300QX1641 • $20
Re-issued from 1980.

1982

469.
25th Christmas Together
BLAC • 450QX2116 • $26

470.
50th Christmas Together
450QX2123 • $20

471.
Arctic Penguin
400QX3003 • $31

472.
Baby's First Christmas
1600QMB9007 • $80

473.
Baby's First Christmas
SEAL • 550QX3023 • $50

474.
Baby's First Christmas
650QX3126 • $35

475.
Baby's First Christmas
SEAL • 1300QX4553 • $35

25

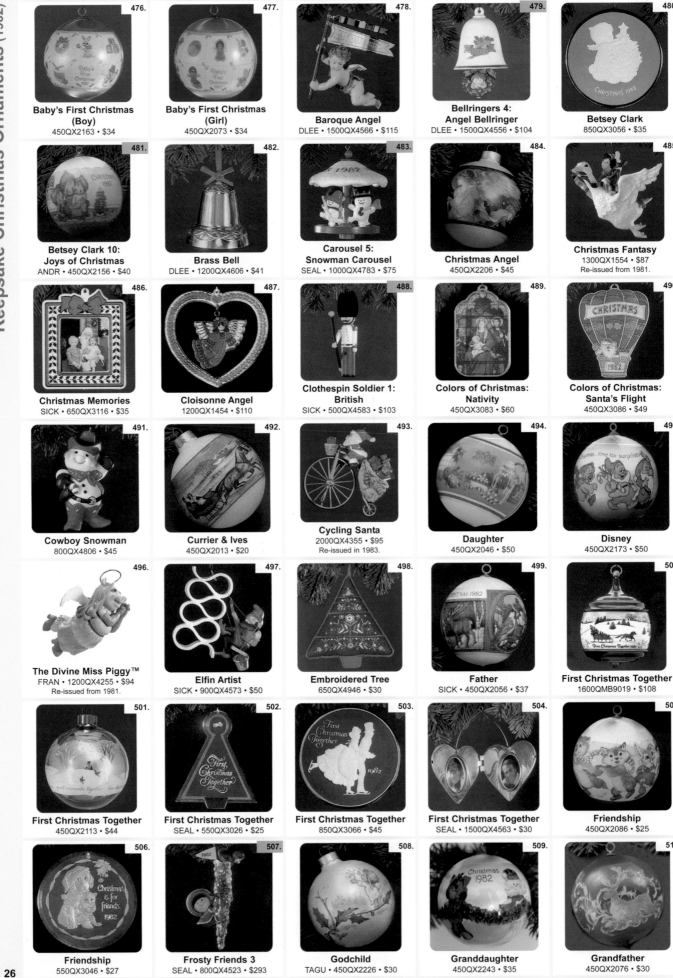

476. Baby's First Christmas (Boy)
450QX2163 • $34

477. Baby's First Christmas (Girl)
450QX2073 • $34

478. Baroque Angel
DLEE • 1500QX4566 • $115

479. Bellringers 4: Angel Bellringer
DLEE • 1500QX4556 • $104

480. Betsey Clark
850QX3056 • $35

481. Betsey Clark 10: Joys of Christmas
ANDR • 450QX2156 • $40

482. Brass Bell
DLEE • 1200QX4606 • $41

483. Carousel 5: Snowman Carousel
SEAL • 1000QX4783 • $75

484. Christmas Angel
450QX2206 • $45

485. Christmas Fantasy
1300QX1554 • $87
Re-issued from 1981.

486. Christmas Memories
SICK • 650QX3116 • $35

487. Cloisonne Angel
1200QX1454 • $110

488. Clothespin Soldier 1: British
SICK • 500QX4583 • $103

489. Colors of Christmas: Nativity
450QX3083 • $60

490. Colors of Christmas: Santa's Flight
450QX3086 • $49

491. Cowboy Snowman
800QX4806 • $45

492. Currier & Ives
450QX2013 • $20

493. Cycling Santa
2000QX4355 • $95
Re-issued in 1983.

494. Daughter
450QX2046 • $50

495. Disney
450QX2173 • $50

496. The Divine Miss Piggy™
FRAN • 1200QX4255 • $94
Re-issued from 1981.

497. Elfin Artist
SICK • 900QX4573 • $50

498. Embroidered Tree
650QX4946 • $30

499. Father
SICK • 450QX2056 • $37

500. First Christmas Together
1600QMB9019 • $108

501. First Christmas Together
450QX2113 • $44

502. First Christmas Together
SEAL • 550QX3026 • $25

503. First Christmas Together
850QX3066 • $45

504. First Christmas Together
SEAL • 1500QX4563 • $30

505. Friendship
450QX2086 • $25

506. Friendship
550QX3046 • $27

507. Frosty Friends 3
SEAL • 800QX4523 • $293

508. Godchild
TAGU • 450QX2226 • $30

509. Granddaughter
450QX2243 • $35

510. Grandfather
450QX2076 • $30

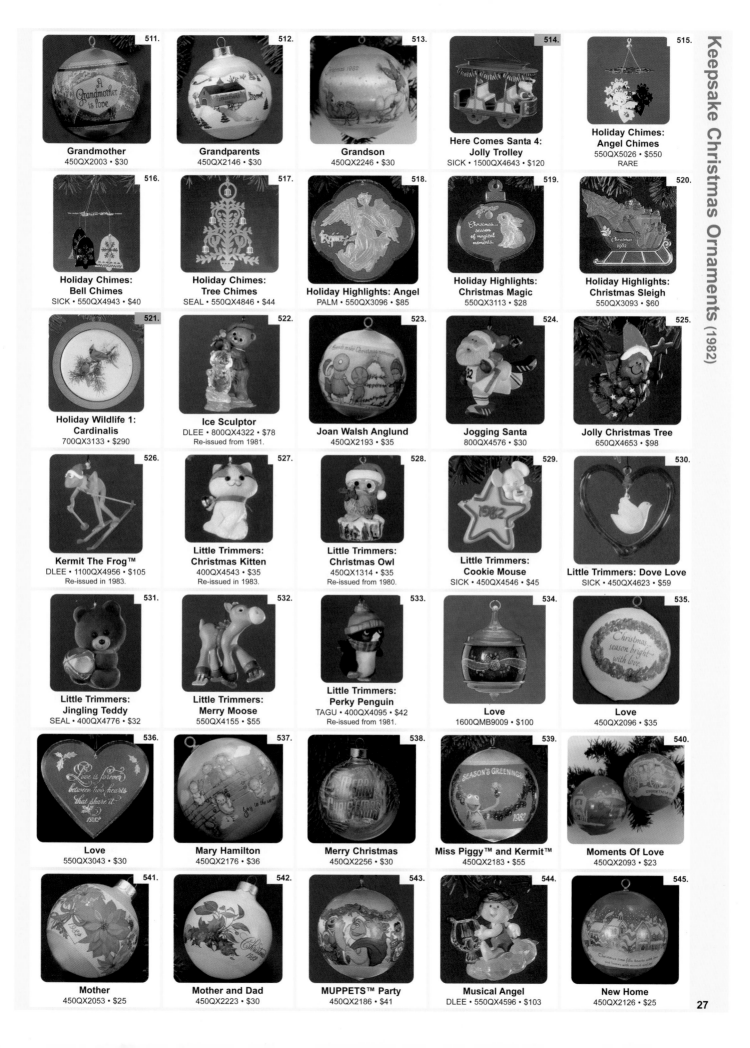

511.
Grandmother
450QX2003 • $30

512.
Grandparents
450QX2146 • $30

513.
Grandson
450QX2246 • $30

514.
Here Comes Santa 4:
Jolly Trolley
SICK • 1500QX4643 • $120

515.
Holiday Chimes:
Angel Chimes
550QX5026 • $550
RARE

516.
Holiday Chimes:
Bell Chimes
SICK • 550QX4943 • $40

517.
Holiday Chimes:
Tree Chimes
SEAL • 550QX4846 • $44

518.
Holiday Highlights: Angel
PALM • 550QX3096 • $85

519.
Holiday Highlights:
Christmas Magic
550QX3113 • $28

520.
Holiday Highlights:
Christmas Sleigh
550QX3093 • $60

521.
Holiday Wildlife 1:
Cardinalis
700QX3133 • $290

522.
Ice Sculptor
DLEE • 800QX4322 • $78
Re-issued from 1981.

523.
Joan Walsh Anglund
450QX2193 • $35

524.
Jogging Santa
800QX4576 • $30

525.
Jolly Christmas Tree
650QX4653 • $98

526.
Kermit The Frog™
DLEE • 1100QX4956 • $105
Re-issued in 1983.

527.
Little Trimmers:
Christmas Kitten
400QX4543 • $35
Re-issued in 1983.

528.
Little Trimmers:
Christmas Owl
450QX1314 • $35
Re-issued from 1980.

529.
Little Trimmers:
Cookie Mouse
SICK • 450QX4546 • $45

530.
Little Trimmers: Dove Love
SICK • 450QX4623 • $59

531.
Little Trimmers:
Jingling Teddy
SEAL • 400QX4776 • $32

532.
Little Trimmers:
Merry Moose
550QX4155 • $55

533.
Little Trimmers:
Perky Penguin
TAGU • 400QX4095 • $42
Re-issued from 1981.

534.
Love
1600QMB9009 • $100

535.
Love
450QX2096 • $35

536.
Love
550QX3043 • $30

537.
Mary Hamilton
450QX2176 • $36

538.
Merry Christmas
450QX2256 • $30

539.
Miss Piggy™ and Kermit™
450QX2183 • $55

540.
Moments Of Love
450QX2093 • $23

541.
Mother
450QX2053 • $25

542.
Mother and Dad
450QX2223 • $30

543.
MUPPETS™ Party
450QX2186 • $41

544.
Musical Angel
DLEE • 550QX4596 • $103

545.
New Home
450QX2126 • $25

27

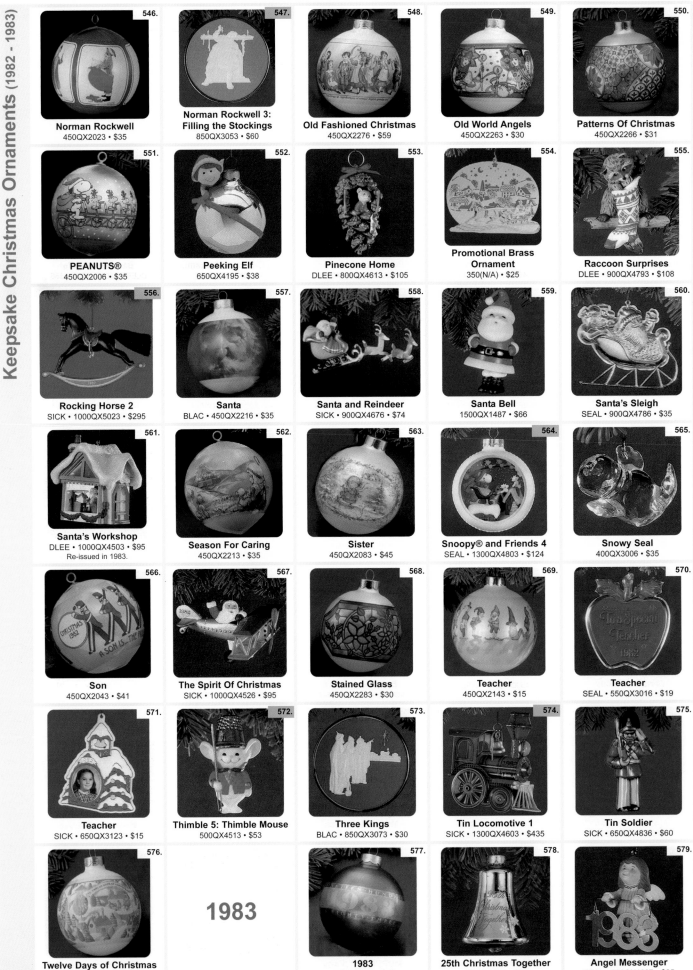

546. Norman Rockwell
450QX2023 • $35

547. Norman Rockwell 3: Filling the Stockings
850QX3053 • $60

548. Old Fashioned Christmas
450QX2276 • $59

549. Old World Angels
450QX2263 • $30

550. Patterns Of Christmas
450QX2266 • $31

551. PEANUTS®
450QX2006 • $35

552. Peeking Elf
650QX4195 • $38

553. Pinecone Home
DLEE • 800QX4613 • $105

554. Promotional Brass Ornament
350(N/A) • $25

555. Raccoon Surprises
DLEE • 900QX4793 • $108

556. Rocking Horse 2
SICK • 1000QX5023 • $295

557. Santa
BLAC • 450QX2216 • $35

558. Santa and Reindeer
SICK • 900QX4676 • $74

559. Santa Bell
1500QX1487 • $66

560. Santa's Sleigh
SEAL • 900QX4786 • $35

561. Santa's Workshop
DLEE • 1000QX4503 • $95
Re-issued in 1983.

562. Season For Caring
450QX2213 • $35

563. Sister
450QX2083 • $45

564. Snoopy® and Friends 4
SEAL • 1300QX4803 • $124

565. Snowy Seal
400QX3006 • $35

566. Son
450QX2043 • $41

567. The Spirit Of Christmas
SICK • 1000QX4526 • $95

568. Stained Glass
450QX2283 • $30

569. Teacher
450QX2143 • $15

570. Teacher
SEAL • 550QX3016 • $19

571. Teacher
SICK • 650QX3123 • $15

572. Thimble 5: Thimble Mouse
500QX4513 • $53

573. Three Kings
BLAC • 850QX3073 • $30

574. Tin Locomotive 1
SICK • 1300QX4603 • $435

575. Tin Soldier
SICK • 650QX4836 • $60

576. Twelve Days of Christmas
450QX2036 • $38

1983

577. 1983
450QX2209 • $40

578. 25th Christmas Together
450QX2247 • $30

579. Angel Messenger
SEAL • 650QX4087 • $85

28

580.
Angels
500QX2197 • $35

581.
The Annunciation
450QX2167 • $50

582.
Baby's First Christmas
1600QMB9039 • $95

583.
Baby's First Christmas
SICK • 750QX3019 • $24

584.
Baby's First Christmas
700QX3029 • $33

585.
Baby's First Christmas
DLEE • 1400QX4027 • $45

586.
**Baby's First Christmas
(Boy)**
450QX2009 • $40

587.
**Baby's First Christmas
(Girl)**
450QX2007 • $40

588.
Baby's Second Christmas
450QX2267 • $45

589.
Baroque Angels
DLEE • 1300QX4229 • $85

590.
Bell Wreath
SICK • 650QX4209 • $46

591.
**Bellringers 5:
Teddy Bellringer**
1500QX4039 • $110

592.
Betsey Clark
SEAL • 650QX4047 • $45

593.
Betsey Clark
900QX4401 • $41

594.
**Betsey Clark 11:
Christmas Happiness**
450QX2119 • $42

595.
Brass Santa
SEAL • 900QX4239 • $31

596.
Caroling Owl
SEAL • 450QX4117 • $42

597.
**Carousel 6:
Santa and Friends**
SICK • 1100QX4019 • $60

598.
Child's Third Christmas
450QX2269 • $35

599.
Christmas Joy
450QX2169 • $41

600.
Christmas Koala
SEAL • 400QX4199 • $41

601.
Christmas Wonderland
450QX2219 • $150
RARE

602.
**Clothespin Soldier 2:
Early American**
SICK • 500QX4029 • $47

603.
**Crown Classics: Enameled
Christmas Wreath**
900QX3119 • $19

604.
**Crown Classics:
Memories To Treasure**
700QX3037 • $43

605.
**Crown Classics:
Mother and Child**
750QX3027 • $40

606.
Currier & Ives
450QX2159 • $31

607.
Cycling Santa
2000QX4355 • $95
Re-issued from 1982.

608.
Daughter
450QX2037 • $70

609.
Diana Doll
DLEE • 900QX4237 • $30

610.
Disney
450QX2129 • $65

611.
Embroidered Heart
SICK • 650QX4217 • $33
Re-issued in 1984.

612.
Embroidered Stocking
SICK • 650QX4796 • $33
Re-issued in 1984.

613.
First Christmas Together
SICK • 450QX2089 • $85

614.
First Christmas Together
750QX3017 • $28

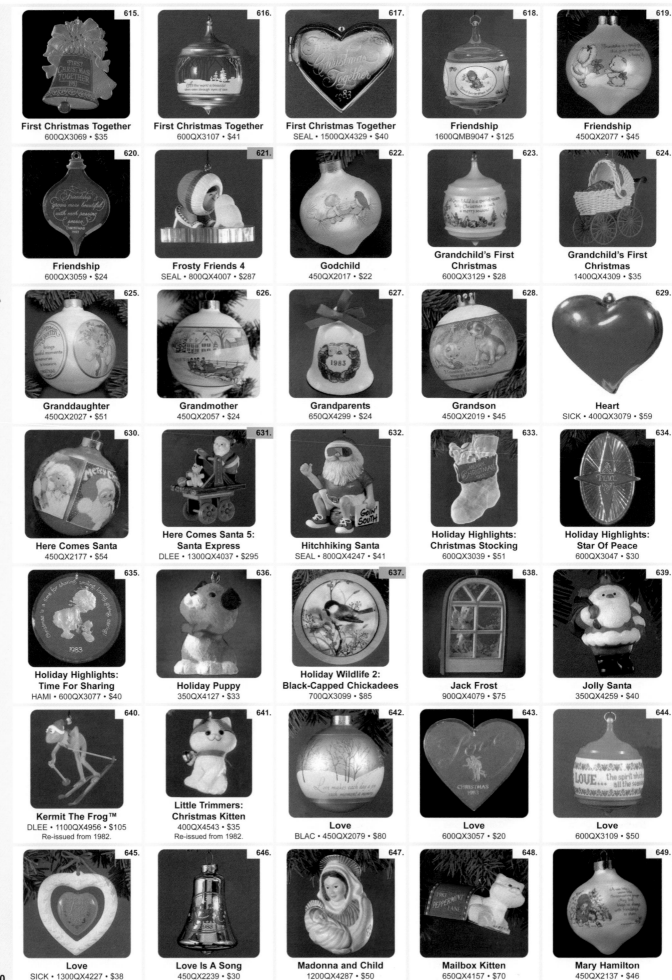

615.
First Christmas Together
600QX3069 • $35

616.
First Christmas Together
600QX3107 • $41

617.
First Christmas Together
SEAL • 1500QX4329 • $40

618.
Friendship
1600QMB9047 • $125

619.
Friendship
450QX2077 • $45

620.
Friendship
600QX3059 • $24

621.
Frosty Friends 4
SEAL • 800QX4007 • $287

622.
Godchild
450QX2017 • $22

623.
Grandchild's First
Christmas
600QX3129 • $28

624.
Grandchild's First
Christmas
1400QX4309 • $35

625.
Granddaughter
450QX2027 • $51

626.
Grandmother
450QX2057 • $24

627.
Grandparents
650QX4299 • $24

628.
Grandson
450QX2019 • $45

629.
Heart
SICK • 400QX3079 • $59

630.
Here Comes Santa
450QX2177 • $54

631.
Here Comes Santa 5:
Santa Express
DLEE • 1300QX4037 • $295

632.
Hitchhiking Santa
SEAL • 800QX4247 • $41

633.
Holiday Highlights:
Christmas Stocking
600QX3039 • $51

634.
Holiday Highlights:
Star Of Peace
600QX3047 • $30

635.
Holiday Highlights:
Time For Sharing
HAMI • 600QX3077 • $40

636.
Holiday Puppy
350QX4127 • $33

637.
Holiday Wildlife 2:
Black-Capped Chickadees
700QX3099 • $85

638.
Jack Frost
900QX4079 • $75

639.
Jolly Santa
350QX4259 • $40

640.
Kermit The Frog™
DLEE • 1100QX4956 • $105
Re-issued from 1982.

641.
Little Trimmers:
Christmas Kitten
400QX4543 • $35
Re-issued from 1982.

642.
Love
BLAC • 450QX2079 • $80

643.
Love
600QX3057 • $20

644.
Love
600QX3109 • $50

645.
Love
SICK • 1300QX4227 • $38

646.
Love Is A Song
450QX2239 • $30

647.
Madonna and Child
1200QX4287 • $50

648.
Mailbox Kitten
650QX4157 • $70

649.
Mary Hamilton
450QX2137 • $46

650.
Miss Piggy™
1300QX4057 • $195

651.
Mom and Dad
PIKE • 650QX4297 • $25

652.
Mother
600QX3067 • $30

653.
Mother's Day
1400QMB3407 • $195
RARE

654.
Mountain Climbing Santa
SEAL • 650QX4077 • $40
Re-issued in 1984.

655.
Mouse In Bell
1000QX4197 • $50

656.
Mouse On Cheese
SICK • 650QX4137 • $50

657.
The MUPPETS™
450QX2147 • $45

658.
Nativity
1600QMB9049 • $150

659.
New Home
450QX2107 • $50

660.
Norman Rockwell
450QX2157 • $56

661.
**Norman Rockwell 4:
Dress Rehearsal**
MCGE • 750QX3007 • $45

662.
**An Old Fashioned
Christmas**
450QX2179 • $30

663.
Old-Fashioned Santa
SICK • 1100QX4099 • $30

664.
Oriental Butterflies
450QX2187 • $35

665.
PEANUTS®
450QX2127 • $49

666.
Peppermint Penguin
650QX4089 • $52

667.
**Porcelain Bear 1:
Cinnamon Teddy**
DUTK • 700QX4289 • $90

668.
Rainbow Angel
DLEE • 550QX4167 • $81

669.
Rocking Horse 3
SICK • 1000QX4177 • $226

670.
Santa
400QX3087 • $39

671.
Santa's Many Faces
600QX3117 • $40

672.
Santa's On His Way
1000QX4269 • $49

673.
Santa's Workshop
DLEE • 1000QX4503 • $95
Re-issued from 1982.

674.
Scrimshaw Reindeer
SEAL • 800QX4249 • $37

675.
Season's Greetings
450QX2199 • $19

676.
Shirt Tales™
450QX2149 • $35

677.
Silver Bell
1200QX1109 • $50
Sold by JC Penny stores.

678.
Sister
450QX2069 • $50

679.
Skating Rabbit
800QX4097 • $53

680.
Ski Lift Santa
800QX4187 • $65

681.
Skiing Fox
DLEE • 800QX4207 • $44

682.
Sneaker Mouse
SEAL • 450QX4009 • $48

683.
**Snoopy® and Friends 5:
Santa Snoopy™**
SICK • 1300QX4169 • $125

684.
Son
450QX2029 • $50

31

685.
Teacher
450QX2249 • $15

686.
Teacher
600QX3049 • $15

687.
Tenth Christmas Together
650QX4307 • $46

688.
Thimble 6: Thimble Elf
500QX4017 • $40

689.
Tin Locomotive 2
SICK • 1300QX4049 • $205

690.
Tin Rocking Horse
SICK • 650QX4149 • $70

691.
Twelve Days Of Christmas
SEAL • 1500QMB4159 • $90
Re-issued in 1984.

692.
Unicorn
1000QX4267 • $81

693.
The Wise Men
450QX2207 • $65

1984

694.
All Are Precious
800QLX7044 • $25
MAGIC • Re-issued in 1985.

695.
Alpine Elf
SEAL • 600QX4521 • $29

696.
Amanda
900QX4321 • $26

697.
Art Masterpiece 1: Madonna
and Child and St. John
MCGE • 650QX3494 • $30

698.
Baby's First Christmas
700QX3001 • $30

699.
Baby's First Christmas
JLEE • 600QX3401 • $60

700.
Baby's First Christmas
DLEE • 1400QX4381 • $50

701.
Baby's First Christmas
1600QX9041 • $85

702.
Baby's First Christmas
(Boy)
450QX2404 • $50

703.
Baby's First Christmas
(Girl)
450QX2401 • $50

704.
Baby's Second Christmas
450QX2411 • $48

705.
Baby-sitter
450QX2531 • $15

706.
Bell Ringer Squirrel
SEAL • 1000QX4431 • $29

707.
Bellringers 6: Elfin Artist
1500QX4384 • $55

708.
Betsey Clark 12:
Days are Merry
500QX2494 • $40

709.
Betsey Clark Angel
900QX4624 • $25

710.
Brass Carousel
900QLX7071 • $83
MAGIC

711.
Chickadee
SICK • 600QX4514 • $55

712.
Child's Third Christmas
450QX2611 • $31

713.
Christmas In The Forest
800QLX7034 • $35
MAGIC

714.
Christmas Memories
650QX3004 • $20

715.
Christmas Owl
SEAL • 600QX4441 • $29

716.
A Christmas Prayer
450QX2461 • $35

717.
City Lights
SIED • 1000QLX7014 • $58
MAGIC

718.
Classical Angel
DLEE • 2750QX4591 • $96
Limited Edition – 24700

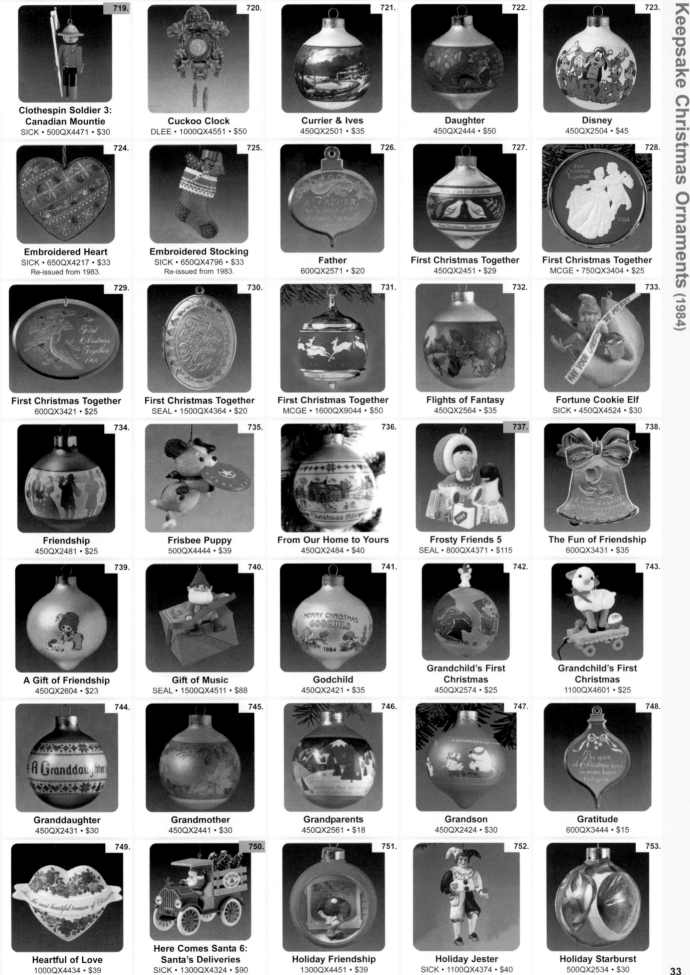

719. Clothespin Soldier 3: Canadian Mountie
SICK • 500QX4471 • $30

720. Cuckoo Clock
DLEE • 1000QX4551 • $50

721. Currier & Ives
450QX2501 • $35

722. Daughter
450QX2444 • $50

723. Disney
450QX2504 • $45

724. Embroidered Heart
SICK • 650QX4217 • $33
Re-issued from 1983.

725. Embroidered Stocking
SICK • 650QX4796 • $33
Re-issued from 1983.

726. Father
600QX2571 • $20

727. First Christmas Together
450QX2451 • $29

728. First Christmas Together
MCGE • 750QX3404 • $25

729. First Christmas Together
600QX3421 • $25

730. First Christmas Together
SEAL • 1500QX4364 • $20

731. First Christmas Together
MCGE • 1600QX9044 • $50

732. Flights of Fantasy
450QX2564 • $35

733. Fortune Cookie Elf
SICK • 450QX4524 • $30

734. Friendship
450QX2481 • $25

735. Frisbee Puppy
500QX4444 • $39

736. From Our Home to Yours
450QX2484 • $40

737. Frosty Friends 5
SEAL • 800QX4371 • $115

738. The Fun of Friendship
600QX3431 • $35

739. A Gift of Friendship
450QX2604 • $23

740. Gift of Music
SEAL • 1500QX4511 • $88

741. Godchild
450QX2421 • $35

742. Grandchild's First Christmas
450QX2574 • $25

743. Grandchild's First Christmas
1100QX4601 • $25

744. Granddaughter
450QX2431 • $30

745. Grandmother
450QX2441 • $30

746. Grandparents
450QX2561 • $18

747. Grandson
450QX2424 • $30

748. Gratitude
600QX3444 • $15

749. Heartful of Love
1000QX4434 • $39

750. Here Comes Santa 6: Santa's Deliveries
SICK • 1300QX4324 • $90

751. Holiday Friendship
1300QX4451 • $39

752. Holiday Jester
SICK • 1100QX4374 • $40

753. Holiday Starburst
500QX2534 • $30

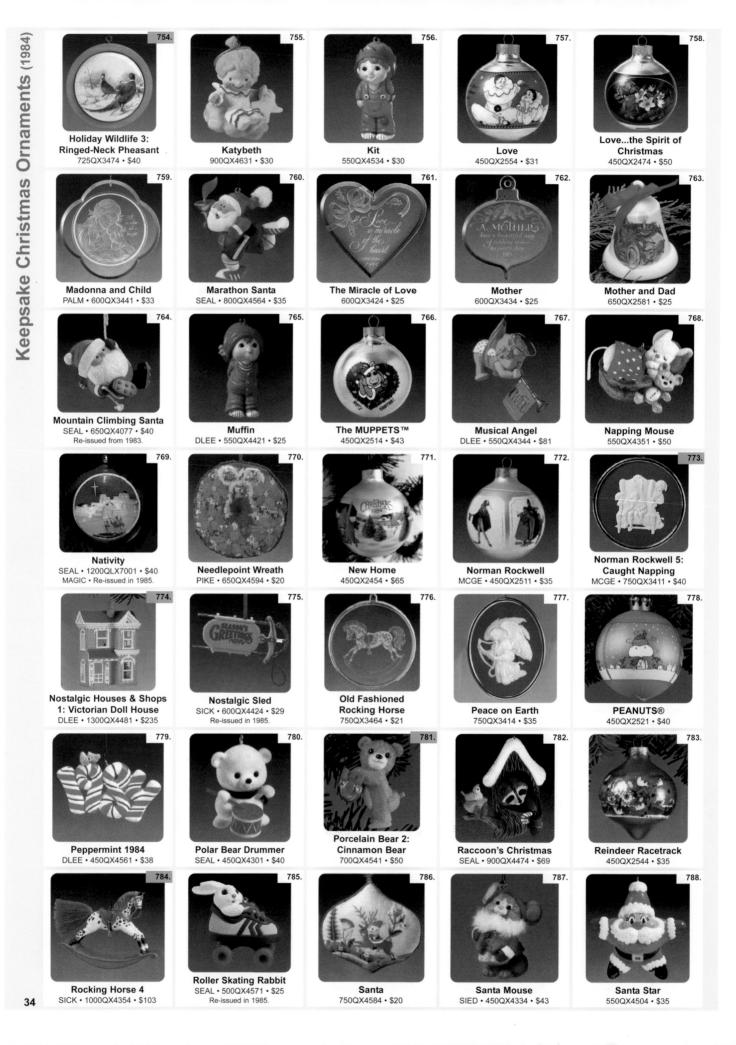

754. Holiday Wildlife 3: Ringed-Neck Pheasant
725QX3474 • $40

755. Katybeth
900QX4631 • $30

756. Kit
550QX4534 • $30

757. Love
450QX2554 • $31

758. Love...the Spirit of Christmas
450QX2474 • $50

759. Madonna and Child
PALM • 600QX3441 • $33

760. Marathon Santa
SEAL • 800QX4564 • $35

761. The Miracle of Love
600QX3424 • $25

762. Mother
600QX3434 • $25

763. Mother and Dad
650QX2581 • $25

764. Mountain Climbing Santa
SEAL • 650QX4077 • $40
Re-issued from 1983.

765. Muffin
DLEE • 550QX4421 • $25

766. The MUPPETS™
450QX2514 • $43

767. Musical Angel
DLEE • 550QX4344 • $81

768. Napping Mouse
550QX4351 • $50

769. Nativity
SEAL • 1200QLX7001 • $40
MAGIC • Re-issued in 1985.

770. Needlepoint Wreath
PIKE • 650QX4594 • $20

771. New Home
450QX2454 • $65

772. Norman Rockwell
MCGE • 450QX2511 • $35

773. Norman Rockwell 5: Caught Napping
MCGE • 750QX3411 • $40

774. Nostalgic Houses & Shops 1: Victorian Doll House
DLEE • 1300QX4481 • $235

775. Nostalgic Sled
SICK • 600QX4424 • $29
Re-issued in 1985.

776. Old Fashioned Rocking Horse
750QX3464 • $21

777. Peace on Earth
750QX3414 • $35

778. PEANUTS®
450QX2521 • $40

779. Peppermint 1984
DLEE • 450QX4561 • $38

780. Polar Bear Drummer
SEAL • 450QX4301 • $40

781. Porcelain Bear 2: Cinnamon Bear
700QX4541 • $50

782. Raccoon's Christmas
SEAL • 900QX4474 • $69

783. Reindeer Racetrack
450QX2544 • $35

784. Rocking Horse 4
SICK • 1000QX4354 • $103

785. Roller Skating Rabbit
SEAL • 500QX4571 • $25
Re-issued in 1985.

786. Santa
750QX4584 • $20

787. Santa Mouse
SIED • 450QX4334 • $43

788. Santa Star
550QX4504 • $35

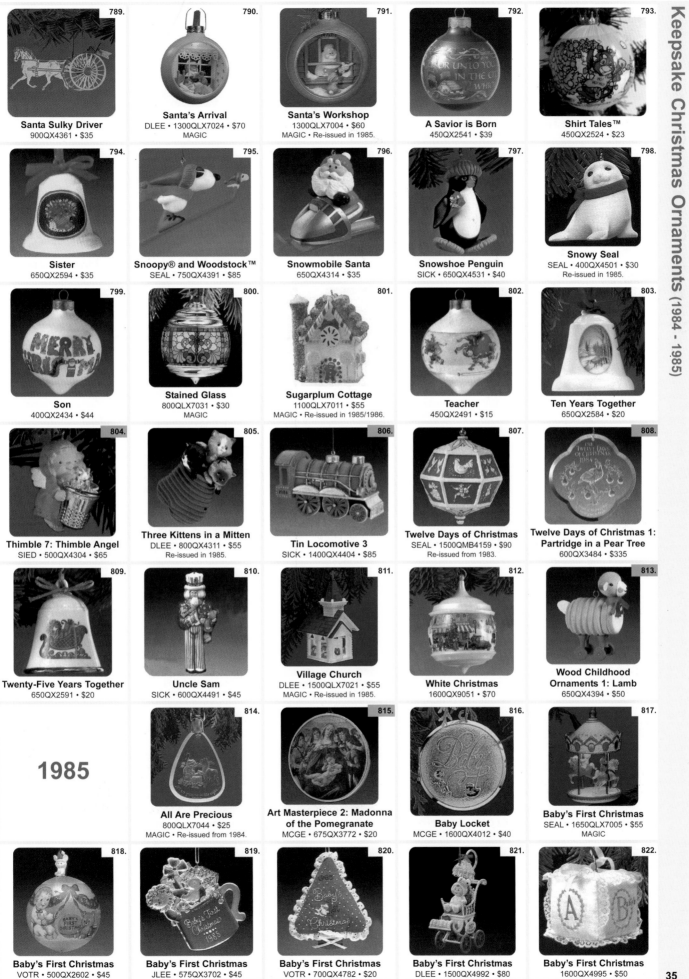

789.
Santa Sulky Driver
900QX4361 • $35

790.
Santa's Arrival
DLEE • 1300QLX7024 • $70
MAGIC

791.
Santa's Workshop
1300QLX7004 • $60
MAGIC • Re-issued in 1985.

792.
A Savior is Born
450QX2541 • $39

793.
Shirt Tales™
450QX2524 • $23

794.
Sister
650QX2594 • $35

795.
Snoopy® and Woodstock™
SEAL • 750QX4391 • $85

796.
Snowmobile Santa
650QX4314 • $35

797.
Snowshoe Penguin
SICK • 650QX4531 • $40

798.
Snowy Seal
SEAL • 400QX4501 • $30
Re-issued in 1985.

799.
Son
400QX2434 • $44

800.
Stained Glass
800QLX7031 • $30
MAGIC

801.
Sugarplum Cottage
1100QLX7011 • $55
MAGIC • Re-issued in 1985/1986.

802.
Teacher
450QX2491 • $15

803.
Ten Years Together
650QX2584 • $20

804.
Thimble 7: Thimble Angel
SIED • 500QX4304 • $65

805.
Three Kittens in a Mitten
DLEE • 800QX4311 • $55
Re-issued in 1985.

806.
Tin Locomotive 3
SICK • 1400QX4404 • $85

807.
Twelve Days of Christmas
SEAL • 1500QMB4159 • $90
Re-issued from 1983.

808.
Twelve Days of Christmas 1:
Partridge in a Pear Tree
600QX3484 • $335

809.
Twenty-Five Years Together
650QX2591 • $20

810.
Uncle Sam
SICK • 600QX4491 • $45

811.
Village Church
DLEE • 1500QLX7021 • $55
MAGIC • Re-issued in 1985.

812.
White Christmas
1600QX9051 • $70

813.
Wood Childhood
Ornaments 1: Lamb
650QX4394 • $50

1985

814.
All Are Precious
800QLX7044 • $25
MAGIC • Re-issued from 1984.

815.
Art Masterpiece 2: Madonna
of the Pomegranate
MCGE • 675QX3772 • $20

816.
Baby Locket
MCGE • 1600QX4012 • $40

817.
Baby's First Christmas
SEAL • 1650QLX7005 • $55
MAGIC

818.
Baby's First Christmas
VOTR • 500QX2602 • $45

819.
Baby's First Christmas
JLEE • 575QX3702 • $45

820.
Baby's First Christmas
VOTR • 700QX4782 • $20

821.
Baby's First Christmas
DLEE • 1500QX4992 • $80

822.
Baby's First Christmas
1600QX4995 • $50

823.
Baby's Second Christmas
600QX4785 • $40

824.
Babysitter
PYDA • 475QX2642 • $15

825.
Baker Elf
SEAL • 575QX4912 • $36

826.
Beary Smooth Ride
SICK • 650QX4805 • $25
Re-issued in 1986.

827.
Betsey Clark
850QX5085 • $40

828.
Betsey Clark 13:
Special Kind of Feeling
PIKE • 500QX2632 • $44

829.
Bottlecap Fun Bunnies
SIED • 775QX4815 • $33

830.
Candle Cameo
PIKE • 675QX3742 • $15

831.
Candy Apple Mouse
SICK • 650QX4705 • $65

832.
Charming Angel
PYDA • 975QX5125 • $26

833.
Children in the Shoe
SEAL • 950QX4905 • $50

834.
Child's Third Christmas
SEAL • 600QX4755 • $20

835.
Chris Mouse 1: Chris Mouse
SIED • 1250QLX7032 • $95
MAGIC

836.
Christmas Eve Visit
1200QLX7105 • $40
MAGIC

837.
Christmas Treats
550QX5075 • $20

838.
Clothespin Soldier 4:
Scottish Highlander
SICK • 550QX4715 • $35

839.
Country Goose
PYDA • 775QX5185 • $15

840.
Dapper Penguin
SEAL • 500QX4772 • $30

841.
Daughter
550QX5032 • $40

842.
A Disney Christmas
475QX2712 • $45

843.
Do Not Disturb Bear
SEAL • 775QX4812 • $35
Re-issued in 1986.

844.
Doggy in a Stocking
550QX4742 • $43

845.
Engineering Mouse
SIED • 550QX4735 • $25

846.
Father
VOTR • 650QX3762 • $15

847.
First Christmas Together
475QX2612 • $28

848.
First Christmas Together
675QX3705 • $25

849.
First Christmas Together
SEAL • 1675QX4005 • $25

850.
First Christmas Together
SICK • 1300QX4935 • $70

851.
First Christmas Together
800QX5072 • $13

852.
Fraggle Rock™ Holiday
475QX2655 • $30

853.
Friendship
PYDA • 675QX3785 • $19

854.
Friendship
PATT • 775QX5062 • $16

855.
From Our House to Yours
PATT • 775QX5202 • $15

856.
Frosty Friends 6
SEAL • 850QX4822 • $155

857.
Godchild
MCGE • 675QX3802 • $20

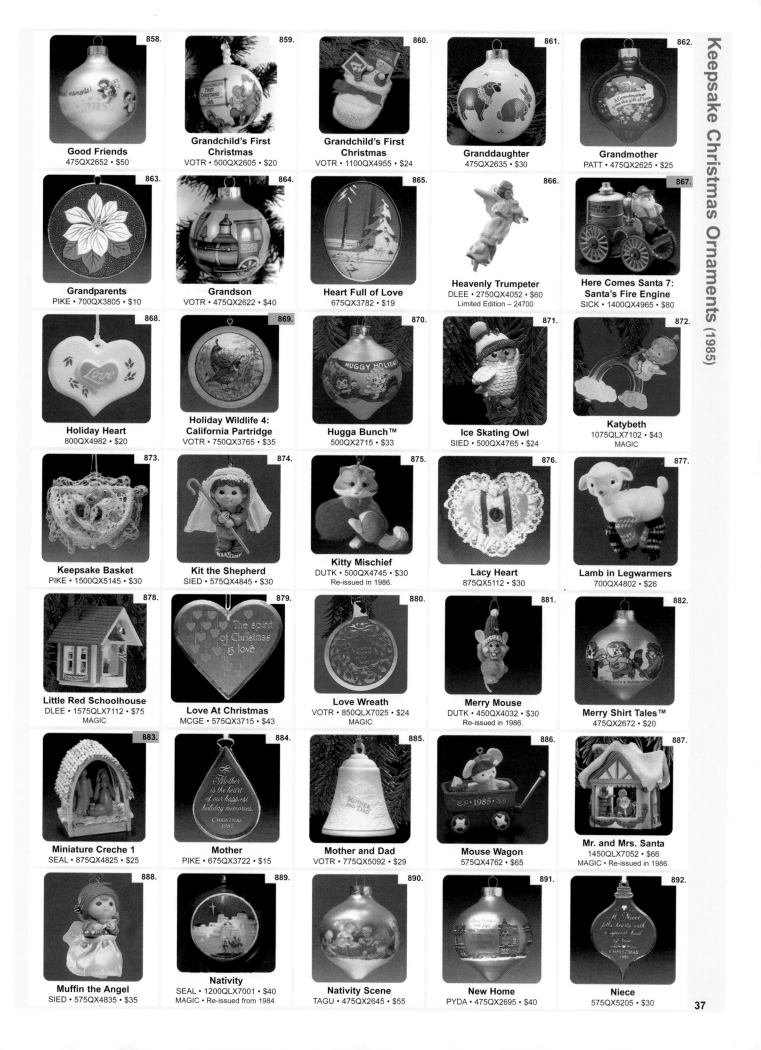

858. **Good Friends**
475QX2652 • $50

859. **Grandchild's First Christmas**
VOTR • 500QX2605 • $20

860. **Grandchild's First Christmas**
VOTR • 1100QX4955 • $24

861. **Granddaughter**
475QX2635 • $30

862. **Grandmother**
PATT • 475QX2625 • $25

863. **Grandparents**
PIKE • 700QX3805 • $10

864. **Grandson**
VOTR • 475QX2622 • $40

865. **Heart Full of Love**
675QX3782 • $19

866. **Heavenly Trumpeter**
DLEE • 2750QX4052 • $60
Limited Edition – 24700

867. **Here Comes Santa 7: Santa's Fire Engine**
SICK • 1400QX4965 • $80

868. **Holiday Heart**
800QX4982 • $20

869. **Holiday Wildlife 4: California Partridge**
VOTR • 750QX3765 • $35

870. **Hugga Bunch™**
500QX2715 • $33

871. **Ice Skating Owl**
SIED • 500QX4765 • $24

872. **Katybeth**
1075QLX7102 • $43
MAGIC

873. **Keepsake Basket**
PIKE • 1500QX5145 • $30

874. **Kit the Shepherd**
SIED • 575QX4845 • $30

875. **Kitty Mischief**
DUTK • 500QX4745 • $30
Re-issued in 1986.

876. **Lacy Heart**
875QX5112 • $30

877. **Lamb in Legwarmers**
700QX4802 • $26

878. **Little Red Schoolhouse**
DLEE • 1575QLX7112 • $75
MAGIC

879. **Love At Christmas**
MCGE • 575QX3715 • $43

880. **Love Wreath**
VOTR • 850QLX7025 • $24
MAGIC

881. **Merry Mouse**
DUTK • 450QX4032 • $30
Re-issued in 1986.

882. **Merry Shirt Tales™**
475QX2672 • $20

883. **Miniature Creche 1**
SEAL • 875QX4825 • $25

884. **Mother**
PIKE • 675QX3722 • $15

885. **Mother and Dad**
VOTR • 775QX5092 • $29

886. **Mouse Wagon**
575QX4762 • $65

887. **Mr. and Mrs. Santa**
1450QLX7052 • $66
MAGIC • Re-issued in 1986.

888. **Muffin the Angel**
SIED • 575QX4835 • $35

889. **Nativity**
SEAL • 1200QLX7001 • $40
MAGIC • Re-issued from 1984.

890. **Nativity Scene**
TAGU • 475QX2645 • $55

891. **New Home**
PYDA • 475QX2695 • $40

892. **Niece**
575QX5205 • $30

37

893. Night Before Christmas
SEAL • 1300QX4494 • $45

894. Norman Rockwell
MCGE • 475QX2662 • $30

895. Norman Rockwell 6:
Jolly Postman
MCGE • 750QX3745 • $35

896. Nostalgic Houses & Shops
2: Old Fashion Toy Shop
DLEE • 1375QX4975 • $127

897. Nostalgic Sled
SICK • 600QX4424 • $29
Re-issued from 1984.

898. Old-Fashioned Doll
1450QX5195 • $38

899. Old-Fashioned Wreath
750QX3735 • $25

900. Peaceful Kingdom
PIKE • 575QX3732 • $40

901. PEANUTS®
475QX2665 • $46

902. Porcelain Bear 3
DUTK • 750QX4792 • $45

903. Porcelain Bird
SICK • 650QX4795 • $38

904. Rainbow Brite™ and
Friends
475QX2682 • $39

905. Rocking Horse 5
SICK • 1075QX4932 • $90

906. Rocking Horse Memories
VOTR • 1000QX5182 • $19

907. Roller Skating Rabbit
SEAL • 500QX4571 • $25
Re-issued from 1984.

908. Santa Claus
675QX3005 • $15

909. Santa Pipe
DUTK • 950QX4942 • $35

910. Santa's Ski Trip
SEAL • 1200QX4962 • $76

911. Santa's Village –
Santa Claus the Movie™
675QX3002 • $15

912. Santa's Workshop
1300QLX7004 • $60
MAGIC • Re-issued from 1984.

913. Season of Beauty
LYLE • 800QLX7122 • $30
MAGIC

914. Sewn Photo Holder
PIKE • 700QX3795 • $20

915. Sheep at Christmas
SICK • 825QX5175 • $35

916. Sister
PATT • 725QX5065 • $28

917. Skateboard Raccoon
DUTK • 650QX4732 • $45
Re-issued in 1986.

918. Snoopy® and Woodstock™
SIED • 750QX4915 • $65

919. Snowflake
PATT • 650QX5105 • $20

920. Snow-Pitching Snowman
DLEE • 450QX4702 • $25
Re-issued in 1986.

921. Snowy Seal
SEAL • 400QX4501 • $30
Re-issued from 1984.

922. Soccer Beaver
DUTK • 650QX4775 • $25
Re-issued in 1986.

923. Son
SIED • 550QX5025 • $62

924. Special Friends
PALM • 575QX3725 • $13

925. The Spirit of Santa Claus
2250QX4985 • $95

926. Stardust Angel
DLEE • 575QX4752 • $47

927. Sugarplum Cottage
1100QLX7011 • $55
MAGIC • Also issued 1984 & 1986.

928.

Sun and Fun Santa
SIED • 775QX4922 • $30

929.

Swinging Angel Bell
SIED • 1100QX4925 • $40

930.

Swiss Cheese Lane
1300QLX7065 • $50
MAGIC

931.

Teacher
600QX5052 • $22

932.

Thimble 8: Thimble Santa
SIED • 550QX4725 • $50

933.

Three Kittens in a Mitten
DLEE • 800QX4311 • $55
Re-issued from 1984.

934.

Tin Locomotive 4
SICK • 1475QX4972 • $70

935.

Trumpet Panda
SEAL • 450QX4712 • $25

936.

**Twelve Days of Christmas 2:
Two Turtle Doves**
PIKE • 650QX3712 • $95

937.

Twenty-Five Years Together
PATT • 800QX5005 • $16

938.

Victorian Lady
950QX5132 • $20

939.

Village Church
DLEE • 1500QLX7021 • $55
MAGIC • Re-issued from 1984.

940.

Whirligig Santa
1250QX5192 • $35

941.

**Windows of the World 1:
Feliz Navidad**
DLEE • 975QX4902 • $98

942.

With Appreciation
675QX3752 • $15

943.

**Wood Childhood
Ornaments 2: Train**
DUTK • 700QX4722 • $60

1986

944.

Acorn Inn
UNRU • 850QX4243 • $29

945.

**Art Masterpiece 3:
Madonna and Child with
the Infant St. John**
MCGE • 675QX3506 • $36

946.

Baby Locket
MCGE • 1600QX4123 • $36

947.

Baby's First Christmas
CROW • 1950QLX7103 • $65
MAGIC

948.

Baby's First Christmas
PATT • 550QX2713 • $37

949.

Baby's First Christmas
PATT • 800QX3792 • $34

950.

Baby's First Christmas
PALM • 600QX3803 • $48

951.

Baby's First Christmas
SICK • 900QX4126 • $85
RARE

952.

Baby's Second Christmas
SIED • 650QX4133 • $37

953.

Baby-Sitter
475QX2756 • $16

954.

Beary Smooth Ride
SICK • 650QX4805 • $25
Re-issued from 1985.

955.

**Betsey Clark: Home for
Christmas 1**
PIKE • 500QX2776 • $32

956.

Bluebird
SICK • 725QX4283 • $120
RARE

957.

Chatty Penguin
CROW • 575QX4176 • $35

958.

Child's Third Christmas
VOTR • 650QX4136 • $22

959.

**Chris Mouse 2:
Chris Mouse Dreams**
DUTK • 1300QLX7056 • $110
MAGIC

960.

Christmas Beauty
PATT • 600QX3223 • $17

961.

**Christmas Classics 1:
The Nutcracker Ballet –
Sugarplum Fairy**
1750QLX7043 • $65
MAGIC

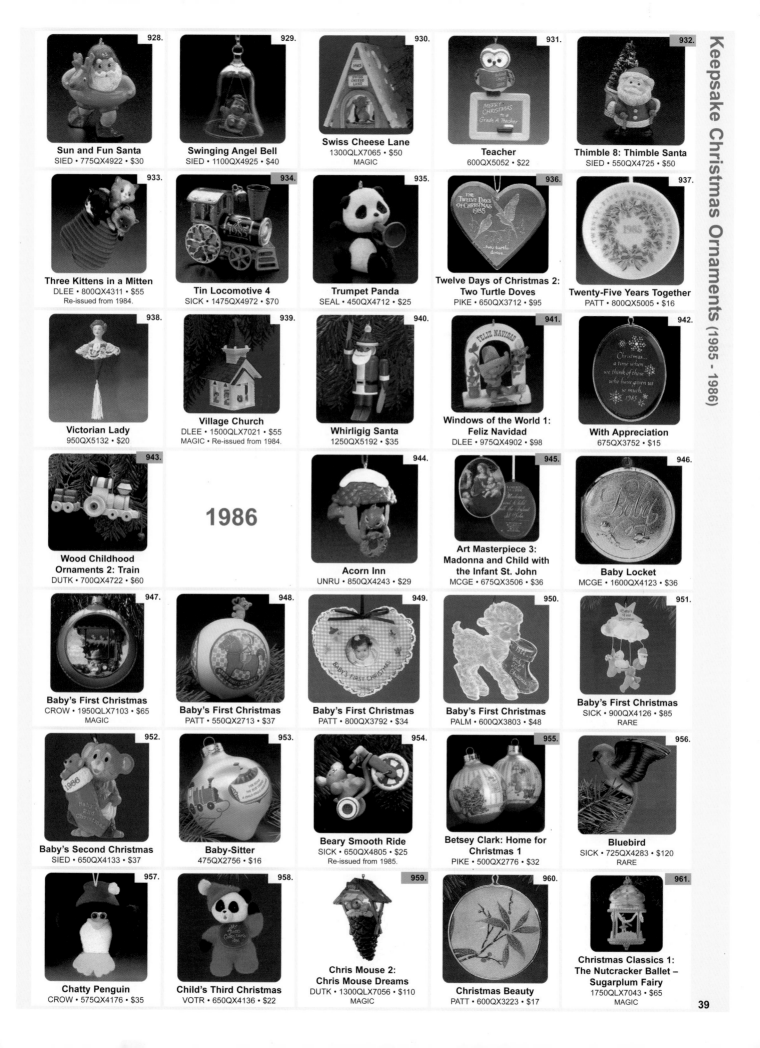

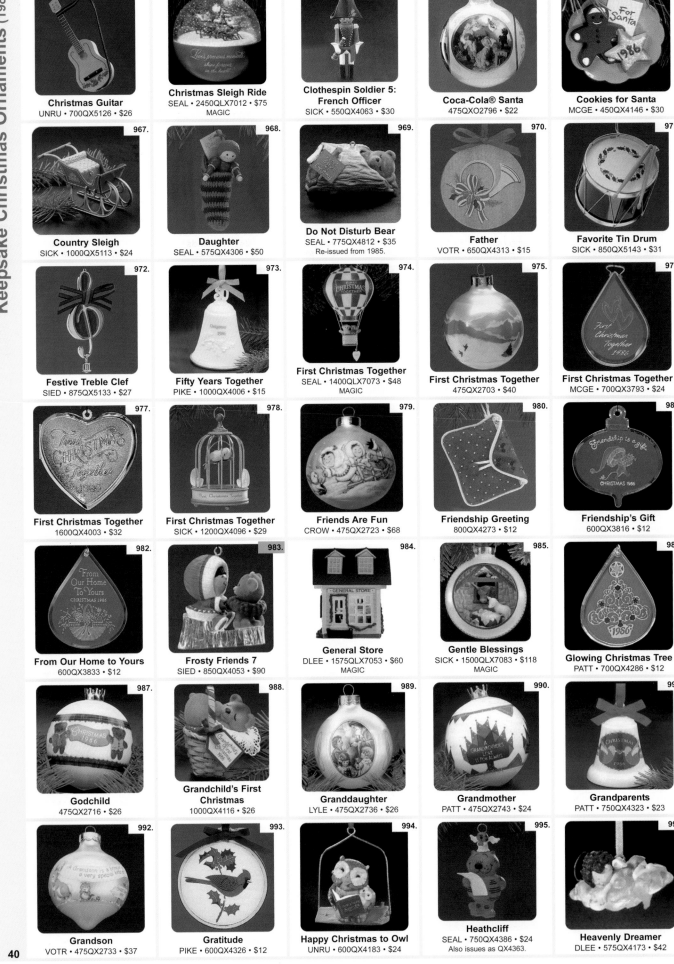

962. Christmas Guitar
UNRU • 700QX5126 • $26

963. Christmas Sleigh Ride
SEAL • 2450QLX7012 • $75
MAGIC

964. Clothespin Soldier 5:
French Officer
SICK • 550QX4063 • $30

965. Coca-Cola® Santa
475QXO2796 • $22

966. Cookies for Santa
MCGE • 450QX4146 • $30

967. Country Sleigh
SICK • 1000QX5113 • $24

968. Daughter
SEAL • 575QX4306 • $50

969. Do Not Disturb Bear
SEAL • 775QX4812 • $35
Re-issued from 1985.

970. Father
VOTR • 650QX4313 • $15

971. Favorite Tin Drum
SICK • 850QX5143 • $31

972. Festive Treble Clef
SIED • 875QX5133 • $27

973. Fifty Years Together
PIKE • 1000QX4006 • $15

974. First Christmas Together
SEAL • 1400QLX7073 • $48
MAGIC

975. First Christmas Together
475QX2703 • $40

976. First Christmas Together
MCGE • 700QX3793 • $24

977. First Christmas Together
1600QX4003 • $32

978. First Christmas Together
SICK • 1200QX4096 • $29

979. Friends Are Fun
CROW • 475QX2723 • $68

980. Friendship Greeting
800QX4273 • $12

981. Friendship's Gift
600QX3816 • $12

982. From Our Home to Yours
600QX3833 • $12

983. Frosty Friends 7
SIED • 850QX4053 • $90

984. General Store
DLEE • 1575QLX7053 • $60
MAGIC

985. Gentle Blessings
SICK • 1500QLX7083 • $118
MAGIC

986. Glowing Christmas Tree
PATT • 700QX4286 • $12

987. Godchild
475QX2716 • $26

988. Grandchild's First
Christmas
1000QX4116 • $26

989. Granddaughter
LYLE • 475QX2736 • $26

990. Grandmother
PATT • 475QX2743 • $24

991. Grandparents
PATT • 750QX4323 • $23

992. Grandson
VOTR • 475QX2733 • $37

993. Gratitude
PIKE • 600QX4326 • $12

994. Happy Christmas to Owl
UNRU • 600QX4183 • $24

995. Heathcliff
SEAL • 750QX4386 • $24
Also issues as QX4363.

996. Heavenly Dreamer
DLEE • 575QX4173 • $42

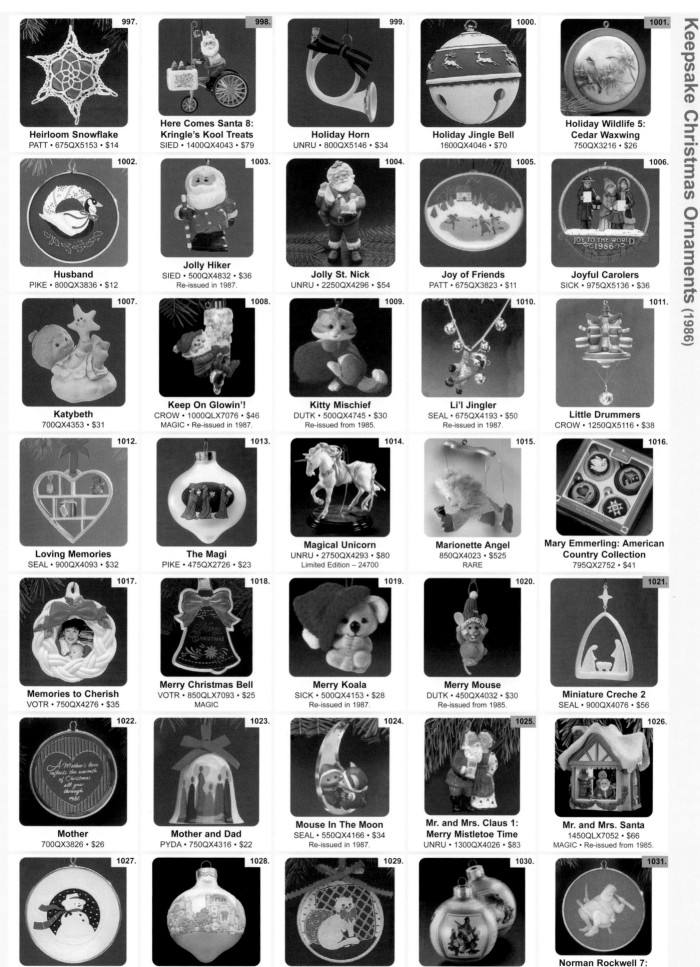

997.
Heirloom Snowflake
PATT • 675QX5153 • $14

998.
Here Comes Santa 8:
Kringle's Kool Treats
SIED • 1400QX4043 • $79

999.
Holiday Horn
UNRU • 800QX5146 • $34

1000.
Holiday Jingle Bell
1600QX4046 • $70

1001.
Holiday Wildlife 5:
Cedar Waxwing
750QX3216 • $26

1002.
Husband
PIKE • 800QX3836 • $12

1003.
Jolly Hiker
SIED • 500QX4832 • $36
Re-issued in 1987.

1004.
Jolly St. Nick
UNRU • 2250QX4296 • $54

1005.
Joy of Friends
PATT • 675QX3823 • $11

1006.
Joyful Carolers
SICK • 975QX5136 • $36

1007.
Katybeth
700QX4353 • $31

1008.
Keep On Glowin'!
CROW • 1000QLX7076 • $46
MAGIC • Re-issued in 1987.

1009.
Kitty Mischief
DUTK • 500QX4745 • $30
Re-issued from 1985.

1010.
Li'l Jingler
SEAL • 675QX4193 • $50
Re-issued in 1987.

1011.
Little Drummers
CROW • 1250QX5116 • $38

1012.
Loving Memories
SEAL • 900QX4093 • $32

1013.
The Magi
PIKE • 475QX2726 • $23

1014.
Magical Unicorn
UNRU • 2750QX4293 • $80
Limited Edition – 24700

1015.
Marionette Angel
850QX4023 • $525
RARE

1016.
Mary Emmerling: American
Country Collection
795QX2752 • $41

1017.
Memories to Cherish
VOTR • 750QX4276 • $35

1018.
Merry Christmas Bell
VOTR • 850QLX7093 • $25
MAGIC

1019.
Merry Koala
SICK • 500QX4153 • $28
Re-issued in 1987.

1020.
Merry Mouse
DUTK • 450QX4032 • $30
Re-issued from 1985.

1021.
Miniature Creche 2
SEAL • 900QX4076 • $56

1022.
Mother
700QX3826 • $26

1023.
Mother and Dad
PYDA • 750QX4316 • $22

1024.
Mouse In The Moon
SEAL • 550QX4166 • $34
Re-issued in 1987.

1025.
Mr. and Mrs. Claus 1:
Merry Mistletoe Time
UNRU • 1300QX4026 • $83

1026.
Mr. and Mrs. Santa
1450QLX7052 • $66
MAGIC • Re-issued from 1985.

1027.
Nephew
625QX3813 • $14

1028.
New Home
CROW • 475QX2746 • $78

1029.
Niece
600QX4266 • $14

1030.
Norman Rockwell
PIKE • 475QX2763 • $41

1031.
Norman Rockwell 7:
Checking Up
PIKE • 775QX3213 • $32

1032.

**Nostalgic Houses & Shops
3: Christmas Candy Shoppe**
DLEE • 1375QX4033 • $300

1033.

Nutcracker Santa
UNRU • 1000QX5123 • $48

1034.

Old-Fashioned Santa
SICK • 1275QXO4403 • $52

1035.

On The Right Track
DUTK • 1500QSP4201 • $50

1036.

Open Me First
FORS • 725QX4226 • $42

1037.

Paddington™ Bear
SIED • 600QX4356 • $37
Also issues as QX4376.

1038.

PEANUTS®
475QX2766 • $62

1039.

Playful Possum
CROW • 1100QX4253 • $38

1040.

Popcorn Mouse
SICK • 675QX4213 • $52

1041.

Porcelain Bear 4
775QX4056 • $41

1042.

Puppy's Best Friend
UNRU • 650QX4203 • $26

1043.

Rah Rah Rabbit
CROW • 700QX4216 • $35

1044.
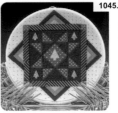
Reindeer Champs 1: Dasher
SIED • 750QX4223 • $148

1045.

Remembering Christmas
875QX5106 • $18

1046.

Rocking Horse 6
SICK • 1075QX4016 • $72

1047.

Santa and His Reindeer
975QXO4406 • $38

1048.

**Santa and Sparky 1:
Lighting the Tree**
2200QLX7033 • $66
MAGIC

1049.

Santa's Hot Tub
SEAL • 1200QX4263 • $59

1050.

Santa's On His Way
UNRU • 1500QLX7115 • $74
MAGIC

1051.

Santa's Panda Pal
500QXO4413 • $20

1052.

Santa's Snack
CROW • 1000QLX7066 • $56
MAGIC

1053.

Season of the Heart
PATT • 475QX2706 • $19

1054.

Sharing Friendship
VOTR • 850QLX7063 • $30
MAGIC

1055.

Shirt Tales™ Parade
475QX2773 • $24

1056.

Sister
VOTR • 675QX3806 • $28

1057.

Skateboard Raccoon
DUTK • 650QX4732 • $45
Re-issued from 1985.

1058.

Ski Tripper
SIED • 675QX4206 • $18

1059.

Snoopy® and Woodstock™
SIED • 800QX4383 • $65

1060.

Snow Buddies
DUTK • 800QX4236 • $38

1061.

Snow-Pitching Snowman
DLEE • 450QX4702 • $25
Re-issued from 1985.

1062.

Soccer Beaver
DUTK • 650QX4775 • $25
Re-issued from 1985.

1063.

Son
SEAL • 575QX4303 • $42

1064.

Special Delivery
SIED • 500QX4156 • $22

1065.

Star Brighteners
VOTR • 600QX3226 • $23

1066.

The Statue of Liberty
PYDA • 600QX3843 • $30

1067.
Sugarplum Cottage
1100QLX7011 • $55
MAGIC • Re-issued from 1984/85.

1068.
Sweetheart
SEAL • 1100QX4086 • $61

1069.
Teacher
TAGU • 475QX2753 • $14

1070.
Ten Years Together
750QX4013 • $29

1071.
Thimble 9:
Thimble Partridge
575QX4066 • $26

1072.
Timeless Love
VOTR • 600QX3796 • $30

1073.
Tin Locomotive 5
SICK • 1475QX4036 • $70

1074.
Tipping the Scales
DUTK • 675QX4186 • $22

1075.
Touchdown Santa
DUTK • 800QX4233 • $38

1076.
Treetop Trio
DLEE • 1100QX4256 • $39
Re-issued in 1987.

1077.
Twelve Days of Christmas 3:
Three French Hens
VOTR • 650QX3786 • $58

1078.
Twenty-Five Years Together
VOTR • 800QX4103 • $30

1079.
Village Express
SICK • 2450QLX7072 • $87
MAGIC • Re-issued in 1987.

1080.
Walnut Shell Rider
SEAL • 600QX4196 • $31
Re-issued in 1987.

1081.
Welcome, Christmas
CROW • 825QX5103 • $34

1082.
Windows of the World 2:
Vrolyk Kerstfeest
SIED • 1000QX4083 • $40

1083.
Wood Childhood
Ornaments 3: Reindeer
CROW • 750QX4073 • $26

1084.
Wynken, Blynken and Nod
DLEE • 975QX4246 • $43

1987

1085.
Angelic Messengers
UNRU • 1875QLX7113 • $93
MAGIC

1086.
Baby Locket
MCGE • 1500QX4617 • $34

1087.
Baby's First Christmas
1350QLX7049 • $80
MAGIC

1088.
Baby's First Christmas
PYDA • 600QX3729 • $32

1089.
Baby's First Christmas
DLEE • 975QX4113 • $35

1090.
Baby's First Christmas
750QX4619 • $47

1091.
Baby's First Christmas
(Boy)
PATT • 475QX2749 • $36

1092.
Baby's First Christmas
(Girl)
PATT • 475QX2747 • $32

1093.
Baby's Second Christmas
DLEE • 575QX4607 • $36

1094.
Babysitter
PIKE • 475QX2797 • $29

1095.
Beary Special
SIED • 475QX4557 • $28

1096.
Betsey Clark: Home for
Christmas 2
PIKE • 500QX2727 • $23

1097.
Bright Christmas
Dreams
SIED • 725QX4737 • $96

1098.
Bright Noel
VOTR • 700QLX7059 • $38
MAGIC

1099.
Carousel Reindeer
SICK • 800QXC5817 • $49

1100.
Child's Third Christmas
CROW • 575QX4599 • $36

43

1101.
Chocolate Chipmunk
SEAL • 600QX4567 • $67

1102.
Chris Mouse 3:
Chris Mouse Glow
SIED • 1100QLX7057 • $78
MAGIC

1103.
Christmas Classics 2:
A Christmas Carol
UNRU • 1600QLX7029 • $58
MAGIC

1104.
Christmas Cuddle
575QX4537 • $41

1105.
Christmas Fun Puzzle
800QX4679 • $31

1106.
Christmas Is Gentle
SEAL • 1750QX4449 • $50
Limited Edition – 24700

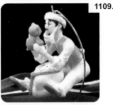

1107.
Christmas Keys
UNRU • 575QX4739 • $29

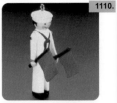

1108.
Christmas Morning
CROW • 2450QLX7013 • $48
MAGIC • Re-issued in 1988.

1109.
Christmas Time Mime
UNRU • 2750QX4429 • $30
Limited Edition – 24700

1110.
Clothespin Soldier 6:
Sailor
SICK • 550QX4807 • $29

1111.
Collector's Plate 1: Light
Shines at Christmas
VOTR • 800QX4817 • $69

1112.
The Constitution
PATT • 650QX3777 • $19

1113.
Country Wreath
PYDA • 575QX4709 • $19

1114.
Currier & Ives:
American Farm Scene
LYLE • 475QX2829 • $41

1115.
Dad
SIED • 600QX4629 • $35

1116.
Daughter
SICK • 575QX4637 • $40

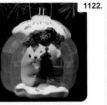

1117.
December Showers
DLEE • 550QX4487 • $31

1118.
Doc Holiday
SEAL • 800QX4677 • $44

1119.
Dr. Seuss®: The
Grinch™'s Christmas
475QX2783 • $189
RARE

1120.
Favorite Santa
DUTK • 2250QX4457 • $38

1121.
Fifty Years Together
SEAL • 800QX4437 • $23

1122.
First Christmas Together
1150QLX7087 • $56
MAGIC

1123.
First Christmas Together
LYLE • 475QX2729 • $31

1124.
First Christmas Together
PYDA • 650QX3719 • $29

1125.
First Christmas Together
800QX4459 • $43

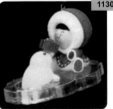

1126.
First Christmas Together
DLEE • 950QX4467 • $37

1127.
First Christmas Together
PATT • 1500QX4469 • $35

1128.
Folk Art Santa
SICK • 525QX4749 • $34

1129.
From Our Home to Yours
PYDA • 475QX2799 • $59

1130.
Frosty Friends 8
SEAL • 850QX4409 • $90

1131.
Fudge Forever
DUTK • 500QX4497 • $40

1132.
Godchild
PYDA • 475QX2767 • $29

1133.
Goldfinch
SICK • 700QX4649 • $84

1134.
Good Cheer Blimp
SICK • 1600QLX7046 • $71
MAGIC

1135.
Grandchild's First
Christmas
SEAL • 900QX4609 • $67

1136.
Granddaughter
VOTR • 600QX3747 • $16

1137.
Grandmother
475QX2779 • $17

1138.
Grandparents
PIKE • 475QX2777 • $22

1139.
Grandson
VOTR • 475QX2769 • $39

1140.
Happy Holidata
SIED • 650QX4717 • $30
Re-issued in 1988.

1141.
Happy Santa
CROW • 475QX4569 • $37

1142.
Heart in Blossom
VOTR • 600QX3727 • $29

1143.
Heavenly Harmony
CROW • 1500QX4659 • $37

1144.
Here Comes Santa 9:
Santa's Woody
CROW • 1400QX4847 • $95

1145.
Holiday Greetings
600QX3757 • $10

1146.
Holiday Heirloom 1
UNRU • 2500QX4857 • $34
Limited Edition – 34600

1147.
Holiday Hourglass
UNRU • 800QX4707 • $36

1148.
Holiday Wildlife 6:
Snow Goose
VOTR • 750QX3717 • $28

1149.
Hot Dogger
UNRU • 650QX4719 • $28

1150.
Husband
VOTR • 700QX3739 • $11

1151.
I Remember Santa
LYLE • 475QX2789 • $40

1152.
Icy Treat
SIED • 450QX4509 • $35

1153.
In a Nutshell
UNRU • 550QX4697 • $30
Re-issued in 1988.

1154.
Jack Frosting
SEAL • 700QX4499 • $53

1155.
Jammie Pies
475QX2839 • $18

1156.
Jogging Through The Snow
DUTK • 725QX4577 • $34

1157.
Jolly Follies
CROW • 850QX4669 • $38

1158.
Jolly Hiker
SIED • 500QX4832 • $36
Re-issued from 1986.

1159.
Joy Ride
SEAL • 1150QX4407 • $75

1160.
Joyous Angels
SEAL • 775QX4657 • $37

1161.
Keep On Glowin'!
CROW • 1000QLX7076 • $46
MAGIC • Re-issued from 1986.

1162.
Keeping Cozy
CROW • 1175QLX7047 • $40
MAGIC

1163.
Lacy Brass Snowflake
1150QLX7097 • $23
MAGIC

1164.
Let It Snow
650QX4589 • $28

1165.
Li'l Jingler
SEAL • 675QX4193 • $50
Re-issued from 1986.

1166.
Little Whittler
DUTK • 600QX4699 • $35

1167.
Love Is Everywhere
LYLE • 475QX2787 • $29

1168.
Loving Holiday
SEAL • 2200QLX7016 • $59
MAGIC

1169.
Memories Are Forever
SEAL • 850QLX7067 • $46
MAGIC

1170.
Meowy Christmas!
PIKE • 1000QLX7089 • $48
MAGIC

1171.

Merry Koala
SICK • 500QX4153 • $28
Re-issued from 1986.

1172.

Miniature Creche 3
SEAL • 900QX4819 • $41

1173.

Mistletoad
CROW • 700QX4687 • $32
Re-issued in 1988.

1174.

Mother
PIKE • 650QX3737 • $22

1175.

Mother and Dad
PIKE • 700QX4627 • $20

1176.

Mouse in the Moon
SEAL • 550QX4166 • $34
Re-issued from 1986.

1177.

**Mr. and Mrs. Claus 2:
Home Cooking**
UNRU • 1325QX4837 • $67

1178.
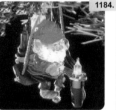
Nature's Decorations
VOTR • 475QX2739 • $38

1179.
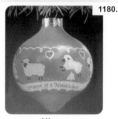
New Home
PATT • 600QX3767 • $34

1180.

Niece
475QX2759 • $13

1181.

Night Before Christmas
CROW • 650QX4517 • $42
Re-issued in 1988.

1182.

**Norman Rockwell 8:
The Christmas Dance**
PALM • 775QX3707 • $20

1183.
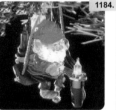
**Norman Rockwell:
Christmas Scenes**
LYLE • 475QX2827 • $30

1184.

North Pole Power & Light
CROW • 295XPR9333 • $22

1185.
**Nostalgic Houses & Shops
4: House on Main Street**
DLEE • 1400QX4839 • $97

1186.

Nostalgic Rocker
SICK • 650QX4689 • $23

1187.

Owliday Wish
PIKE • 650QX4559 • $24
Re-issued in 1988.

1188.

Paddington™ Bear
PIKE • 550QX4727 • $44

1189.

PEANUTS®
475QX2819 • $44

1190.
Porcelain Bear 5
775QX4427 • $22

1191.

Pretty Kitty
CROW • 1100QX4489 • $37

1192.
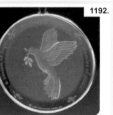
Promise of Peace
PIKE • 650QX3749 • $35

1193.

Raccoon Biker
SIED • 700QX4587 • $35

1194.

Reindeer Champs 2: Dancer
SIED • 750QX4809 • $44

1195.

Reindoggy
SIED • 575QX4527 • $33
Re-issued in 1988.

1196.

Rocking Horse 7
SICK • 1075QX4829 • $85

1197.

**Santa and Sparky 2:
Perfect Portrait**
1950QLX7019 • $74
MAGIC

1198.

Santa at the Bat
SIED • 775QX4579 • $32

1199.

Season For Friendship
VOTR • 850QLX7069 • $20
MAGIC

1200.
Seasoned Greetings
SEAL • 625QX4549 • $30

1201.

Sister
SICK • 600QX4747 • $19

1202.

Sleepy Santa
CROW • 625QX4507 • $41

1203.

Snoopy® and Woodstock™
SIED • 725QX4729 • $61

1204.

Son
SICK • 575QX4639 • $95
RARE

1205.

Special Memories
675QX4647 • $36

1206.
Spots 'n Stripes
550QX4529 • $32

1207.
St. Louie Nick
DUTK • 775QX4539 • $34
Re-issued in 1988.

1208.
Sweetheart
SICK • 1100QX4479 • $34

1209.
Teacher
SIED • 575QX4667 • $29

1210.
Ten Years Together
VOTR • 700QX4447 • $21

1211.
Thimble 10:
Thimble Drummer
SIED • 575QX4419 • $34

1212.
Three Men in a Tub
DLEE • 800QX4547 • $24

1213.
Time for Friends
VOTR • 475QX2807 • $30

1214.
Tin Locomotive 6
SICK • 1475QX4849 • $47

1215.
Train Station
DLEE • 1275QLX7039 • $59
MAGIC

1216.
Treetop Dreams
SEAL • 675QX4597 • $30
Re-issued in 1988.

1217.
Treetop Trio
DLEE • 1100QX4256 • $39
Re-issued from 1986.

1218.
Twelve Days of Christmas 4:
Four Colly Birds
PIKE • 650QX3709 • $40

1219.
Twenty-Five Years Together
PIKE • 750QX4439 • $20

1220.
Village Express
SICK • 2450QLX7072 • $87
MAGIC • Re-issued from 1986.

1221.
Walnut Shell Rider
SEAL • 600QX4196 • $31
Re-issued from 1986.

1222.
Warmth of Friendship
600QX3759 • $10

1223.
Wee Chimney Sweep
SEAL • 625QX4519 • $25

1224.
Windows of the World 3:
Mele Kalikimaka
DLEE • 1000QX4827 • $30

1225.
Wood Childhood
Ornaments 4: Horse
SIED • 750QX4417 • $25

1226.
Word of Love
800QX4477 • $30

1227.
Wreath of Memories
UNRU • GiftQXC5809 • $47

1988

1228.
Americana Drum
SICK • 775QX4881 • $30

1229.
Angelic Minstrel
DLEE • 2950QXC4084 • $42
Limited Edition – 49900

1230.
Arctic Tenor
SIED • 400QX4721 • $17

1231.
Baby Redbird
CHAD • 500QX4101 • $24

1232.
Baby's First Christmas
SEAL • 2400QLX7184 • $70
MAGIC

1233.
Baby's First Christmas
PIKE • 600QX3721 • $32

1234.
Baby's First Christmas
CROW • 975QX4701 • $40

1235.
Baby's First Christmas
750QX4704 • $60
RARE

1236.
Baby's First Christmas
(Boy)
475QX2721 • $32

1237.
Baby's First Christmas
(Girl)
475QX2724 • $32

1238.
Baby's Second Christmas
PIKE • 600QX4711 • $43

1239.
Babysitter
SICK • 475QX2791 • $17

1240.

Bearly Reaching
SICK • 950QLX7151 • $38
MAGIC

1241.

Betsey Clark: Home for Christmas 3
PIKE • 500QX2714 • $26

1242.

Child's Third Christmas
CHAD • 600QX4714 • $28

1243.

Chris Mouse 4: Chris Mouse Star
SIED • 875QLX7154 • $98
MAGIC

1244.

Christmas Classics 3: Night Before Christmas
DLEE • 1500QLX7161 • $43
MAGIC

1245.

Christmas Cuckoo
CROW • 800QX4801 • $31

1246.

Christmas Is Magic
CROW • 1200QLX7171 • $54
MAGIC

1247.

Christmas Is Sharing
SEAL • 1750QXC4071 • $48
Limited Edition – 49900

1248.

Christmas Memories
PATT • 650QX3724 • $35

1249.

Christmas Morning
CROW • 2450QLX7013 • $48
MAGIC • Re-issued from 1987.

1250.
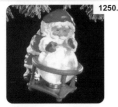
Circling The Globe
CROW • 1050QLX7124 • $47
MAGIC

1251.

Collector's Plate 2: Waiting for Santa
VOTR • 800QX4061 • $36

1252.

Cool Juggler
CROW • 650QX4874 • $24

1253.

Country Express
SICK • 2450QLX7211 • $68
MAGIC

1254.

Cymbals of Christmas
DLEE • 550QX4111 • $49

1255.

Dad
SIED • 700QX4141 • $28

1256.

Daughter
PATT • 575QX4151 • $72

1257.

Feliz Navidad
UNRU • 675QX4161 • $70

1258.

Festive Feeder
SICK • 1150QLX7204 • $61
MAGIC

1259.

Fifty Years Together
675QX3741 • $15

1260.

Filled with Fudge
SEAL • 475QX4191 • $34

1261.
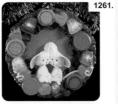
First Christmas Together
SICK • 1200QLX7027 • $51
MAGIC

1262.

First Christmas Together
TAGU • 475QX2741 • $28

1263.

First Christmas Together
VOTR • 675QX3731 • $28

1264.

First Christmas Together
PIKE • 900QX4894 • $32

1265.

Five Years Together
MCGE • 475QX2744 • $15

1266.

From Our Home To Yours
PATT • 475QX2794 • $15

1267.

Frosty Friends 9
SEAL • 875QX4031 • $98

1268.

Glowing Wreath
PATT • 600QX4921 • $19

1269.

Go For The Gold
SIED • 800QX4174 • $25

1270.

Godchild
TAGU • 475QX2784 • $35

1271.

Goin' Cross Country
SICK • 850QX4764 • $15

1272.

Gone Fishing
SIED • 500QX4794 • $26
Re-issued in 1989.

1273.

Granddaughter
VOTR • 475QX2774 • $42

1274.

Grandmother
475QX2764 • $27

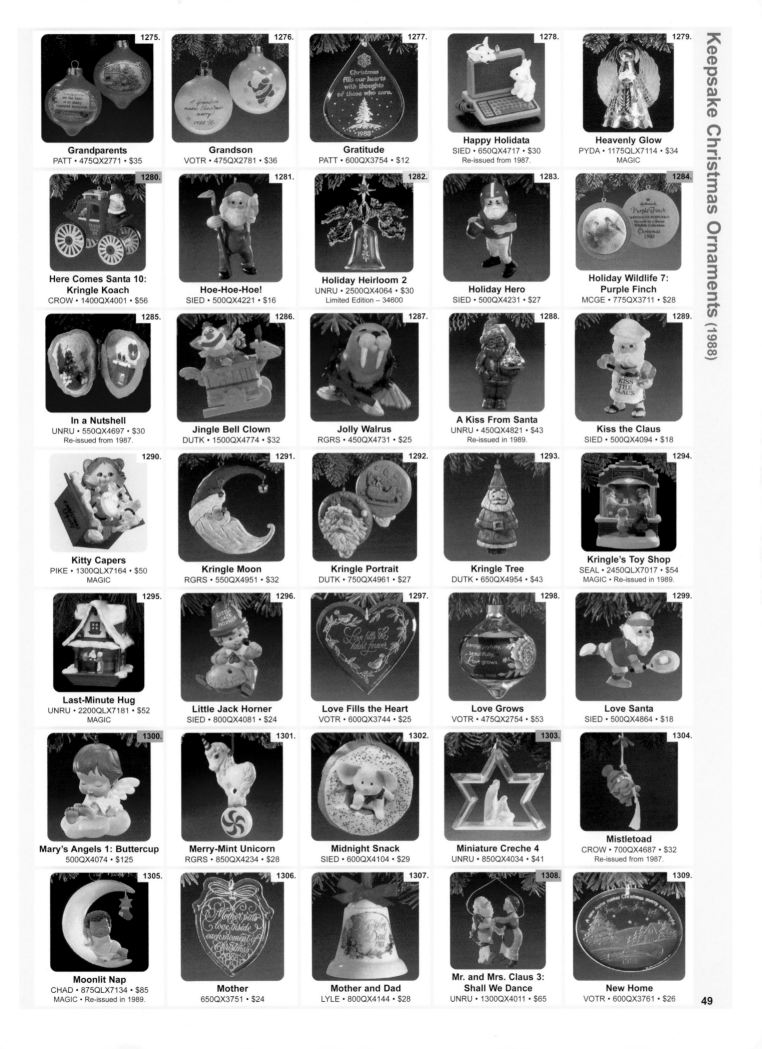

1275.
Grandparents
PATT • 475QX2771 • $35

1276.
Grandson
VOTR • 475QX2781 • $36

1277.
Gratitude
PATT • 600QX3754 • $12

1278.
Happy Holidata
SIED • 650QX4717 • $30
Re-issued from 1987.

1279.
Heavenly Glow
PYDA • 1175QLX7114 • $34
MAGIC

1280.
**Here Comes Santa 10:
Kringle Koach**
CROW • 1400QX4001 • $56

1281.
Hoe-Hoe-Hoe!
SIED • 500QX4221 • $16

1282.
Holiday Heirloom 2
UNRU • 2500QX4064 • $30
Limited Edition – 34600

1283.
Holiday Hero
SIED • 500QX4231 • $27

1284.
**Holiday Wildlife 7:
Purple Finch**
MCGE • 775QX3711 • $28

1285.
In a Nutshell
UNRU • 550QX4697 • $30
Re-issued from 1987.

1286.
Jingle Bell Clown
DUTK • 1500QX4774 • $32

1287.
Jolly Walrus
RGRS • 450QX4731 • $25

1288.
A Kiss From Santa
UNRU • 450QX4821 • $43
Re-issued in 1989.

1289.
Kiss the Claus
SIED • 500QX4094 • $18

1290.
Kitty Capers
PIKE • 1300QLX7164 • $50
MAGIC

1291.
Kringle Moon
RGRS • 550QX4951 • $32

1292.
Kringle Portrait
DUTK • 750QX4961 • $27

1293.
Kringle Tree
DUTK • 650QX4954 • $43

1294.
Kringle's Toy Shop
SEAL • 2450QLX7017 • $54
MAGIC • Re-issued in 1989.

1295.
Last-Minute Hug
UNRU • 2200QLX7181 • $52
MAGIC

1296.
Little Jack Horner
SIED • 800QX4081 • $24

1297.
Love Fills the Heart
VOTR • 600QX3744 • $25

1298.
Love Grows
VOTR • 475QX2754 • $53

1299.
Love Santa
SIED • 500QX4864 • $18

1300.
Mary's Angels 1: Buttercup
500QX4074 • $125

1301.
Merry-Mint Unicorn
RGRS • 850QX4234 • $28

1302.
Midnight Snack
SIED • 600QX4104 • $29

1303.
Miniature Creche 4
UNRU • 850QX4034 • $41

1304.
Mistletoad
CROW • 700QX4687 • $32
Re-issued from 1987.

1305.
Moonlit Nap
CHAD • 875QLX7134 • $85
MAGIC • Re-issued in 1989.

1306.
Mother
650QX3751 • $24

1307.
Mother and Dad
LYLE • 800QX4144 • $28

1308.
**Mr. and Mrs. Claus 3:
Shall We Dance**
UNRU • 1300QX4011 • $65

1309.
New Home
VOTR • 600QX3761 • $26

1310.
Nick the Kick
SIED • 500QX4224 • $22

1311.
Night Before Christmas
CROW • 650QX4517 • $42
Re-issued from 1987.

1312.
Noah's Ark
SICK • 850QX4904 • $60

1313.
Norman Rockwell 9:
And To All a Good Night
MCGE • 775QX3704 • $23

1314.
Norman Rockwell:
Christmas Scenes
LYLE • 475QX2731 • $34

1315.
Nostalgic Houses & Shops
5: Hall Bro's Card Shop
DLEE • 1450QX4014 • $65

1316.
Old-Fashioned Church
SICK • 400QX4981 • $24

1317.
Old-Fashioned Schoolhouse
SICK • 400QX4971 • $28

1318.
Oreo® Chocolate
Sandwich Cookie
UNRU • 400QX4814 • $26
Re-issued in 1989.

1319.
Our Clubhouse
SIED • GiftQXC5804 • $34

1320.
Owliday Wish
PIKE • 650QX4559 • $24
Re-issued from 1987.

1321.
Par for Santa
SIED • 500QX4791 • $22

1322.
Parade of the Toys
SICK • 2450QLX7194 • $53
MAGIC

1323.
Party Line
PIKE • 875QX4761 • $26
Re-issued in 1989.

1324.
PEANUTS®
475QX2801 • $78

1325.
Peek-a-Boo Kitties
CROW • 750QX4871 • $28
Re-issued in 1989.

1326.
Polar Bowler
SIED • 500QX4784 • $20
Re-issued in 1989.

1327.
Porcelain Bear 6
PIKE • 800QX4044 • $31

1328.
Purrfect Snuggle
RGRS • 625QX4744 • $24

1329.
Radiant Tree
LYLE • 1175QLX7121 • $29
MAGIC

1330.
Reindeer Champs 3:
Prancer
SIED • 750QX4051 • $32

1331.
Reindoggy
SIED • 575QX4527 • $33
Re-issued from 1987.

1332.
Rocking Horse 8
SICK • 1075QX4024 • $88

1333.
Sailing! Sailing!
SICK • 850QX4911 • $28

1334.
Santa and Sparky 3:
On With the Show
DLEE • 1950QLX7191 • $48
MAGIC

1335.
Santa Flamingo
PYDA • 475QX4834 • $42

1336.
Shiny Sleigh
PATT • 575QX4924 • $19

1337.
Sister
VOTR • 800QX4994 • $34

1338.
Skater's Waltz
UNRU • 2450QLX7201 • $65
MAGIC

1339.
Sleighful Of Dreams
SICK • 800QXC5801 • $32

1340.
Slipper Spaniel
CROW • 425QX4724 • $24

1341.
Snoopy® and Woodstock™
UNRU • 600QX4741 • $49

1342.
Soft Landing
CHAD • 700QX4751 • $23

1343.
Son
PATT • 575QX4154 • $45

1344.
Song Of Christmas
850QLX7111 • $35
MAGIC

1345.
Sparkling Tree
PATT • 600QX4931 • $24

1346.
Spirit of Christmas
LYLE • 475QX2761 • $31

1347.
Squeaky Clean
PIKE • 675QX4754 • $34

1348.
St. Louie Nick
DUTK • 775QX4539 • $34
Re-issued from 1987.

1349.
Sweet Star
SEAL • 500QX4184 • $36

1350.
Sweetheart
UNRU • 975QX4901 • $28

1351.
Teacher
PIKE • 625QX4171 • $30

1352.
Teeny Taster
SEAL • 475QX4181 • $30
Re-issued in 1989.

1353.
Ten Years Together
PYDA • 475QX2751 • $20

1354.
Thimble 11:
Thimble Snowman
SIED • 575QX4054 • $42

1355.
Tin Locomotive 7
SICK • 1475QX4004 • $56

1356.
The Town Crier
SEAL • 550QX4734 • $20

1357.
Travels with Santa
DLEE • 1000QX4771 • $42

1358.
Tree Of Friendship
850QLX7104 • $15
MAGIC

1359.
Treetop Dreams
SEAL • 675QX4597 • $30
Re-issued from 1987.

1360.
Twelve Days of Christmas 5:
Five Golden Rings
PIKE • 650QX3714 • $39

1361.
Twenty-Five Years Together
PATT • 675QX3734 • $24

1362.
Twirl-About –
Christmas Cardinal
RGRS • 475QX4941 • $22

1363.
Twirl-About – Loving Bear
RGRS • 475QX4934 • $22

1364.
Twirl-About – Starry Angel
RGRS • 475QX4944 • $20

1365.
Uncle Sam Nutcracker
DLEE • 700QX4884 • $37

1366.
Very Strawbeary
DUTK • 475QX4091 • $23

1367.
Windows of the World 4:
Joyeaux Noel
DLEE • 1000QX4021 • $32

1368.
Winter Fun
CHAD • 850QX4781 • $40

1369.
The Wonderful Santacycle
SEAL • 2250QX4114 • $71

1370.
Wood Childhood
Ornaments 5: Airplane
DUTK • 750QX4041 • $31

1371.
Year to Remember
700QX4164 • $22

1989

1372.
Angel Melody
VOTR • 950QLX7202 • $24
MAGIC

1373.
The Animals Speak
FRAN • 1350QLX7232 • $95
MAGIC

1374.
Baby Celebrations: Baby's
Christening Keepsake
700BBY1325 • $40

1375.
Baby Celebrations:
Baby's First Birthday
550BBY1729 • $30

1376.
Baby Partridge
FRAN • 675QX4525 • $16

1377.
Baby's First Christmas
SEAL • 3000QLX7272 • $60
MAGIC

1378.
Baby's First Christmas
FRAN • 675QX3815 • $19

51

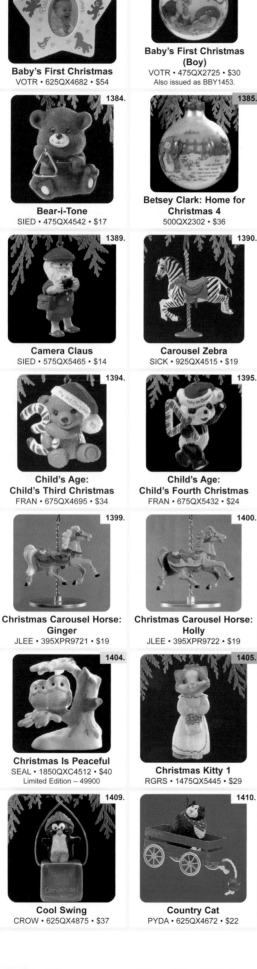

1379.
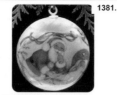
Baby's First Christmas
VOTR • 625QX4682 • $54

1380.
Baby's First Christmas
(Boy)
VOTR • 475QX2725 • $30
Also issued as BBY1453.

1381.
Baby's First Christmas
(Girl)
VOTR • 475QX2722 • $30
Also issued as BBY1553.

1382.

Backstage Bear
SIED • 1350QLX7215 • $38
MAGIC

1383.

Balancing Elf
CHAD • 675QX4895 • $24

1384.

Bear-i-Tone
SIED • 475QX4542 • $17

1385.
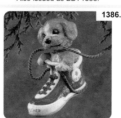
Betsey Clark: Home for
Christmas 4
500QX2302 • $36

1386.

Brother
LYLE • 725QX4452 • $18

1387.
Busy Beaver
DLEE • 1750QLX7245 • $44
MAGIC

1388.

Cactus Cowboy
DUTK • 675QX4112 • $38

1389.
Camera Claus
SIED • 575QX5465 • $14

1390.
Carousel Zebra
SICK • 925QX4515 • $19

1391.
Cherry Jubilee
SICK • 500QX4532 • $26

1392.

Child's Age:
Baby's First Christmas
CHAD • 725QX4492 • $120

1393.
Child's Age:
Baby's Second Christmas
FRAN • 675QX4495 • $40

1394.
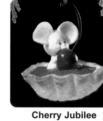
Child's Age:
Child's Third Christmas
FRAN • 675QX4695 • $34

1395.

Child's Age:
Child's Fourth Christmas
FRAN • 675QX5432 • $24

1396.

Child's Age:
Child's Fifth Christmas
RHOD • 675QX5435 • $24

1397.
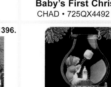
Chris Mouse 5:
Chris Mouse Cookout
RGRS • 950QLX7225 • $78
MAGIC

1398.
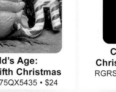
Christmas Carousel Horse:
Display Stand
JLEE • 100XPR9723 • $8

1399.

Christmas Carousel Horse:
Ginger
JLEE • 395XPR9721 • $19

1400.

Christmas Carousel Horse:
Holly
JLEE • 395XPR9722 • $19

1401.

Christmas Carousel Horse:
Snow
JLEE • 395XPR9719 • $32

1402.

Christmas Carousel Horse:
Star
JLEE • 395XPR9720 • $19

1403.

Christmas Classics 4:
Little Drummer Boy
DLEE • 1350QLX7242 • $44
MAGIC

1404.

Christmas Is Peaceful
SEAL • 1850QXC4512 • $40
Limited Edition – 49900

1405.

Christmas Kitty 1
RGRS • 1475QX5445 • $29

1406.

Claus Construction
SEAL • 775QX4885 • $35
Re-issued in 1990.

1407.
Collect A Dream
PIKE • GiftQXC4285 • $35

1408.
Collector's Plate 3:
Morning of Wonder
VOTR • 825QX4612 • $19

1409.
Cool Swing
CROW • 625QX4875 • $37

1410.

Country Cat
PYDA • 625QX4672 • $22

1411.

Cranberry Bunny
RGRS • 575QX4262 • $25

1412.
Crayola® Crayon 1:
Bright Journey
SICK • 875QX4352 • $80

1413.

Dad
JLEE • 725QX4412 • $20

1414.

Daughter
SICK • 625QX4432 • $24

1415.

Deer Disguise
SIED • 575QX4265 • $28

1416.

Feliz Navidad
PYDA • 675QX4392 • $60

1417.

Festive Angel
675QX4635 • $29

1418.

Festive Year
VOTR • 775QX3842 • $14

1419.

Fifty Years Together
RGRS • 875QX4862 • $14

1420.

The First Christmas
775QX5475 • $26

1421.

First Christmas Together
DLEE • 1750QLX7342 • $47
MAGIC

1422.

First Christmas Together
475QX2732 • $29

1423.

First Christmas Together
RHOD • 675QX3832 • $26

1424.

First Christmas Together
RGRS • 975QX4852 • $25

1425.

Five Years Together
475QX2735 • $19

1426.

Forest Frolics 1
PIKE • 2450QLX7282 • $86
MAGIC

1427.

Forty Years Together
RGRS • 875QX5452 • $16

1428.

Friendship Time
JLEE • 975QX4132 • $29

1429.

From Our Home to Yours
PYDA • 625QX3845 • $20

1430.

Frosty Friends 10
SEAL • 925QX4572 • $58

1431.

Gentle Fawn
RGRS • 775QX5485 • $24

1432.

**George Washington
Bicentennial**
625QX3862 • $15

1433.

Gift Bringers 1: St. Nicholas
VOTR • 500QX2795 • $23

1434.

Godchild
FRAN • 625QX3112 • $14

1435.

Goin' South
CROW • 425QX4105 • $24

1436.

Gone Fishing
SIED • 575QX4794 • $26
Re-issued from 1988.

1437.

Graceful Swan
675QX4642 • $19

1438.

Granddaughter
VOTR • 475QX2782 • $29

1439.

**Granddaughter's First
Christmas**
FRAN • 675QX3822 • $14

1440.

Grandmother
LYLE • 475QX2775 • $14

1441.

Grandparents
LYLE • 475QX2772 • $17

1442.

Grandson
PYDA • 475QX2785 • $29

1443.

Grandson's First Christmas
FRAN • 675QX3825 • $13

1444.

Gratitude
VOTR • 675QX3852 • $11

1445.

Gym Dandy
SIED • 575QX4185 • $16

1446.

Hang in There
CROW • 525QX4305 • $41

1447.

Hark! It's Herald 1
CROW • 675QX4555 • $23

1448.

**Here Comes Santa 11:
Christmas Caboose**
CROW • 1475QX4585 • $59

1449.

Here's the Pitch
SIED • 575QX5455 • $22

1450.

Holiday Bell
1750QLX7222 • $39
MAGIC

1451.

Holiday Heirloom 3
UNRU • 2500QXC4605 • $40
Limited Edition – 34600

1452.

Hoppy Holidays
SIED • 775QX4692 • $19

1453.

Horse Weathervane
SICK • 575QX4632 • $16

1454.

Joyful Trio
FRAN • 975QX4372 • $17

1455.

Joyous Carolers
UNRU • 3000QLX7295 • $77
MAGIC

1456.

A Kiss From Santa
UNRU • 450QX4821 • $43
Re-issued from 1988.

1457.

Kringle's Toy Shop
SEAL • 2450QLX7017 • $54
MAGIC • Re-issued from 1988.

1458.

Kristy Claus
SIED • 575QX4245 • $13

1459.

Language of Love
625QX3835 • $24

1460.

Let's Play
CROW • 725QX4882 • $34

1461.

Loving Spoonful
SIED • 1950QLX7262 • $45
MAGIC

1462.

Mail Call
SEAL • 875QX4522 • $18

1463.

Mary's Angels 2: Bluebell
575QX4545 • $165

1464.

Merry-Go-Round Unicorn
RGRS • 1075QX4472 • $25

1465.

Metro Express
SICK • 2800QLX7275 • $88
MAGIC

1466.

Miniature Creche 5
RGRS • 925QX4592 • $20

1467.

Mom and Dad
PIKE • 975QX4425 • $28

1468.

Moonlit Nap
CHAD • 875QLX7134 • $85
MAGIC • Re-issued from 1988.

1469.

Mother
975QX4405 • $26

1470.

Mr. and Mrs. Claus 4: Holiday Duet
UNRU • 1325QX4575 • $58

1471.

New Home
VOTR • 475QX2755 • $24

1472.

Noelle
UNRU • 1975QXC4483 • $47
Limited Edition – 49900

1473.

Norman Rockwell
LYLE • 475QX2762 • $22

1474.

North Pole Jogger
SIED • 575QX5462 • $16

1475.

Nostalgic Houses & Shops 6: U.S. Post Office
DLEE • 1425QX4582 • $69

1476.

Nostalgic Lamb
PYDA • 675QX4665 • $18

1477.
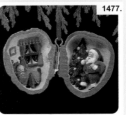
Nutshell Dreams
CHAD • 575QX4655 • $25

1478.
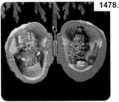
Nutshell Holiday
RGRS • 575QX4652 • $24
Re-issued in 1990.

1479.
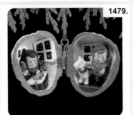
Nutshell Workshop
CHAD • 575QX4872 • $24

1480.
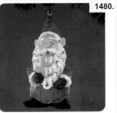
Old-World Gnome
DUTK • 775QX4345 • $20

1481.

On the Links
SIED • 575QX4192 • $24

1482.

Oreo® Chocolate Sandwich Cookie
UNRU • 400QX4814 • $26
Re-issued from 1988.

1483.

The Ornament Express
SICK • 2200QX5805 • $42
Set/3

1484. Owliday Greetings
PIKE • 400QX4365 • $17

1485. Paddington™ Bear
FRAN • 575QX4292 • $32

1486. Party Line
PIKE • 875QX4761 • $26
Re-issued from 1988.

1487. PEANUTS®: A Charlie Brown® Christmas
475QX2765 • $60

1488. Peek-a-Boo Kitties
CROW • 750QX4871 • $28
Re-issued from 1988.

1489. Peppermint Clown
DUTK • 2475QX4505 • $58

1490. Playful Angel
DLEE • 675QX4535 • $26

1491. Polar Bowler
SIED • 575QX4784 • $20
Re-issued from 1988.

1492. Porcelain Bear 7
PIKE • 875QX4615 • $31

1493. Reindeer Champs 4: Vixen
SIED • 775QX4562 • $19

1494. Rocking Horse 9
SICK • 1075QX4622 • $62

1495. Rodney Reindeer
SIED • 675QX4072 • $14

1496. Rooster Weathervane
SICK • 575QX4675 • $14

1497. Rudolph The Red-Nosed Reindeer
CHAD • 1950QLX7252 • $45
MAGIC

1498. Sea Santa
SIED • 575QX4152 • $29

1499. Sister
VOTR • 475QX2792 • $17

1500. Snoopy® and Woodstock™
RHOD • 675QX4332 • $38

1501. Snowplow Santa
SIED • 575QX4205 • $24

1502. Son
SICK • 625QX4445 • $30

1503. Sparkling Snowflake
LYLE • 775QX5472 • $23

1504. Special Delivery
RGRS • 575QX4325 • $18

1505. Spencer® Sparrow, Esq.
PIKE • 675QX4312 • $26
Re-issued in 1990.

1506. Spirit Of St. Nick
SEAL • 2450QLX7285 • $55
MAGIC

1507. Stocking Kitten
PIKE • 675QX4565 • $17
Re-issued in 1990.

1508. Sweet Memories
675QX4385 • $20

1509. Sweetheart
SICK • 975QX4865 • $35

1510. Teacher
SIED • 575QX4125 • $25

1511. Teeny Taster
SEAL • 475QX4181 • $30
Re-issued from 1988.

1512. Ten Years Together
LYLE • 475QX2742 • $29

1513. Thimble 12: Thimble Puppy
RGRS • 575QX4552 • $30

1514. Tin Locomotive 8
SICK • 1475QX4602 • $45

1515. Tiny Tinker
CROW • 1950QLX7174 • $45
MAGIC

1516. TV Break
DLEE • 625QX4092 • $19

1517. Twelve Days of Christmas 6: Six Geese A-Laying
LYLE • 675QX3812 • $20

1518. Twenty-Five Years Together
RGRS • 875QX4855 • $13

55

1519.
Unicorn Fantasy
RHOD • 950QLX7235 • $30
MAGIC

1520.
Visit From Santa
CROW • GiftQXC5802 • $52

1521.
Wiggly Snowman
RHOD • 675QX4892 • $31

1522.
Windows of the World 5:
Frohliche Weihnachten
DLEE • 1075QX4625 • $29

1523.
Winter Surprise 1
FRAN • 1075QX4272 • $25

1524.
Wood Childhood
Ornaments 6: Truck
DUTK • 775QX4595 • $19

1525.
World of Love
475QX2745 • $38

1990

1526.
Across the Miles
VOTR • 675QX3173 • $14

1527.
Angel Kitty
PYDA • 875QX4746 • $24

1528.
Armful Of Joy
FRAN • 975QXC4453 • $32

1529.
Baby Celebrations:
Baby's Christening
JLEE • 1000BBY1326 • $20

1530.
Baby Celebrations: Baby's
First Christmas (Boy)
JLEE • 1000BBY1454 • $28

1531.
Baby Celebrations: Baby's
First Christmas (Girl)
RGRS • 1000BBY1554 • $28

1532.
Baby Unicorn
RGRS • 975QX5486 • $20

1533.
Baby's First Christmas
PALM • 2800QLX7246 • $65
MAGIC

1534.
Baby's First Christmas
RGRS • 675QX3036 • $26

1535.
Baby's First Christmas
PYDA • 775QX4843 • $30

1536.
Baby's First Christmas
FRAN • 975QX4853 • $23

1537.
Baby's First Christmas
(Boy)
475QX2063 • $26

1538.
Baby's First Christmas
(Girl)
475QX2066 • $26

1539.
Bearback Rider
CROW • 975QX5483 • $23

1540.
Beary Good Deal
SIED • 675QX4733 • $17

1541.
Beary Short Nap
SIED • 1000QLX7326 • $28
MAGIC

1542.
Betsey Clark: Home for
Christmas 5
500QX2033 • $24

1543.
Billboard Bunny
JLEE • 775QX5196 • $14

1544.
Blessings of Love
1400QLX7363 • $60
MAGIC

1545.
Born to Dance
PIKE • 775QX5043 • $16

1546.
Brother
SIED • 575QX4493 • $14

1547.
Child Care Giver
675QX3166 • $8

1548.
Children's Express
SICK • 2800QLX7243 • $65
MAGIC

1549.
Child's Age:
Baby's First Christmas
FRAN • 775QX4856 • $65

1550.
Child's Age:
Baby's Second Christmas
FRAN • 675QX4863 • $46

1551.
Child's Age:
Child's Third Christmas
FRAN • 675QX4866 • $28

1552.
Child's Age:
Child's Fourth Christmas
FRAN • 675QX4873 • $18

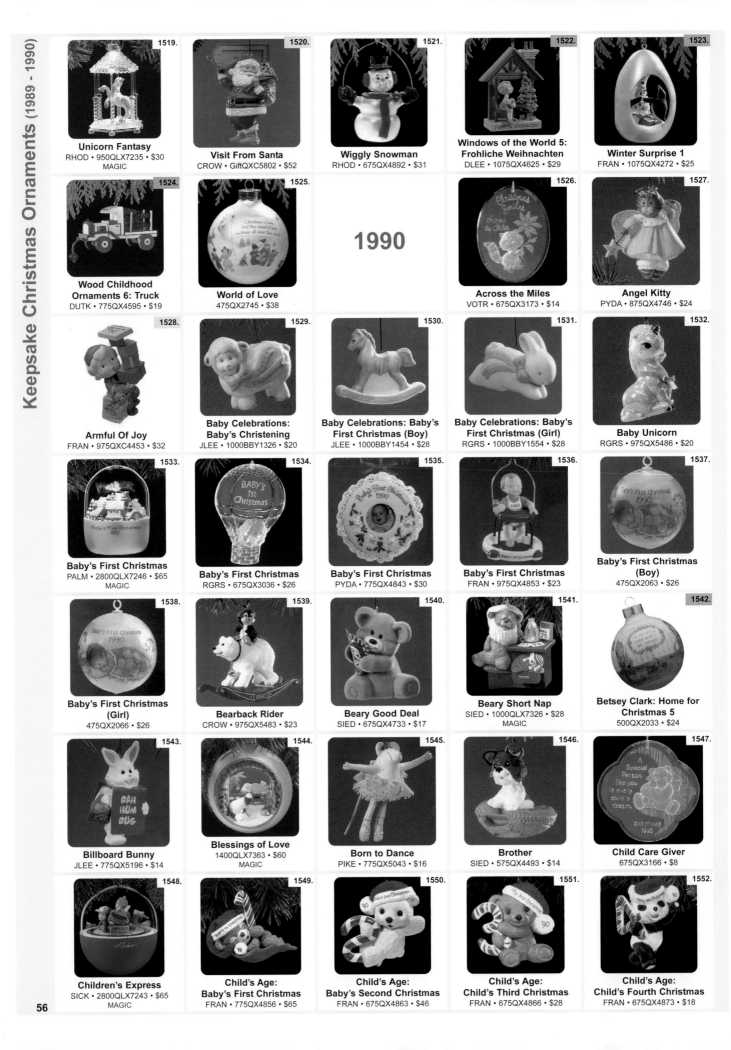

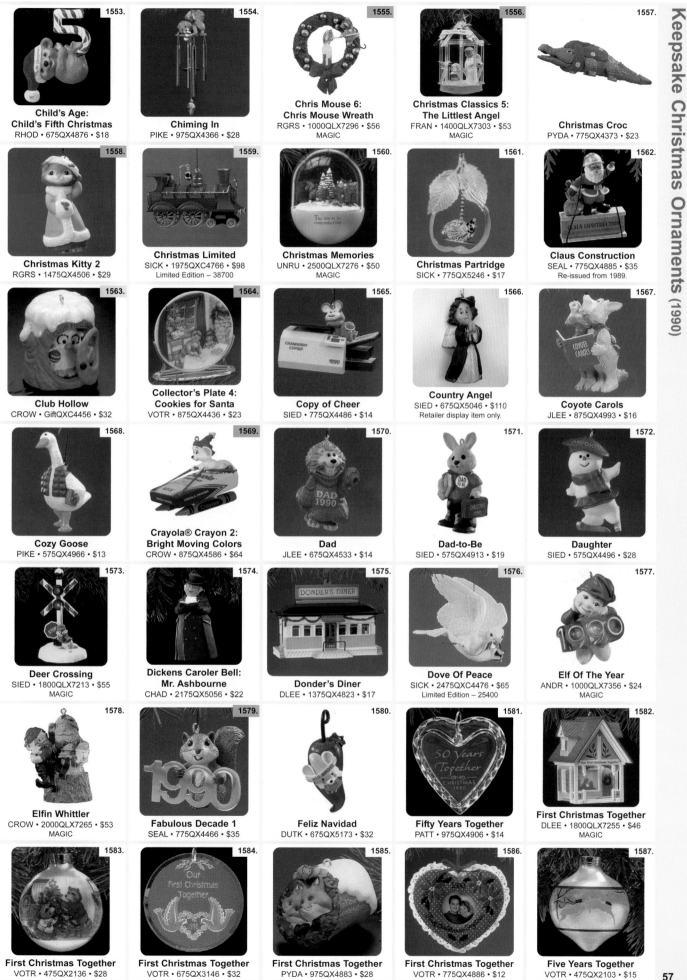

1553.
Child's Age:
Child's Fifth Christmas
RHOD • 675QX4876 • $18

1554.
Chiming In
PIKE • 975QX4366 • $28

1555.
Chris Mouse 6:
Chris Mouse Wreath
RGRS • 1000QLX7296 • $56
MAGIC

1556.
Christmas Classics 5:
The Littlest Angel
FRAN • 1400QLX7303 • $53
MAGIC

1557.
Christmas Croc
PYDA • 775QX4373 • $23

1558.
Christmas Kitty 2
RGRS • 1475QX4506 • $29

1559.
Christmas Limited
SICK • 1975QXC4766 • $98
Limited Edition – 38700

1560.
Christmas Memories
UNRU • 2500QLX7276 • $50
MAGIC

1561.
Christmas Partridge
SICK • 775QX5246 • $17

1562.
Claus Construction
SEAL • 775QX4885 • $35
Re-issued from 1989.

1563.
Club Hollow
CROW • GiftQXC4456 • $32

1564.
Collector's Plate 4:
Cookies for Santa
VOTR • 875QX4436 • $23

1565.
Copy of Cheer
SIED • 775QX4486 • $14

1566.
Country Angel
SIED • 675QX5046 • $110
Retailer display item only.

1567.
Coyote Carols
JLEE • 875QX4993 • $16

1568.
Cozy Goose
PIKE • 575QX4966 • $13

1569.
Crayola® Crayon 2:
Bright Moving Colors
CROW • 875QX4586 • $64

1570.
Dad
JLEE • 675QX4533 • $14

1571.
Dad-to-Be
SIED • 575QX4913 • $19

1572.
Daughter
SIED • 575QX4496 • $28

1573.
Deer Crossing
SIED • 1800QLX7213 • $55
MAGIC

1574.
Dickens Caroler Bell:
Mr. Ashbourne
CHAD • 2175QX5056 • $22

1575.
Donder's Diner
DLEE • 1375QX4823 • $17

1576.
Dove Of Peace
SICK • 2475QXC4476 • $65
Limited Edition – 25400

1577.
Elf Of The Year
ANDR • 1000QLX7356 • $24
MAGIC

1578.
Elfin Whittler
CROW • 2000QLX7265 • $53
MAGIC

1579.
Fabulous Decade 1
SEAL • 775QX4466 • $35

1580.
Feliz Navidad
DUTK • 675QX5173 • $32

1581.
Fifty Years Together
PATT • 975QX4906 • $14

1582.
First Christmas Together
DLEE • 1800QLX7255 • $46
MAGIC

1583.
First Christmas Together
VOTR • 475QX2136 • $28

1584.
First Christmas Together
VOTR • 675QX3146 • $32

1585.
First Christmas Together
PYDA • 975QX4883 • $28

1586.
First Christmas Together
VOTR • 775QX4886 • $12

1587.
Five Years Together
VOTR • 475QX2103 • $15

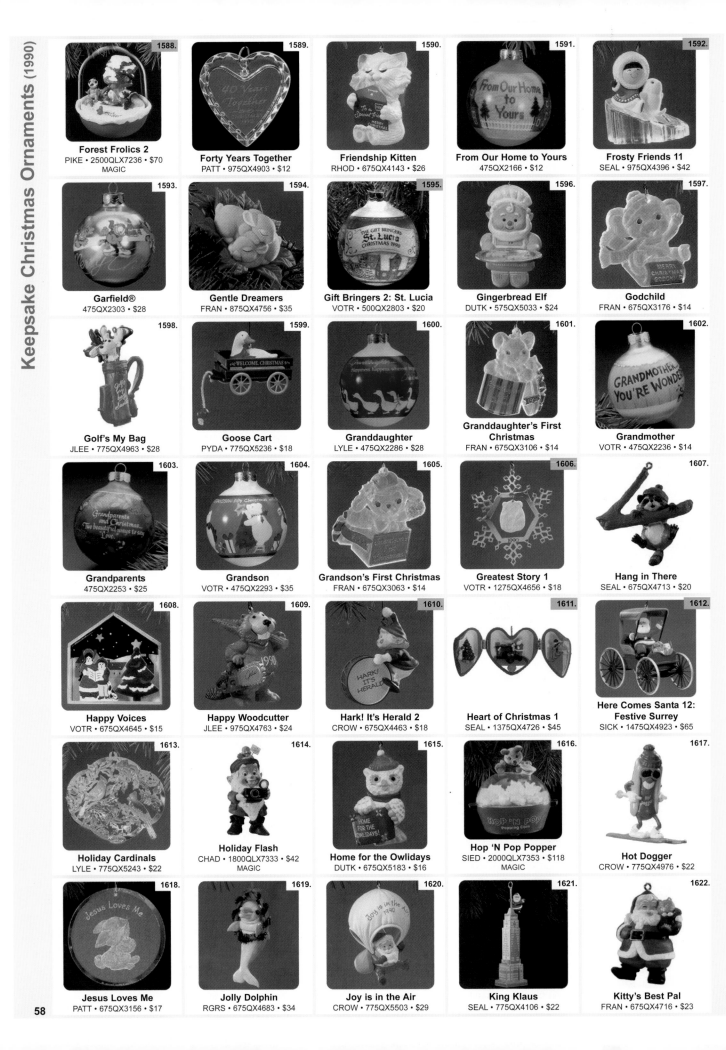

1588. Forest Frolics 2
PIKE • 2500QLX7236 • $70
MAGIC

1589. Forty Years Together
PATT • 975QX4903 • $12

1590. Friendship Kitten
RHOD • 675QX4143 • $26

1591. From Our Home to Yours
475QX2166 • $12

1592. Frosty Friends 11
SEAL • 975QX4396 • $42

1593. Garfield®
475QX2303 • $28

1594. Gentle Dreamers
FRAN • 875QX4756 • $35

1595. Gift Bringers 2: St. Lucia
VOTR • 500QX2803 • $20

1596. Gingerbread Elf
DUTK • 575QX5033 • $24

1597. Godchild
FRAN • 675QX3176 • $14

1598. Golf's My Bag
JLEE • 775QX4963 • $28

1599. Goose Cart
PYDA • 775QX5236 • $18

1600. Granddaughter
LYLE • 475QX2286 • $28

1601. Granddaughter's First Christmas
FRAN • 675QX3106 • $14

1602. Grandmother
VOTR • 475QX2236 • $14

1603. Grandparents
475QX2253 • $25

1604. Grandson
VOTR • 475QX2293 • $35

1605. Grandson's First Christmas
FRAN • 675QX3063 • $14

1606. Greatest Story 1
VOTR • 1275QX4656 • $18

1607. Hang in There
SEAL • 675QX4713 • $20

1608. Happy Voices
VOTR • 675QX4645 • $15

1609. Happy Woodcutter
JLEE • 975QX4763 • $24

1610. Hark! It's Herald 2
CROW • 675QX4463 • $18

1611. Heart of Christmas 1
SEAL • 1375QX4726 • $45

1612. Here Comes Santa 12: Festive Surrey
SICK • 1475QX4923 • $65

1613. Holiday Cardinals
LYLE • 775QX5243 • $22

1614. Holiday Flash
CHAD • 1800QLX7333 • $42
MAGIC

1615. Home for the Owlidays
DUTK • 675QX5183 • $16

1616. Hop 'N Pop Popper
SIED • 2000QLX7353 • $118
MAGIC

1617. Hot Dogger
CROW • 775QX4976 • $22

1618. Jesus Loves Me
PATT • 675QX3156 • $17

1619. Jolly Dolphin
RGRS • 675QX4683 • $34

1620. Joy is in the Air
CROW • 775QX5503 • $29

1621. King Klaus
SEAL • 775QX4106 • $22

1622. Kitty's Best Pal
FRAN • 675QX4716 • $23

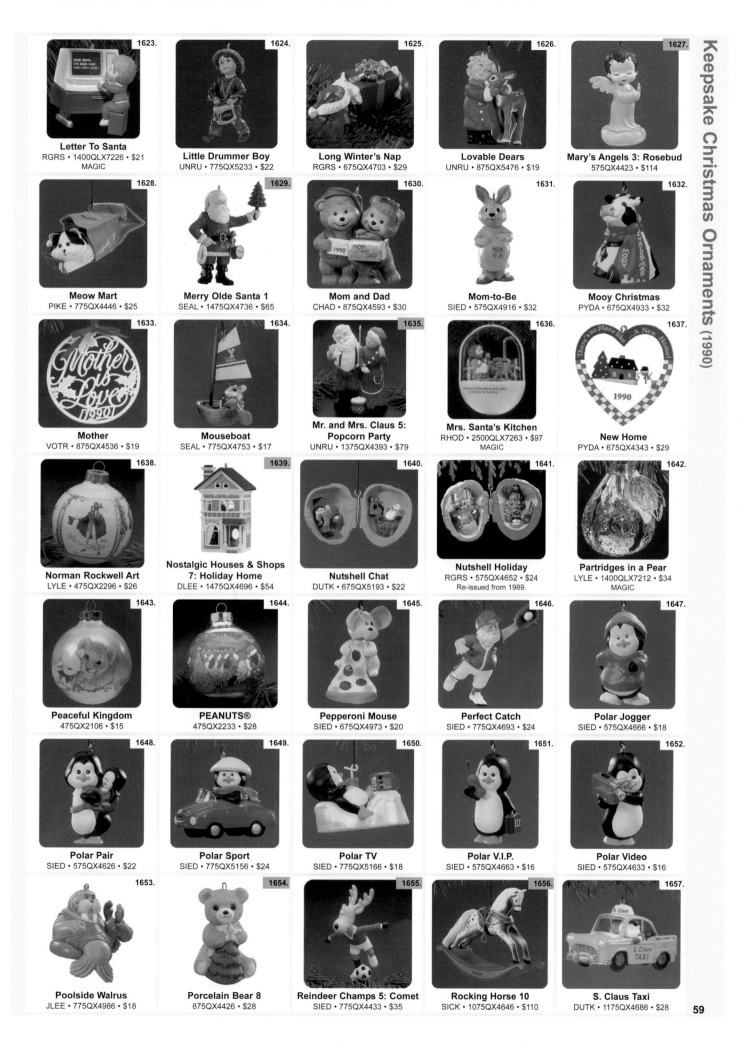

1623.
Letter To Santa
RGRS • 1400QLX7226 • $21
MAGIC

1624.
Little Drummer Boy
UNRU • 775QX5233 • $22

1625.
Long Winter's Nap
RGRS • 675QX4703 • $29

1626.
Lovable Dears
UNRU • 875QX5476 • $19

1627.
Mary's Angels 3: Rosebud
575QX4423 • $114

1628.
Meow Mart
PIKE • 775QX4446 • $25

1629.
Merry Olde Santa 1
SEAL • 1475QX4736 • $65

1630.
Mom and Dad
CHAD • 875QX4593 • $30

1631.
Mom-to-Be
SIED • 575QX4916 • $32

1632.
Mooy Christmas
PYDA • 675QX4933 • $32

1633.
Mother
VOTR • 875QX4536 • $19

1634.
Mouseboat
SEAL • 775QX4753 • $17

1635.
Mr. and Mrs. Claus 5: Popcorn Party
UNRU • 1375QX4393 • $79

1636.
Mrs. Santa's Kitchen
RHOD • 2500QLX7263 • $97
MAGIC

1637.
New Home
PYDA • 675QX4343 • $29

1638.
Norman Rockwell Art
LYLE • 475QX2296 • $26

1639.
Nostalgic Houses & Shops 7: Holiday Home
DLEE • 1475QX4696 • $54

1640.
Nutshell Chat
DUTK • 675QX5193 • $22

1641.
Nutshell Holiday
RGRS • 575QX4652 • $24
Re-issued from 1989.

1642.
Partridges in a Pear
LYLE • 1400QLX7212 • $34
MAGIC

1643.
Peaceful Kingdom
475QX2106 • $15

1644.
PEANUTS®
475QX2233 • $28

1645.
Pepperoni Mouse
SIED • 675QX4973 • $20

1646.
Perfect Catch
SIED • 775QX4693 • $24

1647.
Polar Jogger
SIED • 575QX4666 • $18

1648.
Polar Pair
SIED • 575QX4626 • $22

1649.
Polar Sport
SIED • 775QX5156 • $24

1650.
Polar TV
SIED • 775QX5166 • $18

1651.
Polar V.I.P.
SIED • 575QX4663 • $16

1652.
Polar Video
SIED • 575QX4633 • $16

1653.
Poolside Walrus
JLEE • 775QX4986 • $18

1654.
Porcelain Bear 8
875QX4426 • $28

1655.
Reindeer Champs 5: Comet
SIED • 775QX4433 • $35

1656.
Rocking Horse 10
SICK • 1075QX4646 • $110

1657.
S. Claus Taxi
DUTK • 1175QX4686 • $28

1658.
Santa Schnoz
CROW • 675QX4983 • $31

1659.
Santa's Ho-Ho-Hoedown
CROW • 2500QLX7256 • $94
MAGIC

1660.
Sister
475QX2273 • $26

1661.
Snoopy® and Woodstock™
RHOD • 675QX4723 • $49

1662.
Son
SIED • 575QX4516 • $42

1663.
Song and Dance
RGRS • 2000QLX7253 • $88
MAGIC

1664.
Spencer® Sparrow, Esq.
PIKE • 675QX4312 • $26
Re-issued from 1989.

1665.
Spoon Rider
ANDR • 975QX5496 • $17

1666.
Starlight Angel
RGRS • 1400QLX7306 • $36
MAGIC

1667.
Starship Christmas
SIED • 1800QLX7336 • $50
MAGIC

1668.
Stitches of Joy
JLEE • 775QX5186 • $23

1669.
Stocking Kitten
PIKE • 675QX4565 • $17
Re-issued from 1989.

1670.
Stocking Pals
SEAL • 1075QX5493 • $22

1671.
Sugar Plum Fairy
ANDR • 2775QXC4473 • $58
Limited Edition – 25400

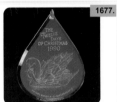

1672.
Sweetheart
RHOD • 1175QX4893 • $19

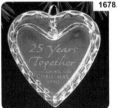

1673.
Teacher
SEAL • 775QX4483 • $11

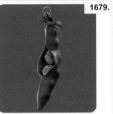

1674.
Ten Years Together
LYLE • 475QX2153 • $14

1675.
Three Little Piggies
CROW • 775QX4996 • $16

1676.
Time for Love
LYLE • 475QX2133 • $24

1677.
Twelve Days of Christmas 7:
Seven Swans A-Swimming
PYDA • 675QX3033 • $28

1678.
Twenty-Five Years Together
PATT • 975QX4896 • $20

1679.
Two Peas in a Pod
ANDR • 475QX4926 • $42

1680.
Welcome, Santa
CROW • 1175QX4773 • $24

1681.
Windows of the World 6:
Nollaig Shona
DLEE • 1075QX4636 • $26

1682.
Winter Surprise 2
FRAN • 1075QX4443 • $22

1991

1683.
Across the Miles
LYLE • 675QX3157 • $13

1684.
All-Star
SIED • 675QX5329 • $19

1685.
Arctic Dome
CROW • 2500QLX7117 • $45
MAGIC

1686.
Baby Celebrations:
Baby's Christening
JLEE • 1000BBY1317 • $17

1687.
Baby Celebrations: Baby's
First Christmas (Boy)
JLEE • 1000BBY1416 • $30

1688.
Baby Celebrations: Baby's
First Christmas (Girl)
RGRS • 1000BBY1514 • $30

1689.
Baby's First Christmas
SEAL • 3000QLX7247 • $124
MAGIC • RARE

1690.
Baby's First Christmas
VOTR • 775QX4869 • $28

1691.
Baby's First Christmas
FRAN • 1775QX5107 • $47

1692.
Baby's First Christmas (Boy)
HAMI • 475QX2217 • $24

1693.
Baby's First Christmas (Girl)
HAMI • 475QX2227 • $28

1694.
Basket Bell Players
SEAL • 775QX5377 • $26

1695.
Beary Artistic
SIED • GiftQXC7259 • $29
MAGIC

1696.
Betsey Clark: Home for Christmas 6
500QX2109 • $22

1697.
The Big Cheese
SIED • 675QX5327 • $14

1698.
Bringing Home The Tree
UNRU • 2800QLX7249 • $64
MAGIC

1699.
Brother
SIED • 675QX5479 • $22

1700.
Child's Age: Baby's First Christmas
FRAN • 775QX4889 • $65

1701.
Child's Age: Baby's Second Christmas
FRAN • 675QX4897 • $36

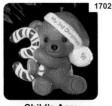
1702.
Child's Age: Child's Third Christmas
FRAN • 675QX4899 • $25

1703.
Child's Age: Child's Fourth Christmas
FRAN • 675QX4907 • $20

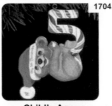
1704.
Child's Age: Child's Fifth Christmas
RHOD • 675QX4909 • $19

1705.
A Child's Christmas
FRAN • 975QX4887 • $14

1706.
Chilly Chap
DLEE • 675QX5339 • $22

1707.
Chris Mouse 7: Chris Mouse Mail
SIED • 1000QLX7207 • $42
MAGIC

1708.
Christmas Carol: Bob Cratchit
UNRU • 1375QX4997 • $31

1709.
Christmas Carol: Ebenezer Scrooge
UNRU • 1375QX4989 • $48

1710.
Christmas Carol: Merry Carolers
UNRU • 2975QX4799 • $89

1711.
Christmas Carol: Mrs. Cratchitt
UNRU • 1375QX4999 • $36

1712.
Christmas Carol: Tiny Tim
UNRU • 1075QX5037 • $34

1713.
Christmas Kitty 3
RGRS • 1475QX4377 • $29

1714.
Christmas Welcome
SICK • 975QX5299 • $28

1715.
Classic American Cars 1: 1957 Corvette®
PALM • 1275QX4319 • $170

1716.
Claus & Co. RR: Caboose
PALM • 395XPR9733 • $13

1717.
Claus & Co. RR: Gift Car
PALM • 395XPR9731 • $11

1718.
Claus & Co. RR: Locomotive
PALM • 395XPR9730 • $29

1719.
Claus & Co. RR: Passenger Car
PALM • 395XPR9732 • $13

1720.
Claus & Co. RR: Trestle Display Stand
PALM • 295XPR9734 • $12

1721.
Collector's Plate 5: Let It Snow!
VOTR • 875QX4369 • $27

1722.
Crayola® Crayon 3: Bright Vibrant Carols
CROW • 975QX4219 • $41

1723.
Cuddly Lamb
RGRS • 675QX5199 • $17

1724.
Dad
JLEE • 775QX5127 • $19

1725.
Dad-to-Be
JLEE • 575QX4879 • $11

1726.
Daughter
SIED • 575QX5477 • $41

61

1727.
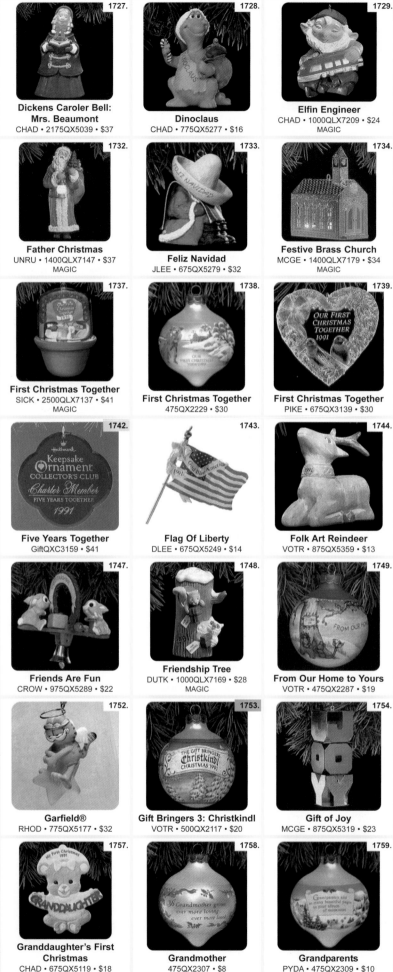
Dickens Caroler Bell: Mrs. Beaumont
CHAD • 2175QX5039 • $37

1728.
Dinoclaus
CHAD • 775QX5277 • $16

1729.

Elfin Engineer
CHAD • 1000QLX7209 • $24
MAGIC

1730.

Extra-Special Friends
AUBE • 475QX2279 • $14

1731.

Fabulous Decade 2
SEAL • 775QX4119 • $40

1732.
Father Christmas
UNRU • 1400QLX7147 • $37
MAGIC

1733.
Feliz Navidad
JLEE • 675QX5279 • $32

1734.
Festive Brass Church
MCGE • 1400QLX7179 • $34
MAGIC

1735.

Fiddlin' Around
VOTR • 775QX4387 • $12

1736.

Fifty Years Together
VOTR • 875QX4947 • $17

1737.
First Christmas Together
SICK • 2500QLX7137 • $41
MAGIC

1738.
First Christmas Together
475QX2229 • $30

1739.

First Christmas Together
PIKE • 675QX3139 • $30

1740.

First Christmas Together
VOTR • 875QX4917 • $22

1741.
Five Years Together
775QX4927 • $14

1742.
Five Years Together
GiftQXC3159 • $41

1743.
Flag Of Liberty
DLEE • 675QX5249 • $14

1744.
Folk Art Reindeer
VOTR • 875QX5359 • $13

1745.

Forest Frolics 3
PIKE • 2500QLX7219 • $65
MAGIC

1746.
Forty Years Together
775QX4939 • $20

1747.
Friends Are Fun
CROW • 975QX5289 • $22

1748.
Friendship Tree
DUTK • 1000QLX7169 • $28
MAGIC

1749.

From Our Home to Yours
VOTR • 475QX2287 • $19

1750.

Frosty Friends 12
PIKE • 975QX4327 • $75

1751.
Galloping Into Christmas
SICK • 1975QXC4779 • $95
Limited Edition – 28400

1752.
Garfield®
RHOD • 775QX5177 • $32

1753.
Gift Bringers 3: Christkindl
VOTR • 500QX2117 • $20

1754.

Gift of Joy
MCGE • 875QX5319 • $23

1755.

Godchild
BISH • 675QX5489 • $24

1756.
Granddaughter
PYDA • 475QX2299 • $30

1757.
Granddaughter's First Christmas
CHAD • 675QX5119 • $18

1758.
Grandmother
475QX2307 • $8

1759.

Grandparents
PYDA • 475QX2309 • $10

1760.

Grandson
PYDA • 475QX2297 • $30

1761.
Grandson's First Christmas
CHAD • 675QX5117 • $17

1762. Greatest Story 2
VOTR • 1275QX4129 • $20

1763. Hark! It's Herald 3
RGRS • 675QX4379 • $20

1764. Heart of Christmas 2
SEAL • 1375QX4357 • $25

1765. Heavenly Angels 1
LYLE • 775QX4367 • $20

1766. Here Comes Santa 13:
Santa's Antique Car
SICK • 1475QX4349 • $53

1767. Hidden Treasure and
Li'l Keeper
CROW • GiftQXC4769 • $38
Set/2

1768. Holiday Glow
PIKE • 1400QLX7177 • $34
MAGIC

1769. Hooked on Santa
JLEE • 775QX4109 • $35

1770. It's A Wonderful Life
DLEE • 2000QLX7237 • $71
MAGIC

1771. Jesus Loves Me
RHOD • 775QX3147 • $14

1772. Jingle Bears
JLEE • 2500QLX7323 • $45
MAGIC

1773. Jolly Wolly Santa
SICK • 775QX5419 • $29

1774. Jolly Wolly Snowman
SICK • 775QX5427 • $30

1775. Jolly Wolly Soldier
SICK • 775QX5429 • $23

1776. Joyous Memories
VOTR • 675QX5369 • $19

1777. Kansas City Santa
UNRU • Gift(N/A) • $655
Edition Size – 700

1778. Kringle's Bumper Cars
SICK • 2500QLX7119 • $45
MAGIC

1779. Mary Engelbreit
475QX2237 • $34

1780. Mary's Angels 4: Iris
CHAD/HAMI • 675QX4279 • $80

1781. Matchbox Memories:
Evergreen Inn
SEAL • 875QX5389 • $13

1782. Matchbox Memories:
Holiday Café
SEAL • 875QX5399 • $13

1783. Matchbox Memories:
Santa's Studio
SEAL • 875QX5397 • $20

1784. Merry Olde Santa 2
JLEE • 1475QX4359 • $89

1785. Mole Family Home
JLEE • 2000QLX7149 • $37
MAGIC

1786. Mom and Dad
AUBE • 975QX5467 • $22

1787. Mom-to-Be
JLEE • 575QX4877 • $15

1788. Mother
PYDA • 975QX5457 • $35

1789. Mr. and Mrs. Claus 6:
Checking His List
UNRU • 1375QX4339 • $35

1790. New Home
BISH • 675QX5449 • $24

1791. Night Before Christmas
SICK • 975QX5307 • $24

1792. Noah's Ark
CROW • 1375QX4867 • $39

1793. Norman Rockwell Art
LYLE • 500QX2259 • $24

1794. Nostalgic Houses & Shops
8: Fire Station
DLEE • 1475QX4139 • $74

1795. Notes of Cheer
SIED • 575QX5357 • $12

1796. Nutshell Nativity
RGRS • 675QX5176 • $28

63

1797.
Nutty Squirrel
PIKE • 575QX4833 • $14

1798.
Old-Fashioned Sled
SICK • 875QX4317 • $19

1799.
On a Roll
CROW • 675QX5347 • $18

1800.
Partridge in a Pear Tree
SICK • 975QX5297 • $19

1801.
Peace on Earth 1: Italy
SICK • 1175QX5129 • $20

1802.
PEANUTS®
500QX2257 • $32

1803.
PEANUTS® 1
RHOD • 1800QLX7229 • $86
MAGIC

1804.
Polar Circus Wagon
SICK • 1375QX4399 • $19

1805.
Polar Classic
SIED • 675QX5287 • $23

1806.
Puppy Love 1
RGRS • 775QX5379 • $115

1807.
Reindeer Champs 6: Cupid
SIED • 775QX4347 • $22

1808.
Rocking Horse 11
SICK • 1075QX4147 • $48

1809.
Salvation Army Band
UNRU • 3000QLX7273 • $90
MAGIC

1810.
Santa Sailor
SEAL • 975QX4389 • $25

1811.
Santa Special
SEAL • 4000QLX7167 • $65
MAGIC • Re-issued in 1992.

1812.
Santa's Hot Line
CROW • 1800QLX7159 • $46
MAGIC

1813.
Santa's Premiere
1075QX5237 • $25

1814.
Secrets For Santa
RGRS • 2375QXC4797 • $46
Limited Edition – 28700

1815.
Sister
LYLE • 675QX5487 • $19

1816.
Ski Lift Bunny
JLEE • 675QX5447 • $16

1817.
Ski Trip
SEAL • 2800QLX7266 • $38
MAGIC

1818.
Snoopy® and Woodstock™
RHOD • 675QX5197 • $37

1819.
Snowy Owl
SICK • 775QX5269 • $22

1820.
Son
SIED • 575QX5469 • $30

1821.
Sparkling Angel
CHAD • 1800QLX7157 • $34
MAGIC

1822.
Starship Enterprise™
NORT • 2000QLX7199 • $290
MAGIC

1823.
Sweet Talk
UNRU • 875QX5367 • $26

1824.
Sweetheart
975QX4957 • $23

1825.
Teacher
RGRS • 475QX2289 • $10

1826.
Ten Years Together
775QX4929 • $14

1827.
Tender Touches:
Fanfare Bear
SEAL • 875QX5337 • $17

1828.
Tender Touches:
Glee Club Bears
SEAL • 875QX4969 • $19

1829.
Tender Touches:
Look Out Below
SEAL • 875QX4959 • $18

1830.
Tender Touches:
Loving Stitches
SEAL • 875QX4987 • $26

1831.
Tender Touches:
Plum Delightful
SEAL • 875QX4977 • $17

1832.
Tender Touches:
Snow Twins
SEAL • 875QX4979 • $20

1833.
Tender Touches:
Yule Logger
SEAL • 875QX4967 • $19

1834.
Terrific Teacher
SICK • 675QX5309 • $10

1835.
Toyland Tower
CROW • 2000QLX7129 • $48
MAGIC

1836.
Tramp and Laddie
FRAN • 775QX4397 • $40

1837.
Twelve Days of Christmas 8:
Eight Maids A-Milking
PYDA • 675QX3089 • $20

1838.
Twenty-Five Years Together
VOTR • 875QX4937 • $12

1839.
Twirl-About –
First Christmas Together
SICK • 875QX4919 • $26

1840.
Under the Mistletoe
PIKE • 875QX4949 • $19

1841.
Up 'N' Down Journey
CROW • 975QX5047 • $25

1842.
Winnie the Pooh:
Christopher Robin
975QX5579 • $41

1843.
Winnie the Pooh:
Kanga and Roo
975QX5617 • $40

1844.
Winnie the Pooh:
Piglet and Eeyore
975QX5577 • $50

1845.
Winnie the Pooh: Rabbit
975QX5607 • $35

1846.
Winnie the Pooh: Tigger
975QX5609 • $85

1847.
Winnie the Pooh:
Winnie the Pooh
975QX5569 • $55

1848.
Winter Surprise 3
LYLE • 1075QX4277 • $36

1992

1849.
Across The Miles
RHOD • 675QX3044 • $10

1850.
Anniversary Year
UNRU • 975QX4851 • $20

1851.
Baby Celebrations:
Baby's Christening
850BBY1331 • $19

1852.
Baby Celebrations: Baby's
First Christmas (Boy)
850BBY1456 • $28

1853.
Baby Celebrations: Baby's
First Christmas (Girl)
850BBY1557 • $19

1854.
Baby's First Christmas
CROW • 2200QLX7281 • $115
MAGIC • RARE

1855.
Baby's First Christmas
ANDR • 1875QX4581 • $49

1856.
Baby's First Christmas
VOTR • 775QX4641 • $36

1857.
Baby's First Christmas
(Boy)
VOTR • 475QX2191 • $25

1858.
Baby's First Christmas
(Girl)
VOTR • 475QX2204 • $25

1859.
Bear Bell Champ
SEAL • 775QX5071 • $19

1860.
Betsey's Country
Christmas 1
500QX2104 • $22

1861.
Brother
CROW • 675QX4684 • $12

1862.
Cheerful Santa
UNRU • 975QX5154 • $22

1863.
Child's Age:
Baby's First Christmas
FRAN • 775QX4644 • $42

1864.
Child's Age:
Baby's Second Christmas
FRAN • 675QX4651 • $35

1865.
Child's Age:
Child's Third Christmas
FRAN • 675QX4654 • $28

1866.
Child's Age:
Child's Fourth Christmas
FRAN • 675QX4661 • $24

1867.
Child's Age:
Child's Fifth Christmas
RHOD • 675QX4664 • $24

1868.
A Child's Christmas
FRAN • 975QX4574 • $17

1869.
Chris Mouse 8:
Chris Mouse Tales
RGRS • 1200QLX7074 • $29
MAGIC

1870.
Christmas Parade
SICK • 3000QLX7271 • $77
MAGIC

1871.
Classic American Cars 2:
1966 Mustang
PALM • 1275QX4284 • $52

1872.
**Coca-Cola® –
Please Pause Here**
DLEE • 1475QX5291 • $32

1873.
Collector's Plate 6:
Sweet Holiday Harmony
VOTR • 875QX4461 • $18

1874.
Continental Express
SICK • 3200QLX7264 • $86
MAGIC

1875.
Cool Fliers
JLEE • 1075QX5474 • $18
Set/2

1876.
Crayola® Crayon 4:
Bright Blazing Colors
CROW • 975QX4264 • $44

1877.
Dad
SIED • 775QX4674 • $22

1878.
Dad-To-Be
JLEE • 675QX4611 • $12

1879.
The Dancing Nutcracker
VOTR • 3000QLX7261 • $62
MAGIC

1880.
Daughter
FRAN • 675QX5031 • $28

1881.
Deck The Hogs
FRAN • 875QX5204 • $25

1882.
Dickens Caroler Bell:
Lord Chadwick
CHAD • 2175QX4554 • $29

1883.
Down-Under Holiday
CROW • 775QX5144 • $16

1884.
Egg Nog Nest
SIED • 775QX5121 • $21

1885.
Elfin Marionette
CHAD • 1175QX5931 • $20

1886.
Elvis
LYLE/RHOD • 1475QX5624 • $34

1887.
Enchanted Clock
CROW • 3000QLX7274 • $55
MAGIC

1888.
Fabulous Decade 3
SEAL • 775QX4244 • $65

1889.
Feathered Friends
SICK • 1400QLX7091 • $35
MAGIC

1890.
Feliz Navidad
ANDR • 675QX5181 • $35

1891.
For My Grandma
775QX5184 • $17

1892.
For The One I Love
LYLE • 975QX4844 • $23

1893.
Forest Frolics 4
PIKE • 2800QLX7254 • $59
MAGIC

1894.
Friendly Greetings
CHAD • 775QX5041 • $12

1895.
Friendship Line
SEAL • 975QX5034 • $25

1896.
From Our Home To Yours
VOTR • 475QX2131 • $12

1897.
Frosty Friends 13
JLEE • 975QX4291 • $49

1898.
Fun On A Big Scale
CROW • 1075QX5134 • $19

1899.
Garfield®
PALM • 775QX5374 • $26

1900.
Genius At Work
CROW • 1075QX5371 • $18

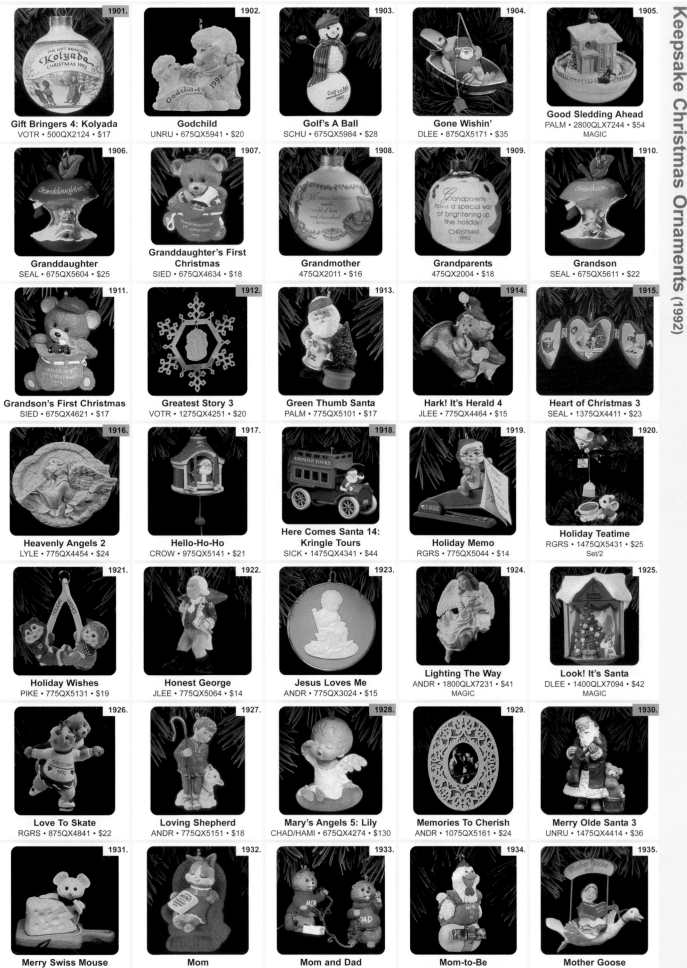

1901.
Gift Bringers 4: Kolyada
VOTR • 500QX2124 • $17

1902.
Godchild
UNRU • 675QX5941 • $20

1903.
Golf's A Ball
SCHU • 675QX5984 • $28

1904.
Gone Wishin'
DLEE • 875QX5171 • $35

1905.
Good Sledding Ahead
PALM • 2800QLX7244 • $54
MAGIC

1906.
Granddaughter
SEAL • 675QX5604 • $25

1907.
Granddaughter's First Christmas
SIED • 675QX4634 • $18

1908.
Grandmother
475QX2011 • $16

1909.
Grandparents
475QX2004 • $18

1910.
Grandson
SEAL • 675QX5611 • $22

1911.
Grandson's First Christmas
SIED • 675QX4621 • $17

1912.
Greatest Story 3
VOTR • 1275QX4251 • $20

1913.
Green Thumb Santa
PALM • 775QX5101 • $17

1914.
Hark! It's Herald 4
JLEE • 775QX4464 • $15

1915.
Heart of Christmas 3
SEAL • 1375QX4411 • $23

1916.
Heavenly Angels 2
LYLE • 775QX4454 • $24

1917.
Hello-Ho-Ho
CROW • 975QX5141 • $21

1918.
Here Comes Santa 14: Kringle Tours
SICK • 1475QX4341 • $44

1919.
Holiday Memo
RGRS • 775QX5044 • $14

1920.
Holiday Teatime
RGRS • 1475QX5431 • $25
Set/2

1921.
Holiday Wishes
PIKE • 775QX5131 • $19

1922.
Honest George
JLEE • 775QX5064 • $14

1923.
Jesus Loves Me
ANDR • 775QX3024 • $15

1924.
Lighting The Way
ANDR • 1800QLX7231 • $41
MAGIC

1925.
Look! It's Santa
DLEE • 1400QLX7094 • $42
MAGIC

1926.
Love To Skate
RGRS • 875QX4841 • $22

1927.
Loving Shepherd
ANDR • 775QX5151 • $18

1928.
Mary's Angels 5: Lily
CHAD/HAMI • 675QX4274 • $130

1929.
Memories To Cherish
ANDR • 1075QX5161 • $24

1930.
Merry Olde Santa 3
UNRU • 1475QX4414 • $36

1931.
Merry Swiss Mouse
SEAL • 775QX5114 • $16

1932.
Mom
RGRS • 775QX5164 • $26

1933.
Mom and Dad
SIED • 975QX4671 • $41

1934.
Mom-to-Be
JLEE • 675QX4614 • $12

1935.
Mother Goose
CROW • 1375QX4984 • $28

1936.

Mr. and Mrs. Claus 7:
Gift Exchange
UNRU • 1475QX4294 • $35

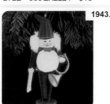

1937.

New Home
PIKE • 875QX5191 • $18

1938.

Norman Rockwell Art
LYLE • 500QX2224 • $18

1939.

North Pole Fire Fighter
SEAL • 975QX5104 • $26

1940.

North Pole Nutcrackers:
Eric The Baker
SICK • 875QX5244 • $18

1941.

North Pole Nutcrackers:
Franz The Artist
SICK • 875QX5261 • $41

1942.

North Pole Nutcrackers:
Frieda The Animals' Friend
SICK • 875QX5264 • $26

1943.

North Pole Nutcrackers:
Ludwig The Musician
SICK • 875QX5281 • $26

1944.

North Pole Nutcrackers:
Max The Tailor
SICK • 875QX5251 • $20

1945.

North Pole Nutcrackers:
Otto The Carpenter
SICK • 875QX5254 • $22

1946.

Nostalgic Houses & Shops
9: Five and Ten Cent Store
DLEE • 1475QX4254 • $52

1947.

Nut Sweet Nut
CROW • 1000QLX7081 • $24
MAGIC

1948.

O Christmas Tree
VOTR • 1075QX5411 • $24

1949.

Our First Christmas
Together
CHAD • 2000QLX7221 • $48
MAGIC

1950.

Our First Christmas
Together
VOTR • 675QX3011 • $18

1951.

Our First Christmas
Together
SEAL • 875QX4694 • $14

1952.

Our First Christmas
Together
JLEE • 975QX5061 • $32

1953.

Owl
SIED • 975QX5614 • $28

1954.

Owliver 1
SIED • 775QX4544 • $16

1955.

Partridge In a Pear Tree
SIED • 875QX5234 • $20

1956.

Peace on Earth 2: Spain
SICK • 1175QX5174 • $24

1957.

PEANUTS®
PYDA • 500QX2244 • $49

1958.

PEANUTS® 2
RHOD • 1800QLX7214 • $55
MAGIC

1959.

Polar Post
SEAL • 875QX4914 • $24

1960.

Puppy Love 2
RGRS • 775QX4484 • $80

1961.

Rapid Delivery
PALM • 875QX5094 • $14

1962.

Reindeer Champs 7: Donder
SIED • 875QX5284 • $30

1963.

Rocking Horse 12
SICK • 1075QX4261 • $38

1964.

Rodney Takes Flight
DLEE • GiftQXC5081 • $24

1965.

Santa and His Reindeer:
Comet and Cupid
CROW • 495XPR9737 • $26

1966.

Santa and His Reindeer:
Dasher and Dancer
CROW • 495XPR9735 • $36

1967.

Santa and His Reindeer:
Donder and Blitzen
CROW • 495XPR9738 • $32

1968.

Santa and His Reindeer:
Prancer and Vixen
CROW • 495XPR9736 • $28

1969.

Santa and His Reindeer:
Santa Claus and Sleigh
CROW • 495XPR9739 • $22

1970.

Santa Maria
CROW • 1275QX5074 • $18

1971.
Santa Special
SEAL • 4000QLX7167 • $65
MAGIC • Re-issued from 1991.

1972.
Santa Sub
CROW • 1800QLX7321 • $42
MAGIC

1973.
Santa with Bag of Toys
Gift(N/A) • $25
Brass or gold-plated cutout, on card.

1974.
A Santa-Full!
FRAN • 975QX5991 • $41

1975.
Santa's Answering Machine
JLEE • 2200QLX7241 • $36
MAGIC

1976.
Santa's Club List
SEAL • GiftQXC7291 • $32
MAGIC

1977.
Santa's Hook Shot
SEAL • 1275QX5434 • $26
Set/2

1978.
Santa's Roundup
JLEE • 875QX5084 • $20

1979.
Secret Pal
RGRS • 775QX5424 • $10

1980.
Shuttlecraft Galileo™ from the Starship Enterprise™
RHOD • 2400QLX7331 • $42
MAGIC

1981.
Silver Star Train Set
SICK • 2800QX5324 • $50
Set/3

1982.
Sister
CROW • 675QX4681 • $18

1983.
Skiing 'Round
JLEE • 875QX5214 • $18

1984.
Skyline: Caboose
SICK • 975QX5321 • $22

1985.
Skyline: Coal Car
SICK • 975QX5401 • $18

1986.
Skyline: Locomotive
SICK • 975QX5311 • $38

1987.
Skyline: Stock Car
SICK • 975QX5314 • $19

1988.
Snoopy® and Woodstock™
RGRS • 875QX5954 • $42

1989.
Son
FRAN • 675QX5024 • $32

1990.
Special Cat
CHAD • 775QX5414 • $19

1991.
Special Dog
CHAD • 775QX5421 • $23

1992.
Spirit Of Christmas Stress
CHAD • 875QX5231 • $18

1993.
Stocked With Joy
SICK • 775QX5934 • $21

1994.
Tasty Christmas
FRAN • 975QX5994 • $29

1995.
Teacher
475QX2264 • $26

1996.
Tobin Fraley Carousel 1
FRAL • 2800QX4891 • $39

1997.
Toboggan Tail
ANDR • 775QX5459 • $13

1998.
Tread Bear
SEAL • 875QX5091 • $32

1999.
Turtle Dreams
JLEE • 875QX4991 • $26

2000.
Twelve Days of Christmas 9: Nine Ladies Dancing
PYDA • 675QX3031 • $24

2001.
Uncle Art's Ice Cream
SIED • 875QX5001 • $21

2002.
Under Construction
PALM • 1800QLX7324 • $40
MAGIC

2003.
V.P. of Important Stuff
SIED • 675QX5051 • $18

2004.
Victorian Skater
UNRU • 2500QXC4067 • $53
Limited Edition – 14700

2005.
Watch Owls
FRAN • 1200QLX7084 • $24
MAGIC

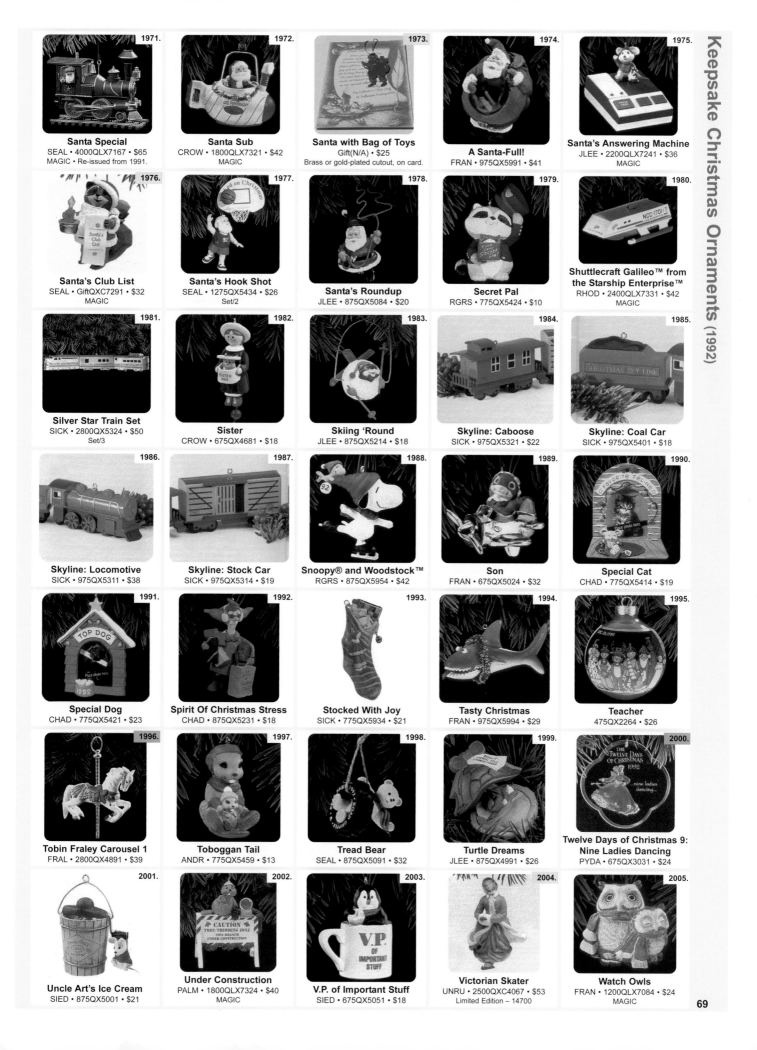

2006.
Winter Surprise 4
FRAN • 1175QX4271 • $24

2007.
World-Class Teacher
SIED • 775QX5054 • $13

2008.
Yuletide Rider
SEAL • 2800QLX7314 • $55
MAGIC

1993

2009.
Across the Miles
FRAN • 875QX5912 • $20

2010.
Anniversary Year Photo Holder
LYLE • 975QX5972 • $18

2011.
Apple for Teacher
SEAL • 775QX5902 • $17

2012.
Baby Celebrations: Baby's Christening
1200BBY2917 • $30

2013.
Baby Celebrations: Baby's First Christmas
FORS • 1200BBY2918 • $23

2014.
Baby Celebrations: Baby's First Christmas
FORS • 1400BBY2919 • $30

2015.
Baby Celebrations: Baby's First Christmas (Boy)
TAGU • 1000BBY1335 • $29

2016.
Baby Celebrations: Baby's First Christmas (Girl)
1000BBY1470 • $32

2017.
Baby Celebrations: Granddaughter's First Christmas
1400BBY2802 • $30

2018.
Baby Celebrations: Grandson's First Christmas
1400BBY2801 • $30

2019.
Baby's First Christmas
FRAN • 2200QLX7365 • $39
MAGIC

2020.
Baby's First Christmas
PALM • 1875QX5512 • $38

2021.
Baby's First Christmas
ANDR • 1075QX5515 • $24

2022.
Baby's First Christmas
RGRS • 775QX5522 • $37

2023.
Baby's First Christmas (Boy)
VOTR • 475QX2105 • $20

2024.
Baby's First Christmas (Girl)
VOTR • 475QX2092 • $20

2025.
Bearingers of Victoria Circle: Abearnathy Bearinger
ANDR/CHAD • 495XPR9747 • $10

2026.
Bearingers of Victoria Circle: Bearnadette Bearinger
ANDR • 495XPR9748 • $10

2027.
Bearingers of Victoria Circle: Fireplace Base
RHOD • 495XPR9749 • $10

2028.
Bearingers of Victoria Circle: Mama Bearinger
ANDR • 495XPR9745 • $10

2029.
Bearingers of Victoria Circle: Papa Bearinger
CHAD • 495XPR9746 • $10

2030.
Beary Gifted
CROW • 775QX5762 • $19

2031.
Bells are Ringing
CROW • 2800QLX7402 • $54
MAGIC

2032.

Betsey's Country Christmas 2
500QX2062 • $19

2033.

Big On Gardening
VOTR • 975QX5842 • $15

2034.

Big Roller
SIED • 875QX5352 • $17

2035.

Bird-Watcher
JLEE • 975QX5252 • $13

2036.

Bowling for ZZZs
FRAN • 775QX5565 • $12

2037.

Brother
RGRS • 675QX5542 • $10

2038.

Bugs Bunny™
SICK • 875QX5412 • $23

2039.

Caring Nurse
FRAN • 675QX5785 • $18

2040.
**Child's Age:
Baby's First Christmas**
CROW • 775QX5525 • $40

2041.
**Child's Age:
Baby's Second Christmas**
FRAN • 675QX5992 • $30

2042.
**Child's Age:
Child's Third Christmas**
FRAN • 675QX5995 • $24

2043.
**Child's Age:
Child's Fourth Christmas**
FRAN • 675QX5215 • $22

2044.
**Child's Age:
Child's Fifth Christmas**
RHOD • 675QX5222 • $19

2045.
A Child's Christmas
FRAN • 975QX5882 • $24

2046.
**Chris Mouse 9:
Chris Mouse Flight**
RGRS • 1200QLX7152 • $29
MAGIC

2047.
Christmas Break
SEAL • 775QX5825 • $18

2048.
Circle of Friendship
GiftQXC2112 • $183

2049.
**Classic American Cars 3:
1956 Ford® Thunderbird™**
PALM • 1275QX5275 • $45

2050.
Clever Cookie
SICK • 775QX5662 • $24

2051.
Coach
PALM • 675QX5935 • $18

2052.
Coca-Cola® – Playful Pals
RGRS • 1475QX5742 • $26

2053.
**Crayola® Crayon 5:
Bright Shining Castle**
CROW • 1075QX4422 • $30

2054.
Curly 'n' Kingly
CROW • 1075QX5285 • $18

2055.
Dad
JLEE • 775QX5855 • $16

2056.
Dad-to-Be
JLEE • 675QX5532 • $10

2057.
Daughter
VOTR • 675QX5872 • $16

2058.
**Dickens Caroler Bell:
Lady Daphne**
CHAD • 2175QX5505 • $31

2059.
Dog's Best Friend
JLEE • 1200QLX7172 • $23
MAGIC

2060.
Dollhouse Dreams
CROW • 2200QLX7372 • $44
MAGIC

2061.
Dunkin' Roo®
775QX5575 • $17

2062.
Elmer Fudd™
LYLE • 875QX5495 • $18

2063.
Fabulous Decade 4
PIKE • 775QX4475 • $19

2064.
Faithful Fire Fighter
VOTR • 775QX5782 • $17

2065.
Feliz Navidad
DLEE • 875QX5365 • $21

2066.
Fills the Bill
SIED • 875QX5572 • $19

2067.
**Folk Art Americana:
Angel in Flight**
SICK • 1575QK1052 • $44

2068.
**Folk Art Americana:
Polar Bear Adventure**
SICK • 1500QK1055 • $85

2069.
**Folk Art Americana:
Riding in the Woods**
SICK • 1575QK1065 • $65

2070.
**Folk Art Americana:
Riding the Wind**
SICK • 1575QK1045 • $50

2071.
**Folk Art Americana:
Santa Claus**
SICK • 1675QK1072 • $140

2072.
Forest Frolics 5
PIKE • 2500QLX7165 • $53
MAGIC

2073.
Frosty Friends 14
JLEE • 975QX4142 • $38

2074.
**Frosty Friends
Complement: Igloo**
SEAL • 2000QX5682 • $50

2075.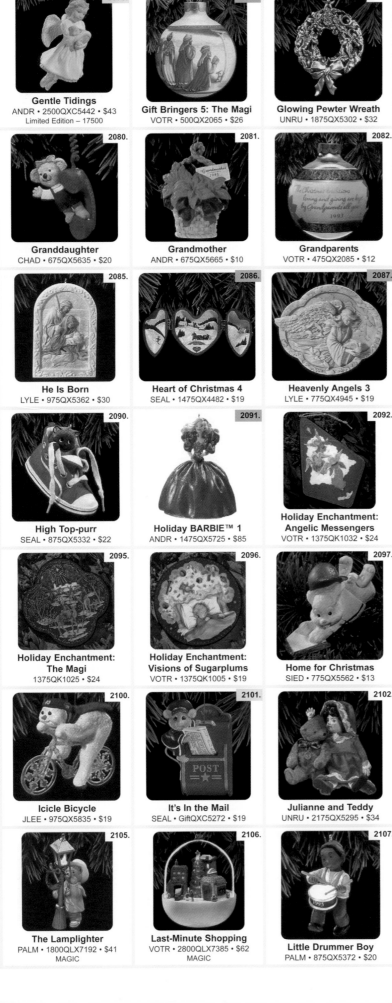
Gentle Tidings
ANDR • 2500QXC5442 • $43
Limited Edition – 17500

2076.
Gift Bringers 5: The Magi
VOTR • 500QX2065 • $26

2077.
Glowing Pewter Wreath
UNRU • 1875QX5302 • $32

2078.
Godchild
CHAD • 875QX5875 • $13

2079.
Grandchild's First Christmas
FRAN • 675QX5552 • $13

2080.
Granddaughter
CHAD • 675QX5635 • $20

2081.
Grandmother
ANDR • 675QX5665 • $10

2082.
Grandparents
VOTR • 475QX2085 • $12

2083.
Grandson
CHAD • 675QX5632 • $20

2084.
Great Connections
RGRS • 1075QX5402 • $24
Set/2

2085.
He Is Born
LYLE • 975QX5362 • $30

2086.
Heart of Christmas 4
SEAL • 1475QX4482 • $19

2087.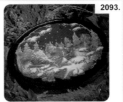
Heavenly Angels 3
LYLE • 775QX4945 • $19

2088.
Here Comes Santa 15: Happy Haul-idays
SICK • 1475QX4102 • $34

2089.
Here Comes Santa Complement: Shopping With Santa
SICK • 2400QX5675 • $40

2090.
High Top-purr
SEAL • 875QX5332 • $22

2091.
Holiday BARBIE™ 1
ANDR • 1475QX5725 • $85

2092.
Holiday Enchantment: Angelic Messengers
VOTR • 1375QK1032 • $24

2093.
Holiday Enchantment: Bringing Home the Tree
CHAD • 1375QK1042 • $19

2094.
Holiday Enchantment: Journey to the Forest
1375QK1012 • $19

2095.
Holiday Enchantment: The Magi
1375QK1025 • $24

2096.
Holiday Enchantment: Visions of Sugarplums
VOTR • 1375QK1005 • $19

2097.
Home for Christmas
SIED • 775QX5562 • $13

2098.
Home on the Range
SICK • 3200QLX7395 • $58
MAGIC

2099.
Howling Good Time
RGRS • 975QX5255 • $19

2100.
Icicle Bicycle
JLEE • 975QX5835 • $19

2101.
It's In the Mail
SEAL • GiftQXC5272 • $19

2102.
Julianne and Teddy
UNRU • 2175QX5295 • $34

2103.
K.C. Angel (Pewter)
UNRU • GiftQXC5445 • $295

2104.
K.C. Angel (Gold)
UNRU • GiftQXC5445C • $1000
VERY RARE • Edition Size – 10

2105.
The Lamplighter
PALM • 1800QLX7192 • $41
MAGIC

2106.
Last-Minute Shopping
VOTR • 2800QLX7385 • $62
MAGIC

2107.
Little Drummer Boy
PALM • 875QX5372 • $20

2108.
Look for the Wonder
DLEE • 1275QX5685 • $20

2109.
Lou Rankin Polar Bear
RHOD • 975QX5745 • $24

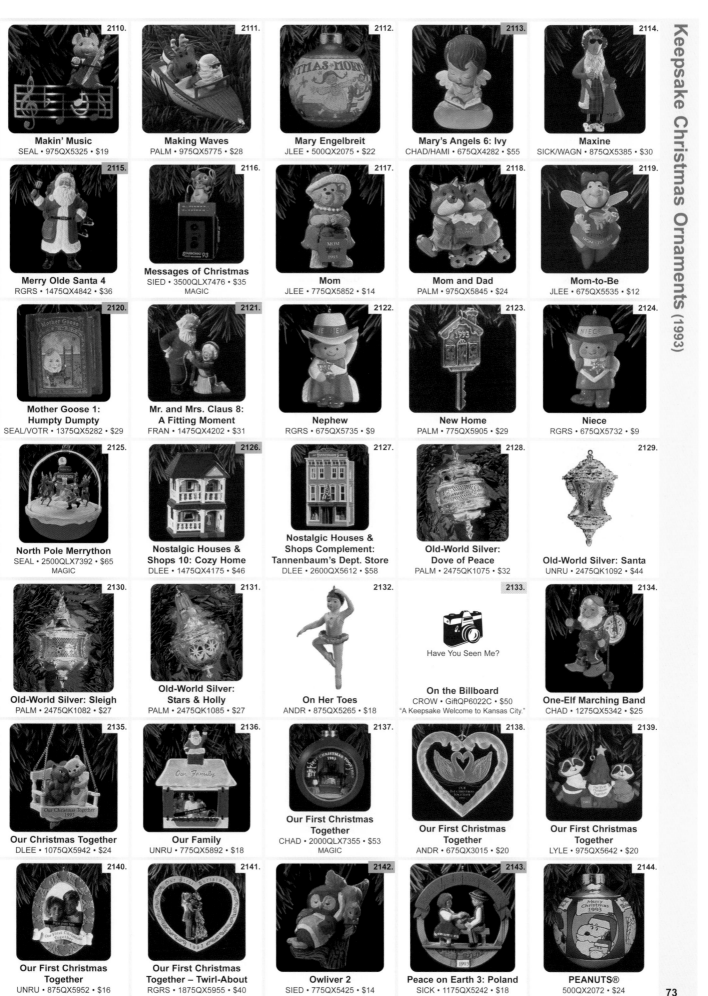

2110. Makin' Music
SEAL • 975QX5325 • $19

2111. Making Waves
PALM • 975QX5775 • $28

2112. Mary Engelbreit
JLEE • 500QX2075 • $22

2113. Mary's Angels 6: Ivy
CHAD/HAMI • 675QX4282 • $55

2114. Maxine
SICK/WAGN • 875QX5385 • $30

2115. Merry Olde Santa 4
RGRS • 1475QX4842 • $36

2116. Messages of Christmas
SIED • 3500QLX7476 • $35
MAGIC

2117. Mom
JLEE • 775QX5852 • $14

2118. Mom and Dad
PALM • 975QX5845 • $24

2119. Mom-to-Be
JLEE • 675QX5535 • $12

2120. Mother Goose 1: Humpty Dumpty
SEAL/VOTR • 1375QX5282 • $29

2121. Mr. and Mrs. Claus 8: A Fitting Moment
FRAN • 1475QX4202 • $31

2122. Nephew
RGRS • 675QX5735 • $9

2123. New Home
PALM • 775QX5905 • $29

2124. Niece
RGRS • 675QX5732 • $9

2125. North Pole Merrython
SEAL • 2500QLX7392 • $65
MAGIC

2126. Nostalgic Houses & Shops 10: Cozy Home
DLEE • 1475QX4175 • $46

2127. Nostalgic Houses & Shops Complement: Tannenbaum's Dept. Store
DLEE • 2600QX5612 • $58

2128. Old-World Silver: Dove of Peace
PALM • 2475QK1075 • $32

2129. Old-World Silver: Santa
UNRU • 2475QK1092 • $44

2130. Old-World Silver: Sleigh
PALM • 2475QK1082 • $27

2131. Old-World Silver: Stars & Holly
PALM • 2475QK1085 • $27

2132. On Her Toes
ANDR • 875QX5265 • $18

2133. Have You Seen Me?
On the Billboard
CROW • GiftQP6022C • $50
"A Keepsake Welcome to Kansas City."

2134. One-Elf Marching Band
CHAD • 1275QX5342 • $25

2135. Our Christmas Together
DLEE • 1075QX5942 • $24

2136. Our Family
UNRU • 775QX5892 • $18

2137. Our First Christmas Together
CHAD • 2000QLX7355 • $53
MAGIC

2138. Our First Christmas Together
ANDR • 675QX3015 • $20

2139. Our First Christmas Together
LYLE • 975QX5642 • $20

2140. Our First Christmas Together
UNRU • 875QX5952 • $16

2141. Our First Christmas Together – Twirl-About
RGRS • 1875QX5955 • $40

2142. Owliver 2
SIED • 775QX5425 • $14

2143. Peace on Earth 3: Poland
SICK • 1175QX5242 • $18

2144. PEANUTS®
500QX2072 • $24

73

2145.
PEANUTS® 3
RHOD • 1800QLX7155 • $48
MAGIC

2146.
PEANUTS® Gang 1
RHOD • 975QX5315 • $48

2147.
Peek-A-Boo Tree
CROW • 1075QX5245 • $24

2148.
Peep Inside
1375QX5322 • $24

2149.
People Friendly
SEAL • 875QX5932 • $16

2150.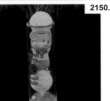
Perfect Match
SIED • 875QX5772 • $17

2151.
Personalized –
Baby Block Photo Holder
FRAN • 1475QP6035 • $29
Re-issued in 1994.

2152.
Personalized –
Cool Snowman
875QP6052 • $30

2153.
Personalized –
Festive Album Photo Holder
VOTR • 1275QP6025 • $18
Re-issued in 1994.

2154.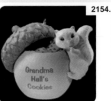
Personalized –
Filled with Cookies
RGRS • 1275QP6042 • $18

2155.
Personalized – Goin' Golfin'
PALM • 1275QP6012 • $30
Re-issued in 1994.

2156.
Personalized –
Here's Your Fortune
SEAL • 1075QP6002 • $18

2157.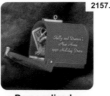
Personalized –
Mailbox Delivery
CROW • 1475QP6015 • $30
Re-issued in 1994 & 1995.

2158.
Personalized –
On the Billboard
CROW • 1275QP6022 • $30
Re-issued in 1994 & 1995.

2159.
Personalized – PEANUTS®
900QP6045 • $20

2160.
Personalized – Playing Ball
FRAN • 1275QP6032 • $25
Re-issued in 1994 & 1995.

2161.
Personalized –
Reindeer in the Sky
875QP6055 • $30

2162.
Personalized – Santa Says
SEAL • 1475QP6005 • $30
Re-issued in 1994.

2163.
The Pink Panther™
PALM • 1275QX5755 • $19

2164.
Popping Good Times
CHAD • 1475QX5392 • $22
Set/2

2165.
Porky Pig™
ANDR • 875QX5652 • $18

2166.
Portraits in Bisque:
Christmas Feast
PIKE • 1375QK1152 • $23

2167.
Portraits in Bisque:
Joy of Sharing
LYLE • 1375QK1142 • $23

2168.
Portraits in Bisque:
Mistletoe Kiss
PIKE • 1375QK1145 • $16

2169.
Portraits in Bisque:
Norman Rockwell –
Filling the Stocking
DUTK • 1375QK1155 • $20

2170.
Portraits in Bisque:
Norman Rockwell –
Jolly Postman
DUTK • 1375QK1162 • $24

2171.
Puppy Love 3
RGRS • 775QX5045 • $40

2172.
Putt-Putt Penguin
JLEE • 975QX5795 • $17

2173.
Quick as a Fox
CROW • 875QX5792 • $17

2174.
Radio News Flash
DLEE • 2200QLX7362 • $37
MAGIC

2175.
Raiding the Fridge
RGRS • 1600QLX7185 • $41
MAGIC

2176.
Ready for Fun
LYLE • 775QX5124 • $16

2177.
Reindeer Champs 8: Blitzen
SIED • 875QX4331 • $18

2178.
Road Runner™ &
Wile E. Coyote™
CHAD • 3000QLX7415 • $63
MAGIC

2179.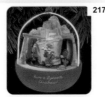
Rocking Horse 13
SICK • 1075QX4162 • $36

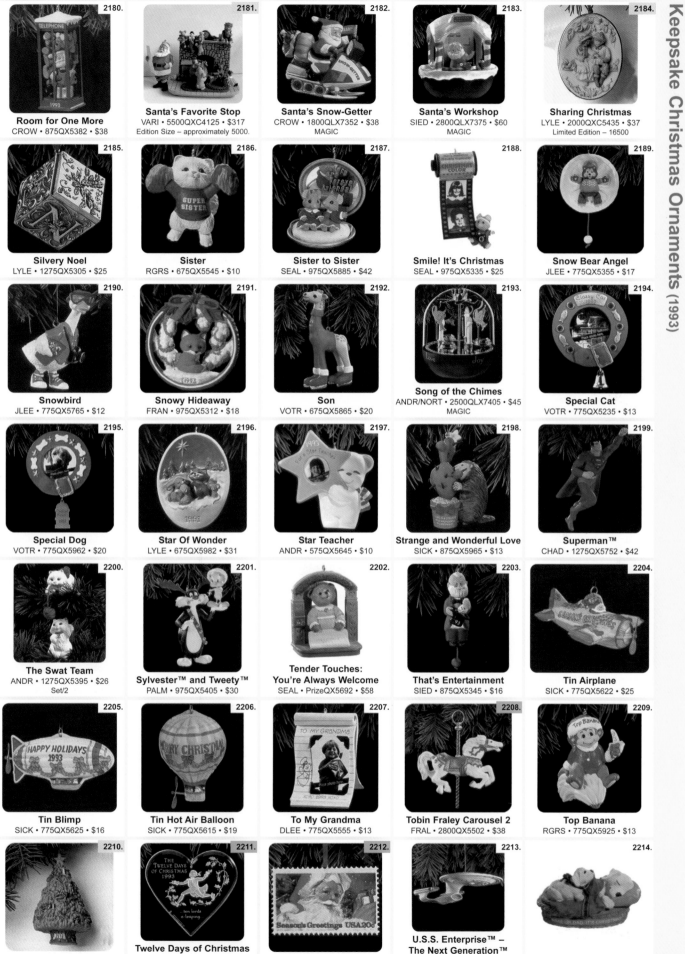

2180.
Room for One More
CROW • 875QX5382 • $38

2181.
Santa's Favorite Stop
VARI • 5500QXC4125 • $317
Edition Size – approximately 5000.

2182.
Santa's Snow-Getter
CROW • 1800QLX7352 • $38
MAGIC

2183.
Santa's Workshop
SIED • 2800QLX7375 • $60
MAGIC

2184.
Sharing Christmas
LYLE • 2000QXC5435 • $37
Limited Edition – 16500

2185.
Silvery Noel
LYLE • 1275QX5305 • $25

2186.
Sister
RGRS • 675QX5545 • $10

2187.
Sister to Sister
SEAL • 975QX5885 • $42

2188.
Smile! It's Christmas
SEAL • 975QX5335 • $25

2189.
Snow Bear Angel
JLEE • 775QX5355 • $17

2190.
Snowbird
JLEE • 775QX5765 • $12

2191.
Snowy Hideaway
FRAN • 975QX5312 • $18

2192.
Son
VOTR • 675QX5865 • $20

2193.
Song of the Chimes
ANDR/NORT • 2500QLX7405 • $45
MAGIC

2194.
Special Cat
VOTR • 775QX5235 • $13

2195.
Special Dog
VOTR • 775QX5962 • $20

2196.
Star Of Wonder
LYLE • 675QX5982 • $31

2197.
Star Teacher
ANDR • 575QX5645 • $10

2198.
Strange and Wonderful Love
SICK • 875QX5965 • $13

2199.
Superman™
CHAD • 1275QX5752 • $42

2200.
The Swat Team
ANDR • 1275QX5395 • $26
Set/2

2201.
Sylvester™ and Tweety™
PALM • 975QX5405 • $30

2202.
**Tender Touches:
You're Always Welcome**
SEAL • PrizeQX5692 • $58

2203.
That's Entertainment
SIED • 875QX5345 • $16

2204.
Tin Airplane
SICK • 775QX5622 • $25

2205.
Tin Blimp
SICK • 775QX5625 • $16

2206.
Tin Hot Air Balloon
SICK • 775QX5615 • $19

2207.
To My Grandma
DLEE • 775QX5555 • $13

2208.
Tobin Fraley Carousel 2
FRAL • 2800QX5502 • $38

2209.
Top Banana
RGRS • 775QX5925 • $13

2210.
Trimmed with Memories
SICK • 1200QXC5432 • $34

2211.
**Twelve Days of Christmas
10: Ten Lords A-Leaping**
CHAD • 675QX3012 • $13

2212.
U.S. Christmas Stamps 1
SICK • 1075QX5292 • $26

2213.
**U.S.S. Enterprise™ –
The Next Generation™**
NORT • 2400QLX7412 • $48
MAGIC

2214.
Wake-Up Call
UNRU • 875QX5262 • $16

75

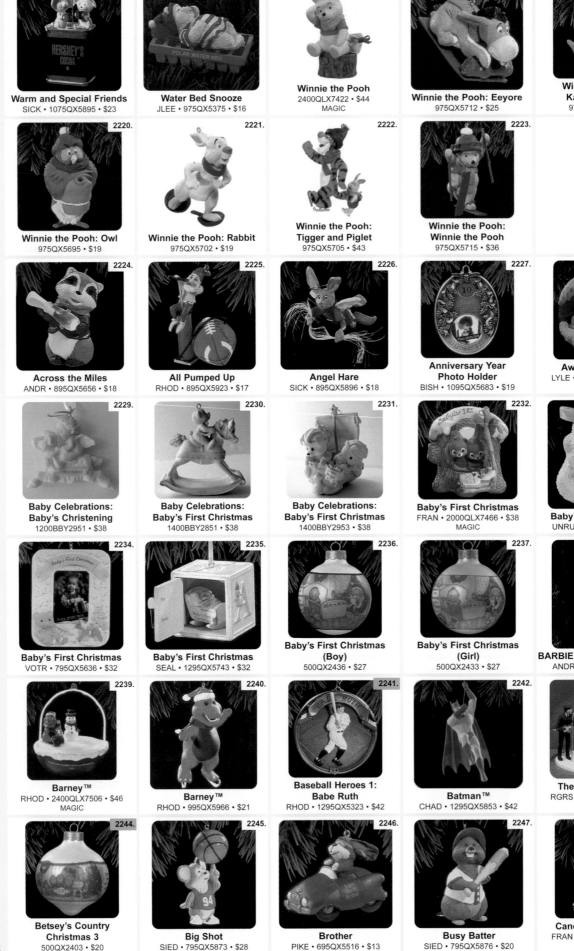

2215.
Warm and Special Friends
SICK • 1075QX5895 • $23

2216.
Water Bed Snooze
JLEE • 975QX5375 • $16

2217.
Winnie the Pooh
2400QLX7422 • $44
MAGIC

2218.
Winnie the Pooh: Eeyore
975QX5712 • $25

2219.
Winnie the Pooh:
Kanga and Roo
975QX5672 • $20

2220.
Winnie the Pooh: Owl
975QX5695 • $19

2221.
Winnie the Pooh: Rabbit
975QX5702 • $19

2222.
Winnie the Pooh:
Tigger and Piglet
975QX5705 • $43

2223.
Winnie the Pooh:
Winnie the Pooh
975QX5715 • $36

1994

2224.
Across the Miles
ANDR • 895QX5656 • $18

2225.
All Pumped Up
RHOD • 895QX5923 • $17

2226.
Angel Hare
SICK • 895QX5896 • $18

2227.
Anniversary Year
Photo Holder
BISH • 1095QX5683 • $19

2228.
Away in a Manger
LYLE • 1600QLX7383 • $37
MAGIC

2229.
Baby Celebrations:
Baby's Christening
1200BBY2951 • $38

2230.
Baby Celebrations:
Baby's First Christmas
1400BBY2851 • $38

2231.
Baby Celebrations:
Baby's First Christmas
1400BBY2953 • $38

2232.
Baby's First Christmas
FRAN • 2000QLX7466 • $38
MAGIC

2233.
Baby's First Christmas
UNRU • 1895QX5633 • $32

2234.
Baby's First Christmas
VOTR • 795QX5636 • $32

2235.
Baby's First Christmas
SEAL • 1295QX5743 • $32

2236.
Baby's First Christmas
(Boy)
500QX2436 • $27

2237.
Baby's First Christmas
(Girl)
500QX2433 • $27

2238.
BARBIE™ 1: 1959 BARBIE™
ANDR • 1495QX5006 • $30

2239.
Barney™
RHOD • 2400QLX7506 • $46
MAGIC

2240.
Barney™
RHOD • 995QX5966 • $21

2241.
Baseball Heroes 1:
Babe Ruth
RHOD • 1295QX5323 • $42

2242.
Batman™
CHAD • 1295QX5853 • $42

2243.
The Beatles Gift Set
RGRS • 4800QX5373 • $124
Set/5

2244.
Betsey's Country
Christmas 3
500QX2403 • $20

2245.
Big Shot
SIED • 795QX5873 • $28

2246.
Brother
PIKE • 695QX5516 • $13

2247.
Busy Batter
SIED • 795QX5876 • $20

2248.
Candy Cane Lookout
FRAN • 1800QLX7376 • $88
MAGIC

2249.

Candy Caper
ANDR • 895QX5776 • $22

2250.

Caring Doctor
RGRS • 895QX5823 • $15

2251.
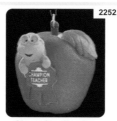
Cat Naps 1
RHOD • 795QX5313 • $36

2252.

Champion Teacher
SIED • 695QX5836 • $13

2253.

Cheers to You!
CROW • 1095QX5796 • $24

2254.

Cheery Cyclists
CROW • 1295QX5786 • $28

2255.
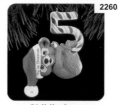
Child Care Giver
VOTR • 795QX5906 • $14

2256.

**Child's Age:
Baby's First Christmas**
CROW • 795QX5713 • $38

2257.

**Child's Age:
Baby's Second Christmas**
CROW • 795QX5716 • $29

2258.

**Child's Age:
Child's Third Christmas**
FRAN • 695QX5723 • $24

2259.

**Child's Age:
Child's Fourth Christmas**
FRAN • 695QX5726 • $24

2260.

**Child's Age:
Child's Fifth Christmas**
RHOD • 695QX5733 • $24

2261.

**Chris Mouse 10:
Chris Mouse Jelly**
RGRS • 1200QLX7393 • $26
MAGIC

2262.

**Christmas Lights:
Home for the Holidays**
PALM • 1575QK1123 • $32

2263.

**Christmas Lights:
Moonbeams**
ANDR • 1575QK1116 • $32

2264.

**Christmas Lights:
Mother and Child**
RGRS • 1575QK1126 • $32

2265.

**Christmas Lights:
Peaceful Village**
CHAD • 1575QK1106 • $32

2266.

**Classic American Cars 4:
1957 Chevrolet® Bel Air**
PALM • 1295QX5422 • $35

2267.

**Classic American Cars 4:
1957 Chevrolet® Bel Air**
PALM • PrizeQX5422C • $975
Edition Size – 40

2268.

Coach
UNRU • 795QX5933 • $17

2269.

**Coca-Cola® –
Relaxing Moment**
FRAN • 1495QX5356 • $28

2270.

Cock-a-Doodle Christmas
VOTR • 895QX5396 • $24

2271.

Collector's Survival Kit
RGRS • GiftQP6042C • $29

2272.

Colors of Joy
SEAL • 795QX5893 • $34

2273.

Conversations with Santa
SEAL • 2800QLX7426 • $43
MAGIC

2274.

Country Showtime
SICK • 2200QLX7416 • $48
MAGIC

2275.

**Crayola® Crayon 6:
Bright Playful Colors**
CROW • 1095QX5273 • $34

2276.

Dad
RGRS • 795QX5463 • $14

2277.

Dad-to-Be
PIKE • 795QX5473 • $18

2278.

Daffy Duck™
PALM • 895QX5415 • $36

2279.
Daughter
ANDR • 695QX5623 • $18

2280.
Dear Santa Mouse
CROW • 1495QX5806 • $22
Set/2

2281.
The Eagle Has Landed
SEAL • 2400QLX7486 • $46
MAGIC

2282.
Extra-Special Delivery
CROW • 795QX5833 • $18

2283.
Fabulous Decade 5
SEAL • 795QX5263 • $36

2284.
Feelin' Groovy
795QX5953 • $24

2285.
A Feline of Christmas
ANDR • 895QX5816 • $28

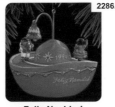
2286.
Feliz Navidad
CROW • 2800QLX7433 • $84
MAGIC

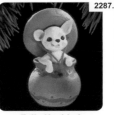
2287.
Feliz Navidad
RGRS • 895QX5793 • $35

2288.
Folk Art Americana: Catching 40 Winks
SICK • 1675QK1183 • $28

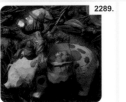
2289.
Folk Art Americana: Going to Town
SICK • 1575QK1166 • $42

2290.
Folk Art Americana: Racing Through the Snow
SICK • 1575QK1173 • $42

2291.
Folk Art Americana: Rarin' To Go
SICK • 1575QK1193 • $34

2292.
Folk Art Americana: Roundup Time
SICK • 1675QK1176 • $34

2293.
Follow the Sun
CROW • 895QX5846 • $16

2294.
For My Grandma
DLEE • 695QX5613 • $14

2295.
Forest Frolics 6
PIKE • 2800QLX7436 • $53
MAGIC

2296.
Fred and Barney – The Flintstones™
RHOD • 1495QX5003 • $28

2297.
Friendly Push
SIED • 895QX5686 • $26

2298.
Friendship Sundae
SICK • 1095QX4766 • $28

2299.
Frosty Friends 15
SEAL • 995QX5293 • $40

2300.
Garden Elves: Daisy Days
CHAD • 995QX5986 • $12

2301.
Garden Elves: Harvest Joy
CHAD • 995QX5993 • $12

2302.
Garden Elves: Tulip Time
CHAD • 995QX5983 • $15

2303.
Garden Elves: Yuletide Cheer
CHAD • 995QX5976 • $15

2304.
Garfield®
1295QX5753 • $26

2305.
Gentle Nurse
LYLE • 695QX5973 • $23

2306.
Gingerbread Fantasy
PALM • 4400QLX7382 • $92
MAGIC

2307.
Godchild
RGRS • 895QX4453 • $22

2308.
Godparent
HAMI • 500QX2423 • $17

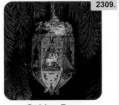
2309.
Golden Bow
PALM • 1000QK1023C • $76
RARER

2310.
Golden Dove of Peace
PALM • 1000QK1075C • $38

2311.
Golden Poinsettia
UNRU • 1000QK1006C • $93
RARER

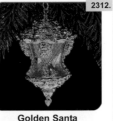
2312.
Golden Santa
UNRU • 1000QK1092C • $64

2313.
Golden Sleigh
PALM • 1000QK1082C • $45

2314.
Golden Stars and Holly
PALM • 1000QK1085C • $45

2315.
Grandchild's First Christmas
UNRU • 795QX5676 • $18

2316.
Granddaughter
PIKE • 695QX5523 • $18

2317.
Grandmother
ANDR • 795QX5673 • $14

2318.
Grandpa
UNRU • 795QX5616 • $14

Grandparents
500QX2426 • $16
2319.

Grandson
PIKE • 695QX5526 • $18
2320.

Happy Birthday, Jesus
LYLE • 1295QX5423 • $23
2321.

Heart of Christmas 5
SEAL • 1495QX5266 • $22
2322.

Hearts in Harmony
ANDR • 1095QX4406 • $20
2323.

Helpful Shepherd
CHAD • 895QX5536 • $22
2324.

Here Comes Santa 16: Makin' Tractor Tracks
SICK • 1495QX5296 • $56
2325.

Here's Your Fortune
SEAL • GiftQP6002C • $40
2 versions.
2326.

Holiday BARBIE™ 2
ANDR • 1495QX5216 • $44
2327.

Holiday Favorites: Dapper Snowman
VOTR • 1375QK1053 • $22
2328.

Holiday Favorites: Graceful Fawn
VOTR • 1175QK1033 • $18
2329.

Holiday Favorites: Jolly Santa
VOTR • 1375QK1046 • $24
2330.

Holiday Favorites: Joyful Lamb
VOTR • 1175QK1036 • $24
2331.

Holiday Favorites: Peaceful Dove
VOTR • 1175QK1043 • $24
2332.

Holiday Hello
SIED • 2495QXR6116 • $42
Recordable.
2333.

Holiday Patrol
RHOD • 895QX5826 • $14
2334.

Holiday Pursuit
FRAN • GiftQXC4823 • $22
2335.

Ice Show
ANDR • 795QX5946 • $17
2336.

In the Pink
ANDR • 995QX5763 • $23
2337.

It's a Strike
SIED • 895QX5856 • $16
2338.

Jingle Bell Band
CROW • 1095QX5783 • $23
2339.

Jolly Holly Santa
LYLE • 2200QXC4833 • $43
2340.

Joyous Song
ANDR • 895QX4473 • $28
2341.

Jump-along Jackalope
FRAN • 895QX5756 • $18
2342.

Keep on Mowin'
SIED • 895QX5413 • $13
2343.

Kickin' Roo
795QX5916 • $16
2344.

Kiddie Car Classics 1: Murray® Champion
PALM • 1395QX5426 • $50
2345.

Kiddie Car Classics 1: Murray® Champion
PALM • PrizeQX5426C • $1000
Edition Size – 40
2346.

Kitty's Catamaran
SEAL • 1095QX5416 • $20
2347.

Klingon Bird of Prey™
NORT • 2400QLX7386 • $40
MAGIC
2348.

Kringle Trolley
CROW • 2000QLX7413 • $43
MAGIC
2349.

Kringle's Kayak
SEAL • 795QX5886 • $26
2350.

Lou Rankin Seal
BISH • 995QX5456 • $20
2351.

Lucinda and Teddy
UNRU • 2175QX4813 • $28
2352.

Magic Carpet Ride
SEAL • 795QX5883 • $22
2353.

2354.
Majestic Deer
UNRU • 2500QXC4836 • $69

2355.
Making It Bright
RHOD • 895QX5403 • $28

2356.
Mary Engelbreit
500QX2416 • $31

2357.
Mary's Angels 7: Jasmine
CHAD/HAMI • 695QX5276 • $42

2358.
Maxine
SICK/WAGN • 2000QLX7503 • $71
MAGIC

2359.
Merry Fishmas
PALM • 895QX5913 • $27

2360.
Merry Olde Santa 5
CHAD • 1495QX5256 • $32

2361.
Mistletoe Surprise
SEAL • 1295QX5996 • $26
Set/2

2362.
Mom
RGRS • 795QX5466 • $14

2363.
Mom and Dad
SIED • 995QX5666 • $40

2364.
Mom-to-Be
PIKE • 795QX5506 • $18

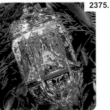

2365.
Mother Goose 2:
Hey Diddle, Diddle
SEAL/VOTR • 1395QX5213 • $36

2366.
Mr. and Mrs. Claus 9:
A Hand Warming Present
UNRU • 1495QX5283 • $34

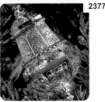

2367.
Mrs. Claus' Cupboard
VARI • 5500QXC4843 • $145
Set/11 • Edition Size – 12000

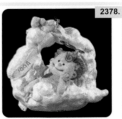

2368.
Mufasa and Simba –
The Lion King
1495QX5406 • $28

2369.
Nephew
FRAN • 795QX5546 • $10

2370.
New Home
ANDR • 895QX5663 • $14

2371.
Niece
FRAN • 795QX5543 • $12

2372.
Norman Rockwell Art
LYLE • 500QX2413 • $18

2373.
Nostalgic Houses & Shops
11: Neighborhood Drugstore
DLEE • 1495QX5286 • $40

2374.
Old-World Silver: Bells
UNRU • 2475QK1026 • $25

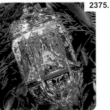

2375.
Old-World Silver: Bows
PALM • 2475QK1023 • $29

2376.
Old-World Silver: Poinsettia
UNRU • 2475QK1006 • $26

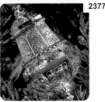

2377.
Old-World Silver:
Snowflakes
UNRU • 2475QK1016 • $29

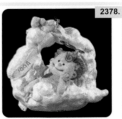

2378.
On Cloud Nine
DLEE • 1200QXC4853 • $25

2379.
Open-and-Shut Holiday
SIED • 995QX5696 • $20

2380.
Our Christmas Together
RGRS • 995QX4816 • $19

2381.
Our Family
ANDR • 795QX5576 • $26

2382.
Our First Christmas
Together
VOTR • 695QX3186 • $26

2383.
Our First Christmas
Together
BISH • 995QX5643 • $28

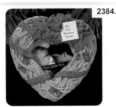

2384.
Our First Christmas
Together
PALM • 895QX5653 • $18

2385.
Our First Christmas
Together
ANDR • 1895QX5706 • $28

2386.
Out of This World Teacher
UNRU • 795QX5766 • $16

2387.
Owliver 3
SIED • 795QX5226 • $18

2388.
PEANUTS® 4
RHOD • 2000QLX7406 • $54
MAGIC

2389.
PEANUTS® Gang 2
BISH • 995QX5203 • $18

2390.
Peekaboo Pup
RGRS • 2000QLX7423 • $38
MAGIC

2391.
Personalized –
Baby Block Photo Holder
FRAN • 1495QP6035 • $29
Re-issued from 1993.

2392.
Personalized –
Computer Cat 'n' Mouse
SEAL • 1295QP6046 • $20
Re-issued in 1995.

2393.
Personalized – Cookie Time
VOTR • 1295QP6073 • $21
Re-issued in 1995.

2394.
Personalized –
Etch-a-Sketch®
CROW • 1295QP6006 • $60
Re-issued in 1995.

2395.
Personalized –
Festive Album Photo Holder
VOTR • 1295QP6025 • $18
Re-issued from 1993.

2396.
Personalized –
From the Heart
RHOD • 1495QP6036 • $20
Re-issued in 1995.

2397.
Personalized – Goin' Fishin'
PALM • 1495QP6023 • $32

2398.
Personalized – Goin' Golfin'
PALM • 1295QP6012 • $30
Re-issued from 1993.

2399.
Personalized –
Mailbox Delivery
CROW • 1495QP6015 • $30
Re-issued from 1993.

2400.
Personalized – Novel Idea
VOTR • 1295QP6066 • $20
Re-issued in 1995.

2401.
Personalized –
On the Billboard
CROW • 1295QP6022 • $30
Also issued in 1993 & 1995.

2402.
Personalized – Playing Ball
FRAN • 1295QP6032 • $25
Also issued in 1993 & 1995.

2403.
Personalized –
Reindeer Rooters
CROW • 1295QP6056 • $34
Re-issued in 1995.

2404.
Personalized – Santa Says
SEAL • 1495QP6005 • $30
Re-issued from 1993.

2405.
Practice Makes Perfect
PALM • 895QX5863 • $12

2406.
Puppy Love 4
RGRS • 795QX5253 • $42

2407.
Red Hot Holiday
RGRS • 795QX5843 • $25

2408.
Reindeer Pro
RHOD • 795QX5926 • $18

2409.
Road Runner™ and
Wile E. Coyote™
CHAD • 1295QX5602 • $28

2410.
Rock Candy Miner
SIED • 2000QLX7403 • $32
MAGIC

2411.
Rocking Horse 14
SICK • 1095QX5016 • $32

2412.
Santa's Lego® Sleigh
CROW • 1095QX5453 • $34

2413.
Santa's Sing-Along
CROW • 2400QLX7473 • $68
MAGIC

2414.
Sarah Plain and Tall:
Country Church
BAUR • 795XPR9450 • $22

2415.
Sarah Plain and Tall:
Hays Train Station
BAUR • 795XPR9452 • $22

2416.
Sarah Plain and Tall:
Mrs. Parkley's
General Store
BAUR • 795XPR9451 • $17

2417.
Sarah Plain and Tall:
Sarah's Maine Home
BAUR • 795XPR9454 • $24

2418.
Sarah Plain and Tall:
Sarah's Prairie Home
BAUR • 795XPR9453 • $26

2419.
Secret Santa
UNRU • 795QX5736 • $18

2420.
A Sharp Flat
CROW • 1095QX5773 • $18

2421.
Simba and Nala –
The Lion King
1295QX5303 • $26
Set/2

2422.
Simba, Sarabi, and
Mufasa – The Lion King
3200QLX7513 • $65
MAGIC • Recalled

2423.
Simba, Sarabi, and
Mufasa – The Lion King
2000QLX7516 • $48
MAGIC

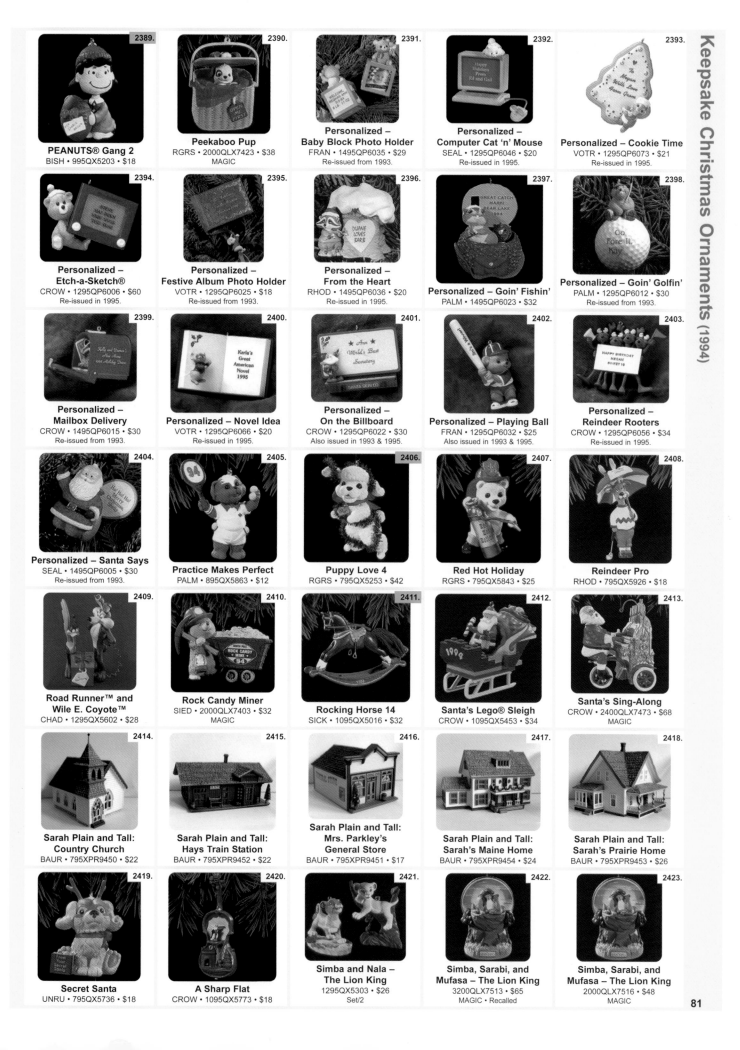

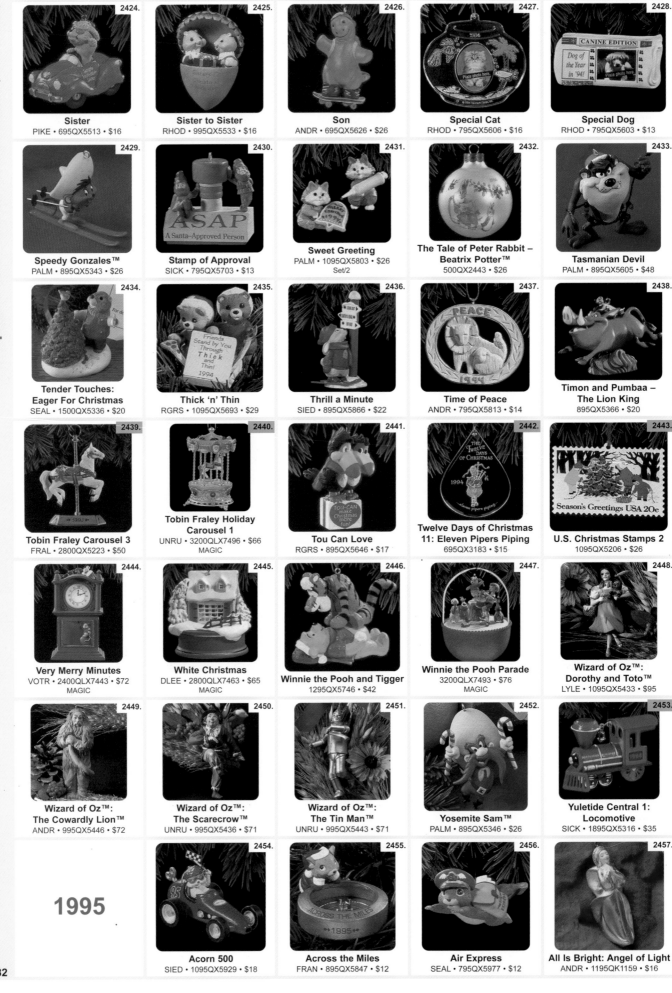

2424. Sister
PIKE • 695QX5513 • $16

2425. Sister to Sister
RHOD • 995QX5533 • $16

2426. Son
ANDR • 695QX5626 • $26

2427. Special Cat
RHOD • 795QX5606 • $16

2428. Special Dog
RHOD • 795QX5603 • $13

2429. Speedy Gonzales™
PALM • 895QX5343 • $26

2430. Stamp of Approval
SICK • 795QX5703 • $13

2431. Sweet Greeting
PALM • 1095QX5803 • $26
Set/2

2432. The Tale of Peter Rabbit –
Beatrix Potter™
500QX2443 • $26

2433. Tasmanian Devil
PALM • 895QX5605 • $48

2434. Tender Touches:
Eager For Christmas
SEAL • 1500QX5336 • $20

2435. Thick 'n' Thin
RGRS • 1095QX5693 • $29

2436. Thrill a Minute
SIED • 895QX5866 • $22

2437. Time of Peace
ANDR • 795QX5813 • $14

2438. Timon and Pumbaa –
The Lion King
895QX5366 • $20

2439. Tobin Fraley Carousel 3
FRAL • 2800QX5223 • $50

2440. Tobin Fraley Holiday
Carousel 1
UNRU • 3200QLX7496 • $66
MAGIC

2441. Tou Can Love
RGRS • 895QX5646 • $17

2442. Twelve Days of Christmas
11: Eleven Pipers Piping
695QX3183 • $15

2443. U.S. Christmas Stamps 2
1095QX5206 • $26

2444. Very Merry Minutes
VOTR • 2400QLX7443 • $72
MAGIC

2445. White Christmas
DLEE • 2800QLX7463 • $65
MAGIC

2446. Winnie the Pooh and Tigger
1295QX5746 • $42

2447. Winnie the Pooh Parade
3200QLX7493 • $76
MAGIC

2448. Wizard of Oz™:
Dorothy and Toto™
LYLE • 1095QX5433 • $95

2449. Wizard of Oz™:
The Cowardly Lion™
ANDR • 995QX5446 • $72

2450. Wizard of Oz™:
The Scarecrow™
UNRU • 995QX5436 • $71

2451. Wizard of Oz™:
The Tin Man™
UNRU • 995QX5443 • $71

2452. Yosemite Sam™
PALM • 895QX5346 • $26

2453. Yuletide Central 1:
Locomotive
SICK • 1895QX5316 • $35

1995

2454. Acorn 500
SIED • 1095QX5929 • $18

2455. Across the Miles
FRAN • 895QX5847 • $12

2456. Air Express
SEAL • 795QX5977 • $12

2457. All Is Bright: Angel of Light
ANDR • 1195QK1159 • $16

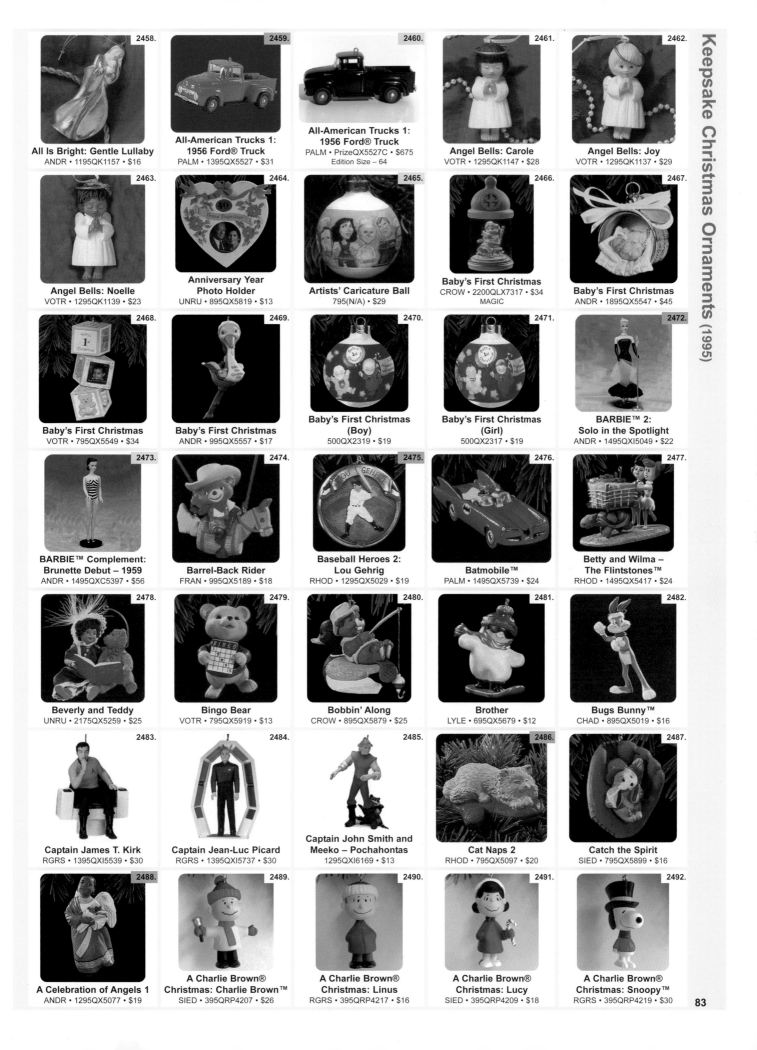

2458.
All Is Bright: Gentle Lullaby
ANDR • 1195QK1157 • $16

2459.
**All-American Trucks 1:
1956 Ford® Truck**
PALM • 1395QX5527 • $31

2460.
**All-American Trucks 1:
1956 Ford® Truck**
PALM • PrizeQX5527C • $675
Edition Size – 64

2461.
Angel Bells: Carole
VOTR • 1295QK1147 • $28

2462.
Angel Bells: Joy
VOTR • 1295QK1137 • $29

2463.
Angel Bells: Noelle
VOTR • 1295QK1139 • $23

2464.
**Anniversary Year
Photo Holder**
UNRU • 895QX5819 • $13

2465.
Artists' Caricature Ball
795(N/A) • $29

2466.
Baby's First Christmas
CROW • 2200QLX7317 • $34
MAGIC

2467.
Baby's First Christmas
ANDR • 1895QX5547 • $45

2468.
Baby's First Christmas
VOTR • 795QX5549 • $34

2469.
Baby's First Christmas
ANDR • 995QX5557 • $17

2470.
**Baby's First Christmas
(Boy)**
500QX2319 • $19

2471.
**Baby's First Christmas
(Girl)**
500QX2317 • $19

2472.
**BARBIE™ 2:
Solo in the Spotlight**
ANDR • 1495QXI5049 • $22

2473.
**BARBIE™ Complement:
Brunette Debut – 1959**
ANDR • 1495QXC5397 • $56

2474.
Barrel-Back Rider
FRAN • 995QX5189 • $18

2475.
**Baseball Heroes 2:
Lou Gehrig**
RHOD • 1295QX5029 • $19

2476.
Batmobile™
PALM • 1495QX5739 • $24

2477.
**Betty and Wilma –
The Flintstones™**
RHOD • 1495QX5417 • $24

2478.
Beverly and Teddy
UNRU • 2175QX5259 • $25

2479.
Bingo Bear
VOTR • 795QX5919 • $13

2480.
Bobbin' Along
CROW • 895QX5879 • $25

2481.
Brother
LYLE • 695QX5679 • $12

2482.
Bugs Bunny™
CHAD • 895QX5019 • $16

2483.
Captain James T. Kirk
RGRS • 1395QXI5539 • $30

2484.
Captain Jean-Luc Picard
RGRS • 1395QXI5737 • $30

2485.
**Captain John Smith and
Meeko – Pochahontas**
1295QXI6169 • $13

2486.
Cat Naps 2
RHOD • 795QX5097 • $20

2487.
Catch the Spirit
SIED • 795QX5899 • $16

2488.
A Celebration of Angels 1
ANDR • 1295QX5077 • $19

2489.
**A Charlie Brown®
Christmas: Charlie Brown™**
SIED • 395QRP4207 • $26

2490.
**A Charlie Brown®
Christmas: Linus**
RGRS • 395QRP4217 • $16

2491.
**A Charlie Brown®
Christmas: Lucy**
SIED • 395QRP4209 • $18

2492.
**A Charlie Brown®
Christmas: Snoopy™**
RGRS • 395QRP4219 • $30

2493.

**A Charlie Brown®
Christmas: Snow Scene**
RGRS • 395QRP4227 • $14

2494.

**Child's Age:
Baby's First Christmas**
CROW • 795QX5559 • $29

2495.

**Child's Age:
Baby's Second Christmas**
CROW • 795QX5567 • $20

2496.

**Child's Age:
Child's Third Christmas**
CROW • 795QX5627 • $20

2497.

**Child's Age:
Child's Fourth Christmas**
FRAN • 695QX5629 • $20

2498.
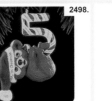
**Child's Age:
Child's Fifth Christmas**
RHOD • 695QX5637 • $24

2499.
**Chris Mouse 11:
Chris Mouse Tree**
RGRS • 1250QLX7307 • $25
MAGIC

2500.

Christmas Eve Bake-Off
VARI • 6000QXC4049 • $84

2501.

Christmas Fever
AUBE • 795QX5967 • $13

2502.

Christmas Morning
FRAN • 1095QX5997 • $15

2503.

Christmas Patrol
ANDR • 795QX5959 • $16

2504.

**Christmas Visitors 1:
St. Nicholas**
RGRS • 1495QX5087 • $22

2505.

**Classic American Cars 5:
1969 Chevrolet® Camaro**
PALM • 1295QX5239 • $23

2506.

**Classic American Cars
Complement: 1958 Ford®
Edsel™ Citation Convertible**
PALM • 1295QXC4167 • $70

2507.

**Coca-Cola® –
Refreshing Gift**
UNRU • 1495QX4067 • $26

2508.

Collecting Memories
SIED • GiftQXC4117 • $16

2509.

Coming to See Santa
PALM • 3200QLX7369 • $65
MAGIC

2510.

Cookie Time
VOTR • GiftQP6073C • $30

2511.

Cows of Bali
ANDR • 895QX5999 • $14

2512.

**Crayola® Crayon 7:
Bright 'n' Sunny Tepee**
ANDR • 1095QX5247 • $22

2513.

**Crayola® Crayon
Complement: Colorful World**
CROW • 1095QX5519 • $22

2514.

Dad
SIED • 795QX5649 • $16

2515.

Dad-to-Be
RHOD • 795QX5667 • $10

2516.

Daughter
PALM • 695QX5677 • $20

2517.

Delivering Kisses
SICK • 1095QX4107 • $30

2518.

Dream On
FRAN • 1095QX6007 • $18

2519.

Dudley the Dragon
PIKE • 1095QX6209 • $16

2520.

Fabulous Decade 6
SEAL • 795QX5147 • $18

2521.

Faithful Fan
SIED • 895QX5897 • $16

2522.

Feliz Navidad
RHOD • 795QX5869 • $20

2523.

Fishing for Fun
SEAL • GiftQXC5207 • $20

2524.

**Folk Art Americana:
Fetching the Firewood**
SICK • 1595QK1057 • $29

2525.
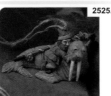
**Folk Art Americana:
Fishing Party**
SICK • 1595QK1039 • $29

2526.

**Folk Art Americana:
Guiding Santa**
SICK • 1895QK1037 • $37

2527.

**Folk Art Americana:
Home from the Woods**
SICK • 1595QXC1059 • $40

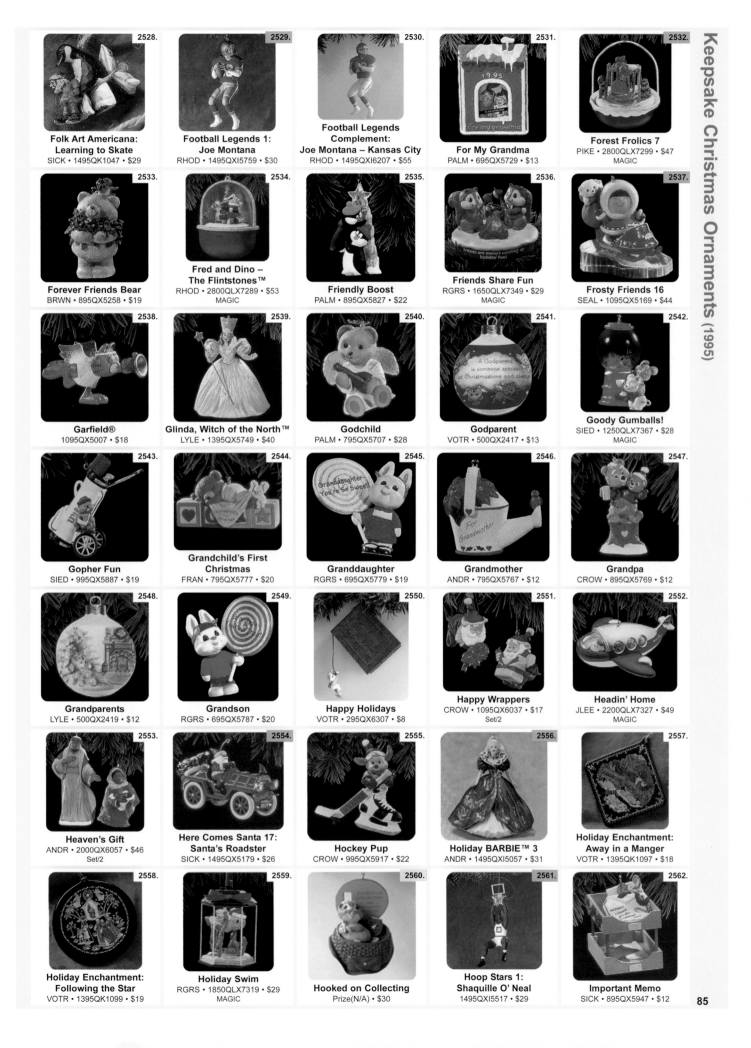

2528.
Folk Art Americana:
Learning to Skate
SICK • 1495QK1047 • $29

2529.
Football Legends 1:
Joe Montana
RHOD • 1495QXI5759 • $30

2530.
Football Legends
Complement:
Joe Montana – Kansas City
RHOD • 1495QXI6207 • $55

2531.
For My Grandma
PALM • 695QX5729 • $13

2532.
Forest Frolics 7
PIKE • 2800QLX7299 • $47
MAGIC

2533.
Forever Friends Bear
BRWN • 895QX5258 • $19

2534.
Fred and Dino –
The Flintstones™
RHOD • 2800QLX7289 • $53
MAGIC

2535.
Friendly Boost
PALM • 895QX5827 • $22

2536.
Friends Share Fun
RGRS • 1650QLX7349 • $29
MAGIC

2537.
Frosty Friends 16
SEAL • 1095QX5169 • $44

2538.
Garfield®
1095QX5007 • $18

2539.
Glinda, Witch of the North™
LYLE • 1395QX5749 • $40

2540.
Godchild
PALM • 795QX5707 • $28

2541.
Godparent
VOTR • 500QX2417 • $13

2542.
Goody Gumballs!
SIED • 1250QLX7367 • $28
MAGIC

2543.
Gopher Fun
SIED • 995QX5887 • $19

2544.
Grandchild's First
Christmas
FRAN • 795QX5777 • $20

2545.
Granddaughter
RGRS • 695QX5779 • $19

2546.
Grandmother
ANDR • 795QX5767 • $12

2547.
Grandpa
CROW • 895QX5769 • $12

2548.
Grandparents
LYLE • 500QX2419 • $12

2549.
Grandson
RGRS • 695QX5787 • $20

2550.
Happy Holidays
VOTR • 295QX6307 • $8

2551.
Happy Wrappers
CROW • 1095QX6037 • $17
Set/2

2552.
Headin' Home
JLEE • 2200QLX7327 • $49
MAGIC

2553.
Heaven's Gift
ANDR • 2000QX6057 • $46
Set/2

2554.
Here Comes Santa 17:
Santa's Roadster
SICK • 1495QX5179 • $26

2555.
Hockey Pup
CROW • 995QX5917 • $22

2556.
Holiday BARBIE™ 3
ANDR • 1495QXI5057 • $31

2557.
Holiday Enchantment:
Away in a Manger
VOTR • 1395QK1097 • $18

2558.
Holiday Enchantment:
Following the Star
VOTR • 1395QK1099 • $19

2559.
Holiday Swim
RGRS • 1850QLX7319 • $29
MAGIC

2560.
Hooked on Collecting
Prize(N/A) • $30

2561.
Hoop Stars 1:
Shaquille O' Neal
1495QXI5517 • $29

2562.
Important Memo
SICK • 895QX5947 • $12

In a Heartbeat
ANDR • 895QX5817 • $16

In Time With Christmas
CROW • 1295QX6049 • $19

Invitation to Tea:
Cozy Cottage Teapot
ANDR • 1595QK1127 • $22

Invitation to Tea:
European Castle Teapot
ANDR • 1595QK1129 • $29

Invitation to Tea:
Victorian Home Teapot
ANDR • 1595QK1119 • $22

Joy to the World
ANDR • 895QX5867 • $14

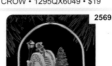
Jumping for Joy
FRAN • 2800QLX7347 • $53
MAGIC

Kiddie Car Classics 2:
1955 Murray® Fire Truck
PALM • 1395QX5027 • $25

Kiddie Car Classics 2:
1955 Murray® Fire Truck
PALM • PrizeQX5027C • $1000
Edition Size – 64

Lego® Fireplace with Santa
CROW • 1095QX4769 • $19

Lou Rankin Bear
SIED • 995QX4069 • $18

The Magic School Bus
RHOD • 1095QX5849 • $22

Mailbox Delivery
CROW • PrizeQP6015C • $45
8 different cities.

Mary Engelbreit
500QX2409 • $22

Mary's Angels 8: Camellia
CHAD/HAMI • 695QX5149 • $35

Merry Olde Santa 6
ANDR • 1495QX5139 • $23

Merry RV
PALM • 1295QX6027 • $18

Mom
SIED • 795QX5647 • $15

Mom and Dad
RGRS • 995QX5657 • $28

Mom-to-Be
RHOD • 795QX5659 • $14

Mother Goose 3:
Jack and Jill
SEAL/VOTR • 1395QX5099 • $22

Mr. and Mrs. Claus 10:
Christmas Eve Kiss
UNRU • 1495QX5157 • $23

Muletide Greetings
CHAD • 795QX6009 • $20

My First Hot Wheels™
CROW • 2800QLX7279 • $48
MAGIC

Nature's Sketchbook:
Backyard Orchard
BAST/LYLE • 1895QK1069 • $30

Nature's Sketchbook:
Christmas Cardinal
BAST/LYLE • 1895QK1077 • $38

Nature's Sketchbook:
Raising a Family
BAST/LYLE • 1895QK1067 • $26

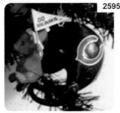
Nature's Sketchbook:
Violets and Butterflies
BAST/LYLE • 1695QK1079 • $37

New Home
ANDR • 895QX5839 • $14

NFL®: Carolina Panthers™
595PNA2035 • $16
Re-issued in 1996.

NFL®: Carolina Panthers™
SIED • 995QSR6227 • $30

NFL®: Chicago Bears™
595BRS2035 • $16
Re-issued in 1996.

NFL®: Chicago Bears™
SIED • 995QSR6237 • $30

NFL®: Dallas Cowboys™
595COW2035 • $16
Re-issued in 1996.

NFL®: Dallas Cowboys™
SIED • 995QSR6217 • $30

2598.
NFL®: Kansas City Chiefs™
595CHF2035 • $16
Re-issued in 1996.

2599.
NFL®: Kansas City Chiefs™
SIED • 995QSR6257 • $30

2600.
**NFL®:
Los Angeles Raiders™**
595RDR2035 • $16
Re-issued in 1996.

2601.
**NFL®:
Los Angeles Raiders™**
SIED • 995QSR6249 • $30

2602.
NFL®: Minnesota Vikings™
595VIK2035 • $16
Re-issued in 1996.

2603.
NFL®: Minnesota Vikings™
SIED • 995QSR6267 • $30

2604.
**NFL®:
New England Patriots™**
595NEP2035 • $16
Re-issued in 1996.

2605.
**NFL®:
New England Patriots™**
SIED • 995QSR6228 • $30

2606.
NFL®: Philadelphia Eagles™
595EAG2035 • $16
Re-issued in 1996.

2607.
NFL®: Philadelphia Eagles™
SIED • 995QSR6259 • $30

2608.
**NFL®:
San Francisco 49ers™**
595FOR2035 • $16
Re-issued in 1996.

2609.
**NFL®:
San Francisco 49ers™**
SIED • 995QSR6239 • $30

2610.
**NFL®:
Washington Redskins™**
595RSK2035 • $16
Re-issued in 1996.

2611.
**NFL®:
Washington Redskins™**
SIED • 995QSR6247 • $30

2612.
North Pole 911
SEAL • 1095QX5957 • $19

2613.
**Nostalgic Houses &
Shops 12: Town Church**
PALM • 1495QX5159 • $29

2614.
**Nostalgic Houses &
Shops Accessories**
JLEE • 895QX5089 • $20
Set/3

2615.
Number One Teacher
SEAL • 795QX5949 • $12

2616.
The Olympic Spirit
795QX3169 • $10

2617.
On the Billboard
GiftQP6022C2 • $50
8 cities – Volunteer Gift.

2618.
On the Ice
CROW • 795QX6047 • $16

2619.
Our Christmas Together
LYLE • 995QX5809 • $24

2620.
Our Family
CHAD • 795QX5709 • $14

2621.
**Our First Christmas
Together**
LYLE • 695QX3177 • $24

2622.
**Our First Christmas
Together**
LYLE • 1695QX5797 • $29

2623.
**Our First Christmas
Together**
SIED • 895QX5799 • $24

2624.
**Our First Christmas
Together**
SEAL • 895QX5807 • $18

2625.
Our Little Blessings
CROW • 1295QX5209 • $20

2626.
Packed with Memories
SEAL • 795QX5639 • $17

2627.
PEANUTS® 5
RHOD • 2450QLX7277 • $59
MAGIC

2628.
PEANUTS® Gang 3
SIED • 995QX5059 • $24

2629.
**Percy, Flit and Meeko –
Pochahontas**
995QXI6179 • $19

2630.
Perfect Balance
SIED • 795QX5927 • $12

2631.
Personalized – Baby Bear
ANDR • 1295QP6157 • $30

2632.
The Personalized – Champ
VOTR • 1295QP6127 • $18

87

2633.
Personalized –
Computer Cat 'n' Mouse
SEAL • 1295QP6046 • $20
Re-issued from 1994.

2634.
Personalized – Cookie Time
VOTR • 1295QP6073 • $21
Re-issued from 1994.

2635.
Personalized –
Etch-A-Sketch®
CROW • 1295QP6006 • $60
Re-issued from 1994.

2636.
Personalized –
From the Heart
RHOD • 1495QP6036 • $20
Re-issued from 1994.

2637.
Personalized – Key Note
SEAL • 1295QP6149 • $30

2638.
Personalized –
Mailbox Delivery
CROW • 1495QP6015 • $30
Re-issued from 1993 & 1994.

2639.
Personalized – Novel Idea
VOTR • 1295QP6066 • $20
Re-issued from 1994.

2640.
Personalized –
On the Billboard
CROW • 1295QP6022 • $30
Re-issued from 1993 & 1994.

2641.
Personalized – Playing Ball
FRAN • 1295QP6032 • $25
Re-issued from 1993 & 1994.

2642.
Personalized –
Reindeer Rooters
CROW • 1295QP6056 • $34
Re-issued from 1994.

2643.
Pez® Santa
FRAN • 795QX5267 • $18

2644.
Pocahontas
1295QXI6177 • $17

2645.
Pocahontas and Capt
John Smith
1495QXI6197 • $20

2646.
Polar Coaster
CROW • 895QX6117 • $18

2647.
Popeye
CHAD • 1095QX5257 • $18

2648.
Puppy Love 5
RGRS • 795QX5137 • $45

2649.
Rejoice!
LYLE • 1095QX5987 • $17

2650.
Rocking Horse 15
SICK • 1095QX5167 • $23

2651.
Rocking Horse Complement:
Pewter Rocking Horse
SICK • 2000QX6167 • $41

2652.
Roller Whiz
SEAL • 795QX5937 • $13

2653.
Romulan Warbird™
NORT • 2400QXI7267 • $39
MAGIC

2654.
Santa In Paris
SICK • 895QX5877 • $29

2655.
Santa's Diner
VOTR • 2450QLX7337 • $34
MAGIC

2656.
Santa's Serenade
CROW • 895QX6017 • $13

2657.
Santa's Visitors –
Norman Rockwell Art
LYLE • 500QX2407 • $29

2658.
Simba, Pumbaa and
Timon – The Lion King
1295QX6159 • $20

2659.
Sister
LYLE • 695QX5687 • $20

2660.
Sister to Sister
VOTR • 895QX5689 • $16

2661.
Ski Hound
RHOD • 895QX5909 • $19

2662.
Son
PALM • 695QX5669 • $20

2663.
Space Shuttle
CROW • 2450QLX7396 • $55
MAGIC

2664.
Special Cat
CHAD • 795QX5717 • $19

2665.
Special Dog
CHAD • 795QX5719 • $18

2666.
Superman™
CHAD • 2800QLX7309 • $38
MAGIC

2667.
Surfin' Santa
CROW • 995QX6019 • $24

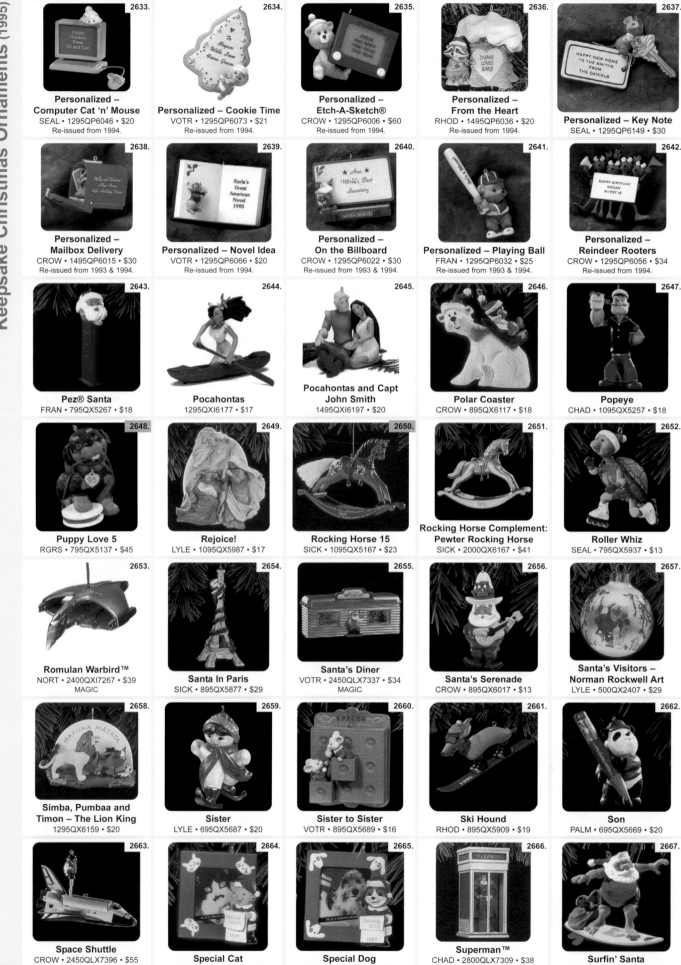

2668.
Sylvester™ and Tweety™
CHAD • 1395QX5017 • $23
Set/2

2669.
**Symbols of Christmas:
Jolly Santa**
ANDR • 1595QK1087 • $19

2670.
**Symbols of Christmas:
Sweet Song**
ANDR • 1595QK1089 • $16

2671.
Takin' a Hike
FRAN • 795QX6029 • $17

2672.
Tender Touches: Wish List
SEAL • 1500QX5859 • $19

2673.
Tennis, Anyone?
AUBE • 795QX5907 • $13

2674.
**Thomas the Tank®
Engine – No. 1**
RHOD • 995QX5857 • $45

2675.
Three Wishes
ANDR • 795QX5979 • $18

2676.
Tobin Fraley Carousel 4
FRAL • 2800QX5069 • $43

2677.
**Tobin Fraley Holiday
Carousel 2**
FRAL • 3200QLX7269 • $60
MAGIC

2678.
Too Much Hunny
2450QLX7297 • $62
MAGIC

2679.
**Turn of the Century
Parade 1: The Fireman**
CROW • 1695QK1027 • $32

2680.
**Twelve Days of Christmas
12: Twelve Drummers
Drumming**
695QX3009 • $14

2681.
Two for Tea
JLEE • 995QX5829 • $22

2682.
U.S. Christmas Stamps 3
1095QX5067 • $19

2683.
Vera the Mouse
895QX5537 • $13

2684.
Victorian Toy Box
LYLE • 4200QLX7357 • $56
MAGIC

2685.
Waiting up for Santa
PALM • 895QX6106 • $14

2686.
Water Sports
SIED • 1495QX6039 • $41
Set/2

2687.
Wee Little Christmas
CROW • 2200QLX7329 • $40
MAGIC

2688.
Wheel of Fortune®
SICK • 1295QX6187 • $19

2689.
Winnie the Pooh and Tigger
1295QX5009 • $30

2690.
The Winning Play
SIED • 795QX5889 • $16

2691.
Yuletide Central 2: Coal Car
SICK • 1895QX5079 • $19

1996

2692.
101 Dalmatians
1295QXI6544 • $16

2693.
Airmail for Santa
RGRS • GiftQXC4194 • $26

2694.
**All God's Children 1:
Christy**
1295QX5564 • $23

2695.
**All-American Trucks 2:
1955 Chevrolet® Cameo**
PALM • 1395QX5241 • $24

2696.
**All-American Trucks 2:
1955 Chevrolet® Cameo**
PALM • PrizeQX5241C • $782
Edition Size – 256

2697.
Antlers Aweigh!
CHAD • 995QX5901 • $26

2698.
Apple for Teacher
AUBE • 795QX6121 • $10

2699.
**At the Ballpark 1:
Nolan Ryan**
RHOD • 1495QXI5711 • $29

2700.
Baby's First Christmas
FRAN • 2200QLX7404 • $42
MAGIC

2701.
Baby's First Christmas
VOTR • 1895QX5744 • $25

2702.
Baby's First Christmas
1095QX5751 • $26

2703.
Baby's First Christmas
ANDR • 995QX5754 • $32

2704.
Baby's First Christmas
SEAL • 795QX5761 • $20

2705.
BARBIE™ 3: Enchanting
Evening BARBIE™
ANDR • 1495QXI6541 • $22

2706.
Baseball Heroes 3:
Satchel Paige
RHOD • 1295QX5304 • $18

2707.
Bounce Pass
SIED • 795QX6031 • $13

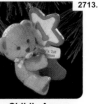
2708.
Bowl 'em Over
SIED • 795QX6014 • $14

2709.
Cat Naps 3
RHOD • 795QX5641 • $20

2710.
A Celebration of Angels 2
ANDR • 1295QX5634 • $16

2711.
Chicken Coop Chorus
CROW • 2450QLX7491 • $42
MAGIC

2712.
Child Care Giver
SIED • 895QX6071 • $10

2713.
Child's Age:
Baby's First Christmas
CROW • 795QX5764 • $38

2714.
Child's Age:
Baby's Second Christmas
CROW • 795QX5771 • $32

2715.
Child's Age:
Child's Third Christmas
CROW • 795QX5774 • $24

2716.
Child's Age:
Child's Fourth Christmas
CROW • 795QX5781 • $24

2717.
Child's Age:
Child's Fifth Christmas
RHOD • 695QX5784 • $24

2718.
Chris Mouse 12:
Chris Mouse Inn
SIED • 1450QLX7371 • $40
MAGIC

2719.
Christmas Joy
UNRU • 1495QX6241 • $23

2720.
Christmas Snowman
BAST/UNRU • 995QX6214 • $28

2721.
Christmas Visitors 2:
Christkindl
VOTR • 1495QX5631 • $15

2722.
Classic American Cars 6:
1959 Cadillac® De Ville
PALM • 1295QX5384 • $23

2723.
Close-Knit Friends
BRIC • 995QX5874 • $23

2724.
Coca-Cola® –
Welcome Guest
UNRU • 1495QX5394 • $20

2725.
Come All Ye Faithful
CROW • 1295QX6244 • $20

2726.
Commander William T. Riker
RGRS • 1495QXI5551 • $28

2727.
Cookie Jar Friends: Carmen
RGRS • 1595QK1164 • $22

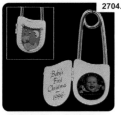
2728.
Cookie Jar Friends: Clyde
AUBE • 1595QK1161 • $20

2729.
Crayola® Crayon 8:
Bright Flying Colors
CROW • 1095QX5391 • $32

2730.
Dad
SIED • 795QX5831 • $20

2731.
Daughter
PALM • 895QX6077 • $26

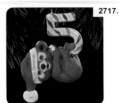
2732.
Dolls of the World 1:
Native American BARBIE™
ANDR • 1495QX5561 • $20

2733.
Emerald City™
CROW • 3200QLX7454 • $120
MAGIC

2734.
Esmeralda and Djali –
Hunchback of Notre Dame
1495QXI6351 • $15

2735.
Evergreen Santa
LYLE • 2200QX5714 • $25

2736.
Fabulous Decade 7
SEAL • 795QX5661 • $28

90

2737.
Fan-tastic Season
CHAD • 995QX5924 • $14

2738.
Father Time
CHAD • 2450QLX7391 • $38
MAGIC

2739.
Feliz Navidad
SICK • 995QX6304 • $17

2740.
**Foghorn Leghorn™ &
Henery Hawk™**
CHAD • 1395QX5444 • $28
Set/2

2741.
**Folk Art Americana:
Caroling Angel**
SICK • 1695QK1134 • $26

2742.
**Folk Art Americana:
Mrs. Claus**
SICK • 1895QK1204 • $29

2743.
**Folk Art Americana:
Santa's Gifts**
SICK • 1895QK1124 • $35

2744.
**Football Legends 2:
Troy Aikman**
RHOD • 1495QXI5021 • $20

2745.
Frosty Friends 17
SEAL • 1095QX5681 • $44

2746.
**Get Hooked on
Collecting Starter Set**
LYLE • 799XPR837 • $12

2747.
Glad Tidings
LYLE • 1495QX6231 • $24

2748.
Goal Line Glory
SEAL • 1295QX6001 • $20
Set/2

2749.
Godchild
RGRS • 895QX5841 • $14

2750.
Granddaughter
RGRS • 795QX5697 • $13

2751.
Grandma
VOTR • 895QX5844 • $25

2752.
Grandpa
VOTR • 895QX5851 • $12

2753.
Grandson
RGRS • 795QX5699 • $12

2754.
**Growth of a Leader –
Boy Scouts®**
995QX5541 • $23

2755.
**Happy Holidays®
BARBIE™ 1**
ANDR • 1495QXC4181 • $56

2756.
Happy Holi-doze
RHOD • 995QX5904 • $12

2757.
Hearts Full of Love
RHOD • 995QX5814 • $28

2758.
**Here Comes Santa 18:
Santa's 4 X 4**
SEAL • 1495QX5684 • $29

2759.
High Style
CHAD • 895QX6064 • $13

2760.
Hillside Express
AUBE • 1295QX6134 • $26

2761.
Holiday BARBIE™ 4
ANDR • 1495QXI5371 • $25

2762.
Holiday Haul
SICK • 1495QX6201 • $28

2763.
Hoop Stars 2: Larry Bird
RHOD • 1495QXI5014 • $24

2764.
Hurrying Downstairs
FRAN • 895QX6074 • $28

2765.
I Dig Golf
RHOD • 1095QX5891 • $13

2766.
Invitation to the Games
MCGE • 1495QXE5511 • $15
Set/2

2767.
It's a Wonderful Life™
CROW • 1495QXI6531 • $32

2768.
Izzy™ – The Mascot
PALM • 995QXE5724 • $10

2769.
Jackpot Jingle
SIED • 995QX5911 • $20

2770.
The Jetsons™
CROW • 2800QLX7411 • $71
MAGIC

2771.
Jolly Wolly Ark
CROW • 1295QX6221 • $22

91

2772.

Journeys Into Space 1: Freedom 7
SEAL • 2400QLX7524 • $69
MAGIC

2773.

Jukebox Party
PALM • 2450QLX7339 • $49
MAGIC

2774.

Kiddie Car Classics 3: Murray® Spitfire
PALM • 1395QX5364 • $23

2775.

Kiddie Car Classics 3: Murray® Spitfire
PALM • PrizeQX5364C • $775
Edition Size – 256

2776.

Kiddie Car Classics Complement: 1937 Steelcraft Auburn by Murray®
PALM • 1595QXC4174 • $58

2777.

Kindly Shepherd
ANDR • 1295QX6274 • $40

2778.

Language of Flowers 1: Pansy
TAGU • 1595QK1171 • $50

2779.

Laverne, Victor and Hugo – Hunchback of Notre Dame
1295QXI6354 • $13

2780.

Let Us Adore Him
LYLE • 1650QLX7381 • $32
MAGIC

2781.

Lighting the Flame
UNRU • 2800QXE7444 • $28
MAGIC

2782.

Lighting the Way
CHAD • 1295QX6124 • $20

2783.

LIONEL® Trains 1: Hudson Steam Locomotive
1895QX5531 • $55

2784.

A Little Song and Dance
CROW • 995QX6211 • $17

2785.

Little Spooners
UNRU • 1295QX5504 • $18

2786.

Madame Alexander® 1: Cinderella
FRAN • 1495QX6311 • $29

2787.

Madonna and Child
RIBE/SICK • 1295QX6324 • $13

2788.

Magi Bells: Balthasar – Frankincense
VOTR • 1395QK1174 • $18

2789.

Magi Bells: Caspar – Myrrh
VOTR • 1395QK1184 • $18

2790.

Magi Bells: Melchior – Gold
VOTR • 1395QK1181 • $16

2791.

Making His Rounds
FRAN • 1495QX6271 • $33

2792.

Marvin the Martian™
CHAD • 1095QX5451 • $24

2793.
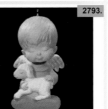
Mary's Angels 9: Violet
CHAD/HAMI • 695QX5664 • $33

2794.

Matchless Memories
CROW • 995QX6061 • $17

2795.

Maxine
CROW/WAGN • 995QX6224 • $28

2796.

Merry Carpoolers
CROW • 1495QX5884 • $25

2797.

Merry Olde Santa 7
CROW • 1495QX5654 • $29

2798.
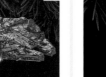
Millennium Falcon™
NORT • 2400QLX7474 • $56
MAGIC

2799.

Mom
LYLE • 795QX5824 • $19

2800.

Mom and Dad
RHOD • 995QX5821 • $26

2801.

Mom-to-Be
UNRU • 795QX5791 • $16

2802.

Mother Goose 4: Mary Had a Little Lamb
SEAL/VOTR • 1395QX5644 • $20

2803.

Mr. Spock
RGRS • 1495QXI5544 • $28

2804.
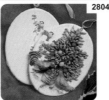
Nature's Sketchbook: Birds' Christmas Tree
BAST/UNRU • 1895QK1114 • $28

2805.

Nature's Sketchbook: Christmas Bunny
BAST/FRAN • 1895QK1104 • $42

2806.

Nature's Sketchbook: Holly Basket
BAST/LYLE • 1895QK1094 • $23

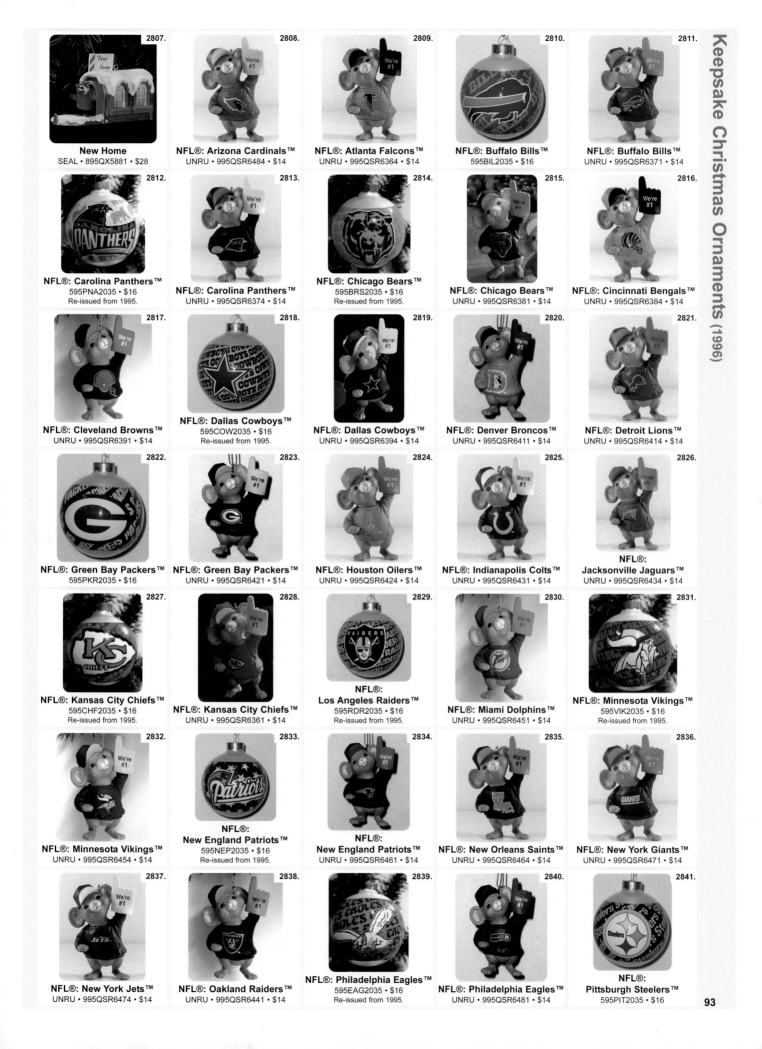

2807.
New Home
SEAL • 895QX5881 • $28

2808.
NFL®: Arizona Cardinals™
UNRU • 995QSR6484 • $14

2809.
NFL®: Atlanta Falcons™
UNRU • 995QSR6364 • $14

2810.
NFL®: Buffalo Bills™
595BIL2035 • $16

2811.
NFL®: Buffalo Bills™
UNRU • 995QSR6371 • $14

2812.
NFL®: Carolina Panthers™
595PNA2035 • $16
Re-issued from 1995.

2813.
NFL®: Carolina Panthers™
UNRU • 995QSR6374 • $14

2814.
NFL®: Chicago Bears™
595BRS2035 • $16
Re-issued from 1995.

2815.
NFL®: Chicago Bears™
UNRU • 995QSR6381 • $14

2816.
NFL®: Cincinnati Bengals™
UNRU • 995QSR6384 • $14

2817.
NFL®: Cleveland Browns™
UNRU • 995QSR6391 • $14

2818.
NFL®: Dallas Cowboys™
595COW2035 • $16
Re-issued from 1995.

2819.
NFL®: Dallas Cowboys™
UNRU • 995QSR6394 • $14

2820.
NFL®: Denver Broncos™
UNRU • 995QSR6411 • $14

2821.
NFL®: Detroit Lions™
UNRU • 995QSR6414 • $14

2822.
NFL®: Green Bay Packers™
595PKR2035 • $16

2823.
NFL®: Green Bay Packers™
UNRU • 995QSR6421 • $14

2824.
NFL®: Houston Oilers™
UNRU • 995QSR6424 • $14

2825.
NFL®: Indianapolis Colts™
UNRU • 995QSR6431 • $14

2826.
NFL®:
Jacksonville Jaguars™
UNRU • 995QSR6434 • $14

2827.
NFL®: Kansas City Chiefs™
595CHF2035 • $16
Re-issued from 1995.

2828.
NFL®: Kansas City Chiefs™
UNRU • 995QSR6361 • $14

2829.
NFL®:
Los Angeles Raiders™
595RDR2035 • $16
Re-issued from 1995.

2830.
NFL®: Miami Dolphins™
UNRU • 995QSR6451 • $14

2831.
NFL®: Minnesota Vikings™
595VIK2035 • $16
Re-issued from 1995.

2832.
NFL®: Minnesota Vikings™
UNRU • 995QSR6454 • $14

2833.
NFL®:
New England Patriots™
595NEP2035 • $16
Re-issued from 1995.

2834.
NFL®:
New England Patriots™
UNRU • 995QSR6461 • $14

2835.
NFL®: New Orleans Saints™
UNRU • 995QSR6464 • $14

2836.
NFL®: New York Giants™
UNRU • 995QSR6471 • $14

2837.
NFL®: New York Jets™
UNRU • 995QSR6474 • $14

2838.
NFL®: Oakland Raiders™
UNRU • 995QSR6441 • $14

2839.
NFL®: Philadelphia Eagles™
595EAG2035 • $16
Re-issued from 1995.

2840.
NFL®: Philadelphia Eagles™
UNRU • 995QSR6481 • $14

2841.
NFL®:
Pittsburgh Steelers™
595PIT2035 • $16

93

2842.

**NFL®:
Pittsburgh Steelers™**
UNRU • 995QSR6491 • $14

2843.

NFL®: San Diego Chargers™
UNRU • 995QSR6494 • $14

2844.

**NFL®:
San Francisco 49ers™**
595FOR2035 • $16
Re-issued from 1995.

2845.

**NFL®:
San Francisco 49ers™**
UNRU • 995QSR6501 • $14

2846.

NFL®: Seattle Seahawks™
UNRU • 995QSR6504 • $14

2847.

NFL®: St. Louis Rams™
595RAM2035 • $16

2848.

NFL®: St. Louis Rams™
UNRU • 995QSR6444 • $14

2849.

**NFL®:
Tampa Bay Buccaneers™**
UNRU • 995QSR6511 • $14

2850.

**NFL®:
Washington Redskins™**
595RSK2035 • $16
Re-issued from 1995.

2851.

**NFL®:
Washington Redskins™**
UNRU • 995QSR6514 • $14

2852.

North Pole Volunteers
SEAL • 4200QLX7471 • $91
MAGIC

2853.

**Nostalgic Houses & Shops
13: Victorian Painted Lady**
PALM • 1495QX5671 • $26

2854.

Olive Oyl and Swee' Pea
CHAD • 1095QX5481 • $19

2855.

Olympic Triumph
SEAL • 1095QXE5731 • $16

2856.

On My Way
TAGU • 795QX5861 • $14

2857.

Our Christmas Together
PALM • 1895QX5794 • $40

2858.

Our Christmas Together
CROW • 895QX5804 • $15

2859.

**Our First Christmas
Together**
VOTR • 695QX3051 • $28

2860.

**Our First Christmas
Together**
1095QX5801 • $24

2861.
**Our First Christmas
Together**
PALM • 995QX5811 • $28

2862.

Over the Rooftops
SEAL • 1450QLX7374 • $35
MAGIC

2863.

Parade of Nations
1095QXE5741 • $12

2864.

**PEANUTS® –
Schroeder and Lucy**
CHAD • 1850QLX7394 • $52
MAGIC

2865.

PEANUTS® Gang 4
FRAN • 995QX5381 • $17

2866.
Peppermint Surprise
PIKE • 795QX6234 • $21

2867.

**Percy the Small Engine –
No. 6**
RHOD • 995QX6314 • $24

2868.

Pez® Snowman
FRAN • 795QX6534 • $18

2869.

Pinball Wonder
CROW • 2800QLX7451 • $55
MAGIC

2870.

Polar Cycle
UNRU • 1295QX6034 • $23

2871.
Prayer for Peace
LYLE • 795QX6261 • $13

2872.

Precious Child
VOTR • 895QX6251 • $13

2873.
Puppy Love 6
RGRS • 795QX5651 • $40

2874.
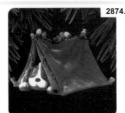
Pup-Tenting
PALM • 795QX6011 • $24

2875.
**Quasimodo – Hunchback
of Notre Dame**
995QXI6341 • $10

2876.
Regal Cardinal
FRAN • 995QX6204 • $40

2877.
Reindeer Rooters
CROW • GiftQP6056C • $395

2878.
Rocking Horse 16
SICK • 1095QX5674 • $20

2879.
Rudolph the Red-Nosed Reindeer®
SIED • GiftQXC7341 • $28
MAGIC

2880.
Sacred Masterworks: Madonna and Child
SICK • 1595QK1144 • $23

2881.
Sacred Masterworks: Praying Madonna
SICK • 1595QK1154 • $23

2882.
Santa
SIED • GiftQXC4164 • $14

2883.
Santa's Toy Shop
VARI • 6000QXC4201 • $130

2884.
Sew Sweet
AUBE • 895QX5921 • $26

2885.
Sharing a Soda
CROW • 2450QLX7424 • $34
MAGIC

2886.
Sister to Sister
LYLE • 995QX5834 • $16

2887.
Slippery Day
2450QLX7414 • $49
MAGIC

2888.
Son
PALM • 895QX6079 • $32

2889.
Special Dog
TAGU • 795QX5864 • $29

2890.
Spider-Man™
CHAD • 1295QX5757 • $42

2891.
Star of the Show
AUBE • 895QX6004 • $17

2892.
Star Trek™ – 30 Years
NORT/RHOD • 4500QXI7534 • $89
Set/2 • MAGIC

2893.
The Statue of Liberty
SEAL • 2450QLX7421 • $60
MAGIC

2894.
Tamika
BRIC/JOHN • 795QX6301 • $12

2895.
Tender Lovin' Care
SEAL • 795QX6114 • $18

2896.
Tender Touches: Welcome Sign
SEAL • 1500QX6331 • $20

2897.
Thank You, Santa
BRIC • 795QX5854 • $17

2898.
This Big!
SEAL • 995QX5914 • $25

2899.
Time for a Treat
SICK • 1195QX5464 • $23

2900.
Tobin Fraley Holiday Carousel 3
FRAN • 3200QLX7461 • $46
MAGIC

2901.
Tonka® Mighty Dump Truck
1395QX6321 • $42

2902.
Toy Shop Santa
UNRU • 1495(N/A) • $38

2903.
Treasured Memories
SICK • 1850QLX7384 • $32
MAGIC

2904.
A Tree for Snoopy®
SIED • 895QX5507 • $18

2905.
Turn of the Century Parade 2: Uncle Sam
CROW • 1695QK1084 • $26

2906.
U.S.S. Voyager™
NORT • 2400QXI7544 • $48
MAGIC

2907.
Video Party
SIED • 2800QLX7431 • $40
MAGIC

2908.
Welcome Him
TAGU • 895QX6264 • $17

2909.
Winnie the Pooh and Piglet
1295QX5454 • $28

2910.
Witch of the West™
LYLE • 1395QX5554 • $32

2911.
The Wizard of Oz™
RGRS • 1295QXC4161 • $85

95

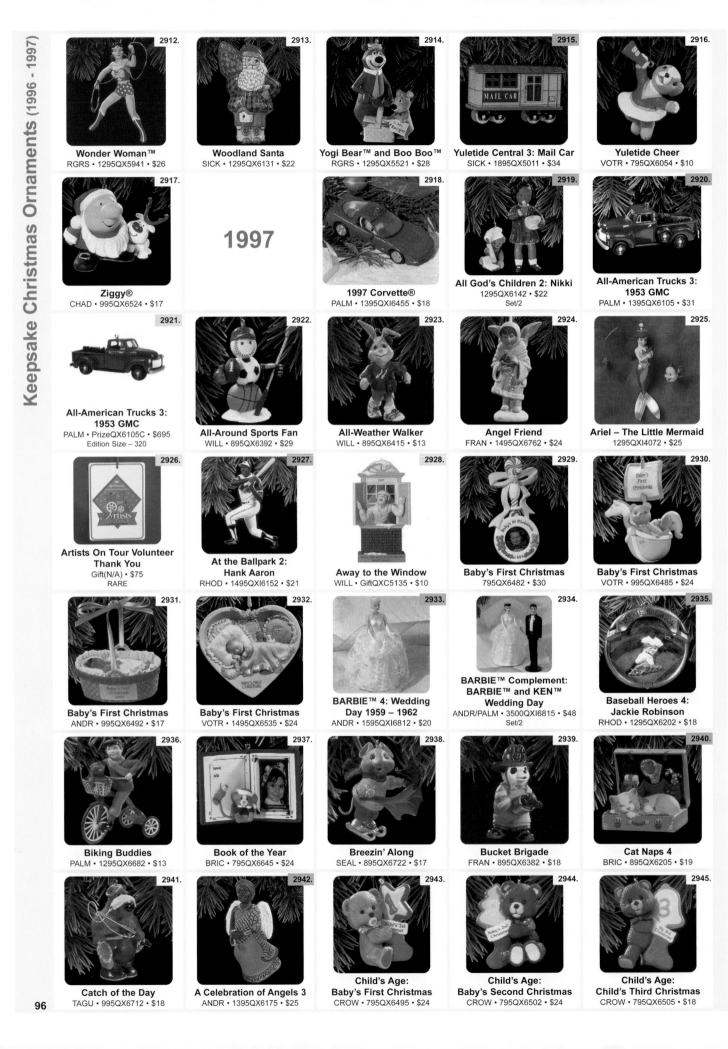

2912.
Wonder Woman™
RGRS • 1295QX5941 • $26

2913.
Woodland Santa
SICK • 1295QX6131 • $22

2914.
Yogi Bear™ and Boo Boo™
RGRS • 1295QX5521 • $28

2915.
Yuletide Central 3: Mail Car
SICK • 1895QX5011 • $34

2916.
Yuletide Cheer
VOTR • 795QX6054 • $10

2917.
Ziggy®
CHAD • 995QX6524 • $17

1997

2918.
1997 Corvette®
PALM • 1395QXI6455 • $18

2919.
All God's Children 2: Nikki
1295QX6142 • $22
Set/2

2920.
All-American Trucks 3:
1953 GMC
PALM • 1395QX6105 • $31

2921.
All-American Trucks 3:
1953 GMC
PALM • PrizeQX6105C • $695
Edition Size – 320

2922.
All-Around Sports Fan
WILL • 895QX6392 • $29

2923.
All-Weather Walker
WILL • 895QX6415 • $13

2924.
Angel Friend
FRAN • 1495QX6762 • $24

2925.
Ariel – The Little Mermaid
1295QXI4072 • $25

2926.
Artists On Tour Volunteer
Thank You
Gift(N/A) • $75
RARE

2927.
At the Ballpark 2:
Hank Aaron
RHOD • 1495QXI6152 • $21

2928.
Away to the Window
WILL • GiftQXC5135 • $10

2929.
Baby's First Christmas
795QX6482 • $30

2930.
Baby's First Christmas
VOTR • 995QX6485 • $24

2931.
Baby's First Christmas
ANDR • 995QX6492 • $17

2932.
Baby's First Christmas
VOTR • 1495QX6535 • $24

2933.
BARBIE™ 4: Wedding
Day 1959 – 1962
ANDR • 1595QXI6812 • $20

2934.
BARBIE™ Complement:
BARBIE™ and KEN™
Wedding Day
ANDR/PALM • 3500QXI6815 • $48
Set/2

2935.
Baseball Heroes 4:
Jackie Robinson
RHOD • 1295QX6202 • $18

2936.
Biking Buddies
PALM • 1295QX6682 • $13

2937.
Book of the Year
BRIC • 795QX6645 • $24

2938.
Breezin' Along
SEAL • 895QX6722 • $17

2939.
Bucket Brigade
FRAN • 895QX6382 • $18

2940.
Cat Naps 4
BRIC • 895QX6205 • $19

2941.
Catch of the Day
TAGU • 995QX6712 • $18

2942.
A Celebration of Angels 3
ANDR • 1395QX6175 • $25

2943.
Child's Age:
Baby's First Christmas
CROW • 795QX6495 • $24

2944.
Child's Age:
Baby's Second Christmas
CROW • 795QX6502 • $24

2945.
Child's Age:
Child's Third Christmas
CROW • 795QX6505 • $18

2946.
Child's Age:
Child's Fourth Christmas
CROW • 795QX6512 • $18

2947.
Child's Age:
Child's Fifth Christmas
CROW • 795QX6515 • $18

2948.
Chris Mouse 13:
Chris Mouse Luminara
SIED • 1495QLX7525 • $30
MAGIC

2949.
Christmas Checkup
SIED • 795QX6385 • $14

2950.
Christmas Visitors 3:
Kolyada
VOTR • 1495QX6172 • $19

2951.
Classic American Cars 7:
1969 Hurst Oldsmobile® 442
PALM • 1395QX6102 • $34

2952.
Classic Cross
VOTR • 1395QX6805 • $24

2953.
The Clauses on Vacation 1
SIED • 1495QX6112 • $22

2954.
Clever Camper
CHAD • 795QX6445 • $14

2955.
Coca-Cola® –
Taking a Break
UNRU • 1495QX6305 • $25

2956.
Commander Data
RGRS • 1495QXI6345 • $30

2957.
Crayola® Crayon 9:
Bright Rocking Colors
TAGU • 1295QX6235 • $23

2958.
Cycling Santa
WILL • 1495QX6425 • $25

2959.
Dad
SIED • 895QX6532 • $20

2960.
Darth Vader™
RHOD • 2400QXI7531 • $36
MAGIC

2961.
Daughter
BRIC • 795QX6612 • $22

2962.
Decorator Taz™
CHAD • 3000QLX7502 • $42
MAGIC

2963.
Dolls of the World 2:
Chinese BARBIE™
RGRS • 1495QX6162 • $20

2964.
Downhill Run
CROW • 995QX6705 • $20

2965.
Dr. Leonard H. McCoy
RGRS • 1495QXI6352 • $35

2966.
Elegance on Ice
LYLE • 995QX6432 • $16

2967.
Enchanted Memories 1:
Cinderella
1495QXD4045 • $28

2968.
Expressly for Teacher
TAGU • 795QX6375 • $14

2969.
Fabulous Decade 8
PIKE • 795QX6232 • $18

2970.
Feliz Navidad
SEAL • 895QX6665 • $40

2971.
First Class Thank You
RGRS • Gift(N/A) • $16

2972.
Football Legends 3:
Joe Namath
RHOD • 1495QXI6182 • $19

2973.
Friendship Blend
LARS/SEAL • 995QX6655 • $18

2974.
Frosty Friends 18
SEAL • 1095QX6255 • $23

2975.
Gift of Friendship –
Winnie the Pooh® Plate
1295QXE6835 • $19

2976.
Glowing Angel
VOTR • 1895QLX7435 • $28
MAGIC

2977.
Godchild
BRIC • 795QX6662 • $14

2978.
God's Gift of Love
LYLE • 1695QX6792 • $50

2979.
Goofy®'s Ski Adventure
1295QXD4042 • $17

2980.
Granddaughter
TAGU • 795QX6622 • $30

97

2981.

Grandma
PIKE • 895QX6625 • $14

2982.

Grandson
TAGU • 795QX6615 • $30

2983.

Gus & Jaq – Cinderella
1295QXD4052 • $28

2984.

**Hallmark Archives 1:
Donald's Surprising Gift**
1295QXD4025 • $19

2985.

Happy Christmas to All!
WILL • GiftQXC5132 • $10

2986.

**Happy Holidays®
BARBIE™ 2**
ANDR • 1595QXC5162 • $53

2987.

Heavenly Song
VOTR • 1295QX6795 • $22

2988.

Hercules®
1295QXI4005 • $24

2989.

**Here Comes Santa 19:
The Claus-Mobile**
TAGU • 1495QX6262 • $25

2990.

**Hockey Greats 1:
Wayne Gretzky**
UNRU • 1595QXI6275 • $25

2991.

Holiday BARBIE™ 5
ANDR • 1595QXI6212 • $20

2992.

Holiday Serenade
FRAN • 2400QLX7485 • $34
MAGIC

2993.

**Holiday Traditions
BARBIE™ Ornament**
RGRS • 1495QHB6002 • $20

2994.

**Hoop Stars 3:
Magic Johnson**
1495QXI6832 • $20

2995.
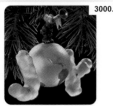
Howdy Doody™
LARS • 1295QX6272 • $18

2996.

The Incredible Hulk™
1295QX5471 • $30

2997.
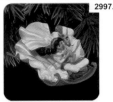
**Jasmine & Aladdin – Aladdin
and the King of Thieves**
1495QXD4062 • $22

2998.
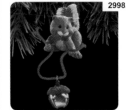
Jingle Bell Jester
PIKE • 995QX6695 • $19

2999.

**Journeys Into Space 2:
Friendship 7**
SEAL • 2400QLX7532 • $64
MAGIC

3000.

Joy to the World
TAGU • 1495QLX7512 • $24
MAGIC

3001.

Juggling Stars
TAGU • 995QX6595 • $17

3002.

**Kiddie Car Classics 4:
Murray® Dump Truck**
PALM • 1395QX6195 • $23

3003.

**Kiddie Car Classics 4:
Murray® Dump Truck**
PALM • PrizeQX6195C • $800
Edition Size – 320

3004.

**Kiddie Car Classics
Complement: 1937 Steelcraft
Airflow by Murray®**
PALM • 1595QXC5185 • $46

3005.

**Language of Flowers 2:
Snowdrop Angel**
TAGU • 1595QX1095 • $20

3006.

Leading the Way
SICK • 1695QX6782 • $34

3007.

**Legend of the Three Kings
1: King Noor – First King**
ANDR • 1295QX6552 • $34

3008.

Lighthouse Greetings 1
FRAN • 2400QLX7442 • $118
MAGIC

3009.

The Lincoln Memorial
SEAL • 2400QLX7522 • $40
MAGIC

3010.

Lion and Lamb
WILL • 795QX6602 • $16

3011.

**LIONEL® Trains 2: 1950
Santa Fe F3 Diesel
Locomotive**
1895QX6145 • $37

3012.

The Lone Ranger™
GOSL • 1295QX6265 • $22

3013.

Love to Sew
TAGU • 795QX6435 • $16

3014.

**Madame Alexander® 2:
Little Red Riding Hood**
FRAN • 1495QX6155 • $22

3015.
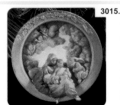
Madonna and Child
LYLE • 1995QLX7425 • $31
MAGIC

3016.
Madonna del Rosario
SICK • 1295QX6545 • $28

3017.
Majestic Wilderness 1:
Snowshoe Rabbits in Winter
1295QX5694 • $29

3018.
Marbles Champion
UNRU • 1095QX6342 • $17

3019.
Marilyn Monroe 1
ANDR • 1495QX5704 • $28

3020.
Mary's Angels 10: Daisy
795QX6242 • $30

3021.
Meadow Snowman
SICK • 1295QX6715 • $28

3022.
Megara and Pegasus –
Hercules
1695QXI4012 • $23

3023.
Merry Olde Santa 8
LYLE • 1495QX6225 • $25

3024.
Michigan J. Frog™
CHAD • 995QX6332 • $20

3025.
Mickey's Holiday Parade 1:
Bandleader Mickey
1395QXD4022 • $22

3026.
Mickey's Long Shot
1095QXD6412 • $18

3027.
Mickey's Snow Angel
995QXD4035 • $16

3028.
Miss Gulch™
LYLE • 1395QX6372 • $48

3029.
Mom
SIED • 895QX6525 • $19

3030.
Mom and Dad
SIED • 995QX6522 • $13

3031.
Mother Goose 5:
Little Boy Blue
SEAL/VOTR • 1395QX6215 • $20

3032.
Motorcycle Chums
SEAL • 2400QLX7495 • $42
MAGIC

3033.
Mr. Potato Head®
SIED • 1095QX6335 • $24

3034.
Mrs. Claus's Story
ESCH/KLIN • 1495(N/A) • $34

3035.
Nativity Tree
UNRU • 1495QX6575 • $26

3036.
Nature's Sketchbook:
Garden Bouquet
BAST/LYLE • 1495QX6752 • $23

3037.
Nature's Sketchbook:
Honored Guests
BAST/FRAN • 1495QX6745 • $29

3038.
NBA®: Charlotte Hornets™
995QSR1222 • $11

3039.
NBA®: Chicago Bulls™
995QSR1232 • $11

3040.
NBA®: Detroit Pistons™
995QSR1242 • $11

3041.
NBA®: Houston Rockets™
995QSR1245 • $11

3042.
NBA®: Indiana Pacers™
995QSR1252 • $11

3043.
NBA®: Los Angeles Lakers™
995QSR1262 • $11

3044.
NBA®: New York
Knickerbockers™
995QSR1272 • $11

3045.
NBA®: Orlando Magic™
995QSR1282 • $11

3046.
NBA®: Phoenix Suns™
995QSR1292 • $11

3047.
NBA®: Seattle Supersonics™
995QSR1295 • $11

3048.
New Home
PIKE • 895QX6652 • $18

3049.
New Pair of Skates
1395QXD4032 • $19

3050.
NFL®: Arizona Cardinals™
SIED • 995QSR5505 • $13

99

3051.
NFL®: Atlanta Falcons™
SIED • 995QSR5305 • $13

3052.
NFL®: Baltimore Ravens™
SIED • 995QSR5352 • $13

3053.
NFL®: Buffalo Bills™
SIED • 995QSR5312 • $13

3054.
NFL®: Carolina Panthers™
SIED • 995QSR5315 • $13

3055.
NFL®: Chicago Bears™
SIED • 995QSR5322 • $13

3056.
NFL®: Cincinnati Bengals™
SIED • 995QSR5325 • $13

3057.
NFL®: Dallas Cowboys™
SIED • 995QSR5355 • $13

3058.
NFL®: Denver Broncos™
SIED • 995QSR5362 • $13

3059.
NFL®: Detroit Lions™
SIED • 995QSR5365 • $13

3060.
NFL®: Green Bay Packers™
SIED • 995QSR5372 • $13

3061.
NFL®: Houston Oilers™
SIED • 995QSR5375 • $13

3062.
NFL®: Indianapolis Colts™
SIED • 995QSR5411 • $13

3063.
**NFL®:
Jacksonville Jaguars™**
SIED • 995QSR5415 • $13

3064.
NFL®: Kansas City Chiefs™
SIED • 995QSR5302 • $13

3065.
NFL®: Miami Dolphins™
SIED • 995QSR5472 • $13

3066.
NFL®: Minnesota Vikings™
SIED • 995QSR5475 • $13

3067.
**NFL®:
New England Patriots™**
SIED • 995QSR5482 • $13

3068.
NFL®: New Orleans Saints™
SIED • 995QSR5485 • $13

3069.
NFL®: New York Giants™
SIED • 995QSR5492 • $13

3070.
NFL®: New York Jets™
SIED • 995QSR5495 • $13

3071.
NFL®: Oakland Raiders™
SIED • 995QSR5422 • $13

3072.
NFL®: Philadelphia Eagles™
SIED • 995QSR5502 • $13

3073.
NFL®: Pittsburgh Steelers™
SIED • 995QSR5512 • $13

3074.
**NFL®:
San Diego Chargers™**
SIED • 995QSR5515 • $13

3075.
**NFL®:
San Francisco 49ers™**
SIED • 995QSR5522 • $13

3076.
NFL®: Seattle Seahawks™
SIED • 995QSR5525 • $13

3077.
NFL®: St. Louis Rams™
SIED • 995QSR5425 • $13

3078.
**NFL®: Tampa Bay
Buccaneers™**
SIED • 995QSR5532 • $13

3079.
**NFL®:
Washington Redskins™**
SIED • 995QSR5535 • $13

3080.
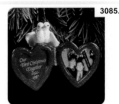
The Night Before Christmas
CROW • 2400QX5721 • $42
Musical.

3081.

**Nostalgic Houses &
Shops 14: Café**
PALM • 1695QX6245 • $24

3082.
Our Christmas Together
1695QX6475 • $19

3083.

**Our First Christmas
Together**
795QX3182 • $14

3084.
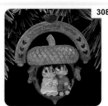
**Our First Christmas
Together**
SEAL • 1095QX6465 • $22

3085.
**Our First Christmas
Together**
PIKE • 895QX6472 • $14

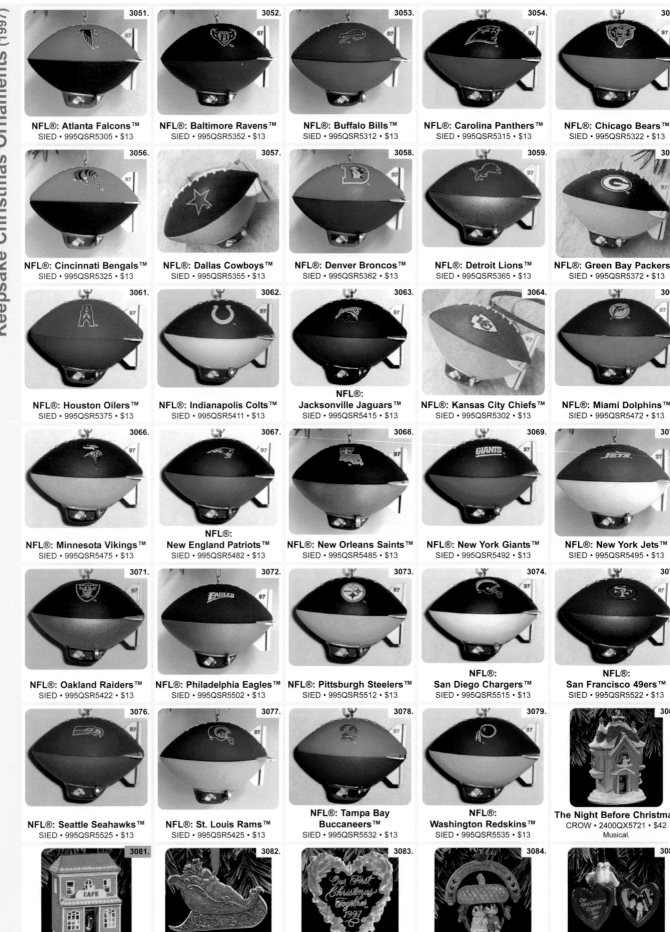

3086.
Phoebus & Esmeralda –
Hunchback of Notre Dame
1495QXD6344 • $20

3087.
Playful Shepherd
TAGU • 995QX6592 • $19

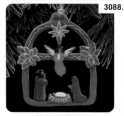
3088.
Praise Him
SICK • 895QX6542 • $30

3089.
Prize Topiary
SEAL • 1495QX6675 • $22

3090.
Puppy Love 7
RGRS • 795QX6222 • $45

3091.
Sailor Bear
UNRU • 1495QX6765 • $19

3092.
Santa Mail
WILL • 1095QX6702 • $28

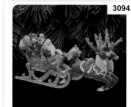
3093.
Santa's Friend
BAST/UNRU • 1295QX6685 • $19

3094.
Santa's Magical Sleigh
UNRU • 2400QX6672 • $37

3095.
Santa's Magical Sleigh
UNRU • PrizeQX6672C • $500
Edition Size – 100.

3096.
Santa's Merry Path
SICK • 1695QX6785 • $29

3097.
Santa's Polar Friend
CHAD • 1695QX6755 • $32

3098.
Santa's Secret Gift
CHAD • 2400QLX7455 • $38
MAGIC

3099.
Santa's Showboat
CROW • 4200QLX7465 • $80
MAGIC

3100.
Santa's Ski Adventure
CHAD • 1295QX6422 • $25

3101.
Scarlett O'Hara™ 1
ANDR • 1495QX6125 • $26

3102.
Sister to Sister
PIKE • 995QX6635 • $24

3103.
Sky's the Limit 1:
The Flight at Kitty Hawk
NORT • 1495QX5574 • $28

3104.
Snoopy® Plays Santa
RGRS • 2200QLX7475 • $55
MAGIC

3105.
Snow Bowling
WILL • 695QX6395 • $13

3106.
Snow White
Anniversary Edition
1695QXD4055 • $25
Set/2

3107.
Snowgirl
TAGU • 795QX6562 • $20

3108.
Snowman Hinged Box
VOTR • 1495QX6772 • $25

3109.
Son
BRIC • 795QX6605 • $20

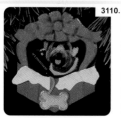
3110.
Special Dog
BRIC • 795QX6632 • $14

3111.
The Spirit of Christmas
LARS • 995QX6585 • $34

3112.
Star Wars™ 1:
Luke Skywalker™
RHOD • 1395QXI5484 • $24

3113.
Stealing a Kiss
TAGU • 1495QX6555 • $20

3114.
Stock Car Champions 1:
Jeff Gordon
SEAL • 1595QXI6165 • $30

3115.
Sweet Discovery
SICK • 1195QX6325 • $24

3116.
Sweet Dreamer
BRIC • 695QX6732 • $30

3117.
Swinging in the Snow
TAGU • 1295QX6775 • $30

3118.
Teapot Party
TAGU • 1895QLX7482 • $29
MAGIC

3119.
Tender Touches:
The Perfect Tree
SEAL • 1500QX6572 • $22

3120.
Thomas Kinkade, Painter of
Light 1: Victorian Christmas
LYLE • 1095QXI6135 • $26

3121.

**Timon & Pumbaa –
The Lion King**
1295QXD4065 • $18

3122.

**Tomorrow's Leader –
Boy Scouts®**
995QX6452 • $18

3123.

Tonka® Mighty Front Loader
1395QX6362 • $31

3124.

Trimming Santa's Tree
VARI • 6000QXC5175 • $95

3125.
**Turn of the Century
Parade 3: Santa Claus**
CROW • 1695QX1215 • $23

3126.
Two-Tone – 101 Dalmatians®
995QXD4015 • $24

3127.

U.S.S. Defiant™
NORT • 2400QXI7481 • $37
MAGIC

3128.

**Victorian Elegance
BARBIE™ Ornament**
ANDR • 1495QHB6004 • $24

3129.

Waitin' on Santa
1295QXD6365 • $24

3130.

The Warmth of the Home
LARS • 1895QXI7545 • $19
MAGIC

3131.

What a Deal!
PIKE • 895QX6442 • $14

3132.
Yoda™
BRIC • 995QXI6355 • $38

3133.
**Yuletide Central 4:
Cargo Car**
SICK • 1895QX5812 • $28

1998

3134.

#1 Student
795QX6646 • $11

3135.

1998 Corvette®
PALM • 2400QLX7605 • $33
MAGIC

3136.

1998 Corvette® Convertible
PALM • 1395QX6416 • $30

3137.

25th Anniversary Elf
SIED • Prize(N/A) • $1000
Edition Size – 5.

3138.

25th Anniversary Mouse
CHAD • Prize(N/A) • $1000
Edition Size – 5.

3139.
25th Anniversary Silver Tree
Gift(N/A) • $32

3140.

**African-American
Holiday BARBIE™ 1**
ANDR • 1595QX6936 • $28

3141.

**All God's Children 3:
Martha Root**
1295QX6363 • $28

3142.

**All-American Trucks 4:
1937 Ford® V-8**
PALM • 1395QX6263 • $34

3143.
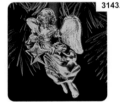
Angelic Flight
ANDR/HAAS • 8500QXI4146 • $85
Limited Edition – 25000

3144.

Angelic Flight (Gold)
ANDR/HAAS • GiftQXI4146C • $1000
Edition Size – approx. 10 • VERY RARE

3145.
**At the Ballpark 3:
Cal Ripken Jr.**
RHOD • 1495QXI4033 • $30

3146.

Baby's First Christmas
TAGU • 995QX6233 • $14

3147.

Baby's First Christmas
ESCH • 995QX6586 • $20

3148.

Baby's First Christmas
KLIN • 895QX6596 • $26

3149.

**BARBIE™ 5: Silken
Flame BARBIE™**
ANDR • 1595QXI4043 • $23

3150.

**Blessed Nativity:
The Holy Family**
LYLE • 2500QX6523 • $45
Set/3 • Re-issued in 1999 & 2000.

3151.

**Blown Glass –
1955 Murray® Fire Truck**
HADD • 3500QBG6909 • $46

3152.

**Blown Glass –
Crown Reflections 1:
Red Poinsettias**
3500QBG6906 • $50

3153.

**Blown Glass – Crown
Reflections Complement:
Pink Poinsettias**
2500QBG6926 • $41

3154.

**Blown Glass – Crown
Reflections Complement:
White Poinsettias**
2500QBG6923 • $69

3155. Blown Glass – Festive Locomotive
TAGU • 3500QBG6903 • $46

3156. Blown Glass – Frosty Friends Complement
SEAL • 4800QBG6907 • $63
Set/2

3157. Blown Glass – Sugarplum Cottage
HADD • 3500QBG6917 • $52

3158. Blown Glass – Sweet Memories
KLIN • 4500QBG6933 • $65
Set/8

3159. Blown Glass – Three Kings: Frankincense
LARS • 2200QBG6896 • $38
Re-issued in 1999.

3160. Blown Glass – Three Kings: Gold
LARS • 2200QBG6836 • $43
Re-issued in 1999.

3161. Blown Glass – Three Kings: Myrrh
LARS • 2200QBG6893 • $38
Re-issued in 1999.

3162. Boba Fett™
RHOD • 1495QXI4053 • $40

3163. Bouncy Baby-sitter
1295QXD4096 • $22

3164. Bugs Bunny™
CHAD • 1395QX6443 • $17

3165. Building a Snowman
1495QXD4133 • $24

3166. Buzz Lightyear – Toy Story
1495QXD4066 • $40

3167. Candlelight Services 1: The Stone Church
SEAL • 1895QLX7636 • $52
MAGIC

3168. Captain Kathryn Janeway
RGRS • 1495QXI4046 • $40

3169. Cat Naps 5
BRIC • 895QX6383 • $20

3170. Catch of the Season
SEAL • 1495QX6786 • $26

3171. A Celebration of Angels 4
ANDR • 1395QX6366 • $35

3172. Chatty Chipmunk
CROW • 995QX6716 • $20

3173. Checking Santa's Files
TAGU • 895QX6806 • $15

3174. A Child is Born
VOTR • 1295QX6176 • $32

3175. Child's Age: Baby's First Christmas
FRAN • 795QX6603 • $45

3176. Child's Age: Baby's Second Christmas
CROW • 795QX6606 • $28

3177. Child's Age: Child's Third Christmas
CROW • 795QX6613 • $22

3178. Child's Age: Child's Fourth Christmas
CROW • 795QX6616 • $22

3179. Child's Age: Child's Fifth Christmas
CROW • 795QX6623 • $22

3180. Christmas Eve Preparations
VARI • 8500QXC4506 • $345
Edition Size – 3900

3181. A Christmas Eve Story – Becky Kelly
TAGU • 1395QX6873 • $23

3182. Christmas Request
FRAN • 1495QX6193 • $28

3183. Christmas Sleigh Ride
CROW • 1295QX6556 • $22

3184. Cinderella at the Ball
2400QXD7576 • $85
MAGIC

3185. Cinderella's Coach
1495QXD4083 • $32

3186. Classic American Cars 8: 1970 Plymouth® Hemi 'Cuda
PALM • 1395QX6256 • $40

3187. The Clauses on Vacation 2
SIED • 1495QX6276 • $18

3188. Collegiate: Florida State Seminoles™
HADD • 995QSR2316 • $14

3189. Collegiate: Michigan Wolverines™
HADD • 995QSR2323 • $14

103

3190.
Collegiate:
North Carolina Tar Heels™
HADD • 995QSR2333 • $14

3191.
Collegiate:
Notre Dame Fighting Irish™
HADD • 995QSR2313 • $14

3192.
Collegiate:
Penn State Nittany Lions™
HADD • 995QSR2326 • $14

3193.
Compact Skater
TAGU • 995QX6766 • $14

3194.
Crayola® Crayon 10:
Bright Sledding Colors
TAGU • 1295QX6166 • $26

3195.
Cross of Peace
KLIN • 995QX6856 • $22

3196.
Cruising into Christmas
CROW • 1695QX6196 • $25

3197.
Dad
KLIN • 895QX6663 • $13

3198.
Daughter
AUBE • 895QX6673 • $19

3199.
Daydreams –
The Little Mermaid
1395QXD4136 • $32

3200.
Decorating Maxine Style
WAGN • 1095QXE6883 • $16

3201.
Dolls of the World 3:
Mexican BARBIE™
RGRS • 1495QX6356 • $30

3202.
Downhill Dash
CROW • 1395QX6776 • $40

3203.
Enchanted Memories 2:
Snow White
1495QXD4056 • $28

3204.
Fabulous Decade 9
PIKE • 795QX6393 • $40

3205.
Fancy Footwork
VOTR • 895QX6536 • $28

3206.
Feliz Navidad
CHAD • 895QX6173 • $17

3207.
Flik – A Bug's Life
1295QXD4153 • $32

3208.
Follow the Leader
SIED • 1695QXC4503 • $35
Set/2

3209.
Football Legends 4:
Emmitt Smith
RHOD • 1495QXI4036 • $50

3210.
Football Legends
Complement:
Joe Montana – Notre Dame
UNRU • 1495QXI6843 • $17

3211.
Forever Friends Bear
BRWN/PIKE • 895QX6303 • $14

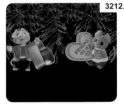

3212.
Friend of My Heart
SEAL • 1495QX6723 • $20
Set/2

3213.
Frosty Friends 19
SEAL • 1095QX6226 • $48

3214.
Future Ballerina
TAGU • 795QX6756 • $17

3215.
Gifted Gardener
CHAD • 795QX6736 • $12

3216.
Godchild
CHAD • 795QX6703 • $25

3217.
Good Luck Dice
HADD • 995QX6813 • $12

3218.
Goofy® Soccer Star
1095QXD4123 • $20

3219.
Granddaughter
FRAN • 795QX6683 • $12

3220.
Grandma's Memories
KLIN • 895QX6686 • $17

3221.
Grandson
FRAN • 795QX6676 • $12

3222.
The Grinch™
CHAD • 1395QXI6466 • $75

3223.
Guardian Friend
LYLE • 895QX6543 • $20

3224.
Hallmark Archives 2:
Ready For Christmas
1295QXD4006 • $32

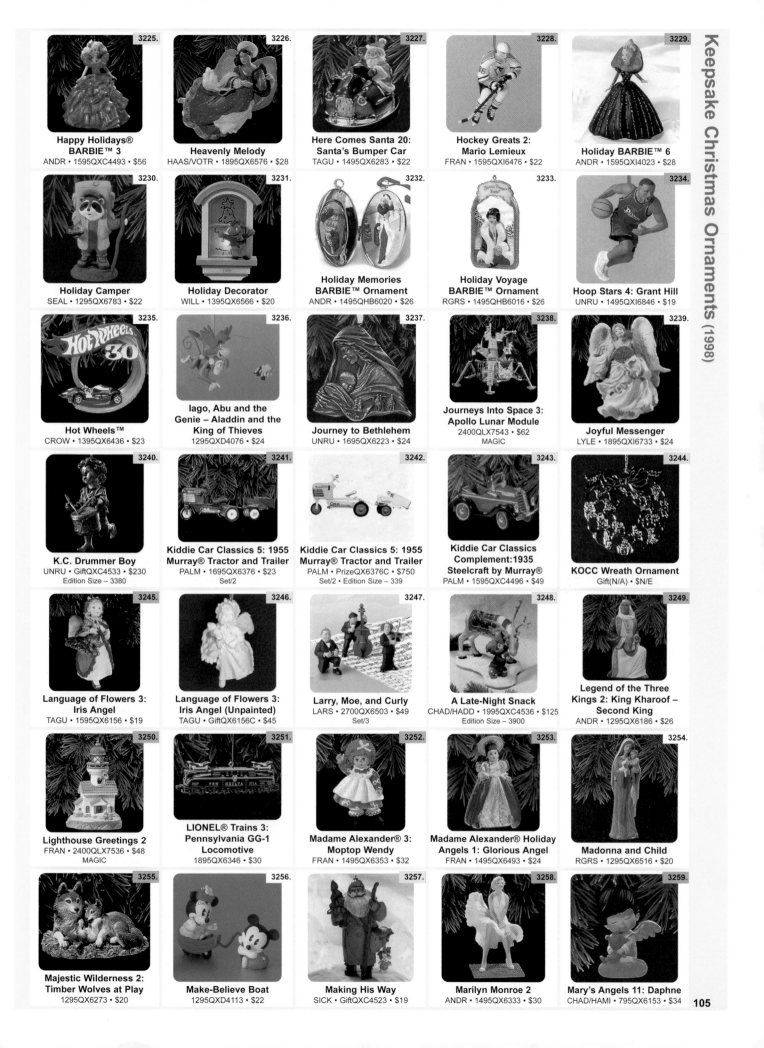

3225.
Happy Holidays®
BARBIE™ 3
ANDR • 1595QXC4493 • $56

3226.
Heavenly Melody
HAAS/VOTR • 1895QX6576 • $28

3227.
Here Comes Santa 20:
Santa's Bumper Car
TAGU • 1495QX6283 • $22

3228.
Hockey Greats 2:
Mario Lemieux
FRAN • 1595QXI6476 • $22

3229.
Holiday BARBIE™ 6
ANDR • 1595QXI4023 • $28

3230.
Holiday Camper
SEAL • 1295QX6783 • $22

3231.
Holiday Decorator
WILL • 1395QX6566 • $20

3232.
Holiday Memories
BARBIE™ Ornament
ANDR • 1495QHB6020 • $26

3233.
Holiday Voyage
BARBIE™ Ornament
RGRS • 1495QHB6016 • $26

3234.
Hoop Stars 4: Grant Hill
UNRU • 1495QXI6846 • $19

3235.
Hot Wheels™
CROW • 1395QX6436 • $23

3236.
Iago, Abu and the
Genie – Aladdin and the
King of Thieves
1295QXD4076 • $24

3237.
Journey to Bethlehem
UNRU • 1695QX6223 • $24

3238.
Journeys Into Space 3:
Apollo Lunar Module
2400QLX7543 • $62
MAGIC

3239.
Joyful Messenger
LYLE • 1895QXI6733 • $24

3240.
K.C. Drummer Boy
UNRU • GiftQXC4533 • $230
Edition Size – 3380

3241.
Kiddie Car Classics 5: 1955
Murray® Tractor and Trailer
PALM • 1695QX6376 • $23
Set/2

3242.
Kiddie Car Classics 5: 1955
Murray® Tractor and Trailer
PALM • PrizeQX6376C • $750
Set/2 • Edition Size – 339

3243.
Kiddie Car Classics
Complement:1935
Steelcraft by Murray®
PALM • 1595QXC4496 • $49

3244.
KOCC Wreath Ornament
Gift(N/A) • $N/E

3245.
Language of Flowers 3:
Iris Angel
TAGU • 1595QX6156 • $19

3246.
Language of Flowers 3:
Iris Angel (Unpainted)
TAGU • GiftQX6156C • $45

3247.
Larry, Moe, and Curly
LARS • 2700QX6503 • $49
Set/3

3248.
A Late-Night Snack
CHAD/HADD • 1995QXC4536 • $125
Edition Size – 3900

3249.
Legend of the Three
Kings 2: King Kharoof –
Second King
ANDR • 1295QX6186 • $26

3250.
Lighthouse Greetings 2
FRAN • 2400QLX7536 • $48
MAGIC

3251.
LIONEL® Trains 3:
Pennsylvania GG-1
Locomotive
1895QX6346 • $30

3252.
Madame Alexander® 3:
Moptop Wendy
FRAN • 1495QX6353 • $32

3253.
Madame Alexander® Holiday
Angels 1: Glorious Angel
FRAN • 1495QX6493 • $24

3254.
Madonna and Child
RGRS • 1295QX6516 • $20

3255.
Majestic Wilderness 2:
Timber Wolves at Play
1295QX6273 • $20

3256.
Make-Believe Boat
1295QXD4113 • $22

3257.
Making His Way
SICK • GiftQXC4523 • $19

3258.
Marilyn Monroe 2
ANDR • 1495QX6333 • $30

3259.
Mary's Angels 11: Daphne
CHAD/HAMI • 795QX6153 • $34

3260.

Maxine
PIKE/WAGN • 995QX6446 • $14

3261.

Memories of Christmas
LARS • 595QX2406 • $23

3262.

Merry Chime
CROW • 995QX6692 • $30

3263.

Merry Olde Santa 9
UNRU • 1595QX6386 • $28

3264.

Mickey and Minnie Handcar
1495QXD4116 • $22

3265.

Mickey's Comet
2400QXD7586 • $40
MAGIC

3266.

Mickey's Favorite Reindeer
1395QXD4013 • $29

3267.

**Mickey's Holiday Parade 2:
Minnie Plays the Flute**
1395QXD4106 • $20

3268.

Miracle in Bethlehem
SEAL • 1295QX6513 • $45

3269.

Mistletoe Fairy
ESCH • 1295QX6216 • $42

3270.

Mom
KLIN • 895QX6656 • $14

3271.

Mom and Dad
KLIN • 995QX6653 • $14

3272.

Mother and Daughter
VOTR • 895QX6696 • $20

3273.

Mrs. Potato Head®
1095QX6886 • $19

3274.

Mulan, Mushu and Cri-Kee
1495QXD4156 • $48
Set/2

3275.

**Munchkinland™ Mayor
and Coroner**
LYLE • 1395QX6463 • $24
Set/2

3276.

National Salute
RHOD • 895QX6293 • $30

3277.

**Nature's Sketchbook:
Country Home**
BAST/FRAN • 1095QX5172 • $25

3278.

NBA®: Charlotte Hornets™
SIED • 995QSR1033 • $11

3279.

NBA®: Chicago Bulls™
SIED • 995QSR1036 • $11

3280.

NBA®: Detroit Pistons™
SIED • 995QSR1043 • $11

3281.

NBA®: Houston Rockets™
SIED • 995QSR1046 • $11

3282.

NBA®: Indiana Pacers™
SIED • 995QSR1053 • $11

3283.

NBA®: Los Angeles Lakers™
SIED • 995QSR1056 • $11

3284.

**NBA®: New York
Knickerbockers™**
SIED • 995QSR1063 • $11

3285.

NBA®: Orlando Magic™
SIED • 995QSR1066 • $11

3286.

NBA®: Seattle Supersonics™
SIED • 995QSR1076 • $11

3287.

NBA®: Utah Jazz™
SIED • 995QSR1083 • $11

3288.

New Arrival
VOTR • 1895QX6306 • $19

3289.

New Christmas Friend
ESCH • GiftQXC4516 • $19

3290.

New Home
SEAL • 995QX6713 • $40

3291.

NFL®: Carolina Panthers™
FRAN • 995QSR5026 • $14

3292.

NFL®: Chicago Bears™
FRAN • 995QSR5033 • $14

3293.

NFL®: Dallas Cowboys™
FRAN • 995QSR5046 • $14

3294.

NFL®: Denver Broncos™
FRAN • 995QSR5053 • $14

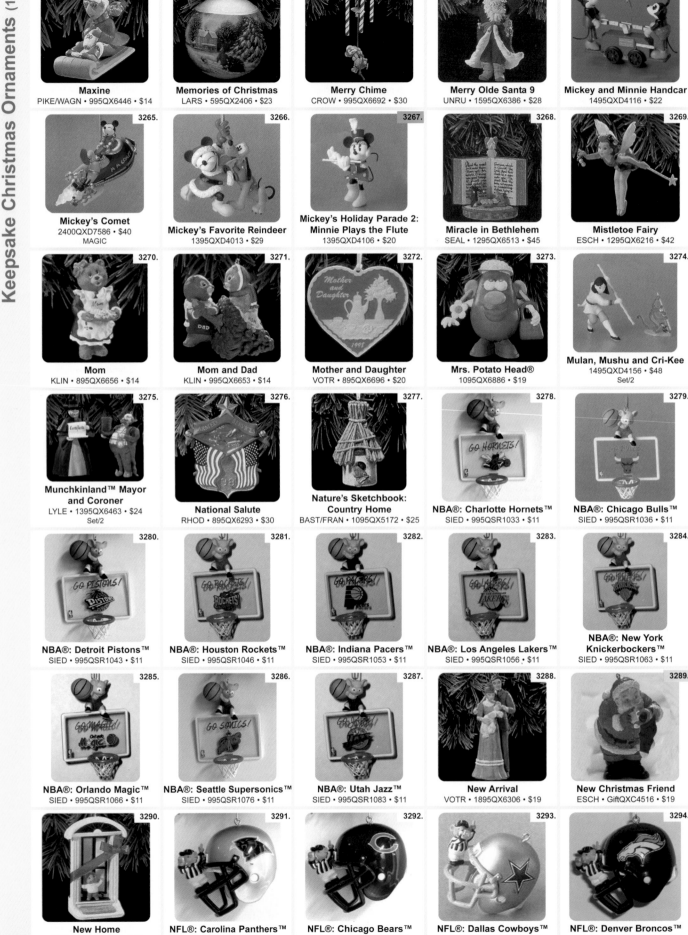

3295.
NFL®: Green Bay Packers™
FRAN • 995QSR5063 • $14

3296.
NFL®: Kansas City Chiefs™
FRAN • 995QSR5013 • $14

3297.
NFL®: Miami Dolphins™
FRAN • 995QSR5096 • $14

3298.
NFL®: Minnesota Vikings™
FRAN • 995QSR5126 • $14

3299.
NFL®: New York Giants™
FRAN • 995QSR5143 • $14

3300.
NFL®: Oakland Raiders™
FRAN • 995QSR5086 • $14

3301.
NFL®: Philadelphia Eagles™
FRAN • 995QSR5153 • $14

3302.
NFL®: Pittsburgh Steelers™
FRAN • 995QSR5163 • $14

3303.
NFL®:
San Francisco 49ers™
FRAN • 995QSR5173 • $14

3304.
NFL®: St. Louis Rams™
FRAN • 995QSR5093 • $14

3305.
NFL®:
Washington Redskins™
FRAN • 995QSR5186 • $14

3306.
Nick's Wish List
ANDR • 895QX6863 • $28

3307.
Night Watch
SIED • 995QX6725 • $28

3308.
North Pole Reserve
SEAL • 1095QX6803 • $20

3309.
Nostalgic Houses &
Shops 15: Grocery Store
PALM • 1695QX6266 • $28

3310.
Nostalgic Houses & Shops
Complement: Halls Station
PALM • 2500QX6833 • $40

3311.
Old West 1:
Pony Express Rider
UNRU • 1395QX6323 • $25

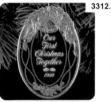

3312.
Our First Christmas
Together
VOTR • 795QX3193 • $19

3313.
Our First Christmas
Together
TAGU • 895QX6636 • $19

3314.
Our First Christmas
Together
VOTR • 1895QX6643 • $19

3315.
Our Song
995QX6183 • $17

3316.
Peekaboo Bears
CROW • 1295QX6563 • $32

3317.
A Perfect Match
RHOD • 1095QX6633 • $24

3318.
Polar Bowler
ESCH • 795QX6746 • $17

3319.
A Pony for Christmas 1
SICK • 1095QX6316 • $35

3320.
A Pony for Christmas 1
SICK • GiftQX6316C • $850
Edition Size – 508

3321.
Princess Aurora –
Sleeping Beauty
1295QXD4126 • $36
Set/2

3322.
Puppy Love 8
RGRS • 795QX6163 • $28

3323.
Purr-fect Little Deer
PIKE • 795QX6526 • $40

3324.
Puttin' Around
RHOD • 895QX6763 • $14

3325.
Rocket to Success
PIKE • 895QX6793 • $11

3326.
Romantic Vacations 1:
Donald and Daisy in Venice
1495QXD4103 • $28

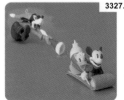

3327.
Runaway Toboggan
1695QXD4003 • $26
Set/2

3328.
Santa's Deer Friend
CHAD • 2400QX6583 • $46

3329.
Santa's Deer Friend
CHAD • PrizeQX6583C • $400
Edition Size – 750

3330.

Santa's Flying Machine
SEAL • 1695QX6573 • $26

3331.

Santa's Hidden Surprise
1495QX6913 • $20

3332.

Santa's Merry Workshop
SEAL • 3200QX6816 • $59
Musical.

3333.

Santa's Show 'n' Tell
CROW • 1895QLX7566 • $26
MAGIC

3334.

Santa's Spin Top
TAGU • 2200QLX7573 • $42
MAGIC

3335.

Scarlett O'Hara™ 2
ANDR • 1495QX6336 • $42

3336.

Sew Gifted
TAGU • 795QX6743 • $17

3337.

**Simba & Nala –
The Lion King**
1395QXD4073 • $34

3338.

Sister to Sister
PIKE • 895QX6693 • $13

3339.

**Sky's the Limit 2: 1917
Curtiss JN-4D "Jenny"**
NORT • 1495QX6286 • $48

3340.

Snow Buddies 1
HADD • 795QX6853 • $53

3341.

Snow Buddies 1
HADD • GiftQX6853C • $414
Edition Size – 800

3342.

Soaring with Angels
SICK • 1695QX6213 • $29

3343.

Son
AUBE • 895QX6666 • $12

3344.

Special Dog
795QX6706 • $20

3345.

Spoonful of Love
TAGU • 895QX6796 • $25

3346.

**Spotlight on Snoopy® 1:
Joe Cool**
SIED • 995QX6453 • $33

3347.

**Spotlight on Snoopy® 1:
Joe Cool**
SIED • PrizeQX6453C • $995
Edition Size – 84

3348.

St. Nicholas Circle
UNRU • 1895QXI7556 • $28
MAGIC

3349.

**Star Wars™ 2:
Princess Leia™**
RHOD • 1395QXI4026 • $24

3350.

**Stock Car Champions 2:
Richard Petty**
SEAL • 1595QXI4143 • $26

3351.

Superman™
1295QX6423 • $16

3352.

Surprise Catch
FRAN • 795QX6753 • $18

3353.

Sweet Rememberings
TAGU • 895QX6876 • $15

3354.
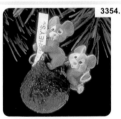
Sweet Treat
KLIN • 1095QX6433 • $28

3355.

**Thomas Kinkade, Painter
of Light 2:
Victorian Christmas II**
WILL • 1095QX6343 • $32

3356.

Tin Locomotive
SICK • 2500QX6826 • $37

3357.

Tonka® Road Grader
1395QX6483 • $32

3358.

Treetop Choir
FRAN • 995QX6506 • $28

3359.

**U.S.S. Enterprise™
NCC-1701-E**
NORT • 2400QXI7633 • $70
MAGIC

3360.

**Unforgettable Villains 1:
Cruella de Vil – 101
Dalmatians**
1495QXD4063 • $28

3361.

Warm and Cozy
SICK • 895QX6866 • $26

3362.

The Washington Monument
SEAL • 2400QLX7553 • $40
MAGIC

3363.

Watchful Shepherd
KLIN • 895QX6496 • $26

3364.

**Winnie the Pooh 1:
A Visit From Piglet**
1395QXD4086 • $24

108

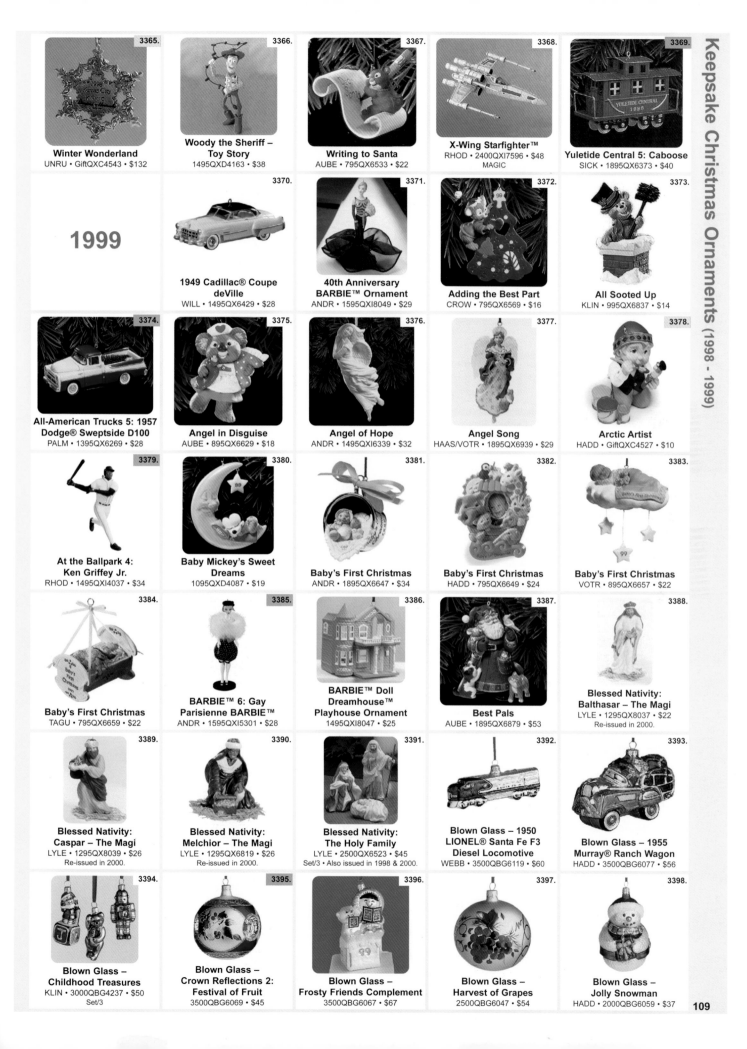

3365.
Winter Wonderland
UNRU • GiftQXC4543 • $132

3366.
Woody the Sheriff –
Toy Story
1495QXD4163 • $38

3367.
Writing to Santa
AUBE • 795QX6533 • $22

3368.
X-Wing Starfighter™
RHOD • 2400QXI7596 • $48
MAGIC

3369.
Yuletide Central 5: Caboose
SICK • 1895QX6373 • $40

1999

3370.
1949 Cadillac® Coupe
deVille
WILL • 1495QX6429 • $28

3371.
40th Anniversary
BARBIE™ Ornament
ANDR • 1595QXI8049 • $29

3372.
Adding the Best Part
CROW • 795QX6569 • $16

3373.
All Sooted Up
KLIN • 995QX6837 • $14

3374.
All-American Trucks 5: 1957
Dodge® Sweptside D100
PALM • 1395QX6269 • $28

3375.
Angel in Disguise
AUBE • 895QX6629 • $18

3376.
Angel of Hope
ANDR • 1495QXI6339 • $32

3377.
Angel Song
HAAS/VOTR • 1895QX6939 • $29

3378.
Arctic Artist
HADD • GiftQXC4527 • $10

3379.
At the Ballpark 4:
Ken Griffey Jr.
RHOD • 1495QXI4037 • $34

3380.
Baby Mickey's Sweet
Dreams
1095QXD4087 • $19

3381.
Baby's First Christmas
ANDR • 1895QX6647 • $34

3382.
Baby's First Christmas
HADD • 795QX6649 • $24

3383.
Baby's First Christmas
VOTR • 895QX6657 • $22

3384.
Baby's First Christmas
TAGU • 795QX6659 • $22

3385.
BARBIE™ 6: Gay
Parisienne BARBIE™
ANDR • 1595QXI5301 • $28

3386.
BARBIE™ Doll
Dreamhouse™
Playhouse Ornament
1495QXI8047 • $25

3387.
Best Pals
AUBE • 1895QX6879 • $53

3388.
Blessed Nativity:
Balthasar – The Magi
LYLE • 1295QX8037 • $22
Re-issued in 2000.

3389.
Blessed Nativity:
Caspar – The Magi
LYLE • 1295QX8039 • $26
Re-issued in 2000.

3390.
Blessed Nativity:
Melchior – The Magi
LYLE • 1295QX6819 • $26
Re-issued in 2000.

3391.
Blessed Nativity:
The Holy Family
LYLE • 2500QX6523 • $45
Set/3 • Also issued in 1998 & 2000.

3392.
Blown Glass – 1950
LIONEL® Santa Fe F3
Diesel Locomotive
WEBB • 3500QBG6119 • $60

3393.
Blown Glass – 1955
Murray® Ranch Wagon
HADD • 3500QBG6077 • $56

3394.
Blown Glass –
Childhood Treasures
KLIN • 3000QBG4237 • $50
Set/3

3395.
Blown Glass –
Crown Reflections 2:
Festival of Fruit
3500QBG6069 • $45

3396.
Blown Glass –
Frosty Friends Complement
3500QBG6067 • $67

3397.
Blown Glass –
Harvest of Grapes
2500QBG6047 • $54

3398.
Blown Glass –
Jolly Snowman
HADD • 2000QBG6059 • $37

3399.
Blown Glass –
The Holy Family
LARS • 3000QBG6127 • $59

3400.
Blown Glass –
Three Kings: Frankincense
LARS • 2200QBG6896 • $38
Re-issued from 1998.

3401.
Blown Glass –
Three Kings: Gold
LARS • 2200QBG6836 • $43
Re-issued from 1998.

3402.
Blown Glass –
Three Kings: Myrrh
LARS • 2200QBG6893 • $38
Re-issued from 1998.

3403.
Blown Glass – U.S.S
Enterprise NCC-1701™
LAPR • 2500QBG6117 • $129

3404.
Blown Glass –
Village Church
SEAL • 3000QBG6057 • $48

3405.
Blown Glass –
Yummy Memories
KLIN • 4500QBG6049 • $83
Set/8

3406.
Blown Glass –
Yummy Memories
KLIN • PrizeQBG6049C • $323
Set/8 • Edition Size – 192

3407.
Bowling's a Ball
KLIN • 795QX6577 • $16

3408.
Candlelight Services 2:
Colonial Church
SEAL • 1895QLX7387 • $29
MAGIC

3409.
Century Stamp: I Love Lucy
995QXI8567 • $29

3410.
Century Stamp:
Silken Flame BARBIE™
995QXI8559 • $19

3411.
Century Stamp: Superman™
995QXI8569 • $18

3412.
Century Stamp:
The Cat in the Hat™ –
Dr. Seuss® Books
995QXI8579 • $15

3413.
Century Stamp: U.S.S
Enterprise NCC-1701™
995QXI8557 • $29

3414.
Century Stamp: Yellow
Submarine™ – The Beatles
995QXI8577 • $22

3415.
Chewbacca™
RHOD • 1495QXI4009 • $32

3416.
Child of Wonder
UNRU • 1495QX6817 • $25

3417.
Child's Age:
Baby's First Christmas
FRAN • 795QX6667 • $20

3418.
Child's Age:
Baby's Second Christmas
FRAN • 795QX6669 • $22

3419.
Child's Age:
Child's Third Christmas
CROW • 795QX6677 • $18

3420.
Child's Age:
Child's Fourth Christmas
CROW • 795QX6687 • $18

3421.
Child's Age:
Child's Fifth Christmas
CROW • 795QX6679 • $18

3422.
The Christmas Story
UNRU • 2200QX6897 • $36

3423.
Classic American Cars 9:
1955 Chevrolet®
Nomad Wagon
PALM • 1395QX6367 • $34

3424.
The Clauses on Vacation 3
SIED • 1495QX6399 • $20

3425.
Clownin' Around
TAGU • 1095QX6487 • $20

3426.
Cocoa Break
KLIN • 1095QX8009 • $23

3427.
Cocoa Break
KLIN • GiftQX8009C • $47

3428.
Collecting Friends
SIED • GiftQXC4679 • $59

3429.
Collegiate:
Arizona Wildcats™
AUBE • 995QSR2429 • $12

3430.
Collegiate:
Duke Blue Devils™
AUBE • 995QSR2437 • $12

3431.
Collegiate:
Florida State Seminoles™
AUBE • 995QSR2439 • $12

3432.
Collegiate:
Georgetown Hoyas™
AUBE • 995QSR2447 • $12

3433.
Collegiate:
Kentucky Wildcats™
AUBE • 995QSR2449 • $12

3434.
Collegiate:
Michigan Wolverines™
AUBE • 995QSR2457 • $12

3435.
Collegiate:
Nebraska Cornhuskers™
AUBE • 995QSR2459 • $12

3436.
Collegiate:
North Carolina Tar Heels™
AUBE • 995QSR2467 • $12

3437.
Collegiate:
Notre Dame Fighting Irish™
AUBE • 995QSR2427 • $12

3438.
Collegiate:
Penn State Nittany Lions™
AUBE • 995QSR2469 • $12

3439.
Counting on Success
PIKE • 795QX6707 • $12

3440.
Cross of Hope
UNRU • 995QX6557 • $23

3441.
Dad
BRIC • 895QX6719 • $14

3442.
Dance for the Season
ESCH • 995QX6587 • $24

3443.
Darth Vader's TIE Fighter™
RHOD • 2400QXI7399 • $35
MAGIC

3444.
Daughter
ESCH • 895QX6729 • $28

3445.
Dolls of the World 4:
Russian BARBIE™
RGRS • 1495QX6369 • $21

3446.
Dorothy and Glinda,
the Good Witch™
LYLE • 2400QX6509 • $47

3447.
Dr. Seuss® Books 1:
The Cat in the Hat™
WILL • 1495QXI6457 • $28
Set/2

3448.
Dumbo's First Flight
1395QXD4117 • $26

3449.
Enchanted Memories 3:
Sleeping Beauty
1495QXD4097 • $32

3450.
Fabulous Decade 10
PIKE • 795QX6357 • $32

3451.
The Family Portrait –
Lady and the Tramp
1495QXD4149 • $35

3452.
Favorite Bible Stories 1:
David and Goliath
LARS • 1395QX6447 • $22

3453.
Feliz Navidad Santa
TAGU • 895QX6999 • $18

3454.
Flame-Fighting Friends
TAGU • 1495QX6619 • $19

3455.
The Flash™
RGRS • 1295QX6469 • $20

3456.
Football Legends 5:
Dan Marino
RHOD • 1495QXI4029 • $38

3457.
For My Grandma
LYLE • 795QX6747 • $17

3458.
Forecast for Fun
TAGU • 1495QX6869 • $24

3459.
Frosty Friends 20
SEAL • 1295QX6297 • $30

3460.
G.I. Joe® – Action Soldier
CROW • 1395QX6537 • $19

3461.
Gift Bearers 1
TAGU • 1295QX6437 • $32

3462.
Godchild
TAGU • 795QX6759 • $17

3463.
Goofy® as Santa's Helper
1295QXD4079 • $25

3464.
Granddaughter
SEAL • 895QX6739 • $26

3465.
Grandson
SEAL • 895QX6737 • $26

3466.
Hallmark Archives 3:
Minnie Trims the Tree
1295QXD4059 • $23

3467.
Handled with Care
RHOD • 895QX6769 • $13

3468.
Happy Holidays®
BARBIE™ 4
ANDR • 1595QXC4507 • $59

111

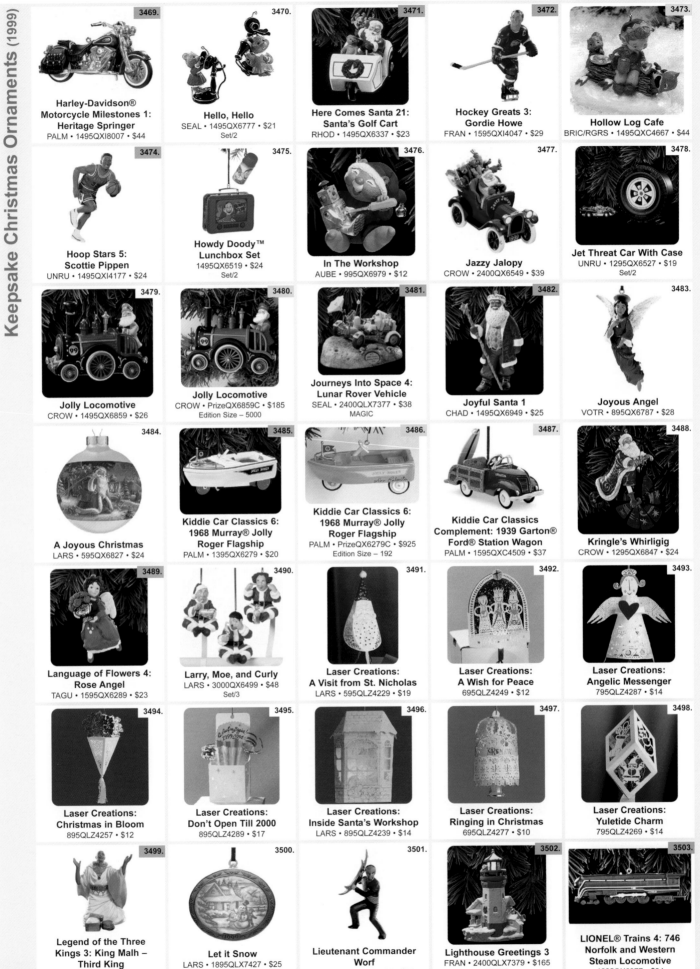

3469.
Harley-Davidson®
Motorcycle Milestones 1:
Heritage Springer
PALM • 1495QXI8007 • $44

3470.
Hello, Hello
SEAL • 1495QX6777 • $21
Set/2

3471.
Here Comes Santa 21:
Santa's Golf Cart
RHOD • 1495QX6337 • $23

3472.
Hockey Greats 3:
Gordie Howe
FRAN • 1595QXI4047 • $29

3473.
Hollow Log Cafe
BRIC/RGRS • 1495QXC4667 • $44

3474.
Hoop Stars 5:
Scottie Pippen
UNRU • 1495QXI4177 • $24

3475.
Howdy Doody™
Lunchbox Set
1495QX6519 • $24
Set/2

3476.
In The Workshop
AUBE • 995QX6979 • $12

3477.
Jazzy Jalopy
CROW • 2400QX6549 • $39

3478.
Jet Threat Car With Case
UNRU • 1295QX6527 • $19
Set/2

3479.
Jolly Locomotive
CROW • 1495QX6859 • $26

3480.
Jolly Locomotive
CROW • PrizeQX6859C • $185
Edition Size – 5000

3481.
Journeys Into Space 4:
Lunar Rover Vehicle
SEAL • 2400QLX7377 • $38
MAGIC

3482.
Joyful Santa 1
CHAD • 1495QX6949 • $25

3483.
Joyous Angel
VOTR • 895QX6787 • $28

3484.
A Joyous Christmas
LARS • 595QX6827 • $24

3485.
Kiddie Car Classics 6:
1968 Murray® Jolly
Roger Flagship
PALM • 1395QX6279 • $20

3486.
Kiddie Car Classics 6:
1968 Murray® Jolly
Roger Flagship
PALM • PrizeQX6279C • $925
Edition Size – 192

3487.
Kiddie Car Classics
Complement: 1939 Garton®
Ford® Station Wagon
PALM • 1595QXC4509 • $37

3488.
Kringle's Whirligig
CROW • 1295QX6847 • $24

3489.
Language of Flowers 4:
Rose Angel
TAGU • 1595QX6289 • $23

3490.
Larry, Moe, and Curly
LARS • 3000QX6499 • $48
Set/3

3491.
Laser Creations:
A Visit from St. Nicholas
LARS • 595QLZ4229 • $19

3492.
Laser Creations:
A Wish for Peace
695QLZ4249 • $12

3493.
Laser Creations:
Angelic Messenger
795QLZ4287 • $14

3494.
Laser Creations:
Christmas in Bloom
895QLZ4257 • $12

3495.
Laser Creations:
Don't Open Till 2000
895QLZ4289 • $17

3496.
Laser Creations:
Inside Santa's Workshop
LARS • 895QLZ4239 • $14

3497.
Laser Creations:
Ringing in Christmas
695QLZ4277 • $10

3498.
Laser Creations:
Yuletide Charm
795QLZ4269 • $14

3499.
Legend of the Three
Kings 3: King Malh –
Third King
ANDR • 1395QX6797 • $26

3500.
Let it Snow
LARS • 1895QLX7427 • $25
MAGIC

3501.
Lieutenant Commander
Worf
RGRS • 1495QXI4139 • $26

3502.
Lighthouse Greetings 3
FRAN • 2400QLX7379 • $165
MAGIC

3503.
LIONEL® Trains 4: 746
Norfolk and Western
Steam Locomotive
1895QX6377 • $34

3504.
LIONEL® Trains
Complement: 746 Norfolk
and Western Tender
1495QX6497 • $38

3505.
Little Cloud Keeper
HADD • 1695QX6877 • $28

3506.
The Lollipop Guild™
LYLE • 1995QX8029 • $46
Set/3

3507.
Lucy Gets in Pictures
VOTR • 1395QX6547 • $25

3508.
Madame Alexander® 4:
Red Queen – Alice in
Wonderland®
FRAN • 1495QX6379 • $22

3509.
Madame Alexander®
Holiday Angels 2:
Angel of the Nativity
FRAN • 1495QX6419 • $34

3510.
Majestic Wilderness 3:
Curious Raccoons
1295QX6287 • $20

3511.
Marilyn Monroe 3
ANDR • 1495QX6389 • $28

3512.
Mary's Angels 12: Heather
CHAD/HAMI • 795QX6329 • $28

3513.
Mary's Bears
HAMI/TAGU • 1295QX5569 • $18

3514.
Merry Motorcycle
SICK • 895QX6637 • $17

3515.
Merry Olde Santa 10
RHOD • 1595QX6359 • $26

3516.
Mickey's Holiday Parade 3:
Donald Plays the Cymbals
1395QXD4057 • $36

3517.
Military on Parade
CROW • 1095QX6639 • $30

3518.
Milk 'n' Cookies Express
CHAD • 895QX6839 • $16

3519.
Millennium Princess
BARBIE™
RGRS • 1595QXI4019 • $38

3520.
Millennium Princess
BARBIE™ (African-American)
RGRS • 1595QXI6449 • $34

3521.
Millennium Snowman
SEAL • 895QX8059 • $38

3522.
Millennium Snowman
SEAL • GiftQX8059C1 • $303
Store recruitment gift.

3523.
Mischievous Kittens 1
AUBE • 995QX6427 • $96

3524.
Mischievous Kittens 1
AUBE • PrizeQX6427C • $435
Edition Size – 5000

3525.
Mom
BRIC • 895QX6717 • $14

3526.
Mom and Dad
SEAL • 995QX6709 • $19

3527.
Mother and Daughter
VOTR • 895QX6757 • $34

3528.
Muhammad Ali
UNRU • 1495QXI4147 • $19

3529.
A Musician of Note
HADD • 795QX6567 • $17

3530.
My Sister, My Friend
TAGU • 995QX6749 • $17

3531.
Naboo Starfighter™
WEBB • 1895QXI7613 • $32

3532.
NBA®: Charlotte Hornets™
KLIN • 1095QSR1057 • $12

3533.
NBA®: Chicago Bulls™
KLIN • 1095QSR1019 • $12

3534.
NBA®: Detroit Pistons™
KLIN • 1095QSR1027 • $12

3535.
NBA®: Houston Rockets™
KLIN • 1095QSR1029 • $12

3536.
NBA®: Indiana Pacers™
KLIN • 1095QSR1037 • $12

3537.
NBA®: Los Angelas Lakers™
KLIN • 1095QSR1039 • $12

3538.
NBA®: New York Knicks™
KLIN • 1095QSR1047 • $12

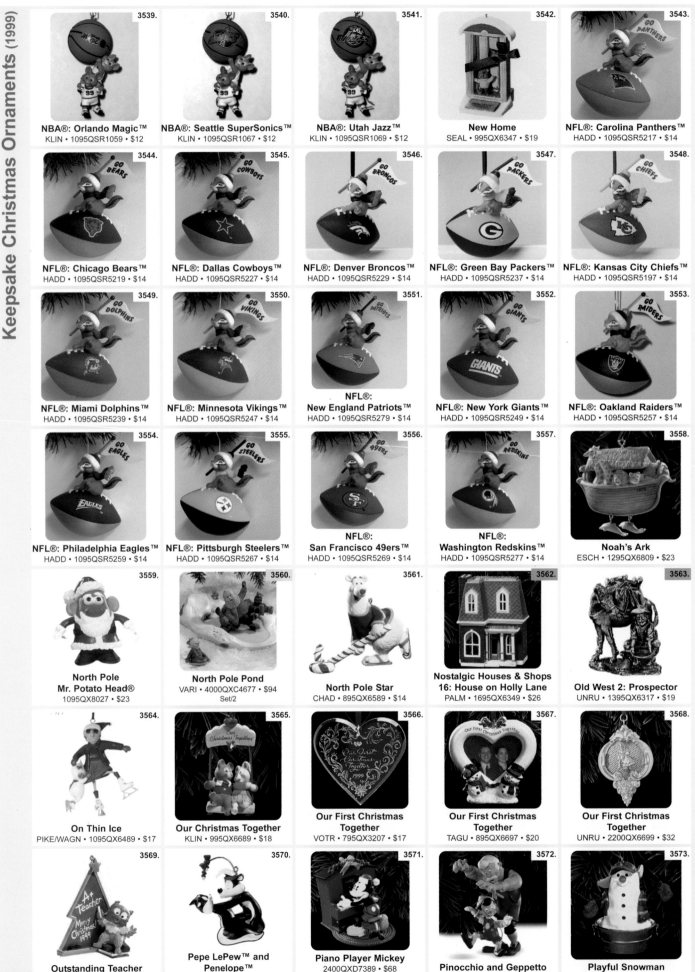

3539.
NBA®: Orlando Magic™
KLIN • 1095QSR1059 • $12

3540.
NBA®: Seattle SuperSonics™
KLIN • 1095QSR1067 • $12

3541.
NBA®: Utah Jazz™
KLIN • 1095QSR1069 • $12

3542.
New Home
SEAL • 995QX6347 • $19

3543.
NFL®: Carolina Panthers™
HADD • 1095QSR5217 • $14

3544.
NFL®: Chicago Bears™
HADD • 1095QSR5219 • $14

3545.
NFL®: Dallas Cowboys™
HADD • 1095QSR5227 • $14

3546.
NFL®: Denver Broncos™
HADD • 1095QSR5229 • $14

3547.
NFL®: Green Bay Packers™
HADD • 1095QSR5237 • $14

3548.
NFL®: Kansas City Chiefs™
HADD • 1095QSR5197 • $14

3549.
NFL®: Miami Dolphins™
HADD • 1095QSR5239 • $14

3550.
NFL®: Minnesota Vikings™
HADD • 1095QSR5247 • $14

3551.
**NFL®:
New England Patriots™**
HADD • 1095QSR5279 • $14

3552.
NFL®: New York Giants™
HADD • 1095QSR5249 • $14

3553.
NFL®: Oakland Raiders™
HADD • 1095QSR5257 • $14

3554.
NFL®: Philadelphia Eagles™
HADD • 1095QSR5259 • $14

3555.
NFL®: Pittsburgh Steelers™
HADD • 1095QSR5267 • $14

3556.
**NFL®:
San Francisco 49ers™**
HADD • 1095QSR5269 • $14

3557.
**NFL®:
Washington Redskins™**
HADD • 1095QSR5277 • $14

3558.
Noah's Ark
ESCH • 1295QX6809 • $23

3559.
**North Pole
Mr. Potato Head®**
1095QX8027 • $23

3560.
North Pole Pond
VARI • 4000QXC4677 • $94
Set/2

3561.
North Pole Star
CHAD • 895QX6589 • $14

3562.
**Nostalgic Houses & Shops
16: House on Holly Lane**
PALM • 1695QX6349 • $26

3563.
Old West 2: Prospector
UNRU • 1395QX6317 • $19

3564.
On Thin Ice
PIKE/WAGN • 1095QX6489 • $17

3565.
Our Christmas Together
KLIN • 995QX6689 • $18

3566.
**Our First Christmas
Together**
VOTR • 795QX3207 • $17

3567.
**Our First Christmas
Together**
TAGU • 895QX6697 • $20

3568.
**Our First Christmas
Together**
UNRU • 2200QX6699 • $32

3569.
Outstanding Teacher
KLIN • 895QX6627 • $11

3570.
**Pepe LePew™ and
Penelope™**
CHAD • 1295QX6507 • $25

3571.
Piano Player Mickey
2400QXD7389 • $68
MAGIC

3572.
Pinocchio and Geppetto
1695QXD4107 • $24

3573.
Playful Snowman
SICK • 1295QX6867 • $23

114

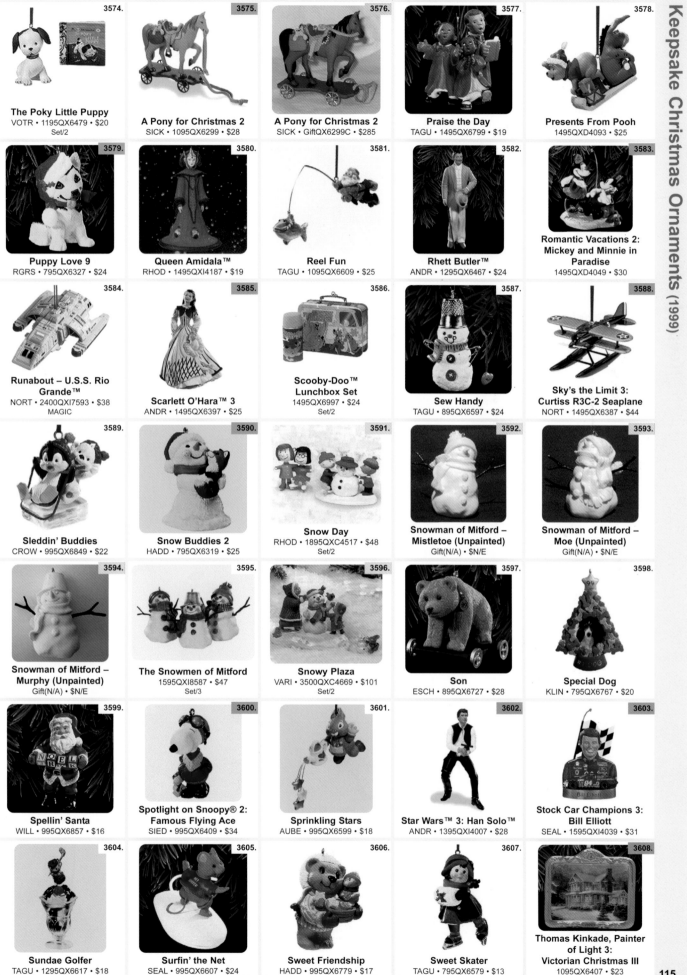

3574.
The Poky Little Puppy
VOTR • 1195QX6479 • $20
Set/2

3575.
A Pony for Christmas 2
SICK • 1095QX6299 • $28

3576.
A Pony for Christmas 2
SICK • GiftQX6299C • $285

3577.
Praise the Day
TAGU • 1495QX6799 • $19

3578.
Presents From Pooh
1495QXD4093 • $25

3579.
Puppy Love 9
RGRS • 795QX6327 • $24

3580.
Queen Amidala™
RHOD • 1495QXI4187 • $19

3581.
Reel Fun
TAGU • 1095QX6609 • $25

3582.
Rhett Butler™
ANDR • 1295QX6467 • $24

3583.
**Romantic Vacations 2:
Mickey and Minnie in
Paradise**
1495QXD4049 • $30

3584.
**Runabout – U.S.S. Rio
Grande™**
NORT • 2400QXI7593 • $38
MAGIC

3585.
Scarlett O'Hara™ 3
ANDR • 1495QX6397 • $25

3586.
**Scooby-Doo™
Lunchbox Set**
1495QX6997 • $24
Set/2

3587.
Sew Handy
TAGU • 895QX6597 • $24

3588.
**Sky's the Limit 3:
Curtiss R3C-2 Seaplane**
NORT • 1495QX6387 • $44

3589.
Sleddin' Buddies
CROW • 995QX6849 • $22

3590.
Snow Buddies 2
HADD • 795QX6319 • $25

3591.
Snow Day
RHOD • 1895QXC4517 • $48
Set/2

3592.
**Snowman of Mitford –
Mistletoe (Unpainted)**
Gift(N/A) • $N/E

3593.
**Snowman of Mitford –
Moe (Unpainted)**
Gift(N/A) • $N/E

3594.
**Snowman of Mitford –
Murphy (Unpainted)**
Gift(N/A) • $N/E

3595.
The Snowmen of Mitford
1595QXI8587 • $47
Set/3

3596.
Snowy Plaza
VARI • 3500QXC4669 • $101
Set/2

3597.
Son
ESCH • 895QX6727 • $28

3598.
Special Dog
KLIN • 795QX6767 • $20

3599.
Spellin' Santa
WILL • 995QX6857 • $16

3600.
**Spotlight on Snoopy® 2:
Famous Flying Ace**
SIED • 995QX6409 • $34

3601.
Sprinkling Stars
AUBE • 995QX6599 • $18

3602.
Star Wars™ 3: Han Solo™
ANDR • 1395QXI4007 • $28

3603.
**Stock Car Champions 3:
Bill Elliott**
SEAL • 1595QXI4039 • $31

3604.
Sundae Golfer
TAGU • 1295QX6617 • $18

3605.
Surfin' the Net
SEAL • 995QX6607 • $24

3606.
Sweet Friendship
HADD • 995QX6779 • $17

3607.
Sweet Skater
TAGU • 795QX6579 • $13

3608.
**Thomas Kinkade, Painter
of Light 3:
Victorian Christmas III**
1095QX6407 • $23

115

3609. Tigger Plays Soccer
1095QXD4119 • $22

3610. A Time of Peace
LARS • 895QX6807 • $16

3611. Tonka® 1956 Suburban Pumper No. 5
1395QX6459 • $42

3612. Town and Country 1: Farm House
SICK • 1595QX6439 • $23

3613. Town and Country Complement: Red Barn
SICK • 1595QX6947 • $23

3614. The Toymaker's Gift
CHAD • GiftQXC4519 • $16

3615. Unforgettable Villains 2: Snow White's Jealous Queen
1495QXD4089 • $24

3616. Waiting for a Hug
CHAD • GiftQXC4537 • $29

3617. Warm Welcome
HADD • 1695QLX7417 • $26
MAGIC

3618. Welcome to 2000
LARS • 1095QX6829 • $36

3619. Winnie the Pooh 2: Honey Time
1395QXD4129 • $25

3620. Winnie the Pooh and Christopher Robin®, Too 1: Playing with Pooh
1395QXD4197 • $24

3621. Wintertime Treat
UNRU • 1295QX6989 • $23

3622. Woody's Roundup – Toy Story
1395QXI4207 • $28

3623. Zebra Fantasy
SICK • 1495QX6559 • $23

2000

3624. 102 Dalmatians
1295QXI5231 • $40

3625. 1962 BARBIE™ Hatbox Doll Case
995QX6791 • $19

3626. Alice Meets the Cheshire Cat
1495QXD4011 • $23

3627. All Things Beautiful
VARI • 1395QX8351 • $16

3628. All-American Trucks 6: 1978 Dodge® Li'l Red Express Truck
PALM • 1395QX6581 • $28

3629. Angel of Promise
ANDR • 1495QXI4144 • $22

3630. Angel-Blessed Tree
ANDR/RGRS • 895QX8241 • $14

3631. Angelic Bell
BRIC • 1695QXC4504 • $28

3632. Angelic Trio
HADD • 1095QX8234 • $28

3633. Angels Over Bethlehem
RHOD • 1895QLX7563 • $35
MAGIC

3634. Arnold Palmer
UNRU • 1495QXI4324 • $19

3635. At the Ballpark 5: Mark McGwire
RHOD • 1495QXI5361 • $23

3636. At the Ballpark Complement: Ken Griffey, Jr.
1495QXI5251 • $22

3637. Baby's First Christmas
HADD • 895QX8031 • $14

3638. Baby's First Christmas
SEAL • 1095QX8034 • $14

3639. Baby's First Christmas
AUBE • 1895QX8041 • $32

3640. BARBIE™ 2000
ANDR • 1995QXC4602 • $120

3641. BARBIE™ 7: BARBIE™ Commuter Set
ANDR • 1595QX6814 • $26
Set/2

3642. BARBIE™ Angel of Joy™
RGRS • 1495QXI6861 • $20

116

3643.
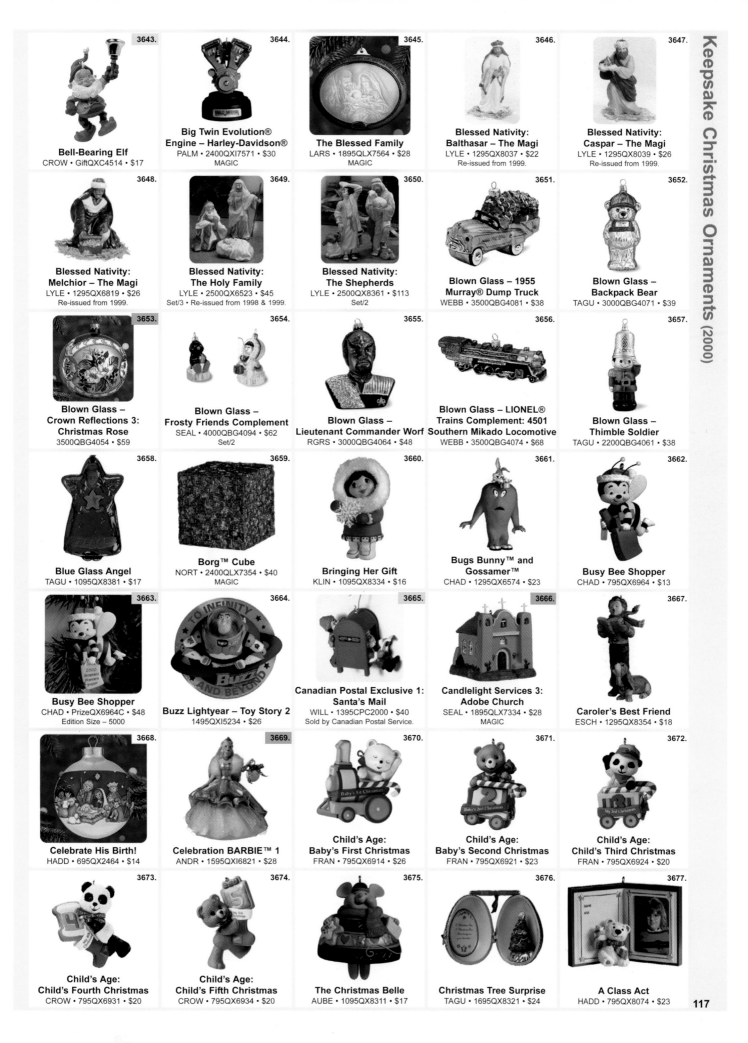
Bell-Bearing Elf
CROW • GiftQXC4514 • $17

3644.
**Big Twin Evolution®
Engine – Harley-Davidson®**
PALM • 2400QXI7571 • $30
MAGIC

3645.
The Blessed Family
LARS • 1895QLX7564 • $28
MAGIC

3646.
**Blessed Nativity:
Balthasar – The Magi**
LYLE • 1295QX8037 • $22
Re-issued from 1999.

3647.
**Blessed Nativity:
Caspar – The Magi**
LYLE • 1295QX8039 • $26
Re-issued from 1999.

3648.
**Blessed Nativity:
Melchior – The Magi**
LYLE • 1295QX6819 • $26
Re-issued from 1999.

3649.
**Blessed Nativity:
The Holy Family**
LYLE • 2500QX6523 • $45
Set/3 • Re-issued from 1998 & 1999.

3650.
**Blessed Nativity:
The Shepherds**
LYLE • 2500QX8361 • $113
Set/2

3651.
**Blown Glass – 1955
Murray® Dump Truck**
WEBB • 3500QBG4081 • $38

3652.
**Blown Glass –
Backpack Bear**
TAGU • 3000QBG4071 • $39

3653.
**Blown Glass –
Crown Reflections 3:
Christmas Rose**
3500QBG4054 • $59

3654.
**Blown Glass –
Frosty Friends Complement**
SEAL • 4000QBG4094 • $62
Set/2

3655.
**Blown Glass –
Lieutenant Commander Worf**
RGRS • 3000QBG4064 • $48

3656.
**Blown Glass – LIONEL®
Trains Complement: 4501
Southern Mikado Locomotive**
WEBB • 3500QBG4074 • $68

3657.
**Blown Glass –
Thimble Soldier**
TAGU • 2200QBG4061 • $38

3658.
Blue Glass Angel
TAGU • 1095QX8381 • $17

3659.
Borg™ Cube
NORT • 2400QLX7354 • $40
MAGIC

3660.
Bringing Her Gift
KLIN • 1095QX8334 • $16

3661.
**Bugs Bunny™ and
Gossamer™**
CHAD • 1295QX6574 • $23

3662.
Busy Bee Shopper
CHAD • 795QX6964 • $13

3663.
Busy Bee Shopper
CHAD • PrizeQX6964C • $48
Edition Size – 5000

3664.
Buzz Lightyear – Toy Story 2
1495QXI5234 • $26

3665.
**Canadian Postal Exclusive 1:
Santa's Mail**
WILL • 1395CPC2000 • $40
Sold by Canadian Postal Service.

3666.
**Candlelight Services 3:
Adobe Church**
SEAL • 1895QLX7334 • $28
MAGIC

3667.
Caroler's Best Friend
ESCH • 1295QX8354 • $18

3668.
Celebrate His Birth!
HADD • 695QX2464 • $14

3669.
Celebration BARBIE™ 1
ANDR • 1595QXI6821 • $28

3670.
**Child's Age:
Baby's First Christmas**
FRAN • 795QX6914 • $26

3671.
**Child's Age:
Baby's Second Christmas**
FRAN • 795QX6921 • $23

3672.
**Child's Age:
Child's Third Christmas**
FRAN • 795QX6924 • $20

3673.
**Child's Age:
Child's Fourth Christmas**
CROW • 795QX6931 • $20

3674.
**Child's Age:
Child's Fifth Christmas**
CROW • 795QX6934 • $20

3675.
The Christmas Belle
AUBE • 1095QX8311 • $17

3676.
Christmas Tree Surprise
TAGU • 1695QX8321 • $24

3677.
A Class Act
HADD • 795QX8074 • $23

117

3678.
Classic American Cars 10:
1969 Pontiac®
GTO™ – The Judge
PALM • 1395QX6584 • $28

3679.
Close-Knit Friends
SEAL • 1495QX8204 • $26
Set/2

3680.
Collegiate:
Alabama Crimson Tide™
995QSR2344 • $12

3681.
Collegiate: Florida Gators™
995QSR2324 • $12

3682.
Collegiate:
Florida State Seminoles™
995QSR2341 • $12

3683.
Collegiate:
Kentucky Wildcats™
995QSR2291 • $12

3684.
Collegiate:
Michigan Wolverines™
995QSR2271 • $12

3685.
Collegiate:
Nebraska Cornhuskers™
995QSR2321 • $12

3686.
Collegiate:
North Carolina Tar Heels™
995QSR2304 • $12

3687.
Collegiate:
Notre Dame Fighting Irish™
995QSR2284 • $12

3688.
Collegiate:
Penn State Nittany Lions™
995QSR2311 • $12

3689.
Collegiate:
Tennessee Volunteers™
995QSR2334 • $12

3690.
Cool Character
SICK • 1295QX8271 • $19

3691.
Cool Decade 1
HADD • 795QX6764 • $24

3692.
Cool Decade 1
HADD • GiftQX6764C • $80

3693.
Dad
CHAD • 895QX8071 • $13

3694.
Dale Earnhardt
SEAL • 1495QXI6754 • $60

3695.
Dancin' In Christmas
TAGU • 795QX6971 • $13

3696.
Darth Maul™
ANDR • 1495QXI6885 • $29

3697.
Daughter
ESCH • 895QX8081 • $26

3698.
Dog Dish Dilemma
1295QXD4044 • $24

3699.
Dousin' Dalmatian
SEAL • 995QX8024 • $25

3700.
Dr. Seuss® Books 2:
One Fish Two Fish Red
Fish Blue Fish™
WILL • 1495QX6781 • $40

3701.
Dressing Cinderella
1295QXD4109 • $27

3702.
Fashion Afoot 1
ESCH • 1495QX8341 • $22

3703.
Favorite Bible Stories 2:
Jonah and the Great Fish
LARS • 1395QX6701 • $26

3704.
Feliz Navidad
RGRS • 895QX8214 • $26

3705.
The Fishing Hole
VISK • 1295QX6984 • $15

3706.
Football Legends 6:
John Elway
RHOD • 1495QXI6811 • $22

3707.
Friendly Greeting
ESCH • 995QX8174 • $23

3708.
Friends in Harmony
FRAN • 995QX8001 • $16

3709.
Frosty Friends 21
SEAL • 1095QX6601 • $19

3710.
Frosty Friends 21
SEAL • PrizeQX6601C • $285
Edition Size – 5000

3711.
Frosty Friends Complement:
Frosty Friends
SEAL • 1895QX8524 • $25
Set/4

3712.
G.I. Joe® – Action Pilot
CROW • 1395QX6734 • $26

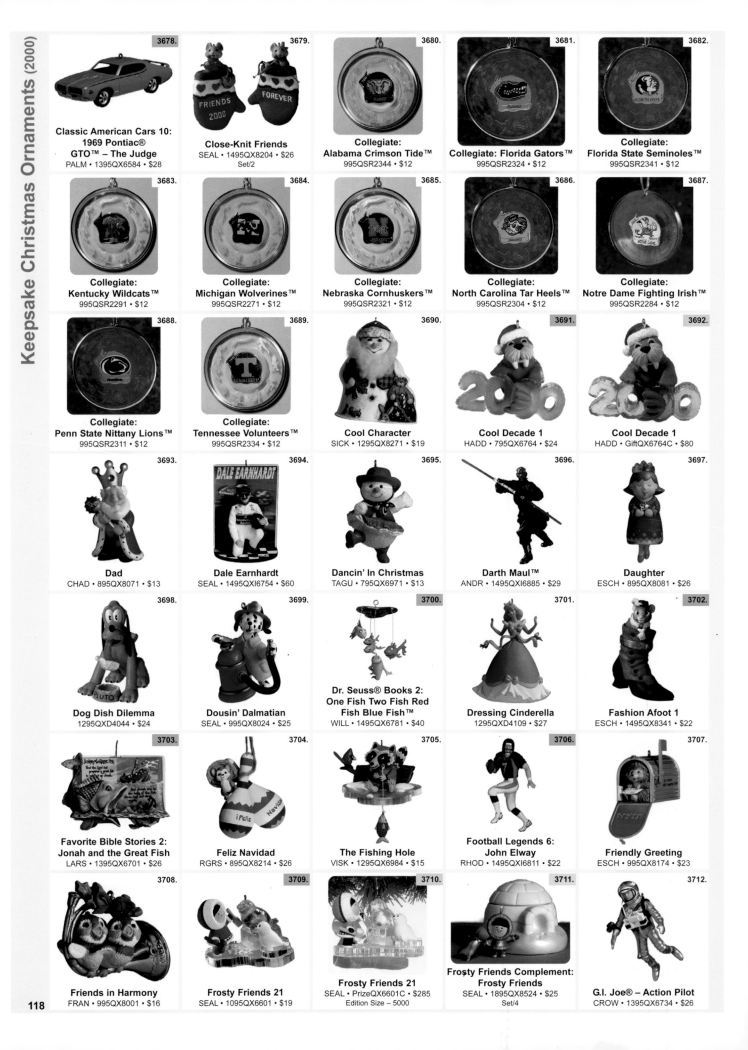

3713.
Gift Bearers 2
TAGU • 1295QX6651 • $40

3714.
Gifts for the Grinch™
KLIN • 1295QXI5344 • $31

3715.
Gingerbread Church
LAPR • 995QX8244 • $20

3716.
Godchild
TAGU • 795QX8161 • $18

3717.
Gold-Star Teacher
PIKE • 795QX6951 • $12

3718.
Gold-Star Teacher
PIKE • GiftQX6951C • $28

3719.
Golfer Supreme
SEAL • 1095QX6991 • $19

3720.
The Good Book
UNRU • 1395QX8254 • $26

3721.
Graceful Glory
HAAS/VOTR • 1895QX8304 • $28

3722.
Granddaughter
FORS • 895QX8091 • $23

3723.
Grandma's House
LARS • 1095QX8141 • $16

3724.
Grandson
FORS • 895QX8094 • $23

3725.
The Great Oz™
CROW • 3200QLX7361 • $59
MAGIC

3726.
Gungan™ Submarine
RHOD • 2400QXI7351 • $40
MAGIC

3727.
Happy Holidays®
BARBIE™ 5
ANDR • 1595QXC4494 • $60

3728.
Harley-Davidson®
BARBIE™
RGRS • 1495QXI8554 • $19

3729.
Harley-Davidson®
Motorcycle Milestones 2:
Fat Boy
PALM • 1495QXI6774 • $27

3730.
Harry Potter™:
Harry Potter™
BRIC • 1295QXE4381 • $28

3731.
Harry Potter™:
Hedwig the Owl™
BRIC • 795QXE4394 • $28

3732.
Harry Potter™:
Hermione Granger™
BRIC • 1295QXE4391 • $28

3733.
Harry Potter™:
Hogwarts™ Charms
KLIN • 1295QXE4404 • $35
Set/6

3734.
Harry Potter™:
Hogwarts™ Crest
BRIC • 1495QXE4411 • $30

3735.
Harry Potter™:
Professor Dumbledore™
BRIC • 1295QXE4384 • $28

3736.
Here Comes Santa 22:
Sleigh X-2000
WILL • 1495QX6824 • $23

3737.
Hockey Greats 4:
Eric Lindros
FRAN • 1595QXI6801 • $28

3738.
A Holiday Gathering
1095QX8561 • $19

3739.
Holly Berry Bell
FORS • 1495QX8291 • $19

3740.
Hoop Stars 6: Karl Malone
UNRU • 1495QXI6901 • $28

3741.
Hooray for the U.S.A.
CHAD • 995QX8281 • $17

3742.
Hopalong Cassidy™
Lunchbox Set
1495QX6714 • $24
Set/2

3743.
Hot Wheels™ 1968
Deora Car
UNRU • 1495QXI6891 • $23
Set/3

3744.
Hot Wheels™ 1968
Deora Car
UNRU • 1495QXI6891G • $23
Set/3

3745.
Imperial Stormtrooper™
KLIN • 1495QXI6711 • $28

3746.
Jeannie –
I Dream of Jeannie™
ANDR • 1495QXI8564 • $24
Set/2

3747.
Jingle Bell Kringle
CROW • GiftQXC4481 • $20

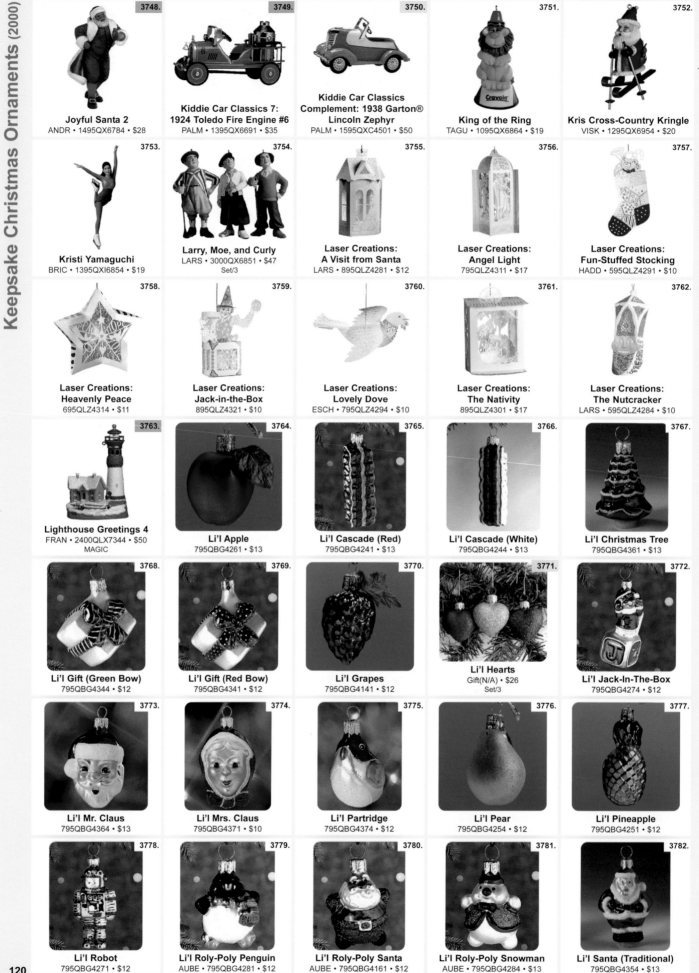

3748.
Joyful Santa 2
ANDR • 1495QX6784 • $28

3749.
Kiddie Car Classics 7:
1924 Toledo Fire Engine #6
PALM • 1395QX6691 • $35

3750.
Kiddie Car Classics
Complement: 1938 Garton®
Lincoln Zephyr
PALM • 1595QXC4501 • $50

3751.
King of the Ring
TAGU • 1095QX6864 • $19

3752.
Kris Cross-Country Kringle
VISK • 1295QX6954 • $20

3753.
Kristi Yamaguchi
BRIC • 1395QXI6854 • $19

3754.
Larry, Moe, and Curly
LARS • 3000QX6851 • $47
Set/3

3755.
Laser Creations:
A Visit from Santa
LARS • 895QLZ4281 • $12

3756.
Laser Creations:
Angel Light
795QLZ4311 • $17

3757.
Laser Creations:
Fun-Stuffed Stocking
HADD • 595QLZ4291 • $10

3758.
Laser Creations:
Heavenly Peace
695QLZ4314 • $11

3759.
Laser Creations:
Jack-in-the-Box
895QLZ4321 • $10

3760.
Laser Creations:
Lovely Dove
ESCH • 795QLZ4294 • $10

3761.
Laser Creations:
The Nativity
895QLZ4301 • $17

3762.
Laser Creations:
The Nutcracker
LARS • 595QLZ4284 • $10

3763.
Lighthouse Greetings 4
FRAN • 2400QLX7344 • $50
MAGIC

3764.
Li'l Apple
795QBG4261 • $13

3765.
Li'l Cascade (Red)
795QBG4241 • $13

3766.
Li'l Cascade (White)
795QBG4244 • $13

3767.
Li'l Christmas Tree
795QBG4361 • $13

3768.
Li'l Gift (Green Bow)
795QBG4344 • $12

3769.
Li'l Gift (Red Bow)
795QBG4341 • $12

3770.
Li'l Grapes
795QBG4141 • $12

3771.
Li'l Hearts
Gift(N/A) • $26
Set/3

3772.
Li'l Jack-In-The-Box
795QBG4274 • $12

3773.
Li'l Mr. Claus
795QBG4364 • $13

3774.
Li'l Mrs. Claus
795QBG4371 • $10

3775.
Li'l Partridge
795QBG4374 • $12

3776.
Li'l Pear
795QBG4254 • $12

3777.
Li'l Pineapple
795QBG4251 • $12

3778.
Li'l Robot
795QBG4271 • $12

3779.
Li'l Roly-Poly Penguin
AUBE • 795QBG4281 • $12

3780.
Li'l Roly-Poly Santa
AUBE • 795QBG4161 • $12

3781.
Li'l Roly-Poly Snowman
AUBE • 795QBG4284 • $13

3782.
Li'l Santa (Traditional)
795QBG4354 • $13

3783. Li'l Snowman (Traditional)
795QBG4351 • $12

3784. Li'l Stars (Metallic Look)
995QBG4221 • $28
Set/3

3785. Li'l Stars (Patriotic)
995QBG4214 • $35
Set/3

3786. Li'l Stars (Traditional)
995QBG4224 • $28
Set/3

3787. Li'l Swirl (Green)
795QBG4234 • $12

3788. Li'l Swirl (Red)
795QBG4231 • $12

3789. Li'l Teddy Bear
795QBG4264 • $12

3790. LIONEL® Trains 5: LIONEL® General Steam Locomotive
1895QX6684 • $31

3791. LIONEL® Trains Complement: 700E J-1E Hudson Steam Locomotive
2200QXI5261 • $53

3792. LIONEL® Trains Complement: General Steam Locomotive Tender
1595QX6834 • $35

3793. Loggin' On To Santa
PIKE • 1295QX8224 • $14

3794. The Lone Ranger™
UNRU • 1595QX6941 • $40

3795. "Lucy Is Enciente"
VOTR • 1595QX6884 • $75

3796. The Lullabye League™
LYLE • 1995QX6604 • $32
Set/3

3797. Madame Alexander® 5: Christmas Holly
FRAN • 1495QX6611 • $32

3798. Madame Alexander® Holiday Angels 3: Twilight Angel
FRAN • 1495QX6614 • $54

3799. Majestic Wilderness 4: Foxes in the Forest
1295QX6794 • $36

3800. Mary's Angels 13: Marguerite
CHAD/HAMI • 795QX6571 • $35

3801. Mary's Angels Complement: Mary's Angels
CHAD/HAMI • 1895QLX7561 • $68
MAGIC

3802. Max
795QX8584 • $26

3803. Memories of Christmas
SICK • 1295QX8264 • $19

3804. Merry Ballooning
BRIC/HADD • 1695QX8384 • $24

3805. Mickey's Bedtime Reading
1095QXD4077 • $28

3806. Mickey's Holiday Parade 4: Baton Twirler Daisy
1395QXD4034 • $26

3807. Mickey's Sky Rider
1895QXD4159 • $32

3808. Millennium Express
CROW • 4200QLX7364 • $105
MAGIC

3809. Millennium Snowma'am
895QXI5241 • $14

3810. Millennium Time Capsule
UNRU • 1895QX8044 • $26

3811. Mischievous Kittens 2
AUBE • 995QX6641 • $19

3812. Mom
CHAD • 895QX8064 • $13

3813. Mom and Dad
BRIC • 995QX8061 • $19

3814. Mother and Daughter
RGRS • 995QX8154 • $28

3815. Mr. Monopoly™
SIED • 1095QX8101 • $17

3816. Mrs. Claus's Holiday
KLIN • 995QX8011 • $14

3817. Nature's Sketchbook: Snowy Garden
BAST/LYLE • 1395QX8284 • $26

3818.
New Home
SEAL • 895QX8171 • $28

3819.
New Millennium Baby
VOTR • 1095QX8581 • $17

3820.
The Newborn Prince –
Bambi
1395QXD4194 • $20

3821.
NFL®: Cleveland Browns™
SIED • 995QSR5161 • $14

3822.
NFL®: Dallas Cowboys™
SIED • 995QSR5121 • $14

3823.
NFL®: Denver Broncos™
SIED • 995QSR5111 • $14

3824.
NFL®: Green Bay Packers™
SIED • 995QSR5114 • $14

3825.
NFL®: Kansas City Chiefs™
SIED • 995QSR5131 • $14

3826.
NFL®: Miami Dolphins™
SIED • 995QSR5144 • $14

3827.
NFL®: Minnesota Vikings™
SIED • 995QSR5164 • $14

3828.
NFL®: Pittsburgh Steelers™
SIED • 995QSR5124 • $14

3829.
NFL®:
San Francisco 49ers™
SIED • 995QSR5134 • $14

3830.
NFL®:
Washington Redskins™
SIED • 995QSR5151 • $14

3831.
North Pole Network
SEAL • 1095QX6994 • $18

3832.
Northern Art Bear
LAPR • 895QX8294 • $26

3833.
Nostalgic Houses &
Shops 17: Schoolhouse
PALM • 1495QX6591 • $32

3834.
Off to Neverland! –
Peter Pan
1295QXD4004 • $31

3835.
Old West 3: Mountain Man
UNRU • 1595QX6594 • $40

3836.
Our Christmas Together
KLIN • 995QX8054 • $14

3837.
Our Family
AUBE • 795QX8211 • $24

3838.
Our First Christmas
Together
VOTR • 795QX3104 • $13

3839.
Our First Christmas
Together
SIED • 895QX8051 • $13

3840.
Our First Christmas
Together
UNRU • 1095QX8701 • $19

3841.
Our Lady of Guadalupe
VISK • 1295QX8231 • $23

3842.
A Pony for Christmas 3
SICK • 1295QX6624 • $22

3843.
A Pony for Christmas 3
SICK • GiftQX6624C • $86

3844.
The Proud Collector
SEAL • GiftQXC4511 • $28

3845.
Puppy Love 10
RGRS • 795QX6554 • $15

3846.
Qui-Gon Jinn™
ANDR • 1495QXI6741 • $26

3847.
A Reader to the Core
AUBE • 995QX6974 • $26

3848.
Rhett Butler™
ANDR • 1295QX6674 • $28

3849.
Ringing Reindeer
ESCH • GiftQXC4484 • $22

3850.
Robot Parade 1
WILL • 1695QX6771 • $19

3851.
Romantic Vacations 3:
Donald and Daisy
at Lovers' Lodge
1495QXD4031 • $28

3852.
Safe in Noah's Ark
HADD • 1095QX8514 • $20

3853.
Santa's Chair
CHAD • 1295QX8314 • $25

3854.
Scarlett O'Hara™ 4
ANDR • 1495QX6671 • $42

3855.
Scooby-Doo™
RGRS • 1295QXI8394 • $29

3856.
Scuffy the Tugboat™
VOTR • 1195QX6871 • $18
Set/2

3857.
Self-Portrait
PIKE/WAGN • 1095QX6644 • $22

3858.
Seven of Nine™
RGRS • 1495QX6844 • $28

3859.
Signature Snowman
HADD • 995QXC4524 • $17

3860.
Sister to Sister
VOTR • 1295QX8144 • $19

3861.
**Sky's the Limit 4:
Spirit of St. Louis**
NORT • 1495QX6634 • $65

3862.
**A Snoopy® Christmas:
Charlie Brown™**
SIED • 495QRP4191 • $14

3863.
**A Snoopy® Christmas:
Linus**
SIED • 495QRP4204 • $9

3864.
**A Snoopy® Christmas:
Lucy**
SIED • 495QRP4174 • $9

3865.
**A Snoopy® Christmas:
Snoopy™**
SIED • 495QRP4184 • $14

3866.
**A Snoopy® Christmas:
Woodstock™ on Doghouse**
SIED • 495QRP4211 • $10

3867.
Snow Buddies 3
HADD • 795QX6654 • $26

3868.
Snow Girl
ESCH • 995QX8274 • $23

3869.
The Snowmen of Mitford
1995QXI5244 • $26
Set/4

3870.
Son
ESCH • 895QX8084 • $14

3871.
**Spotlight on Snoopy® 3:
The Detective**
SIED • 995QX6564 • $22

3872.
**Star Wars™ 4:
Obi-Wan Kenobi™**
RHOD • 1495QXI6704 • $32

3873.
Stroll Round the Pole
AUBE • 1095QX8164 • $14

3874.
**Super Friends™
Lunchbox Set**
1495QX6724 • $19
Set/2

3875.
**Surprise Package –
Blue's Clues™**
BRIC • 1095QXI8391 • $23

3876.
Tending Her Topiary
KLIN • 995QX8004 • $13

3877.
Time for Joy
CROW • 2400QX6904 • $48

3878.
Together We Serve
WILL • 995QX8021 • $16

3879.
Tonka® Dump Truck
1395QX6681 • $26

3880.
**Town and Country 2:
Bait Shop with Boat**
SICK • 1595QX6631 • $23

3881.
Toy Shop Serenade
HADD • 1695QX8301 • $23

3882.
Toymaker Santa 1
CROW • 1495QX6751 • $23

3883.
Treasure Tree
VARI • 6500QXC4521 • $140
Set/19 • Limited Edition – 25000

3884.
Tree Guy
CHAD • 895QX6961 • $13

3885.
**Unforgettable Villains 3:
Sleeping Beauty's
Maleficent**
1495QXD4001 • $35

3886.
**VeggieTales® –
Bob the Tomato™ and
Larry the Cucumber™**
LYLE • 995QXI4334 • $20

3887.
A Visit from St. Nicholas
LARS • 1095QX8344 • $17

123

3888.
Warm Kindness
HADD • 895QX8014 • $32

3889.
Warmed by Candleglow
LARS • 695QX2471 • $17

3890.
Winnie the Pooh 3:
A Blustery Day
1395QXD4021 • $23

3891.
Winnie the Pooh and
Christopher Robin®, Too 2:
Story Time with Pooh
1395QXD4024 • $20

3892.
Winnie the Pooh:
Piglet's Jack-in-the-Box
1495QXD4187 • $20

3893.
Winnie the Pooh:
Pooh Chooses the Tree
1295QXD4157 • $32

3894.
Winter Fun with
BARBIE™ and Kelly™
ESCH • 1595QXI6561 • $22

3895.
Winterberry Santa
CHAD • 1495QXI4331 • $19

3896.
The Yellow Submarine™
- The Beatles
WILL • 1395QXI6841 • $28

3897.
Yule Tide Runner
KLIN • 995QX6981 • $32

2001

3898.
1950s BARBIE™ Ornament
ANDR • 1495QXI8882 • $32

3899.
1961 BARBIE™ Hatbox Case
995QX6922 • $17

3900.
1968 Silhouette™ and Case
WEBB • 1495QX6605 • $19
Set/2

3901.
2000 Oscar Mayer
Wienermobile™
WEBB • 1295QX6935 • $25

3902.
2001 Jeep™ Sport Wrangler
WEBB • 1495QXI6362 • $34

3903.
2001 Time Capsule
VISK • 995QX2802 • $22

3904.
2001 Vacation
WEBB • 995QX2822 • $16

3905.
All-American Trucks 7: 1959
Chevrolet® El Camino™
PALM • 1395QX6072 • $32

3906.
All-Sport Santa
RHOD • 995QX8332 • $16

3907.
All-Star Kid Memory Keeper
VOTR • 995QX2805 • $18

3908.
America for Me!
FORS • 995QX2882 • $31

3909.
Anakin Skywalker™
ANDR • 1495QX6942 • $25

3910.
Angel of Faith
LYLE • 1495QXI5375 • $30

3911.
Angel's Whisper
LYLE • 995QX8852 • $18

3912.
At the Ballpark 6:
Sammy Sosa
RHOD • 1495QXI6375 • $25

3913.
At the Ballpark Complement:
Mickey Mantle –
New York Yankees™
RHOD • 1495QXI6804 • $45

3914.
Baby's First Christmas
AUBE • 895QX8355 • $32

3915.
Baby's First Christmas
HADD • 895QX8362 • $16

3916.
Baby's First Christmas
RGRS • 995QX8482 • $17

3917.
Baby's First Christmas
(Boy)
HADD • 895QX8365 • $19

3918.
Baby's First Christmas
(Girl)
HADD • 895QX8372 • $18

3919.
Bambi Discovers Winter
2400QXD7541 • $38
MAGIC

3920.
BARBIE™ 2001
ANDR • 1995QXC4531 • $89

3921.
BARBIE™ 8: BARBIE™
in Busy Gal™ Fashion
RGRS • 1595QX6965 • $23
Set/2

3922.
BARBIE™ and Kelly™
on the Ice
BRIC • 1595QXI6915 • $20

3923.
BARBIE™ Angel Ornament
RGRS • 1595QXI6925 • $23
Set/2

3924.
BARBIE™ as the Sugar
Plum Princess
ANDR • 1595QXI6132 • $36
Set/2

3925.
Beautiful Cross
UNRU • 995QX8825 • $19

3926.
Beginning Ballet
AUBE • 1295QX2875 • $16

3927.
Bell-Ringing Santa –
Mickey Mouse
995QXD4125 • $19

3928.
Blown Glass – LIONEL®
I-400E Blue
Comet Locomotive
WEBB • 3500QBG4355 • $60

3929.
Blown Glass – Q
RGRS • 2400QBG4345 • $48

3930.
Blue and Periwinkle –
Blue's Clues™
KLIN • 995QXI6142 • $18

3931.
Canadian Postal Exclusive 2:
Friendly Greetings
ESCH • 1395QX8174C • $38
Sold by Canadian Postal Service.

3932.
Candlelight Services 4:
Brick Church
SEAL • 1895QLX7552 • $34
MAGIC

3933.
Captain Benjamin Sisko
RGRS • 1495QX6865 • $24

3934.
Carving Santa
LARS • 1295QX8265 • $18

3935.
Carving Santa
LARS • PrizeQX8265C • $698
Edition Size – 54

3936.
Celebration BARBIE™ 2
ANDR • 1595QXI5202 • $26

3937.
Child's Age:
Baby's First Christmas
FRAN • 795QX8375 • $24

3938.
Child's Age:
Baby's Second Christmas
FRAN • 795QX8382 • $20

3939.
Child's Age:
Child's Third Christmas
FRAN • 795QX8385 • $15

3940.
Child's Age:
Child's Fourth Christmas
FRAN • 795QX8392 • $15

3941.
Child's Age:
Child's Fifth Christmas
CROW • 795QX8395 • $15

3942.
Christmas Brings Us
Together
LARS • 995QX8285 • $29

3943.
The Christmas Cone
SICK • 895QX8875 • $16

3944.
Christmas Parrot
VISK • 895QX8175 • $20

3945.
Cinderella's Castle
1800QXD4172 • $31

3946.
Classic American
Cars 11: 1953 Buick®
Roadmaster Skylark
PALM • 1395QX6872 • $40

3947.
Coca-Cola® – Cool Sport
HADD • 1495QHB9002 • $15

3948.
Collegiate:
Alabama Crimson Tide™
RHOD • 995QSR2132 • $12

3949.
Collegiate:
Florida Gators™
RHOD • 995QSR2165 • $12

3950.
Collegiate:
Florida State Seminoles™
RHOD • 995QSR2162 • $12

3951.
Collegiate:
Kentucky Wildcats™
RHOD • 995QSR2152 • $12

3952.
Collegiate:
Michigan Wolverines™
RHOD • 995QSR2142 • $12

3953.
Collegiate:
Nebraska Cornhuskers™
RHOD • 995QSR2135 • $12

3954.
Collegiate:
North Carolina Tar Heels™
RHOD • 995QSR2155 • $12

3955.
Collegiate:
Notre Dame Fighting Irish™
RHOD • 995QSR2145 • $12

3956.
Collegiate:
Penn State Nittany Lions™
RHOD • 995QSR2122 • $12

3957.

Collegiate:
Tennessee Volunteers™
RHOD • 995QSR2125 • $12

3958.

Color Crew Chief
TAGU • 1095QX6185 • $20

3959.

Cooking for Christmas:
Creative Cutter
ESCH • 995QX8865 • $16

3960.

Cooking for Christmas:
Creative Cutter
ESCH • PrizeQX8865C • $60
Edition Size – 5000

3961.
Cooking for Christmas:
Santa Sneaks a Sweet
UNRU • 1595QX8862 • $25

3962.

Cooking for Christmas:
Sharing Santa's Snacks
AUBE • 895QX8212 • $23

3963.

Cooking for Christmas:
Sharing Santa's Snacks
AUBE • GiftQX8212C • $62

3964.

Cool Decade 2
HADD • 795QX6992 • $22

3965.

Cool Decade 2
HADD • GiftQX6992C • $70
Edition Size – 15000

3966.
Cool Patriot
SEAL • 995QX8059C2 • $28

3967.

Cozy Home
VOTR • 995QX8965 • $17

3968.

A Cup of Friendship
CHAD • 995QX8472 • $17

3969.

Dad
SICK • 895QX8422 • $20

3970.

Dale Jarrett
WEBB • 1495QXI5205 • $23

3971.
Daughter
SICK • 895QX8425 • $22

3972.

Disney's School Bus
Lunchbox Set
1495QXD4115 • $35
Set/2

3973.

Donald Goes Motoring
1295QXD4122 • $20

3974.

Dr. Seuss® Books 3:
Horton™ Hatches the Egg
WILL • 1495QX6282 • $30
Set/2

3975.

Farewell Scene –
Gone With The Wind™
ANDR • 2400QLX7562 • $50
MAGIC

3976.

Fashion Afoot 2
ESCH • 1495QX8105 • $22

3977.

Favorite Bible Stories 3:
Daniel in the Lions' Den
LARS • 1395QX8122 • $26

3978.

Feliz Navidad
FORS • 995QX8185 • $13

3979.

The First Walgreen's
Drugstore
995QGO3082 • $22

3980.

Football Legends 7:
Brett Favre
RHOD • 1495QXI5232 • $48

3981.

Football Legends
Complement: Steve Young –
San Francisco 49ers™
UNRU • 1495QXI6305 • $44

3982.

Four-Alarm Friends
CROW • 995QX8325 • $18

3983.

Friendly Elves
FORS • 1495QX8805 • $15
Set/2

3984.

Frostlight Faeries:
Beaded Snowflakes (Blue)
995QP1712 • $17
Set/3 • Re-issued in 2002.

3985.
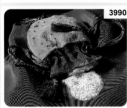
Frostlight Faeries: Beaded
Snowflakes (Periwinkle)
995QP1725 • $28
Set/3 • Re-issued in 2002.

3986.

Frostlight Faeries: Beaded
Snowflakes (Violet)
995QP1732 • $28
Set/3 • Re-issued in 2002.

3987.
Frostlight Faeries:
Faerie Brilliana
ESCH • 1495QP1672 • $34

3988.
Frostlight Faeries:
Faerie Candessa
ESCH • 1495QP1665 • $25

3989.
Frostlight Faeries:
Faerie Delandra
ESCH • 1495QP1685 • $34

3990.
Frostlight Faeries:
Faerie Dust
595QP1752 • $18

3991.
Frostlight Faeries:
Faerie Estrella
ESCH • 1495QP1695 • $22

3992.
Frostlight Faeries:
Faerie Floriella
ESCH • 1495QP1692 • $29

3993.
Frostlight Faeries:
Frostlight Fir Tree
4500QP1762 • $69

3994.
Frostlight Faeries:
Frostlight Flowers
1595QP1705 • $20

3995.
Frostlight Faeries:
Glistening Icicles
1295QP1742 • $34
Set/12

3996.
Frostlight Faeries:
Snowflake Garland
1295QP1745 • $17

3997.
Frosty Friends 22
SEAL • 1095QX8012 • $24

3998.
Frosty Friends 22
SEAL • 1095QX8012C • $48

3999.
G.I. Joe® – Fighter Pilot
CROW • 1395QX6045 • $29

4000.
Gift Bearers 3
TAGU • 1295QX8115 • $28

4001.
Godchild
TAGU • 795QX8452 • $22

4002.
Gouda Reading
KLIN • 995QX2855 • $24

4003.
Graceful Angel Bell
VOTR • 1295QX8182 • $17

4004.
Graceful Reindeer
KLIN • 2095QX8912 • $25
Set/3

4005.
Grandchild's First
Christmas
VOTR • 895QX8485 • $14

4006.
Granddaughter
PIKE • 895QX8435 • $14

4007.
Grandmother
PIKE • 995QX8445 • $17

4008.
Grandson
PIKE • 895QX8442 • $13

4009.
Guiding Star
VISK • 995QX8962 • $12

4010.
Happy Snowman
AUBE • 895QX8942 • $19

4011.
Harley-Davidson® BARBIE™
PALM/RGRS • 1595QXI8885 • $35

4012.
Harley-Davidson®
Motorcycle Milestones 3:
1957 XL Sportster®
PALM • 1495QXI8125 • $44

4013.
Harry Potter™ –
The Mirror of Erised™
WILL • 1595QXI8645 • $24

4014.
Harry Potter™ –
The Potions Master
LARS • 1495QXI8652 • $24

4015.
Harry Potter™:
Fluffy™ on Guard
BRIC • 1295QXE4415 • $32

4016.
Harry Potter™:
Hagrid™ and Norbert
the Dragon™
FORS • 1595QXE4412 • $29

4017.
Harry Potter™:
Harry Potter™
1295QXE4402 • $25

4018.
Harry Potter™:
Hermione Granger™'s Trunk
PIKE • 1495QXE4422 • $31
Set/6

4019.
Harry Potter™:
Hogwarts™ School Crests
LAPR • 1295QXE4452 • $35
Set/5

4020.
Harry Potter™:
Ron Weasley and Scabbers™
BRIC • 1295QXE4405 • $26

4021.
Hello Dumbo
1295QXD4162 • $23

4022.
Here Comes Santa 23:
Santa's Snowplow
UNRU • 1495QX8065 • $25

4023.
Hockey Greats 5:
Jaromir Jagr
FRAN • 1595QXI6852 • $25

4024.
Hockey Greats Complement:
Mario Lemieux
FRAN • 1595QXI6155 • $23

4025.
Holiday Spa Tweety™
CHAD • 995QX6945 • $20

4026.
Hoop Stars 7: Tim Duncan
UNRU • 1495QXI5235 • $29

127

4027.
I Love My Dog
RGRS • 795QX8802 • $17

4028.
It Had to be You
UNRU • 995QX2815 • $20

4029.
Jar Jar Binks™
RHOD • 1495QX6882 • $24

4030.
The Jetsons™ Lunchbox Set
LAPR • 1495QX6312 • $18
Set/2

4031.
Jolly Santa Bells
AUBE • 1995QX8915 • $32
Set/3

4032.
Jolly Visitor
LARS • 695QX2235 • $11

4033.
Journey to Bethlehem Bell
BRIC • 1495QX8386 • $25

4034.
Joyful Santa 3
ANDR • 1495QX8152 • $23

4035.
Kiddie Car Classics 8: 1930 Custom Biplane
PALM • 1395QX6975 • $38

4036.
Kiddie Car Classics Complement: 1958 Custom Corvette®
WEBB • 1795QXC4505 • $55

4037.
Kiss the Cook
SIED • 995QX2852 • $17

4038.
Kris and the Kringles 1
CROW • 2400QX8112 • $34
MAGIC

4039.
The Land of Christmastime
VARI • 1295QX8282 • $17

4040.
Laptop Santa
RHOD • 795QX8972 • $18

4041.
Lazy Afternoon
FRAN • 995QX8335 • $16

4042.
Legend Of Santa Claus
ANDR • 4000QXC4585 • $75
Set/5

4043.
Lighthouse Greetings 5
FRAN • 2400QLX7572 • $42
MAGIC

4044.
Lionel Plays with Words
CROW • 1495QXI6902 • $15

4045.
LIONEL® Trains 6: LIONEL® Chessie Steam Special Locomotive
1895QX6092 • $32

4046.
LIONEL® Trains Complement: LIONEL® Chessie Steam Special Tender
1395QX6285 • $98

4047.
Local Clubs Pop
HADD • GiftQXC4512 • $24

4048.
"Lucy Does a TV Commercial"
VOTR • 1595QX6862 • $32

4049.
Madame Alexander® 6: Victorian Christmas
FRAN • 1495QX6855 • $23

4050.
Madame Alexander® Little Women 1: Margaret "Meg" March
FORS • 1595QX6315 • $23

4051.
A Magical Dress for Briar Rose – Sleeping Beauty
1495QXD4202 • $24

4052.
Mary and Joseph
UNRU • 1895QX8195 • $28

4053.
Mary Hamilton Angel Chorus
HAMI/LAPR • 695QX2232 • $14

4054.
Mary's Angels 14: Chrysantha
CHAD/HAMI • 795QX6985 • $28

4055.
Mary's Angels 14: Chrysantha
CHAD/HAMI • GiftQX6985C • $89
Edition Size – 15000

4056.
Merry Carolers
2400QXD7585 • $37
Musical.

4057.
Mickey's Holiday Parade 5: Pluto Plays Triangle
1395QXD4112 • $29

4058.
Mickey's Sweetheart Minnie Mouse
995QXD4192 • $17

4059.
Minnie's Sweetheart Mickey Mouse
995QXD4195 • $17

4060.
Mischievous Kittens 3
AUBE • 995QX8025 • $44

4061.
Miss Rose – Snowman of Mitford (Unpainted)
TAGU • Gift(N/A) • $35
Edition Size – 15000

4062.
Mistletoe Miss 1
AUBE • 1495QX8092 • $22

4063.
Mitford Snowman Jubilee
TAGU • 1995QX2825 • $56
Set/4

4064.
Mom
SICK • 895QX8415 • $23

4065.
Mom and Dad
PIKE • 995QX8462 • $17

4066.
Monsters, Inc.
1295QXI6145 • $44

4067.
Moose's Merry Christmas
LARS • 1295QX8835 • $44

4068.
Mother and Daughter
VOTR • 995QX6962 • $18

4069.
Mrs. Claus's Chair
CHAD • 1295QX6955 • $20

4070.
Mrs. Potts and Chip –
Beauty and the Beast
1295QXD4165 • $23
Set/2

4071.
The Mystery Machine™
CHAD • 1395QX6295 • $26

4072.
Naboo Royal Starship™
WEBB • 1895QX8475 • $31

4073.
Nature's Sketchbook:
My First Snowman
BAST/LYLE • 995QX4442 • $24

4074.
Nesting Nativity
SICK • 2000QXC4502 • $39
Set/5

4075.
NFL®: Cleveland Browns™
GOSL • 995QSR5572 • $14

4076.
NFL®: Dallas Cowboys™
GOSL • 995QSR5622 • $14

4077.
NFL®: Denver Broncos™
GOSL • 995QSR5545 • $14

4078.
NFL®: Green Bay Packers™
GOSL • 995QSR5625 • $14

4079.
NFL®: Kansas City Chiefs™
GOSL • 995QSR5542 • $14

4080.
NFL®: Miami Dolphins™
GOSL • 995QSR5555 • $14

4081.
NFL®: Minnesota Vikings™
GOSL • 995QSR5575 • $14

4082.
NFL®: Pittsburgh Steelers™
GOSL • 995QSR5565 • $14

4083.
NFL®:
San Francisco 49ers™
GOSL • 995QSR5562 • $14

4084.
NFL®:
Washington Redskins™
GOSL • 995QSR5552 • $14

4085.
Night Before Christmas:
Hung With Care
TAGU • 495QRP4485 • $7

4086.
Night Before Christmas:
Not Even a Mouse
RGRS • 495QRP4482 • $6

4087.
Night Before Christmas:
Santa
CHAD • 495QRP4495 • $8

4088.
Night Before Christmas:
Tiny Reindeer
UNRU • 495QRP4492 • $10

4089.
No. 1 Teacher
FRAN • 995QX2865 • $16

4090.
Noah's Ark
ESCH • 1295QX2835 • $21

4091.
Noche de Paz
SICK • 1295QX8192 • $19

4092.
Nostalgic Houses &
Shops 18: Service Station
PALM • 1495QX8045 • $34

4093.
Nostalgic Houses &
Shops 18: Service Station
PALM • PrizeQX8045C • $925
Edition Size – 54

4094.
Old-World Santa
SICK • 995QX8975 • $18

4095.
One Little Angel
895QX8935 • $18

4096.
Our Christmas Together
VISK • 1995QX8412 • $30
Set/4

4097.
Our Family
LYLE • 895QX8995 • $30

4098.
Our Family
LYLE • GiftQX8995C • $35
Edition Size – 15000

4099.
Our First Christmas Together
VOTR • 795QX3162 • $19

4100.
Our First Christmas Together
CHAD • 895QX6012 • $16

4101.
Our First Christmas Together
KLIN • 995QX8405 • $17

4102.
A Partridge in a Pear Tree
VOTR • 1295QX8215 • $22

4103.
Pat the Bunny
KLIN • 995QX8582 • $14

4104.
PEANUTS® Pageant
HADD • 1495QX2832 • $25
Set/2

4105.
Peek-a-Boo Present
WILL • 995QX8302 • $14

4106.
Peggy Fleming
ANDR • 1495QXI6845 • $20

4107.
Penguins at Play
KLIN • 995QX8982 • $36

4108.
A Perfect Blend
KLIN • 995QX8985 • $19

4109.
A Perfect Christmas!
KLIN • 1295QXI6895 • $18

4110.
A Pony for Christmas 4
SICK • 1295QX6995 • $20

4111.
A Pony for Christmas 4
SICK • GiftQX6995C • $53

4112.
Poppy Field – The Wizard of Oz™
CROW • 2400QLX7565 • $42
MAGIC

4113.
Portrait of Scarlett
ANDR • 1595QX2885 • $48

4114.
Puppy Love 11
RGRS • 795QX6982 • $14

4115.
Raggedy Andy®
RGRS • 1095QX8574 • $19

4116.
Raggedy Ann®
RGRS • 1095QX8571 • $23

4117.
Ready Teddy
TAGU • 995QX8842 • $18

4118.
Robot Parade 2
WILL • 1495QX8162 • $20

4119.
Rocking Reindeer
VISK • 1295QX8261 • $19

4120.
Safe and Snug 1
FORS • 1295QX8342 • $17

4121.
Safe and Snug 1
FORS • PrizeQX8342C • $748
Edition Size – 54

4122.
Samantha "Sam" Stephens – Bewitched™
CHAD • 1495QXI6892 • $24

4123.
Santa Marionette
CROW • 1395QXC4525 • $26

4124.
Santa's Day Off
RGRS • 995QX2872 • $16

4125.
Santa's Sweet Surprise
VOTR • 1495QX8275 • $25

4126.
Santa's Workshop
PIKE • 995QX2812 • $19

4127.
Sew Sweet Angel
TAGU • 995QX2862 • $19

4128.
Sisters
VISK • 895QX8455 • $18

4129.
Skating Sugar Bear Bell
HAMI/TAGU • 995QX6005 • $17

4130.
Sky's the Limit 5: Gee Bee R-1 Super Sportster®
NORT • 1495QX8005 • $94

4131.
Snoozing Santa
CROW • 1895QX8165 • $23

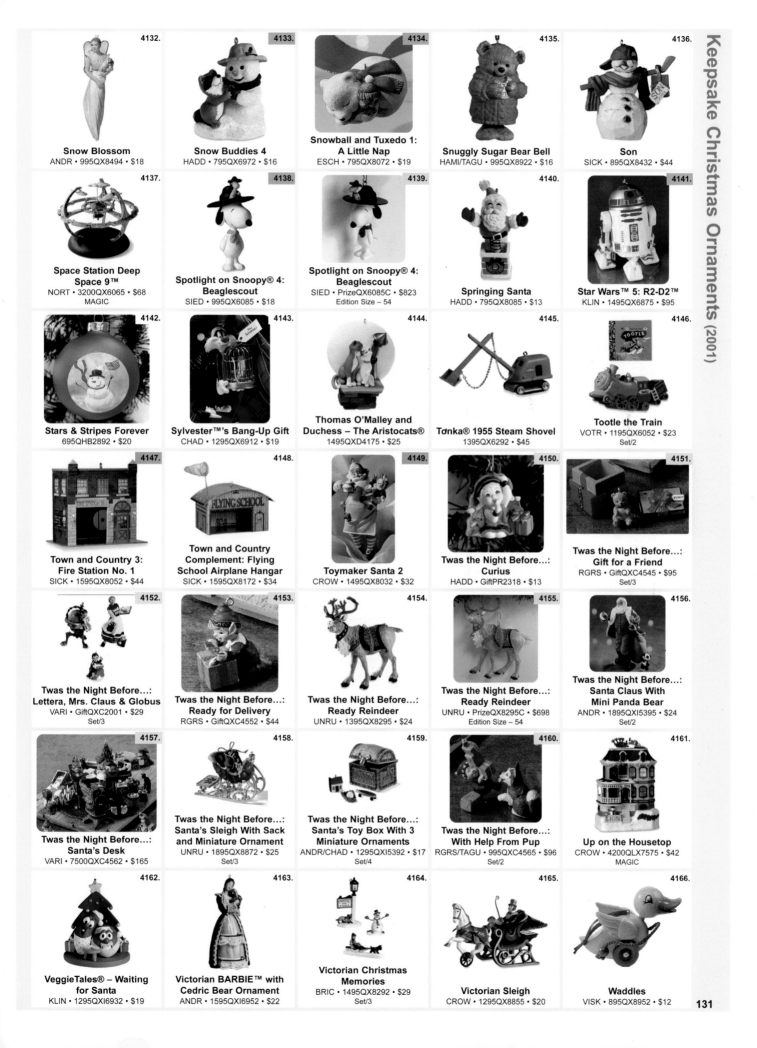

4132.
Snow Blossom
ANDR • 995QX8494 • $18

4133.
Snow Buddies 4
HADD • 795QX6972 • $16

4134.
Snowball and Tuxedo 1:
A Little Nap
ESCH • 795QX8072 • $19

4135.
Snuggly Sugar Bear Bell
HAMI/TAGU • 995QX8922 • $16

4136.
Son
SICK • 895QX8432 • $44

4137.
Space Station Deep
Space 9™
NORT • 3200QX6065 • $68
MAGIC

4138.
Spotlight on Snoopy® 4:
Beaglescout
SIED • 995QX6085 • $18

4139.
Spotlight on Snoopy® 4:
Beaglescout
SIED • PrizeQX6085C • $823
Edition Size – 54

4140.
Springing Santa
HADD • 795QX8085 • $13

4141.
Star Wars™ 5: R2-D2™
KLIN • 1495QX6875 • $95

4142.
Stars & Stripes Forever
695QHB2892 • $20

4143.
Sylvester™'s Bang-Up Gift
CHAD • 1295QX6912 • $19

4144.
Thomas O'Malley and
Duchess – The Aristocats®
1495QXD4175 • $25

4145.
Tonka® 1955 Steam Shovel
1395QX6292 • $45

4146.
Tootle the Train
VOTR • 1195QX6052 • $23
Set/2

4147.
Town and Country 3:
Fire Station No. 1
SICK • 1595QX8052 • $44

4148.
Town and Country
Complement: Flying
School Airplane Hangar
SICK • 1595QX8172 • $34

4149.
Toymaker Santa 2
CROW • 1495QX8032 • $32

4150.
Twas the Night Before…:
Curius
HADD • GiftPR2318 • $13

4151.
Twas the Night Before…:
Gift for a Friend
RGRS • GiftQXC4545 • $95
Set/3

4152.
Twas the Night Before…:
Lettera, Mrs. Claus & Globus
VARI • GiftQXC2001 • $29
Set/3

4153.
Twas the Night Before…:
Ready for Delivery
RGRS • GiftQXC4552 • $44

4154.
Twas the Night Before…:
Ready Reindeer
UNRU • 1395QX8295 • $24

4155.
Twas the Night Before…:
Ready Reindeer
UNRU • PrizeQX8295C • $698
Edition Size – 54

4156.
Twas the Night Before…:
Santa Claus With
Mini Panda Bear
ANDR • 1895QXI5395 • $24
Set/2

4157.
Twas the Night Before…:
Santa's Desk
VARI • 7500QXC4562 • $165

4158.
Twas the Night Before…:
Santa's Sleigh With Sack
and Miniature Ornament
UNRU • 1895QX8872 • $25
Set/3

4159.
Twas the Night Before…:
Santa's Toy Box With 3
Miniature Ornaments
ANDR/CHAD • 1295QXI5392 • $17
Set/4

4160.
Twas the Night Before…:
With Help From Pup
RGRS/TAGU • 995QXC4565 • $96
Set/2

4161.
Up on the Housetop
CROW • 4200QLX7575 • $42
MAGIC

4162.
VeggieTales® – Waiting
for Santa
KLIN • 1295QXI6932 • $19

4163.
Victorian BARBIE™ with
Cedric Bear Ornament
ANDR • 1595QXI6952 • $22

4164.
Victorian Christmas
Memories
BRIC • 1495QX8292 • $29
Set/3

4165.
Victorian Sleigh
CROW • 1295QX8855 • $20

4166.
Waddles
VISK • 895QX8952 • $12

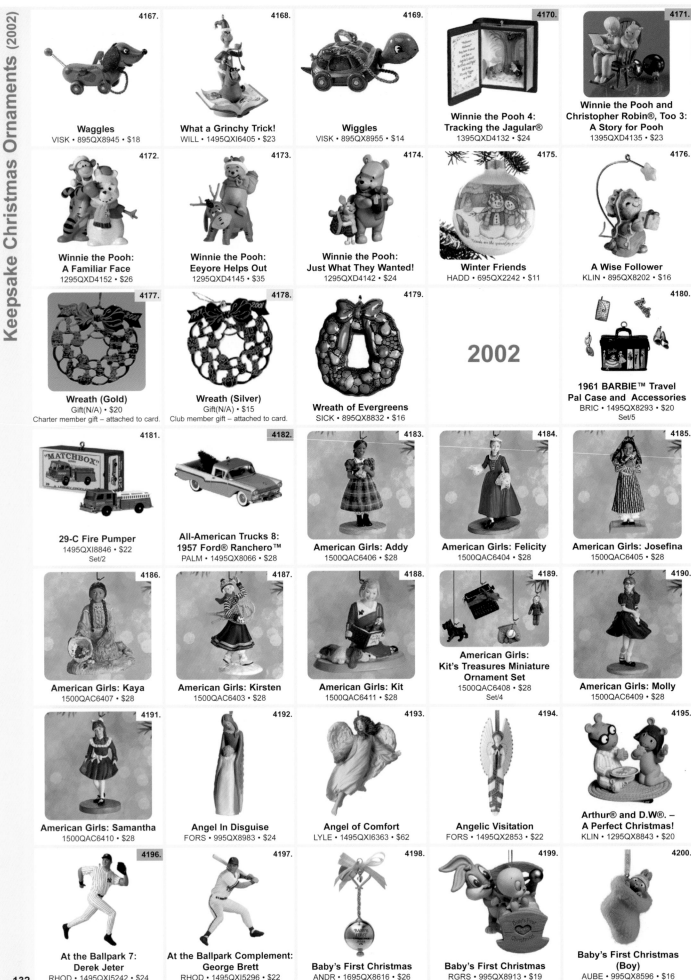

4167.
Waggles
VISK • 895QX8945 • $18

4168.
What a Grinchy Trick!
WILL • 1495QXI6405 • $23

4169.
Wiggles
VISK • 895QX8955 • $14

4170.
Winnie the Pooh 4:
Tracking the Jagular®
1395QXD4132 • $24

4171.
Winnie the Pooh and
Christopher Robin®, Too 3:
A Story for Pooh
1395QXD4135 • $23

4172.
Winnie the Pooh:
A Familiar Face
1295QXD4152 • $26

4173.
Winnie the Pooh:
Eeyore Helps Out
1295QXD4145 • $35

4174.
Winnie the Pooh:
Just What They Wanted!
1295QXD4142 • $24

4175.
Winter Friends
HADD • 695QX2242 • $11

4176.
A Wise Follower
KLIN • 895QX8202 • $16

4177.
Wreath (Gold)
Gift(N/A) • $20
Charter member gift – attached to card.

4178.
Wreath (Silver)
Gift(N/A) • $15
Club member gift – attached to card.

4179.
Wreath of Evergreens
SICK • 895QX8832 • $16

2002

4180.
1961 BARBIE™ Travel
Pal Case and Accessories
BRIC • 1495QX8293 • $20
Set/5

4181.
29-C Fire Pumper
1495QXI8846 • $22
Set/2

4182.
All-American Trucks 8:
1957 Ford® Ranchero™
PALM • 1495QX8066 • $28

4183.
American Girls: Addy
1500QAC6406 • $28

4184.
American Girls: Felicity
1500QAC6404 • $28

4185.
American Girls: Josefina
1500QAC6405 • $28

4186.
American Girls: Kaya
1500QAC6407 • $28

4187.
American Girls: Kirsten
1500QAC6403 • $28

4188.
American Girls: Kit
1500QAC6411 • $28

4189.
American Girls:
Kit's Treasures Miniature
Ornament Set
1500QAC6408 • $28
Set/4

4190.
American Girls: Molly
1500QAC6409 • $28

4191.
American Girls: Samantha
1500QAC6410 • $28

4192.
Angel In Disguise
FORS • 995QX8983 • $24

4193.
Angel of Comfort
LYLE • 1495QXI6363 • $62

4194.
Angelic Visitation
FORS • 1495QX2853 • $22

4195.
Arthur® and D.W.® –
A Perfect Christmas!
KLIN • 1295QX8843 • $20

4196.
At the Ballpark 7:
Derek Jeter
RHOD • 1495QXI5242 • $24

4197.
At the Ballpark Complement:
George Brett
RHOD • 1495QXI5296 • $22

4198.
Baby's First Christmas
ANDR • 1695QX8616 • $26

4199.
Baby's First Christmas
RGRS • 995QX8913 • $19

4200.
Baby's First Christmas
(Boy)
AUBE • 995QX8596 • $16

4201.
Baby's First Christmas
(Girl)
AUBE • 995QX8806 • $16

4202.
Back to School
FRAN • 995QX8696 • $17

4203.
Baking Memories
RGRS • 1295QX6956 • $26

4204.
Ballet Photo Holder
LYLE • 995QX2873 • $17

4205.
BARBIE™ 2002
ANDR • 2390QXC4653 • $80

4206.
BARBIE™ 9: Sophisticated
Lady BARBIE™
ANDR • 1595QX8203 • $32

4207.
BARBIE™ as Rapunzel
ANDR • 1495QXI5326 • $28
Set/2

4208.
BARBIE™ as Snowflake
ANDR • 1495QXI8303 • $25

4209.
The Beatles – Yellow
Submarine™ Lunchbox Set
1495QXI5313 • $23
Set/2

4210.
Belle – Beauty and the Beast
1295QXD4946 • $26

4211.
Between Us:
A Heartful of Grateful
WILL • 995QP1523 • $23

4212.
Between Us: Always Near
KLIN • 995QP1503 • $23

4213.
Between Us: Display Base
995QP1553 • $17

4214.
Between Us:
Dreams Have Wings
WILL • 995QP1536 • $23

4215.
Between Us: Kindred Spirits
KLIN • 995QP1546 • $36

4216.
Between Us:
Like a Snowflake…
WILL • 995QP1533 • $23

4217.
Between Us:
Lucky Sisters… Lucky Us
KLIN • 995QP1516 • $22

4218.
Between Us: Make a Wish
VISK • 995QP1526 • $23

4219.
Between Us: Mom
KLIN • 995QP1543 • $20

4220.
Between Us: You Inspire Me
KLIN • 995QP1513 • $25

4221.
The Biggest Fan
SIED • 995QX8733 • $20

4222.
Blushing Bride BARBIE™
ANDR • 1995QXI5323 • $22
Blonde hair.

4223.
Blushing Bride BARBIE™
ANDR • 1995QXI5323 • $22
Brunette hair.

4224.
Blushing Bride BARBIE™
ANDR • 1995QXI5323 • $28
Auburn hair.

4225.
Buzz Lightyear – Toy Story
1495QXD4606 • $32
MAGIC

4226.
Calling All Firefighters
SEAL • 995QX8746 • $20

4227.
Calling the Caped
Crusader – Batman™
CHAD • 1495QXI8856 • $28

4228.
Canadian Postal Exclusive 3:
Write to Santa
1495CPC8102 • $40
Sold by Canadian Postal Service.

4229.
Candlelight Services 5:
Country Church
UNRU • 1895QLX7653 • $40
MAGIC

4230.
Castle in the Forest –
Beauty and the Beast
1800QXD4953 • $40

4231.
Celebration BARBIE™ 3
ANDR • 1595QXI8163 • $34

4232.
Change of Heart – How The
Grinch Stole Christmas™
WILL • 1495QXI5273 • $19

4233.
Checking the List
CHAD • 1495QX8493 • $28

4234.
Cheer for Fun! BARBIE™
RGRS • 1495QXI8306 • $23

4235.
Child's Age:
Baby's First Christmas
FRAN • 795QX8326 • $20

133

4236.
Child's Age:
Baby's Second Christmas
FRAN • 795QX8333 • $19

4237.
Child's Age:
Child's Third Christmas
FRAN • 795QX8336 • $14

4238.
Child's Age:
Child's Fourth Christmas
FRAN • 795QX8343 • $14

4239.
Child's Age:
Child's Fifth Christmas
FRAN • 795QX8346 • $14

4240.
Christmas Around The World
LAPR • 695QX8436 • $26

4241.
Christmas Fairy
1495QX8396 • $22

4242.
Christmas Floral
695QX2963 • $13

4243.
Christmas Growth Chart
AUBE • 1295QX8896 • $23

4244.
Christmas Habitat – Tweety™
FRAN • 995QX2913 • $22

4245.
Christmas In The Kitchen
WEBB • 1295QX8956 • $32

4246.
Christmas Tree Gift Clip
RHOD • 995QX2896 • $17

4247.
Cinderella
995QXD4956 • $22

4248.
Circus Mountain Railroad
CROW • 4200QLX7686 • $56
MAGIC

4249.
**Classic American
Cars 12: 1970 Ford®
Mach 1 Mustang™**
PALM • 1495QX8073 • $68

4250.
Club Star Ornaments
VARI • ($N/E)QXC4693 • $75
Set/3

4251.
Cool Decade 3
HADD • 795QX8016 • $50

4252.
Cool Friends
VOTR • 995QX8706 • $20

4253.
Dad
VISK • 995QX8936 • $16

4254.
Daughter
VISK • 995QX8946 • $20

4255.
Death Star™
RHOD • 2400QLX7656 • $35
MAGIC

4256.
**Decorating
Scooby-Doo™ Style**
KLIN • 1295QX8256 • $20

4257.
Deer Creek Cottage
UNRU • 1495QXI5276 • $20

4258.
Delta Flyer™
NORT • 2400QLX7663 • $55
MAGIC

4259.
The Doctor
RGRS • 1495QX8226 • $28

4260.
**Don't Get Into Mischief,
Beatrix Potter™**
VOTR • 995QX2906 • $19

4261.
Dorothy & Scarecrow™
LYLE • 1595QX8246 • $20

4262.
**Dr. Seuss® Books 4:
Green Eggs and Ham™**
WILL • 1495QX8083 • $28

4263.
**E.T. The Extraterrestrial™
20th Anniversary**
RHOD • 1495QXI5333 • $23

4264.
Family Photo Holder
VISK • 1295QX8693 • $26

4265.
Fashion Afoot 3
ESCH • 1495QX8116 • $28

4266.
Fill 'Er Up! Daffy Duck™
995QX8266 • $20

4267.
First Snow
AUBE • 1295QX8403 • $23

4268.
First Snow
AUBE • PrizeQX8403C • $62
Edition Size – approximately 5000.

4269.
**The First Snow –
Blue's Clues™**
KLIN • 995QXI5266 • $20

4270.
Fishin' Mission
SIED • 995QX8736 • $26

134

4271.
Football Legends 8:
Kurt Warner
RHOD • 1495QXI8143 • $28

4272.
Friendship Hearts
1495QX8713 • $28
Set/2

4273.
Frostlight Faeries: Faerie
Gabriella and Faerie Castle
Ornament Stand
ESCH • 3500QXC4656 • $150
Set/2 • MAGIC

4274.
Frostlight Faeries, Too:
Baby Brilliana
HADD • 1495QP1683 • $20

4275.
Frostlight Faeries, Too:
Baby Candessa
ESCH • 1495QP1676 • $20

4276.
Frostlight Faeries, Too:
Baby Delandra
HADD • 1495QP1666 • $20

4277.
Frostlight Faeries, Too:
Baby Estrella
ESCH • 1495QP1663 • $20

4278.
Frostlight Faeries, Too:
Baby Floriella
HADD • 1495QP1673 • $20

4279.
Frostlight Faeries, Too:
Beaded Snowflakes (Blue)
995QP1712 • $17
Set/3 • Re-issued from 2001.

4280.
Frostlight Faeries, Too:
Beaded Snowflakes
(Periwinkle)
995QP1725 • $28
Set/3 • Re-issued from 2001.

4281.
Frostlight Faeries, Too:
Beaded Snowflakes
(Violet)
995QP1732 • $28
Set/3 • Re-issued from 2001.

4282.
Frosty Friends 23
SEAL • 1095QX8053 • $34

4283.
Frosty Friends Complement:
Porcelain Box
SEAL • 1895QXC4573 • $75

4284.
G.I. Joe® Lunchbox Set
GENT • 1495QX8286 • $20
Set/2

4285.
Gardener's Christmas
Corner
HADD • 995QX2866 • $26

4286.
Gift Bearers 4
TAGU • 1295QX8883 • $34

4287.
Gingerbread Cottage
WILL • 1995QLX7683 • $38
MAGIC

4288.
God With Us
695QX8893 • $13

4289.
Godchild
BRIC • 1295QX8953 • $20

4290.
Goofy® Clockworks
1495QXD4923 • $23

4291.
Granddaughter
TAGU • 995QX8663 • $13

4292.
Grandma
LARS • 695QX8676 • $12

4293.
Grandson
TAGU • 995QX8666 • $13

4294.
The Great Ski Challenge
1295QXD4926 • $23

4295.
Harley-Davidson®
Motorcycle Milestones 4:
FX-1200 Super Glide®
PALM • 1495QXI8123 • $25

4296.
Harry Potter™ –
Quidditch™ Season
WILL • 2400QXI8656 • $40

4297.
Harry Potter™ –
The Invisibility Cloak
CHAD • 1295QXI8663 • $34

4298.
Having Fun With Friends
AUBE • GiftQXC4553 • $25

4299.
Here Comes Santa 24:
North Pole Towing Service
UNRU • 1495QX8106 • $29

4300.
Holiday Treat Taz™
CHAD • 995QX8263 • $20

4301.
Hoop Stars 8: Kevin Garnett
UNRU • 1495QXI8146 • $23

4302.
Hope Cross
MCGE • 995QX8886 • $23

4303.
Hope, Joy, and Love
TAGU • 1595QX8433 • $28
Set/3

4304.
Horse of a Different Color™
CROW • 3600QLX7673 • $60
MAGIC

4305.
I Don't Do Jolly!
PIKE/WAGN • 1995QX2806 • $40

4306.
Jango Fett™
1495QXI4386 • $46

4307.
Jesus and Friends
KLIN • 1495QX2843 • $26

4308.
Job Switching – I Love
Lucy® 50th Anniversary
RGRS • 1695QXI5316 • $26

4309.
A Joyful Noise
KLIN • 1495QX2816 • $32

4310.
Juice Machine and
Revvin' Heaven
WEBB • 1495QX8236 • $23
Set/2

4311.
Kiddie Car Classics 9:
1928 Jingle Bell Express
1395QX8076 • $22

4312.
Kris and the Kringles 2
CROW • 2400QX8173 • $38
MAGIC

4313.
The Light Within
VOTR • 1295QX2846 • $23

4314.
Lighthouse Greetings 6
FRAN • 2400QLX7646 • $58
MAGIC

4315.
LIONEL® Trains 7:
Blue Comet 400E
Steam Locomotive
1895QX8166 • $29

4316.
LIONEL® Trains Complement:
Blue Comet 400T Oil Tender
1295QX8243 • $32

4317.
LIONEL® Trains Complement:
Blue Comet Passenger Car
1295QX8833 • $95

4318.
Look Out Below!
Sylvester™ & Tweety™
KLIN • 995QX8273 • $20

4319.
Loving Angel
KLIN • 995QX8366 • $34

4320.
Luke Skywalker™
RHOD • 1495QX8206 • $38

4321.
Madame Alexander® 7:
Winter Wonderland
FRAN • 1495QX8086 • $36

4322.
Madame Alexander®
Little Women 2:
Josephine "Jo" March
FORS • 1595QX8126 • $105

4323.
Madeline and Genevieve
RGRS • 1295QXI5286 • $26
Set/2

4324.
Malibu BARBIE™ Lunchbox
GENT • 1995QXC4686 • $85
Set/6

4325.
Mary's Angels 15: Willow
CHAD/HAMI • 795QX8013 • $22

4326.
Mary's Angels 15: Willow
CHAD/HAMI • PrizeQX8013C • $95
Edition Size – approximately 5000.

4327.
Mary's Angels Complement:
Heavenly Carols
CHAD/HAMI • 1695QXI7713 • $28

4328.
Medal For America
GOSL • 995QX2936 • $20

4329.
Memories of Christmas:
Christmas Joy
SICK • 1295QP1413 • $26

4330.
Memories of Christmas:
Flicker Flame Lights
1495QP1443 • $23
Set/7

4331.
Memories of Christmas:
Gentle Angel
TAGU • 1495QP1426 • $28

4332.
Memories of Christmas:
Joyous Angel
TAGU • 1495QP1433 • $20

4333.
Memories of Christmas:
Snowflakes
VOTR • 1295QP1436 • $23
Set/3

4334.
Memories of Christmas:
Snowy Friend
SICK • 995QP1406 • $32

4335.
Memories of Christmas:
Winter Angel
SICK • 995QP1423 • $28

4336.
Memories of Christmas:
Winter's Ride
SICK • 1295QP1416 • $26

4337.
Memories of Christmas:
Yuletide Santa
ESCH • 995QP1403 • $33

4338.
Merry Music Makers
CROW • 2400QX8523 • $35

4339.
Mickey's Holiday Parade 6:
Goofy Toots the Tuba
1395QXD4903 • $32

4340.
Mickey's Skating Party
995QXD4913 • $25

4341.
Mischievous Kittens 4
AUBE • 995QX8046 • $19

4342.
Mistletoe Miss 2
AUBE • 1495QX8113 • $26

4343.
Mom
VISK • 995QX8933 • $23

4344.
Mother and Daughter
Ornaments
1495QX2926 • $28
Set/2

4345.
Mother-Daughter
Photo Holder
VOTR • 1295QX8683 • $26

4346.
My First Christmas
Memory Book
LAPR/LYLE • 1295QX8613 • $23

4347.
Naughty or Nice? Elf
VISK • 995QX2823 • $23

4348.
New Home
UNRU • 1295QX8636 • $23

4349.
Nostalgic Houses &
Shops 19: Victorian Inn
PALM • 1495QX8103 • $55

4350.
Nostalgic Houses & Shops
Complement: Clara's
Hallmark Shop
PALM • 1995QXC4583 • $125

4351.
Obi Wan Kenobi™
1495QXI8216 • $40

4352.
Oddball, Domino and Little
Dipper – 102 Dalmatians
1295QXD4936 • $23

4353.
One Cool Snowboarder
CHAD • 995QX2876 • $28

4354.
Our Christmas Together
HADD • 995QX8623 • $20

4355.
Our Christmas Together
FORS • 1495QX8926 • $24

4356.
Our First Christmas
ANDR • 1895QX8816 • $32

4357.
Our First Christmas
Together
VOTR • 795QX3233 • $13

4358.
Our First Christmas
Together
VOTR • 995QX8626 • $20

4359.
Peace on Earth
Harmony Bell
VOTR • 995QX8393 • $24

4360.
Perfect Harmony:
A Kind World
VOTR • 995QP1203 • $17

4361.
Perfect Harmony:
A New Hope
VOTR • 995QP1213 • $17

4362.
Perfect Harmony:
Display Stand
1000QP1236 • $14

4363.
Perfect Harmony: Hope
VOTR • 995QP1206 • $17

4364.
Perfect Harmony: Joy
VOTR • 995QP1233 • $17

4365.
Perfect Harmony: Love
VOTR • 995QP1226 • $17

4366.
Perfect Harmony: Peace
VOTR • 995QP1216 • $17

4367.
Perfect Harmony:
Peace & Goodwill
VOTR • 995QP1223 • $17

4368.
Playful Minnie
995QXD4906 • $17

4369.
A Pony for Christmas 5
SICK • 1295QX8056 • $25

4370.
Puppy Love 12
RGRS • 795QX8006 • $14

4371.
Rainbow Snowman
TAGU • 995QX8283 • $38

4372.
Robot Parade 3
WILL • 1495QX8133 • $23

4373.
Safe and Snug 2
FORS • 1295QX8036 • $23

4374.
Santa and His
Sweetest Friends
1995QX2923 • $26
Set/4

4375.
Santa's Big Night: Christmas
Morning Treasures
VARI • 1895QXI5346 • $28
Set/3

4376. Santa's Big Night: Christmas Tree With Decorations
KLIN • 1895QX4476 • $29

4377. Santa's Big Night: Curius the Elf
HADD • GiftQXC4623 • $26

4378. Santa's Big Night: Family Room
VARI • 7500QXC4566 • $150

4379. Santa's Big Night: Santa's Big Night
VARI • GiftQXC2002 • $28
Set/4

4380. Santa's Big Night: Snowman
BRIC • GiftQXC4613 • $21

4381. Santa's Mailbox
SICK • 1295QX6943 • $23

4382. Santa's Racin' Sleigh – NASCAR®
RHOD • 1495QXI5306 • $28

4383. Santa's Workshop Lunchbox
LAPR/VISK • 1895QXC4586 • $80
Set/4

4384. Scarlett O'Hara™
ANDR • 1595QX8253 • $40

4385. Scooby-Doo™ and Shaggy
KLIN • 1695QXI5283 • $24

4386. Sisters
FORS • 1295QX8686 • $36

4387. Sky's the Limit 6: Staggerwing
NORT • 1495QX8093 • $55

4388. Slave I Starship™
1895QXI8223 • $36

4389. Snow Belles
AUBE • 1595QX8446 • $35
Set/3

4390. Snow Buddies 5
HADD • 795QX8003 • $32

4391. Snow Buddies 5
HADD • PrizeQX8003C • $85

4392. Snow Cub Club: Calvin Carver
SEAL • 495QRP4646 • $8

4393. Snow Cub Club: Dexter Next
SEAL • 495QRP4633 • $8

4394. Snow Cub Club: Gracie Skates
SEAL • 495QRP4643 • $11

4395. Snow Cub Club: Hollyday Hill Display Base
SEAL • 495QRP4683 • $8

4396. Snow Cub Club: Wendy Whoosh
SEAL • 495QRP4626 • $8

4397. Snowball and Tuxedo 2: The Wishing Star
ESCH • 795QX8033 • $32

4398. Snuggle Time – Mickey and Minnie
1495QXD4916 • $28

4399. Son
VISK • 995QX8943 • $20

4400. A Song For The Lamb Of God
CROW • 1495QX8376 • $28

4401. Sooo Fast™ Custom Car Set
1695QX8876 • $26
Set/2

4402. Special Cat
RGRS • 995QX2863 • $14

4403. Special Dog
RGRS • 995QX8716 • $17

4404. Spotlight on Snoopy® 5: Literary Ace
SIED • 995QX8043 • $24

4405. Star Gazer Shepherd
TAGU • 995QX2836 • $20

4406. Star Wars™ 6: Darth Vader™
RHOD • 1495QX8136 • $36

4407. Sulley and Mike – Monsters, Inc.
1495QXD4613 • $40

4408. Sunday Evening Sleigh Ride
LARS • 1495QX2903 • $23

4409. Sweet Tooth Treats 1
AUBE • 1495QX8193 • $34
Set/4

4410. Teacher
HADD • 995QX8973 • $16

4411. Tee's the Season
SIED • 1295QX8726 • $23

4412. Teetering Toddler
TAGU • 1495QX8916 • $23

4413. Thank You Hug
AUBE • 995QX2893 • $14

4414. "Thank You" Ball
695QX8986 • $8

4415. Thanks, Coach!
RHOD • 995QX8976 • $14

4416. Thanks, Mom!
VOTR • 995QX8963 • $14

4417. Threadbear
995QX2916 • $28

4418. Three Kings Lantern
LARS • 1295QX8853 • $23

4419. Tickle Tickle Santa
CROW • 1995QX2826 • $36

4420. A Time to Believe
CROW • 1895QX8506 • $26

4421. Tinker Bell – Peter Pan
1495QXD4943 • $33

4422. Toddler Photo Holder
AUBE • 1295QX2856 • $20

4423. Tonka® 1961 Cement Truck
1495QX8233 • $24

4424. Topping the Tree
KLIN • 1495QX6953 • $24

4425. Town and Country 4: Grandmother's House and Covered Bridge
SICK • 1695QX8156 • $43
Set/2

4426. Toymaker Santa 3
CROW • 1295QX8096 • $75

4427. Treasures and Dreams 1: Jewelry Box Ballet
CROW • 1995QX8183 • $40
MAGIC

4428. True Love is Our Love
UNRU • 1495QX8923 • $31

4429. Tucked In Tenderly
HADD • 995QX2886 • $17

4430. U.S.S. Enterprise™
NORT • 2400QXI2943 • $44
Set/2

4431. Up Up and Away
CROW • 995QX8466 • $23

4432. VeggieTales®
KLIN • 1295QXI5293 • $22

4433. A Very Carrot Christmas - Bugs Bunny™
WILL • 995QX8276 • $20

4434. Village Toy Shop
FRAN • 2400QLX7676 • $33
MAGIC

4435. We Call Him Santa
LYLE • 1295QX2883 • $26

4436. Welcoming the Savior
VISK • 1295QX8356 • $20

4437. White Poinsettia
695QX2953 • $13

4438. The Wild Thornberrys™
SIED • 1295QXI5263 • $19

4439. Winnie the Pooh 5: School Days
1395QXD4983 • $23

4440. Winnie the Pooh: Piglet's First Ride
1295QXD4963 • $20

4441. Winnie the Pooh: Skating in Circles
2400QXD7526 • $42
MAGIC

4442. Winnie the Pooh: Tigger's Springy Tree
995QXD4966 • $23

4443. Winter Wonderland 1: Bringing Home the Tree
UNRU • 1295QX8186 • $32

4444. Woodland Friends
AUBE • 1495QX8536 • $23

4445. Woodland Frolic
AUBE • 1495QX8543 • $23
Set/3

2003

4446.
Woody and Bullseye –
Toy Story
1495QXD4933 • $25

4447.
Worldwide Celebration
FORS • 1295QX2833 • $23

4448.
A Year To Remember – 2002
MCGE • 2400QX2813 • $35

4449.
You're A Star
WILL • 995QX8966 • $20

4450.
100 Years of Fun
CROW • 1995QXI8769 • $42

4451.
The 1990s Batmobile™
WEBB • 1495QXI8297 • $25

4452.
Adoption 2003
VOTR • 1295QXG2497 • $19

4453.
Adventures of a Book Lover
995QXG8589 • $18

4454.
All-American Trucks 9: 1972
Chevrolet® Cheyenne Super
PALM • 1495QX8117 • $24

4455.
The Amazing Little Tree
SIED • 2400QXI7517 • $46

4456.
American Girls: Addy
FORS • 1500QAC6412 • $19

4457.
American Girls: Felicity
ESCH • 1500QAC6413 • $17

4458.
American Girls: Josefina
ESCH • 1500QAC6415 • $19

4459.
American Girls: Kaya
LYLE • 1500QAC6414 • $16

4460.
American Girls: Kirsten
LYLE • 1500QAC6416 • $16

4461.
American Girls: Kit
BRIC • 1500QAC6417 • $16

4462.
American Girls: Molly
PALM • 1500QAC6418 • $16

4463.
American Girls: Samantha
LYLE • 1500QAC6419 • $22

4464.
American Patriot Santa
1495QXG2549 • $23

4465.
Amiga Por Siempre
1495QXG2529 • $20

4466.
Angel at My Side
FORS • 995QXG8659 • $26

4467.
Angel of Serenity
ANDR • 1495QXG8999 • $28

4468.
Angels of Virtue
ESCH • 1595QXG8839 • $19
Set/3

4469.
Angels We Have Heard
KLIN • 2400QLX7527 • $44
MAGIC

4470.
Angels We Have Heard
KLIN • PrizeQLX7527C • $695
MAGIC • Edition Size – 75

4471.
Arthur® and Pal –
A Perfect Christmas!
995QXI8359 • $13

4472.
At the Ballpark 8:
Jason Giambi
RHOD • 1495QX2449 • $22

4473.
At the Ballpark Complement:
Ted Williams –
Boston Red Sox™
RHOD • 1495QXI8397 • $28

4474.
Away to the Manger
LARS • 995QXG8669 • $28

4475.
Baby's First Christmas
HADD • 1295QXG8719 • $22

4476.
Baby's First Christmas
VOTR • 1495QXG8729 • $22

4477.
Baby's First Christmas
KLIN • 995QXG8737 • $18

4478.
BARBIE™ 10:
Mailbu BARBIE™
1595QX8107 • $22

4479.
BARBIE™ 2003
RGRS • 1995QXC4589 • $68

4480.
BARBIE™ Fashion Model:
BARBIE™ In The Pink
ANDR • 2500QXI8439 • $32

4481.
BARBIE™ Ornament
Photo Holder
1495QXI4269 • $19

4482.
BARBIE™ Swan Lake
1495QXI8447 • $32
Set/2

4483.
Basket of Joy
VOTR • 995QXG8599 • $14

4484.
Bearing the Colors
995QXG2499 • $14

4485.
Bubble Bath –
Sylvester™ and Tweety™
CHAD • 1495QXI8277 • $19

4486.
Bugs Bunny™ and Daffy
Duck™ – Back In Action
CHAD • 1495QXI4329 • $23

4487.
Bugs the Barnstormer –
Bugs Bunny™
WILL • 1695QXI8279 • $23

4488.
Burrton, Coldwell and
Windfield
1495QXG2557 • $20
Set/3

4489.
Canadian Postal Exclusive 4:
Letter to Santa
TAGU • 1499CPC2003 • $30
Sold by Canadian Postal Service.

4490.
Candlelight Services 6:
Fieldstone Church
SEAL • 1895QX7429 • $29
MAGIC

4491.
Captain Jonathan Archer
RGRS • 1495QXI8349 • $22

4492.
Caroling at the Door
TAGU • 1495QXG8819 • $19

4493.
The Cat Arrives! –
The Cat in the Hat™
WILL • 995QXI8379 • $26

4494.
Celebrate, Decorate, Enjoy!
FRAN • 695QXG8779 • $10

4495.
Celebration BARBIE™ 4
1595QX2459 • $34

4496.
Celebration BARBIE™ 4
(African-American)
1595QXI4357 • $34

4497.
Child's Age:
Baby's Second Christmas
FRAN • 895QXG8699 • $15

4498.
Child's Age:
Child's Third Christmas
FRAN • 895QXG8707 • $15

4499.
Child's Age:
Child's Fourth Christmas
FRAN • 895QXG8709 • $15

4500.
Child's Age:
Child's Fifth Christmas
FRAN • 895QXG8717 • $15

4501.
Child's Age:
My First Christmas (Boy)
HADD • 995QXG8697 • $34

4502.
Child's Age:
My First Christmas (Girl)
KLIN • 995QXG2487 • $24

4503.
Christmas Tree Dreams
LARS • 2400QLX7477 • $35
MAGIC

4504.
Christmas Tree Gift Clip
995QXG8637 • $14

4505.
Christmas Window 1:
Christmas Window 2003
CROW • 1995QXC3003 • $48

4506.
Christmastime in the City
FRAN • 1295QXG8817 • $20

4507.
The Church Choir
WEBB • 1695QXG2429 • $24

4508.
Cinderella and Prince
Charming – Cinderella
1695QXD5139 • $24

4509.
Classic American
Cars 13: 1963 Corvette®
Sting Ray Coupe
PALM • 1495QX8129 • $48

4510.
Click Your Heels
RGRS • 3200QXI7487 • $44

4511.
Coach of the Year
995QXG8639 • $12

4512.
Commemorative Bells
VARI • 4000QXC4617 • $70
Set/3

4513.
Cool Decade 4
HADD • 795QX8079 • $22

4514.
Cool Decade 4
HADD • GiftQX8079C • $65
Edition Size – 5000

141

4515. Countdown to Christmas
LARS • 1995QLX7529 • $25
MAGIC

4516. Cross of Glory
MCGE • 995QXG8977 • $16

4517. Dad
AUBE • 995QXG8889 • $13

4518. Dancer in Flight
FORS • 1295QXG8619 • $23

4519. Daughter
AUBE • 995QXG8899 • $14

4520. The Decision
AUBE • 995QXG8569 • $16

4521. The Decision
AUBE • GiftQXG8569C • $34

4522. Defending the Flag
WILL • 1295QXG8577 • $19

4523. Delicious Christmas
1495QXG8657 • $19

4524. Disney's It's A Small World After All
8500QXC4689 • $150
Set/3

4525. Dorothy and Tin Man™
LYLE • 1595QXI8299 • $20

4526. Dr. Seuss® Books 5: Hop on Pop
WILL • 1495QX8179 • $34

4527. Feliz Navidad
1295QXG8689 • $22

4528. Fire Brigade 1: 1929 Chevrolet® Fire Engine
WEBB • 1895QX8449 • $60

4529. Fire Brigade 1: 1929 Chevrolet® Fire Engine
WEBB • 1895QX8449C • $95

4530. First Christmas Together
895QXG3257 • $19

4531. Flying Over London – Peter Pan
1495QXD5137 • $20

4532. Football Legends 9: Jerry Rice – San Francisco 49ers™
RHOD • 1495QX2457 • $28

4533. Football Legends Complement: Jerry Rice – Oakland Raiders™
RHOD • 1495QXI4267 • $24

4534. Forever Friend
1495QXG8967 • $25

4535. Friendship
695QXG8879 • $14

4536. Frostlight Faeries: Frostlight Faerie Sisters
ESCH • 2495QXG2479 • $44
Set/3

4537. Frosty Friends 24
SEAL • 1295QX8089 • $34

4538. Gift Bearers 5
TAGU • 1295QX8239 • $65

4539. A Gift for Raggedy Ann®
FRAN • 1295QXI8417 • $17

4540. Gift of Love
TAGU • 1895QXC4299 • $59

4541. Gift of Peace
TAGU • 1895QRP4249 • $19

4542. Glad Tidings Angel
TAGU • 1895QRP4249 • $19

4543. Glory Shining Down
MURR • 1095QXG8667 • $16

4544. Godchild
1295QXG8939 • $28

4545. Goofy® Helps Out
1295QXD5037 • $23

4546. Gopher Par
HADD • 995QXG8587 • $17

4547. Grandchild's First Christmas
TAGU • 995QXG2437 • $17

4548. Granddaughter
VISK • 995QXG8907 • $17

4549. Grandson
VISK • 995QXG8909 • $19

4550.
The Grinch™ and Cindy-Lou Who™ – How the Grinch Stole Christmas™
CHAD • 1495QXI8377 • $22
Set/2

4551.
Harley-Davidson® Motorcycle Milestones 5: 100th Anniversary Ultra Classic Electra Glide®
PALM • 1495QX8169 • $34

4552.
Harley-Davidson® Motorcycle Milestones Complement: Around the World
PALM/WEBB • 4400QXI7489 • $55

4553.
Harley-Davidson® Motorcycle Milestones Complement: Serial Number One & 2003 Ultra Classic Electra Glide®
PALM • 2800QXI8317 • $42
Set/2

4554.
Harry Potter™ – Platform Nine 3/4™
CHAD • 1295QXI4279 • $20

4555.
Here Comes Santa 25: Santa's Big Rig
SICK • 1495QX8167 • $23

4556.
Here Comes Santa 25: Santa's Big Rig
SICK • PrizeQX8167C1 • $100
Edition Size – 5000

4557.
Here Comes Santa 25: Santa's Big Rig
SICK • PrizeQX8167C2 • $950
Edition Size – 75

4558.
Holiday Adventure
KLIN • 1495QXI8289 • $19

4559.
Holiday Advice Booth – Lucy
1495QXI4257 • $24

4560.
Home Bright Home – Mickey and Pluto
1495QXD2509 • $23

4561.
Home for the Holidays
1695QXG8837 • $25

4562.
Hoop Stars 9: Kobe Bryant
UNRU • 1495QX8237 • $24

4563.
Hot Wheels™ Lunchbox Set
GENT • 1495QXI8427 • $19
Set/2

4564.
I'll Be Home for Christmas
CROW • 1995QLX7519 • $34
MAGIC

4565.
I'll Be Home for Christmas
CROW • GiftQLX7519C • $46
MAGIC

4566.
In Excelsis Deo
LARS • 1495QXG2427 • $23

4567.
Jack-in-the-Box Memories 1: Pop! Goes the Snowman
VISK • 1495QX8457 • $45

4568.
Jimmie Johnson
RHOD • 1495QXI8389 • $20

4569.
Jingle All the Way! – Tweety™
CHAD • 1495QXI8267 • $19

4570.
Jingle Bells
695QXG8777 • $14

4571.
Just for You
AUBE • GiftQXC4567 • $24

4572.
Kiddie Car Classics 10: 1949 Gillham™ Sport
PALM • 1395QX8139 • $24
Set/2

4573.
Kris and the Kringles 3
CROW • 2400QX7439 • $75
MAGIC

4574.
Kris Kringle
VISK • 995PR2917 • $12

4575.
Lighthouse Greetings 7
FRAN • 2400QX7409 • $78
MAGIC

4576.
LIONEL® Holiday Special Train Set
7500QXC4587 • $125
Set/3

4577.
LIONEL® Trains 8: 4449 Daylight Steam Locomotive
1895QX8087 • $23

4578.
LIONEL® Trains Complement: Daylight Observation Car
1295QXI8327 • $22

4579.
LIONEL® Trains Complement: Daylight Oil Tender
1295QXI8249 • $22

4580.
The List
UNRU • 1295QXG8829 • $22

4581.
Little Christmas Helper
HADD • 1295QXG8747 • $22

4582.
Love Ya, Grandma!
KLIN • 995QXG8917 • $14

4583.
Love Ya, Grandma!
KLIN • GiftQXG8917C • $25

4584.
Love Ya, Grandpa!
KLIN • 995QXG8919 • $14

4585. "Lucy's Italian Movie" – I Love Lucy®
RGRS • 1695QXI8387 • $25

4586. Madame Alexander® 8: Holiday Snowflake Skater
FRAN • 1495QX8137 • $24

4587. Madame Alexander® Little Women 3: Elizabeth "Beth" March
FORS • 1595QX8187 • $30

4588. Madeline
RGRS • 1295QXI8409 • $19

4589. Marlin and Nemo – Finding Nemo
1295QXD5147 • $60

4590. Mary's Angels 16: Sweet William
CHAD/HAMI • 795QX8119 • $23

4591. Mary's Angels 16: Sweet William
CHAD/HAMI • PrizeQX8119C • $109
Edition Size – 5000

4592. Merriweather
GiftWD2875 • $10

4593. Merry Christmas World!
PALM • 1995QLX7449 • $28
MAGIC

4594. Merry Glitzmas!
1495QLX7537 • $19
MAGIC

4595. Mighty Tonka® Crane
1495QXI8367 • $30

4596. Mischievous Kittens 5
AUBE • 995QX8109 • $16

4597. Mischievous Kittens 5
AUBE • PrizeQX8109C • $95
Edition Size – 5000

4598. Mistletoe Miss 3
AUBE • 1495QX8219 • $20
Set/2

4599. Mistletoe Time – Mickey and Minnie
1495QXD5057 • $24

4600. The Mistletot Faeries
TAGU • 1995QXC3001 • $38

4601. Model 8420 Tractor – John Deere
1495QXI4259 • $29

4602. Mom
AUBE • 995QXG8887 • $14

4603. Moose on the Loose
LARS • 995QXG8579 • $24

4604. Moose on the Loose
LARS • PrizeQXG8579C • $695
Edition Size – 75

4605. Mother and Daughter
WILL • 1295QXG8949 • $32

4606. Mr. Potato Head®
SIED • 1295QXI4277 • $20

4607. Mufasa and Simba – The Lion King
1295QXD5087 • $24
Set/2

4608. Nature's Sketchbook: Nature's Sketchbook 1
BAST/FRAN • 995QX8679 • $29

4609. New Home
1295QXG8957 • $19

4610. Noah's Ark
SICK • 1695QXG8997 • $25

4611. Nostalgic Houses & Shops 20: The Grand Theater
PALM • 1495QX8149 • $22

4612. Nostalgic Houses & Shops Complement: Town Hall and Mayor's Christmas Tree
PALM • 1995QX2467 • $36

4613. Nostalgic Houses & Shops Complement: Town Hall and Mayor's Christmas Tree
PALM • PrizeQX2467C • $748
Edition Size – 75

4614. Nuestra Familia
VISK • 1295QXG2537 • $18

4615. Nurse With a Magic Touch
VOTR • 995QXG8567 • $22

4616. Nutcracker Soldier
LARS • 1695QXC4599 • $49

4617. On Frozen Pond: Kermit™ and Miss Piggy™
1495QXI4289 • $19

4618. On Track: Deora II and Sweet Sixteen II
1695QXI8429 • $19

4619. Our Best Buddy – Buzz Lightyear and Woody – Toy Story
1495QXD5129 • $17

4620.

Our Family
VISK • 1295QXG8947 • $22

4621.

Our First Christmas
VOTR • 1895QXG8877 • $29

4622.

Our Love Story Photo Holder
1295QXG8859 • $18

4623.

Padme Amidala™
1495QXI8339 • $19

4624.

Pals at the Pole
KLIN • 1495QXG8827 • $18

4625.

Pals at the Pole
KLIN • PrizeQXG8827C • $50

4626.

Parents-to-Be
VOTR • 1295QXG2469 • $19

4627.

Play It Again, Santa!
WILL • 2400QLX7469 • $32
MAGIC

4628.

Polar Coaster
CROW • 4200QLX7459 • $50
MAGIC

4629.

A Pony for Christmas 5
SICK • GiftQX8056C • $54

4630.

A Pony for Christmas 6
SICK • 1295QX8229 • $50

4631.

A Pony for Christmas 6
SICK • GiftQX8229C • $60

4632.

Pretty As a Princess
1295QXD5079 • $28

4633.

Primera Navidad de Bebé
HADD • 1295QXG2517 • $16

4634.

Puppy Love 13
RGRS • 795QX8127 • $22

4635.

Red Power Ranger™ – Power Rangers: Ninja Storm™
1295QXD2439 • $18

4636.

Rock 'n' Roll Stitch – Lilo & Stitch
995QXD2447 • $29

4637.

Rockin' & Rollin'!
CROW • 3200QLX7457 • $41
MAGIC

4638.

Ruff and Tuff Hero
FRAN • 995QXG8557 • $16

4639.

Safe and Snug 3
FORS • 1295QX8217 • $18

4640.

Santa's Magical Sleigh
WEBB • 1895QRP4247 • $30

4641.

Santa's on His Way
CHAD • 1495QXG8809 • $23

4642.

Santa's on His Way
CHAD • GiftQXG8809C • $44

4643.

Scarlett O'Hara™
ANDR • 1595QXI8307 • $32

4644.

Scarlett O'Hara™ and Rhett Butler™
1895QXI4287 • $88

4645.

School Photo Holder
VISK • 995QXG8929 • $16

4646.

Scooby-Doo™ Takes Aim
KLIN • 995QXI8287 • $17

4647.

The Scorpion™
NORT/RGRS • 3200QXI7509 • $43
MAGIC

4648.

Shrek® and Donkey
CHAD • 1495QXG8759 • $29
Set/2

4649.

Sister-to-Sister
1695QXG8969 • $22
Set/2

4650.

Skating To and Fro
BRIC/RDON • 1995QXC3002 • $35

4651.

Sky's the Limit 7: 1936 Stinson Reliant
NORT • 1495QX8147 • $23

4652.

S'Mittens
KLIN • 1295QXG8857 • $19
Set/2

4653.

Snackercize!
CROW • 1995QLX7581 • $26
MAGIC

4654.

Snow Angel
SIED • 995QXG8749 • $18

145

4655.
Snow Buddies 6
HADD • 795QX8097 • $20

4656.
Snowball and Tuxedo 3:
Snowshoe Taxi
ESCH • 795QX8227 • $22

4657.
Snowie Rolie –
Rolie Polie Olie
1295QXD2477 • $18

4658.
Snowman Surprise
CROW • 1295QXG8807 • $19

4659.
Snowman's Land:
Display Wreath
HADD • 1995QP1139 • $35

4660.
Snowman's Land:
I'm Snow Angel!
HADD • 995QP1109 • $14

4661.
Snowman's Land:
Snow Ho Ho!
HADD • 995QP1107 • $14

4662.
Snowman's Land: Snow
News is Good News!
HADD • 995QP1117 • $16

4663.
Snowman's Land:
Snow Place Like Home!
HADD • 995QP1129 • $14

4664.
Snowman's Land: Snow
Time Like the Present!
HADD • 995QP1137 • $14

4665.
Snowman's Land:
Snow What Fun!
HADD • 995QP1127 • $14

4666.
Snowman's Land:
Snowbody Does It Better!
HADD • 995QP1119 • $24

4667.
Snowy Push 'n' Pull
AUBE • 1995QLX8259 • $28
MAGIC

4668.
Son
AUBE • 995QXG8897 • $14

4669.
Spaghetti Supper –
Lady and the Tramp
1495QXD5099 • $22

4670.
Special Cat
VISK • 995QXG8609 • $13

4671.
Special Dog
VISK • 995QXG8607 • $13

4672.
Special Event Photo Holder
1295QXG8959 • $20

4673.
Special Friend
995QXG8927 • $17

4674.

Spotlight on Snoopy® 6:
Joe Cool
SIED • 995QX8099 • $16

4675.
Star of Belief
GOSL • 1495QXC4619 • $28

4676.
Star Wars™ 7: C-3PO™
KLIN • 1495QX8177 • $23

4677.
Steamboat Willie –
Mickey Mouse
2400QXD5047 • $31
MAGIC

4678.
Stuck on You
HADD • 995QXG8867 • $16

4679.
Sub-Commander T'Pol
RGRS • 1495QXI8757 • $23

4680.
Sweet Tooth Treats 2
AUBE • 1495QX8199 • $23
Set/4

4681.
Sweetest Little Angel
KLIN • 1695QLX7574 • $26
MAGIC

4682.
Taz™ as the Nutcracker
CHAD • 995QXI8269 • $14

4683.
Teachers Rule
RHOD • 995QXG8629 • $14

4684.
This is the Life
VISK • 995QXG8597 • $22

4685.
TIE Fighter™
RHOD • 2400QXI7507 • $31

4686.
Toddler Photo Holder
KLIN • 995QXG8739 • $24

4687.
Town and Country 5:
Schoolhouse and Flagpole
SICK • 1695QX8247 • $22
Set/2

4688.
Toymaker Santa 4
CROW • 1295QX8159 • $48

4689.

Treasures and Dreams 2:
Jewelry Box Carousel
CROW • 1995QX8197 • $38
MAGIC

4690. Uncle Sam Nutcracker
VISK • 995QXG2489 • $13

4691. VeggieTales®
RHOD • 1295QXI4337 • $19

4692. A Visit From Santa:
A Christmas Story
HADD • 995QP1429 • $13

4693. A Visit From Santa:
A Very Good Girl
HADD • 1295QP1477 • $18

4694. A Visit From Santa:
A Very Merry Snowman
AUBE • 1495QP1417 • $18

4695. A Visit From Santa:
Giddy-Up, Christmas!
AUBE • 1295QP1437 • $18

4696. A Visit From Santa:
Gifts for Everyone
HADD • 1695QP1409 • $25

4697. A Visit From Santa:
Oh, What Fun!
HADD • 1295QP1427 • $18

4698. A Visit From Santa:
Sweet Little Lad
AUBE • 995QP1469 • $14

4699. A Visit From Santa:
Sweet Shopper
AUBE • 995QP1447 • $16

4700. A Visit From Santa:
Winter Trimmers
995QP1497 • $14
Set/6

4701. Waiting For Santa
VISK • 1995QRP4327 • $24
Set/5

4702. What Child Is This
HADD • 1295QXG8989 • $32

4703. What Child Is This
HADD • PrizeQXG8989C • $695
Edition Size – 75

4704. Winnie the Pooh 6:
Little Rain Cloud
1395QXD5117 • $20

4705. Winnie the Pooh:
A Boost for Piglet
1495QXD5069 • $24

4706. Winnie the Pooh:
Our Friendship
1295QXD5067 • $25

4707. Winnie the Pooh:
Soccer Tigger-Style
995QXD5119 • $13

4708. Winnie the Pooh:
Twinkle, Twinkle
1295QXD8767 • $22

4709. Winter Wonderland 2:
Sleigh Ride
UNRU • 1295QX8207 • $28

4710. Words of Love
1495QXG8869 • $25
Set/8

4711. World-Famous Christmas
Decorator Snoopy®
SIED • 1995QXC3004 • $48

4712. Wreath of Peace
FRAN • 995QXG8687 • $18

4713. Yoda™
1495QXI8337 • $36

4714. You've Got Games
LARS • 995QXG8627 • $19

2004

4715. Adoption 2004
BRIC • 1295QXG5641 • $19

4716. Affection for Confections
1895QRP4291 • $28
Set/2

4717. ¡Al Mundo Paz!
VOTR • 1495QXG5471 • $23

4718. All-American Trucks 10:
2000 Ford® F-150
PALM • 1495QX8154 • $20

4719. Amazing Number 53 –
Herbie, The Love Bug
1495QXD5071 • $23

4720. American Girls:
Addy With Coin
FORS • 1500QAC6421 • $22

4721. American Girls:
Felicity With Horse Brush
BRIC • 1500QAC6431 • $22

4722. American Girls:
Josefina With Memory Box
RGRS • 1500QAC6434 • $18

4723. American Girls:
Kaya With Moccasins
LYLE • 1500QAC6461 • $22

147

4724.
American Girls:
Kirsten With Swedish Tine
LYLE • 1500QAC6424 • $22

4725.
American Girls:
Kit With Notebook
PALM • 1500QAC6441 • $22
Set/2

4726.
American Girls:
Molly With Envelope
PALM • 1500QAC6444 • $22

4727.
American Girls:
Samantha With Sampler
RGRS • 1500QAC6451 • $26

4728.
An Angel's Touch
FORS • 1295QXG5634 • $18

4729.
Anakin Skywalker™
KLIN • 1495QXI4071 • $30

4730.
Angel of Compassion
LYLE • 1495QXG5381 • $23

4731.
Anything For A Friend
KLIN • 1495QXG5511 • $24

4732.
Ariel – The Little Mermaid
1295QXD5061 • $20

4733.
At the Ballpark 9:
Barry Bonds – San
Francisco Giants™
RHOD • 1495QX8551 • $18

4734.
At the Ballpark Complement:
Willie Mays –
San Francisco Giants™
RHOD • 1495QXI5314 • $23

4735.
Baby's First Christmas
AUBE • 995QXG5711 • $17

4736.
Baby's First Christmas
AUBE • 1295QXG5714 • $20

4737.
Baby's First Christmas
1295QXG5724 • $20

4738.
Baby's First Christmas
AUBE • 1895QXG5731 • $30

4739.
"The Ballet"
RGRS • 1695QXI5311 • $26

4740.
Bambi and Friends
1695QXD5044 • $26

4741.
BARBIE™ 11: Smasheroo
BARBIE™ Ornament
1595QX8591 • $25

4742.
BARBIE™ as The Princess
and The Pauper Ornament
1895QXI8614 • $30

4743.
BARBIE™ Fashion Model:
Lisette BARBIE™ Ornament
ANDR • 2500QXI8541 • $40

4744.
BARBIE™s 45th
Anniversary Ornament
ANDR • 2500QHB6601 • $34
MAGIC

4745.
BARBIE™s 45th Shoe
Tree Ornament
1995QHB6604 • $38

4746.
Beak To Beak
FEUR • 995QXG5331 • $24

4747.
Billions of Dreams
BARBIE™ Ornament
RGRS • 1995QXC4009 • $51

4748.
Born To Shop
WILL • 995QXG5414 • $26

4749.
Buzz Lightyear and The
Claw – Toy Story
1495QXD8671 • $23

4750.
Canadian Postal Exclusive 5:
Santa Writes Back
PAON • 1499CPC2004 • $36
Sold by Canadian Postal Service.

4751.
Candlelight Services 7:
Colonial Church
LARS • 1895QX8451 • $35
MAGIC

4752.
The Caped Crusader –
Batman™
CHAD • 1495QXI4041 • $24
MAGIC

4753.
Carousel Ride 1:
Majestic Lion
KLIN • 1295QX8464 • $23

4754.
Carousel Ride Complement:
Carousel Ride Display
KLIN • 4500QX8481 • $51
Re-issued in 2005.

4755.
Catch of the Day
VISK • 995QXG5541 • $14

4756.
Celebration BARBIE™ 5
1595QX8604 • $31

4757.
Celebration BARBIE™ 5
(African-American)
1595QXI8664 • $25

4758.
Child's Age:
Child's Third Christmas
FRAN • 895QXG5764 • $14

4759.
Child's Age:
Child's Fourth Christmas
FRAN • 895QXG5771 • $14

4760.
Child's Age:
Child's Fifth Christmas
FRAN • 895QXG5774 • $14

4761.
Child's Age:
My First Christmas (Boy)
HADD • 995QXG5661 • $29

4762.
Child's Age:
My First Christmas (Girl)
KLIN • 995QXG5671 • $18

4763.
Child's Age:
My Second Christmas (Boy)
HADD • 995QXG5664 • $15

4764.
Child's Age:
My Second Christmas (Girl)
KLIN • 995QXG5674 • $15

4765.
Child's Age:
My Third Christmas (Boy)
HADD • 995QXG5681 • $15

4766.
Child's Age:
My Third Christmas (Girl)
KLIN • 995QXG5691 • $15

4767.
Child's Age:
My Fourth Christmas (Boy)
HADD • 995QXG5684 • $15

4768.
Child's Age:
My Fourth Christmas (Girl)
KLIN • 995QXG5694 • $15

4769.
Child's Age:
My Fifth Christmas (Boy)
HADD • 995QXG5701 • $15

4770.
Child's Age:
My Fifth Christmas (Girl)
KLIN • 995QXG5704 • $15

4771.
Christmas Cookies!
WILL • 2500QLX7611 • $68
MAGIC

4772.
**Christmas Crossing –
Thomas The Tank®**
WILL • 1295QXI8661 • $45

4773.
**Christmas Eve Snack –
Tweety™**
FRAN • 1295QXI4001 • $20

4774.
**Christmas Window 2:
Christmas Window 2004**
AUBE • 1995QXC4003 • $36

4775.
**"City on the Edge
of Forever"**
RGRS • 2800QXI4094 • $44
MAGIC

4776.
**Classic American Cars
14: 1966 Oldsmobile®
Toronado Coupe**
PALM • 1495QX8151 • $29

4777.
Commander Trip Tucker
RGRS • 1495QXI4091 • $20

4778.
Cookie Doe
KEGR • 995QXG5441 • $29

4779.
Cool Decade 5
HADD • 795QX8134 • $28

4780.
Cool Decade 5
HADD • PrizeQX8134C • $84

4781.
A Cool Holiday!
ESCH • 3200QLX7621 • $42
MAGIC

4782.
Cuando Él Nació
VISK • 1295QXG5361 • $20

4783.
Dad
995QXG5551 • $15

4784.
Dancer En Pointe
KLIN • 1295QXG5394 • $23

4785.
Daughter
995QXG5561 • $15

4786.
Deck The Halls! – Tweety™
FRAN • 1495QXI4004 • $28
MAGIC

4787.
**Dorothy and the
Cowardly Lion™**
LYLE • 1595QXI4021 • $24

4788.
**Dr. Seuss® Books 6:
Yertle The Turtle™**
WILL • 1495QX8421 • $24

4789.
Electrical Spectacle!
4200QLX7624 • $60
MAGIC

4790.
Father Christmas 1
ESCH • 1895QX8471 • $32

4791.
Feliz Navidad
KEGR • 1295QXG5504 • $55

4792.
Finishing Touch
AUBE • GiftQXC4008 • $18

4793.
**Fire Brigade 2:
American LaFrance 700
Series Pumper**
WEBB • 1895QX8424 • $29
MAGIC

4794.
Fire Brigade 2:
American LaFrance 700
Series Pumper
WEBB • 1895QX8424C • $55
Edition Size – 6400

4795.
First Christmas Together
1295QXG5334 • $34

4796.
Football Legends 10:
Peyton Manning –
Indianapolis Colts™
RHOD • 1495QX8521 • $38

4797.
For A Friend
TAGU • 995QXG5604 • $16

4798.
For Grandma
995QXG5574 • $16

4799.
For Grandpa
995QXG5581 • $16

4800.
Frodo Baggins –
The Lord of the Rings™
DIRH • 1495QXI8624 • $24

4801.
Frostlight Faeries, Too:
Collection
ESCH • 1995QXG5531 • $30
Set/3

4802.
Frosty Friends 25
1295QX8331 • $23

4803.
Frosty Friends 25
PrizeQX8331C • $105

4804.
Frosty Friends Complement:
Winterfest
1695QX8474 • $41
25 years of Frosty Friends.

4805.
Frosty Fun
KLIN • 2495QRP4304 • $36

4806.
G.I. Joe®
1495QXI8601 • $23

4807.
Garage Ramp Race
WEBB • 995QXI8631 • $16

4808.
Gift Bearers 6
TAGU • 1295QX8401 • $17

4809.
Gift of Friendship
RHOD • 1295QXG5611 • $20

4810.
Gingerbread Home
CROW • 1295QXI5294 • $24

4811.
Go Teams!
LARS • 995QXG5401 • $16

4812.
Godchild
AUBE • 1295QXG5644 • $20

4813.
Grandchild's First
Christmas
VOTR • 995QXG5741 • $16

4814.
Granddaughter
995QXG5571 • $14

4815.
Grandson
995QXG5564 • $14

4816.
The Grinch™ and Max –
How The Grinch Stole
Christmas™
WILL • 1495QXI8534 • $23

4817.
Happy Birthday, Jesus
995QXG5354 • $19

4818.
Harley-Davidson®
Motorcycle Milestones 6:
2002 VRSCA V-Rod
PALM • 1495QX8184 • $30

4819.
Harry Potter™ and
Hedwig™
FEUR • 1495QXI4044 • $20
Set/2

4820.
Heads-Up Play
RGRS • 1295QXI4061 • $24

4821.
Hidden Wishes
KEGR • 1995QXC4001 • $31

4822.
Holiday Hug
FRAN • 1495QXI5284 • $24

4823.
Hoop Stars 10: Jason Kidd –
New Jersey Nets™
UNRU • 1495QX8531 • $24

4824.
I'm Melting! Melting!
CROW • 3600QXI4024 • $105
MAGIC

4825.
Jack Skellington – The
Nightmare Before
Christmas™
CHAD • 1695QXI8644 • $39

4826.
Jack-in-the-Box
Memories 2:
Pop! Goes the Santa
VISK • 1495QX8411 • $28
MAGIC

4827.
Jolly Old Kris Jingle
LYLE • 1295QXG5501 • $20

4828.
Jolly Old Kris Jingle
LYLE • GiftQXG5501C • $30

150

4829.
Joyful Christmas Village
LARS • 3400QXC4007 • $95

4830.
A Joyful Noise
FORS • 1295QXG5374 • $29

4831.
Joyful Trio
ANDR • 1295QXG5481 • $26

4832.
Kaleidoscope Fairy
KEGR/VOTR • 995QXG5461 • $16

4833.
Keepsake Kids: "Countdown to Christmas" Tree
STGR • 3995QKK3001 • $40
Re-issued in 2005.

4834.
Keepsake Kids: From a Stable So Small Storybook Set
2495QKK3014 • $30
Set/7 • Re-issued in 2005.

4835.
Keepsake Kids: Jolly Ol' St. Nicholas Storybook and Ornaments
2495QKK3011 • $30
Set/6 • Re-issued in 2005.

4836.
Keepsake Kids: My Very Own Christmas Tree
1495QKK3004 • $26
Re-issued in 2005 and 2006.

4837.
Kiddie Car Classics 11: 1935 Timmy Racer
WEBB • 1395QX8444 • $23

4838.
Kindred Spirits
KLIN • 1295QXG5781 • $17

4839.
Kris and the Kringles 4
CROW • 2400QX8114 • $36
MAGIC

4840.
Lighthouse Greetings 8
FRAN • 2400QX8104 • $35
MAGIC

4841.
LIONEL® Trains 9: 1939 Hiawatha Steam Locomotive
1895QX8454 • $30

4842.
LIONEL® Trains Complement: Hiawatha Observation Car
1295QXI4104 • $20

4843.
LIONEL® Trains Complement: Hiawatha Tender
1295QXI4101 • $20

4844.
LIONELville®
CROW • 4400QXI4111 • $94
MAGIC

4845.
Little Nurse, Big Heart
AUBE • 995QXG5424 • $16

4846.
Love To Dance! – Snoopy™
WILL • 2400QXI4114 • $36
MAGIC

4847.
Lunch Wagon for Porky Pig™
1495QXI4051 • $24
Set/2

4848.
Madame Alexander® 9: Dancing Clara
FRAN • 1495QX8111 • $30

4849.
Madame Alexander® Little Women 4: Amy March
FORS • 1595QX8404 • $32

4850.
Mary's Angels 17: Sweet Pea
CHAD/HAMI • 795QX8324 • $38

4851.
Mary's Angels 17: Sweet Pea
CHAD/HAMI • PrizeQX8324C • $95

4852.
Maxine's Crabby Mall-idays
DIRH/WAGN • 1995QLX7641 • $30
MAGIC

4853.
Merry Christmas, Snoopy™!
BRIC • 1495QXI4081 • $33

4854.
Mischievous Kittens 6
AUBE • 995QX8194 • $24

4855.
Model 4010 Tractor – John Deere
1495QXI5291 • $20

4856.
Mom
995QXG5544 • $15

4857.
Monkey See – Curious George™
995QXI8654 • $16

4858.
Mother and Daughter
VOTR • 1295QXG5651 • $19

4859.
Mr. Incredible – The Incredibles
1295QXD5081 • $23

4860.
My Christmas Slippers
HADD • 1495QLX7554 • $25
MAGIC

4861.
Nature's Sketchbook: Nature's Sketchbook 2
BAST/FRAN • 995QX8554 • $16

4862.
New Home
SICK • 1295QXG5621 • $19

4863.
Nick and Christopher 1: Downhill Delivery
LARS • 1295QX2834 • $19

4864.
Noah's Ark
VISK • 1695QXG5371 • $25
MAGIC

4865.
North Pole Patriot
KLIN • 1295QXG5451 • $20

4866.
North Pole Patriot
KLIN • GiftQXG5451C • $75

4867.
**Nostalgic Houses &
Shops 21: Barber Shop
& Beauty Shop**
PALM • 1495QX8181 • $28

4868.
Nuestra Familia
RHOD • 1295QXG5744 • $24

4869.
Nutcracker King
SICK • 1695QXC4006 • $30

4870.
**Oddball, Little Dipper, and
Domino – 102 Dalmatians**
1495QXD5074 • $23

4871.
On, Tweety™! On, Daffy™!
DIRH • 1995QXI4011 • $31

4872.
Our Christmas
ESCH • 1295QXG5341 • $26

4873.
Our Christmas
ESCH • 1495QXG5344 • $29

4874.
Our Family
RHOD • 1295QXG5601 • $20

4875.
Our First Christmas
FORS • 1895QXG5351 • $29

4876.
**Our First Christmas
Together**
895QXG5324 • $14

4877.
Over Par Snowman
RHOD • 995QXG5421 • $16

4878.
Parents-To-Be
FRAN • 1295QXG5734 • $28

4879.
The PEANUTS® Games
DIRH • 1895QXI8691 • $28
Set/4

4880.
**Pedal Power –
Kermit The Frog™**
1495QXI5304 • $23

4881.
**Peppermint Candy Cane
BARBIE™ Ornament**
1495QXI8544 • $28

4882.
Plotting The Course
LARS • 1995QXC4002 • $30

4883.
**Pocket Watch Ornament –
Mickey Mouse**
2400QXD5001 • $36

4884.
**The Polar Express™ –
First Gift of Christmas!**
1495QSR5811 • $20

4885.
**The Polar Express™ – First
Gift Of Christmas Bell**
1295PXA2019 • $75
Re-issued in 2005.

4886.
**The Polar Express™ –
Journey of the Train**
CHAD • 1695QSR5804 • $26
MAGIC

4887.
**The Polar Express™ –
Journey Water Globe**
PALM • 3995QSR5814 • $59
MAGIC

4888.
**The Polar Express™ –
The Magic Bell**
RHOD • 2400QSR5801 • $95
MAGIC

4889.
A Pony for Christmas 7
SICK • 1295QX8221 • $23

4890.
A Pony for Christmas 7
SICK • GiftQX8221C • $95

4891.
Primera Navidad De Bebe
AUBE • 1295QXG5751 • $20

4892.
Puppy Love 14
RGRS • 895QX8441 • $32

4893.
Queen Of Cuisine
TAGU • 1295QP1831 • $19

4894.
Queen Of Cuisine
TAGU • 1295QP1841 • $19

4895.
Queen Of Cuisine
TAGU • 1295QP1844 • $19

4896.
Queen Of Do-It-Yourself
TAGU • 1295QP1821 • $26

4897.
Queen Of Fitness
TAGU • 1295QP1811 • $22

4898.
Queen Of Multi-Tasking
TAGU • 1295QP1814 • $22

4899.
Queen Of Shoes
TAGU • 1295QP1801 • $32

4900.
Queen Of Shopping
TAGU • 1295QP1824 • $32

4901.
Queen Of The Garden
TAGU • 1295QP1804 • $25

4902.
Rainbow Brite™ and Starlite
ESCH • 1295QXI8681 • $28

4903.
Reaching For Christmas
HADD • 1495QXG5474 • $23

4904.
Red Power Ranger™
1495QXI8604 • $23

4905.
Rudolph and Santa –
Rudolph the Red-Nosed
Reindeer™
CHAD • 1295QXG5654 • $32
MAGIC

4906.
Santa Paws
BRIC • 1295QXI4054 • $22

4907.
Santa To The Rescue
LARS • 995QXG5431 • $16

4908.
Santa, Look At Me!
1495QXG5484 • $20
Set/2

4909.
Santas From Around The
World: Display Wreath
2495PR3134 • $36

4910.
Santas From Around
The World: Germany
SICK • 1295QP1704 • $34

4911.
Santas From Around
The World: Ireland
BRIC/KEGR • 1295QP1714 • $30

4912.
Santas From Around
The World: Italy
KEGR/VOTR • 1295QP1724 • $48

4913.
Santas From Around
The World: Mexico
VISK • 1295QP1721 • $49

4914.
Santas From Around
The World: Norway
KEGR/PALM • 1295QP1711 • $23

4915.
Santas From Around
The World: Russia
HADD/KEGR • 1295QP1701 • $23

4916.
Santas From Around
The World: USA
KEGR/VOTR • 1295QP1731 • $34

4917.
Santas From Around
The World: USA
KEGR/VOTR • 1295QP1734 • $38

4918.
Santa's Hula-day!
VISK • 2800QLX7631 • $45
MAGIC

4919.
Scarlett O'Hara™
1595QXI4031 • $31

4920.
Scarlett O'Hara™ and
Rhett Butler™
1895QXI4034 • $44

4921.
School Days
995QXG5624 • $16

4922.
Season of the Heart
KEGR/TAGU • 4000QXC4015 • $95

4923.
Sew Merry, Sew Bright
TAGU • 995QXG5434 • $22

4924.
Sharing The Stars
1995QXC4004 • $36
MAGIC

4925.
Shining Promise
MCGE • 1295QXG5364 • $28

4926.
Silent Night
FORS • 2500QLX7591 • $38
MAGIC

4927.
Sisters
ANDR • 1295QXG5594 • $20

4928.
Sisters
ANDR • 1295QXG5761 • $20

4929.
Sittin' on Santa's Lap
HADD • 2500QLX7594 • $31
MAGIC

4930.
Sky's the Limit 8: Spartan
Model 7-W Executive
NORT • 1495QX8391 • $32

4931.
Small World
3200QXD5021 • $49
Musical.

4932.
Sneaking a Treat
1895QRP4294 • $28

4933.
Snow Buddies 7
HADD • 895QX8131 • $30

153

4934. Snow Sculpture – Mickey Mouse
995QXD5014 • $25

4935. Snow White and the Seven Dwarfs
3600QXD5064 • $55
MAGIC

4936. Snowball and Tuxedo 4: Fancy Footwork
ESCH • 795QX8414 • $19

4937. Snowflake Fun
KEGR • 1595QXG5524 • $25
Set/3

4938. Snowy Day
695QXG5454 • $11

4939. So Much To Do!
WILL • 995PR3035 • $13

4940. Son
995QXG5554 • $15

4941. The Sorcerer's Apprentice – Fantasia
1495QXD5011 • $23

4942. Special Cat
TAGU • 995QXG5591 • $16

4943. Special Dog
TAGU • 995QXG5584 • $23

4944. Special Event
1295QXG5614 • $19

4945. Spider-Man™
RGRS • 1495QXI8611 • $26

4946. Spotlight on Snoopy® 7: The Winning Ticket
DIRH • 995QX8371 • $20

4947. Stanley and Dennis – Playhouse Disney
1295QXD8674 • $20
Set/2

4948. Star Destroyer™ and Blockade Runner™
RHOD • 2800QXI4064 • $50
MAGIC

4949. Star Wars™ 8: Chewbacca™ and C-3PO™
KLIN • 1495QX8431 • $24

4950. Star Wars™: A New Hope Theater One-Sheet
RHOD • 1995QXI4074 • $31

4951. Sweet Tooth Treats 3
AUBE • 1495QX8191 • $24
Set/4

4952. Sweet Tooth Treats 3
AUBE • PrizeQX8191C • $42

4953. Sweetest Little Shepherd
KLIN • 1695QLX7634 • $28
MAGIC

4954. Swinging On A Star
KLIN • 1695QXC4005 • $35

4955. Teacher
FEUR • 995QXG5631 • $16

4956. That Holy Night
LYLE • 1695QXG5391 • $40
Set/3

4957. Those Who Serve
FORS • 1295QXG5444 • $20

4958. Three Beautiful Princesses
1695QXD5054 • $28

4959. Thrill Drivers Corkscrew Race
WEBB • 1495QXI8634 • $24

4960. Ticktock Workshop
CROW • 2800QLX7614 • $44
MAGIC

4961. Tinker Bell – Peter Pan
1695QXD4232 • $26

4962. Tonka® Giant Bulldozer
1495QXI5281 • $24

4963. Tony Stewart – NASCAR®
1495QXI8651 • $24

4964. Town and Country 6: Hometown Church
SICK • 1695QX8201 • $33
Set/2

4965. Toymaker Santa 5
CROW • 1295QX8124 • $44

4966. Treasures and Dreams 3: Jewelry Box Gazebo
CROW • 1995QX8121 • $31
MAGIC

4967. Triple-Decker Treat
CHAD • 995QXG5491 • $22

4968. VeggieTales® – Drummer Boy
895QXG4454 • $18

154

4969.

Victorian Christmas
1695QXG5521 • $26

4970.

Vulcan™ Command Ship
NORT • 2800QXI4084 • $50
MAGIC

4971.

Walt Disney's Snow White
and The Seven Dwarfs
3600QXD5064 • $65
MAGIC

4972.

Whirlwind Decorating –
Taz™
CHAD • 1495QXI4014 • $24
MAGIC

4973.

Winnie the Pooh 7:
A Sticky Situation
1495QXD5084 • $22

4974.

Winnie the Pooh:
100 Acre Express
1995QXD5034 • $31

4975.

Winnie the Pooh:
Amigos Por Siempre
1295QXG5754 • $20

4976.

Winnie the Pooh:
Baby's First Christmas
1495QXG5721 • $22

4977.

Winnie the Pooh:
Friends Forever
1295QXG5024 • $21

4978.

Winnie the Pooh:
Stocking Stuffers
1495QXD5041 • $23

4979.

Winnie the Pooh:
The Winning Bounce
995QXD8561 • $16

4980.

Winnie the Pooh:
Wings For Eeyore
1495QXD5031 • $26

4981.

Winter Garden
VOTR • 1295QXG5534 • $24

4982.

Winter In Paris –
Madeline™
RGRS • 1295QXI5321 • $20

4983.

Winter Wonderland 3:
Building a Snowman
UNRU • 1295QX8251 • $36

4984.

A Wish For Peace
BEST • 2400QXC4013 • $39

4985.

World-Class Shoppers –
Mickey and Minnie
1895QXD5004 • $45

4986.

Yule Express
SICK • 1995QLX7644 • $31
MAGIC

2005

4987.

50 Years of Music and Fun –
Disney's Mickey
Mouse Club®
1995QXD4075 • $24
MAGIC

4988.

All Decked Out
FEUR • 1495QXC5006 • $55

4989.

All-American Trucks 11:
2003 Chevrolet®
Silverado™ SS
PALM • 1495QX2032 • $24

4990.

Anakin Skywalker™'s
Jedi™ Starfighter™
FRAN/PALM • 2800QXI6192 • $50

4991.

And the Winner is...
1495QXI6195 • $20

4992.

Angel of Grace
LYLE • 1495QXG4375 • $40

4993.

Angel on Earth
FORS • 995QXG4372 • $12

4994.

Arctic Adventurers
KLIN • 1295QXG4452 • $19

4995.

Arctic Adventurers
KLIN • GiftQXG4452C • $45

4996.

At the Ballpark 10:
Albert Pujols –
St. Louis Cardinals™
RHOD • 1495QX2282 • $32

4997.

Baby's First Christmas
AUBE • 1295QXG4592 • $26

4998.

Baby's First Christmas
HADD • 995QXG4602 • $12

4999.

Baby's First Christmas
VISK • 1295QXG4622 • $14

5000.

Baby's First Christmas
HADD • 1895QXG4625 • $28

5001.

BARBIE™ 12:
Fashion Luncheon™
BARBIE™ Ornament
1595QX2305 • $28

5002.

BARBIE™ and the Magic
of Pegasus
2500QXI6415 • $34

155

5003.
BARBIE™ as Titania™
Ornament
1495QXI6412 • $19

5004.
BARBIE™ Fairytopia™
Ornament
1895QXI6512 • $24
MAGIC

5005.
BARBIE™ Fashion
Model: Delphine™
BARBIE™ Ornament
ANDR • 2500QXI6432 • $34

5006.
The Batcycle™
CHAD • 1495QXI8902 • $20

5007.
The Beauty of Birds 1:
Northern Cardinal
KEGR/VOTR • 1495QX2135 • $28

5008.
Best in Show
VISK • 995QXG4705 • $14

5009.
Best Night of the Week –
Wonderful World of Disney
2400QXD4085 • $32
MAGIC

5010.
Buzz Lightyear and RC
Racer – Toy Story
1495QXD4225 • $22

5011.
Candlelight Services 8:
Central Tower Church
LARS • 1895QX2262 • $28

5012.
Carousel Ride 2:
Proud Giraffe
KLIN • 1295QX2012 • $95

5013.
Carousel Ride Complement:
Carousel Ride Display
KLIN • 4500QX8481 • $51
Re-issued from 2004.

5014.
Celebration BARBIE™ 6
1595QX2202 • $32

5015.
Celebration BARBIE™ 6
(African-American)
1595QXI6422 • $32

5016.
Charlie Brown
Christmas Ball
GiftPR3731 • $26

5017.
A Charlie Brown®
Christmas
3000QFM6482 • $50
Musical Snowglobe.

5018.
Chicken Little
1295QXD4815 • $18

5019.
Child's Age:
Child's Fourth Christmas
FRAN • 895QXG4532 • $20

5020.
Child's Age:
Child's Fifth Christmas
FRAN • 895QXG4535 • $20

5021.
Child's Age:
My First Christmas (Boy)
HADD • 995QXG4542 • $14

5022.
Child's Age:
My First Christmas (Girl)
KLIN • 995QXG4565 • $14

5023.
Child's Age:
My Second Christmas (Boy)
HADD • 995QXG4545 • $14

5024.
Child's Age:
My Second Christmas (Girl)
KLIN • 995QXG4572 • $14

5025.
Child's Age:
My Third Christmas (Boy)
HADD • 995QXG4552 • $14

5026.
Child's Age:
My Third Christmas (Girl)
KLIN • 995QXG4575 • $14

5027.
Child's Age:
My Fourth Christmas (Boy)
HADD • 995QXG4555 • $14

5028.
Child's Age:
My Fourth Christmas (Girl)
KLIN • 995QXG4582 • $14

5029.
Child's Age:
My Fifth Christmas (Boy)
HADD • 995QXG4562 • $14

5030.
Child's Age:
My Fifth Christmas (Girl)
KLIN • 995QXG4585 • $14

5031.
Christmas At Last!
7500QXC5012 • $95

5032.
Christmas Countdown
CROW • 1495QXG4455 • $20

5033.
Christmas Window 3:
Christmas Window 2005
HADD • 1995QXC5003 • $45

5034.
Christmas With the Family –
Lady and the Tramp
1695QXD4235 • $24

5035.
City Sidewalks
CROW • 4400QLX7635 • $64
MAGIC

5036.
Classic American
Cars 15: 1968
Pontiac® Firebird™
PALM • 1495QX2025 • $22

5037.
Classic American Cars
Complement: Ford®
Thunderbird™ 50th
Anniversary Set
PALM • 2400QXI6172 • $32
Set/2

5038.
Clone Trooper™ Lieutenant
KLIN/RGRS • 1495QXI6175 • $42

5039.
Color Me Curious –
Curious George™
995QXI6222 • $16

5040.
Cool Decade 6
HADD • 795QX2195 • $19

5041.
Cool Decade 6
HADD • PrizeQX2195C • $895
Edition Size – 96

5042.
The Crabby Caroler –
Maxine
DIRH/WAGN • 1995QLX7592 • $29
MAGIC

5043.
Crack the Whip! –
PEANUTS®
DIRH • 2400QXI6292 • $38
MAGIC

5044.
Cutest Kitty
VISK • 995QXG4712 • $14

5045.
Dad
FORS • 995QXG4672 • $18

5046.
Darth Vader™
KLIN • 1895QXI6185 • $38

5047.
Daughter
FORS • 995QXG4682 • $22

5048.
Designer Spotlight™
BARBIE™ Ornament
RGRS • 1995QXC5008 • $180

5049.
Dr. Seuss® Books 7: Oh,
the Places You'll Go!
WILL • 1495QX2112 • $22

5050.
Dreaming Big
FEUR • 995QXG4325 • $18

5051.
Duck Dodgers™ and
Marvin The Martian™
WILL • 1495QXI8765 • $19

5052.
Every Kid's a Star:
Academics
STGR • 995QXG4795 • $12

5053.
Every Kid's a Star:
Ballet
BEST • 995QXG4782 • $12

5054.
Every Kid's a Star:
Baseball/Softball
BEST • 995QXG4762 • $12

5055.
Every Kid's a Star:
Basketball
BEST • 995QXG4752 • $12

5056.
Every Kid's a Star:
Camping
BEST • 995QXG4775 • $12

5057.
Every Kid's a Star:
Cheerleading
BEST • 995QXG4785 • $12

5058.
Every Kid's a Star:
Football
STGR • 995QXG4772 • $12

5059.
Every Kid's a Star:
Music
STGR • 995QXG4792 • $12

5060.
Every Kid's a Star:
Ornament Display Stand
595QXG4802 • $9

5061.
Every Kid's a Star:
Soccer
BEST • 995QXG4755 • $12

5062.
Every Kid's a Star:
Volleyball
BEST • 995QXG4765 • $12

5063.
Fairy Messengers 1:
Poinsettia Fairy
KLIN • 995QX2145 • $28

5064.
Family Ties
FORS • 1295QXG4742 • $26

5065.
Father Christmas 2
ESCH • 1895QX2155 • $26

5066.
Feliz Navidad
KEGR/VISK • 1295QXG4492 • $22

5067.
Fire Brigade 3: 1938
Chevrolet® Fire Engine
WEBB • 1895QX2035 • $29
MAGIC

5068.
Fire Brigade 3: 1938
Chevrolet® Fire Engine
WEBB • 1995QX2035C • $46
MAGIC

5069.
First Christmas Together
895QXG4392 • $20

5070.
First Christmas Together
FORS • 1295QXG4402 • $26

5071.
Football Legends 11:
Michael Vick –
Atlanta Falcons™
GARC • 1495QX2292 • $20

5072.
For Grandma
995QXG4695 • $14

157

5073.
For Grandpa
995QXG4702 • $14

5074.
For You, Teacher!
RHOD • 995QXG4315 • $12

5075.
Friends at Large –
Madagascar™
GARC • 1295QXI6495 • $18

5076.
Frosty Friends 26
SEAL • 1295QX2325 • $26

5077.
Frosty Friends 26
SEAL • PrizeQX2325C • $1095
Edition Size – 96

5078.
G.I. Joe®
1495QXI6262 • $19

5079.
Gandalf the Grey™ –
The Lord of the Rings™
FORS • 1495QXI6232 • $22

5080.
Gardener's Paradise
VOTR • 1295QXG4285 • $19

5081.
Gift Bearers 7
TAGU • 1295QX2222 • $24

5082.
Gift Bearers 7 (Unpainted)
TAGU • GiftQX2222C • $30

5083.
Godchild
LYLE • 995QXG4735 • $24

5084.
Grandchild's First
Christmas
SICK • 995QXG4612 • $12

5085.
Granddaughter
RGRS • 995QXG4692 • $28

5086.
Grandson
RGRS • 995QXG4685 • $28

5087.
Happy Hues
TAGU • 1295QXI6225 • $18

5088.
A Happy Snowman
AUBE • 995PR3570 • $14

5089.
Harley-Davidson®
Motorcycle Milestones 7:
2000 Softtail® Deuce™
PALM • 1495QX2042 • $24

5090.
Harry Potter™ –
Quidditch™ Match
FEUR • 1495QXI8915 • $20

5091.
The Heart of the Season
695QXG4645 • $16

5092.
Here Comes Santa 9:
Santa's Woody
Special Edition
CROW • 1495QXE2355 • $44

5093.
Holiday Serenade
KEGR • 2400QXG4422 • $34
MAGIC

5094.
Holiday Sledding –
Raggedy Ann and Andy®
FRAN • 1495QXI6282 • $20
Set/2

5095.
Hoop Stars 11:
Carmelo Anthony –
Denver Nuggets™
FEUR • 1495QX2345 • $32

5096.
I.C. Pete's Frozen Treats
HADD • 1995QLX7595 • $28
MAGIC

5097.
Illuminations:
Santa's Christmas Magic
2500QLM7952 • $25

5098.
Illuminations:
Snowflake Snowballs
6000QLM7932 • $60
Set/9

5099.
Illuminations:
Snowflake Snowballs
2500QLM7975 • $25
Set/3

5100.
Illuminations:
Starlight Starbright
2500QLM7982 • $25

5101.
Illuminations:
Sugarplum Dreams
2500QLM7922 • $25

5102.
Illuminations:
Watching for Santa
2500QLM7925 • $25

5103.
"It's Christmas Eve!"
CHAD • 2800QXC5007 • $58

5104.
Jack-in-the-Box Memories
3: Pop! Goes the Reindeer
VISK • 1495QX2125 • $24
MAGIC

5105.
The Journey of the Kings
CROW • 1895QXG4382 • $24
MAGIC

5106.
The Joy of Music
FALT • 995QXG4322 • $19

5107.
The Joy of Nursing
AUBE • 995QXG4305 • $12

5108.
Joyful Bells
FALT • 695QXG4425 • $19

5109.
Joyful Jumping Jacks
FALT • 1695QXG4462 • $18
Set/3

5110.
Joyful Tidings: Arianne
VARI • 1295QP1822 • $14

5111.
Joyful Tidings: Azura
FORS/KEGR • 1295QP1825 • $16

5112.
Joyful Tidings: Cordelia
VARI • 1295QP1805 • $14

5113.
Joyful Tidings: Cordelia
VARI • 1295QP1832 • $14

5114.
Joyful Tidings: Cordelia
VARI • 1295QP1835 • $14

5115.
Joyful Tidings: Display Wreath
2495QP1842 • $25

5116.
Joyful Tidings: Esmeralda
VARI • 1295QP1812 • $14

5117.
Joyful Tidings: Gilda
KEGR/VOTR • 1295QP1815 • $14

5118.
Keepsake Kids: "Countdown to Christmas" Tree
STGR • 3995QKK3001 • $40
Re-issued from 2004.

5119.
Keepsake Kids: From a Stable So Small Storybook Set
2495QKK3014 • $30
Set/7 • Re-issued from 2004.

5120.
Keepsake Kids: Jolly Ol' St. Nicholas Storybook and Ornaments
2495QKK3011 • $30
Set/6 • Re-issued from 2004.

5121.
Keepsake Kids: My Very Own Christmas Tree
1495QKK3004 • $26
Also issued in 2004 and 2006.

5122.
Keepsake Kids: Nativity Play Set
VISK • 3995QKK3025 • $40
Set/8

5123.
Keepsake Kids: Pickles, The Elf "Find Me, If You Can" Game
995QKK3072 • $12

5124.
Keepsake Kids: Santa's Workshop Play Set
VISK • 3995QKK3032 • $40
Set/8

5125.
Keepsake Kids: Three Kings From Afar
2495QKK3002 • $25
Set/6 • Re-issued in 2006.

5126.
Keepsake Kids: Where's Pickles?
2495QKK3015 • $25
Set/6

5127.
Khan
RGRS • 1495QXI6202 • $19

5128.
Kiddie Car Classics 12: 1926 Murray® Steelcraft Speedster
PALM • 1395QX2295 • $20

5129.
The Kiss
1295QXG4412 • $32

5130.
Kris and the Kringles 5
CROW • 2400QX2185 • $29

5131.
Kris and the Kringles 5
CROW • PrizeQX2185C • $900
Edition Size – 96

5132.
L.A.at Last! – I Love Lucy®
GARC • 1695QXI6252 • $26

5133.
Leap of Love
VISK • 995QXG4395 • $14

5134.
Leonardo – Teenage Mutant Ninja Turtles™
GARC • 1295QXI6435 • $18

5135.
Light of Liberty
KEGR • 1295QXG4332 • $19

5136.
Lighthouse Greetings 9
FRAN • 2400QX2272 • $55
MAGIC

5137.
LIONEL® Trains 10: Pennsylvania B6 Steam Locomotive
1895QX2052 • $32

5138.
LIONEL® Trains Complement: No. 714 Boxcar
1295QXI6125 • $19

5139.
LIONEL® Trains Complement: No. 717 Caboose
1295QX2122 • $19

5140.
LIONEL® Trains Complement: Pennsylvania B6 Tender
1295QXI6122 • $19

5141.
Little Helpers: Baking Cookies
FORS • 1295QXG4445 • $16

5142.
Little Helpers: Hanging the Wreath
BRIC • 1295QXG4442 • $14

5143.
Little Helpers: Mailing A Letter to Santa
FEUR • 1295QXG4435 • $14

5144.
Little Shepherd
FALT • 995QXG4345 • $12

5145.
Locutus of Borg™
RGRS • 2800QXI6205 • $39

5146.
Madame Alexander® 10: Sweet Irish Dancer
FRAN • 1495QX2055 • $32

5147.
Mailbox Melodies
CROW • 3200QLX7632 • $39
MAGIC

5148.
Make Way! – Taz™
CHAD • 1295QXI8772 • $19

5149.
Mary's Angels 18: Forsythia
CHAD/HAMI • 795QX2315 • $14

5150.
Mary's Angels 18: Forsythia
CHAD/HAMI • PrizeQX2315C • $58

5151.
Matt Kenseth
GENT • 1495QXI6272 • $19

5152.
Melody of Praise
1295QXG4365 • $16

5153.
Merry Mayhem Workshop
VARI • 7500QXC5013 • $125

5154.
Mighty Simba – The Lion King
1495QXD4222 • $19
MAGIC

5155.
Mighty Tonka® Wrecker
1495QXI6255 • $19

5156.
Mischievous Kittens 7
AUBE • 995QX2225 • $18

5157.
Mischievous Kittens 7
AUBE • PrizeQX2225C • $995
Edition Size ñ 96

5158.
Model B Tractor – John Deere
1495QXI6245 • $22

5159.
Mom
FORS • 995QXG4665 • $18

5160.
Mooster Fix-It
LARS • 1295QXG4272 • $24

5161.
Mosaic of Faith
VOTR • 1295QXG4352 • $16

5162.
Mother and Daughter
VOTR • 1295QXG4745 • $20

5163.
Muscle Cars
GOSL/PALM • 3400QXC5009 • $200
Set/3

5164.
Nació el Amor
GARC • 1295QXG4362 • $19

5165.
Nature's Sketchbook: Nature's Sketchbook 3
BAST/FRAN • 995QX2115 • $20

5166.
New Home
VOTR • 1295QXG4635 • $40

5167.
Nick and Christopher 2: Hockey Thrills
LARS • 1295QX2152 • $16

5168.
Nick and Christopher 2: Hockey Thrills
LARS • GiftQX2152C • $48

5169.
Noah's Ark
BRIC • 1495QXG4355 • $20

5170.
Nostalgic Houses & Shops 22: Victorian Home
PALM • 1495QX2322 • $28

5171.
Nostalgic Houses & Shops 22: Victorian Home
PALM • 1295QX2322C • $58

5172.
Nuestra Familia
1295QXG4732 • $16

5173.
O Kitchen Rack
KEGR • 995QXG4282 • $12

5174.
Off to See the Wizard! – The Wizard of Oz™
LYLE • 1995QXI8925 • $30

5175.
Once Upon a Starry Night
TAGU • 1295QXG4385 • $14

5176.
One Cute Cookie
995QXG4632 • $12

5177.
The Opening Game
TAGU • 1995QXC5002 • $38

5178.
Order Up!
1895QRP4082 • $28
Set/2

5179.
Our Christmas
KEGR • 1295QXG4405 • $22

5180.
Our Family
1295QXG4725 • $34

5181.
Our First Christmas
ANDR • 1895QXG4415 • $34

5182.
Over the Rainbow –
The Wizard of Oz™
RHOD • 2800QXI8932 • $39

5183.
Packed With Love
995QXG4642 • $12

5184.
Parents-to-Be
FRAN • 1295QXG4605 • $19

5185.
PEANUTS® Christmas
Pageant
DIRH/RGRS • 2600QXC5011 • $200
MAGIC

5186.
Peek-a-Boo! – Sylvester™
and Tweety™
GARC • 1495QXI8755 • $19

5187.
Pinball Action – Bugs
Bunny™ and Daffy Duck™
FEUR • 2400QXI8775 • $32

5188.
The Polar Express™ – First
Gift Of Christmas Bell
1295PXA2019 • $75
Re-issued from 2004.

5189.
The Polar Express™ –
Jingle Bell Memories
BEST/CROW • 1495QXI6462 • $22

5190.
A Pony for Christmas 8
SICK • 1295QX2265 • $22

5191.
A Pony for Christmas 8
SICK • GiftQX2265C • $58

5192.
Primera Navidad de Bebé
AUBE • 1295QXG4595 • $14

5193.
Puppy Love 15
RGRS • 895QX2312 • $20

5194.
Puppy Love 15
RGRS • GiftQX2312C • $55

5195.
A Putter for Santa
RHOD • 995QXG4312 • $14

5196.
Queen of Chocolate
TAGU • 1295QEC1851 • $22

5197.
Rockin' With Santa
VISK • 2800QLX7622 • $85
MAGIC

5198.
Ruby Slippers –
The Wizard of Oz™
GOSL • 1995QXC5004 • $95

5199.
Rudolph® and Bumble™
The Abominable
Snowmonster
1495QXG4475 • $18

5200.
Santa Beagle and
Friends:PEANUTS®
1495QXI6485 • $28

5201.
Santa Knows!
GARC • 2400QLX7612 • $35
MAGIC

5202.
Santa Nutcracker
CHAD • 1695QXC5005 • $42

5203.
Santas From Around
The World: England
KEGR • 1295QXG4822 • $16

5204.
Santa's Helpers –
Mickey and Pluto
1495QXD4012 • $18

5205.
Santa's Little Shopper
AUBE • 995QXG4302 • $12

5206.
Santa's Magic Sack
LARS • 1295QXG4465 • $16

5207.
Santa's Magic Sack
LARS • GiftQXG4465NC • $16

5208.
Santa's Magic Sack
LARS • PrizeQXG4465OC • $36

5209.
Santa's Magic Sack
LARS • 1295QXG4472 • $36

5210.
Santa's Midnight Ride:
Dash Away All
CHAD • 2995QP1762 • $35

5211.
Santa's Midnight Ride:
Ready for Flight
ESCH • 1495QP1745 • $30
Set/2

5212.
Santa's Midnight Ride:
Two for the Skies
ESCH • 1495QP1755 • $30
Set/2

5213.
Scarlett O'Hara™
and Rhett Butler™ –
Gone With the Wind™
1895QXI6015 • $22

5214.
Scarlett O'Hara™:
Gone With the Wind™
1595QXI6002 • $20

5215.
A Season to Sing –
Kermit the Frog™
1295QXI6242 • $16

5216.
Shake it, Santa!
VISK • GiftWD3533 • $28

5217.
Shiver-Me Tim Brrr
KLIN • 1695QLX7582 • $20
MAGIC

5218.
Shrek® and Princess
Fiona – Shrek 2®
CHAD • 1495QXI6492 • $18

5219.
Silent Night
1495QXG4482 • $24

5220.
Sisters
FORS • 1295QXG4715 • $19

5221.
Sisters
FORS • 1295QXG4722 • $15

5222.
Skating Lessons – Bambi
1695QXD4242 • $20

5223.
Sky's the Limit 9:
1931 Laird Super Solution
NORT • 1495QX2045 • $18

5224.
Snow Bear Buddies
RGRS • 995QXG4432 • $12

5225.
Snow Bear Buddies
RGRS • GiftQXG4432C • $40

5226.
Snow Buddies 8
HADD • 895QX2245 • $12

5227.
Snow Buddies 8
HADD • PrizeQX2245C • $N/E

5228.
Snow Day Magic
HADD • 1995QXC5001 • $26

5229.
Snowball and Tuxedo 5:
Two Sweet!
ESCH • 795QX2192 • $14

5230.
Snowtop Lodge 1:
Skylar A. Woolscarf
ESCH • 1895QX2405 • $24

5231.
Soda Shop Sweethearts
1695QRP4072 • $22

5232.
Son
FORS • 995QXG4675 • $22

5233.
The Sorcerer's
Apprentice – Fantasia
3200QXD4082 • $40
MAGIC

5234.
Space Alien Alert! –
Power Rangers SPD™
FEUR • 1495QXI6505 • $18

5235.
Speak! – Scooby-Doo™
RHOD • 1695QXI8905 • $20

5236.
Special Edition Repaint
Rocking Horse
SICK • 1295QXE2352 • $38

5237.
Spider-Man™
RGRS • 1495QXI6265 • $18

5238.
Spirit of St. Nick
WILL • 1995QLX7645 • $40
MAGIC

5239.
Spirit of St. Nick
WILL • 1995QLX7645C • $56
MAGIC

5240.
Spotlight on Snoopy® 8:
Snoopy™ the Magnificent
LARS • 995QX2132 • $12

5241.
Star Wars™ 9:
Princess Leia™
KLIN • 1495QX2015 • $18

5242.
Sweeeeet Friendship –
Finding Nemo
1495QXD4812 • $18

5243.
Sweet Tooth Treats 4
AUBE • 1495QX2175 • $18
Set/4

5244.
Sweet Tooth Treats 4
AUBE • PrizeQX2175C • $46
Set/4

5245.
Thomas the Tank® Engine
WILL • 1295QXI6235 • $22

5246.
Tinker Bell – Peter Pan
1495QXD4265 • $18

5247.
To My Gouda Friend
DIRH • 995QXG4662 • $14

5248.
Touchdown, Snoopy®!
FEUR • 1495QXI6285 • $18

5249.
Toyland Treasures
HADD • 3200QLX7625 • $39
MAGIC

5250.
Toymaker Santa 6
CROW • 1295QX2205 • $18

5251.
Toymaker Santa 6
CROW • PrizeQX2205C • $58

5252.
Treasures and Dreams 4:
Jewelry Box Carol
CROW • 1995QX2172 • $24
MAGIC

5253.
Tree-Napper at Work –
Dr. Seuss's® How the
Grinch Stole Christmas™
WILL • 1295QXI6162 • $16

5254.
Trim A Tiny Tree
FALT • 995QXG4295 • $12

5255.
Triple Dippin'!
HADD • GiftWD3532 • $12

5256.
True Patriot –
Mickey Mouse®
995QXD4005 • $14

5257.
Tweety™ Plays an Angel
GARC • 1695QXI8762 • $20
MAGIC

5258.
U.S.S. Enterprise™
NCC-1701-A
NORT • 2800QXI6215 • $59
MAGIC

5259.
Wedding Day Dance –
Cinderella
2400QXD4245 • $28
MAGIC

5260.
Winnie the Pooh 8:
Rainy Day Rescue
1495QXD4102 • $16

5261.
Winnie the Pooh:
Amigos de Verdad
1295QXG4655 • $16

5262.
Winnie the Pooh:
Baby's First Christmas
1495QXG4615 • $16

5263.
Winnie the Pooh:
Bounce Practice – Tigger
1295QXD4092 • $16

5264.
Winnie the Pooh: Getting
Ready for Christmas
3200QXD4212 • $36

5265.
Winnie the Pooh:
Gift Exchange
1495QXD4105 • $18

5266.
Winnie the Pooh:
True Friends
1295QXG4652 • $16

5267.
Winnie the Pooh:
Unlikely Friends – Pooh's
Heffalump Movie™
1295QXD4215 • $22

5268.
Winter Wonderland 4:
Ice-Skaters' Delight
BEST/UNRU • 1295QX2182 • $20

5269.
Yankee Doodle Santa
FRAN • 1295QXG4335 • $16

5270.
You've Been Caught!
BRIC • 995QXG4292 • $16

2006

5271.
A+ Teacher
TAGU • 1000QXG2603

5272.
"All In" for Fun!
TAGU • 1000QXG2283

5273.
All Is Calm
ESCH • 1400QXG2683

5274.
All-American Trucks 12:
1948 Ford® Pickup
PALM • 1500QX2376

5275.
Always a Princess
1500QMP4018

5276.
Always Remembered
TAGU • 1250QXG2673

5277.
Anakin Skywalker™ and
Obi-Wan Kenobi™
KLIN • 2800QXI6186
MAGIC

5278.
Angel of Life
LYLE • 1500QXG2686

5279.
Art & Crafts
BEST • 1250QXG3336

5280.
At the Ballpark 11:
Alex Rodriguez –
New York Yankees
1500QX2336

5281.
Baby's First Christmas
HADD • 1250QXG2823

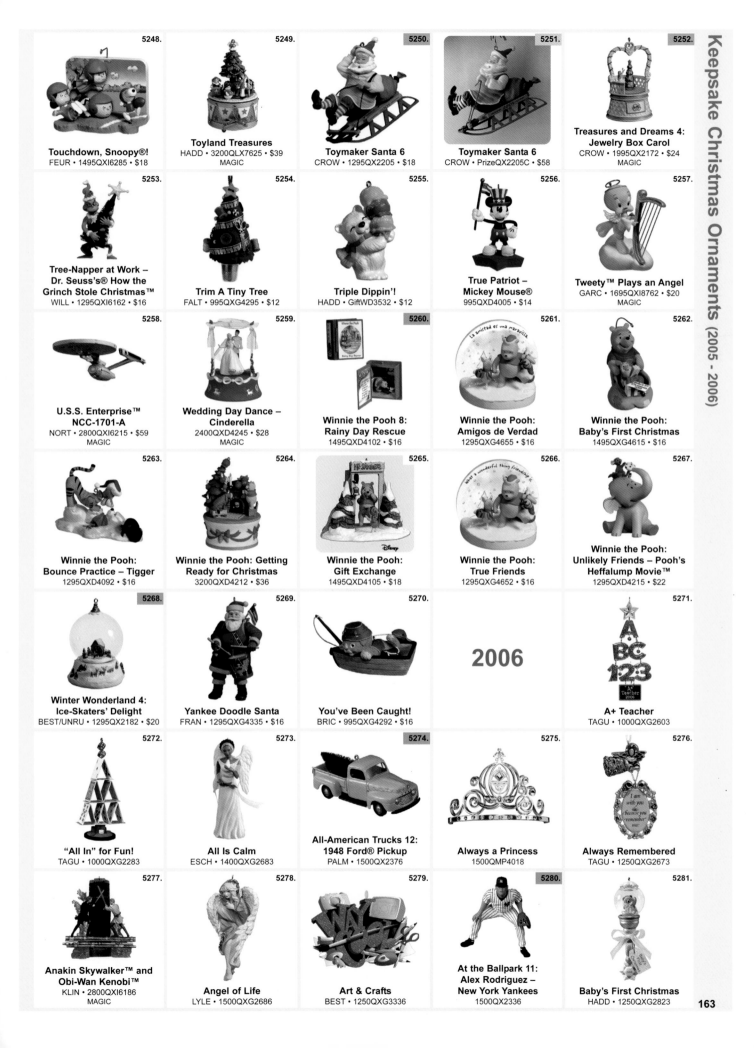

5282.
Baby's First Christmas
HADD • 1250QXG2826

5283.
Baby's First Christmas
HADD • 1250QXG2833

5284.
Baby's First Christmas
BRIC • 1650QXG2836

5285.
Bananas for You
VISK • 1000QXG3253

5286.
BARBIE™ 13:
Evening Splendor BARBIE™
1600QX2373

5287.
BARBIE™ 13:
Evening Splendor BARBIE™
1500QXE4463
Limited Edition

5288.
BARBIE™ Fairytopia™
Ornament
ANDR • 1500QXI6206
Set/2

5289.
BARBIE™ in The Twelve
Dancing Princesses
ANDR • 2000QXI6346
MAGIC

5290.
BARBIE™ Shoe Tree
SICK • 1850QXI6343

5291.
The Bat Signal™
CHAD/FORS • 1650QXI6153
MAGIC

5292.
Bathtime – Dumbo
1500QXD8353

5293.
The Beauty of Birds 2:
Black-Capped Chickadee
KEGR/VOTR • 1500QX2506

5294.
Belle's Grand Entrance –
Beauty and the Beast
1650QXD8363

5295.
Bright Memories
FORS • 1000QXG3083

5296.
Bunny Hug
HADD • 1000QXE3223
Limited Edition – 2006

5297.
Buzz Lightyear, Space
Ranger – Toy Story
1500QXD8376
MAGIC

5298.
Candlelight Services 9:
Old Stone Church
LARS • 2000QX2313
MAGIC

5299.
Caregivers –
Angels Among Us
RGRS • 1000QXG2643

5300.
Carousel Ride 3:
Prancing Reindeer
KLIN • 1250QX2486

5301.
Catching Snowflakes
HADD • 1500QXE3256
Limited Edition – 2006

5302.
Celebration BARBIE™ 7
ANDR • 1600QX2393

5303.
Celebrity Style
KLIN • 1250QXG3173

5304.
A Charlie Brown™
Christmas Tree
2000QXC6004
MAGIC

5305.
A Charmed Life –
First Christmas Together
"Promise Tree"
VOTR • 1850QXG2733

5306.
Cheery Cargo –
Thomas the Tank® Engine
WILL • 1250QXI3186
Set/2

5307.
Child's Age:
Child's Fifth Christmas
FRAN • 900QXG2906

5308.
Child's Age:
My First Christmas (Boy)
HADD • 1000QXG2856

5309.
Child's Age:
My First Christmas (Girl)
KLIN • 1000QXG2883

5310.
Child's Age:
My Second Christmas (Boy)
HADD • 1000QXG2863

5311.
Child's Age:
My Second Christmas (Girl)
KLIN • 1000QXG2886

5312.
Child's Age:
My Third Christmas (Boy)
HADD • 1000QXG2866

5313.
Child's Age:
My Third Christmas (Girl)
KLIN • 1000QXG2893

5314.
Child's Age:
My Fourth Christmas (Boy)
HADD • 1000QXG2873

5315.
Child's Age:
My Fourth Christmas (Girl)
KLIN • 1000QXG2896

5316.
Child's Age:
My Fifth Christmas (Boy)
HADD • 1000QXG2876

5317.
Child's Age:
My Fifth Christmas (Girl)
KLIN • 1000QXG2903

5318.
Chocolate Treasures
TAGU • 1250QXG2286

5319.
Christmas Belle
KEGR/VOTR • 1500QXG3023

5320.
A Christmas Broadcast
WILL • 2400QLX7596
MAGIC

5321.
A Christmas Greeting –
Hoops & Yoyo
WILL • 1650QXG2243
MAGIC

5322.
Christmas Window 4:
Christmas Window 2006
AUBE • 2000QXC6003

5323.
Cinderella's Slipper
1250QMP4017

5324.
Classic American Cars 16:
1961 Chevrolet® Impala®
PALM • 1500QX2356

5325.
Coach
FEUR • 1000QXG2236

5326.
Cool Decade 7
HADD • 850QX2463

5327.
Dad
KLIN • 1000QXG2916

5328.
Daughter
KLIN • 1000QXG2926

5329.
Dear Santa
AUBE • 1250QXG2306

5330.
Deck the Halls,
Charlie Brown™
2400QXI6166
MAGIC

5331.
Decorating Scooby-style
RGRS • 1250QXI6146

5332.
Dorothy and the Munchkins –
The Wizard of Oz™
CROW • 3200QXI6106
MAGIC

5333.
Dr. Seuss® Books 8:
Fox in Socks™
WILL • 1500QX2353

5334.
Dreaming of Christmas
1500QXD8306

5335.
ESPN
FEUR • 1500QXI6313
MAGIC

5336.
Fairy Messengers 2:
Pansy Fairy
KLIN • 1000QX2563

5337.
Fashion
BEST • 1250QXG3353

5338.
Father Christmas 3
ESCH • 1850QX2566

5339.
Fire Brigade 4: 1961 GMC®
WEBB • 1850QX2326
MAGIC

5340.
Have You Seen Me?
Fire Brigade 4: 1961 GMC®
WEBB • ($N/E)QX2326C
MAGIC

5341.
Firefighters
LYLE • 1000QXG2656

5342.
First Christmas Together
FRAN • 1500QXG2716

5343.
Football Legends 12:
Donovan McNabb –
Philadelphia Eagles
1500QX2386

5344.
Frosty Friends 1
MAHO • 1450QXE4496
Limited Edition

5345.
Frosty Friends 27
VISK • 1250QX2513

5346.
Frosty Friends Complement:
Snow Globe
HADD • 2800QXE3313

5347.
Get Your Kicks!
1000QXG6386

5348.
A Glimpse of Santa
LYLE • 2800QXC6007
MAGIC

5349.
Glinda the Good Witch
Arrives! – The Wizard of Oz™
LYLE • 1500QXI6103

5350.
Godchild
FORS • 1000QXG3213

5351.
Goodcuppa Coffee
WEBB • 1250QXG2276

165

5352.
Granddaughter
KLIN • 1000QXG2936

5353.
Grandma
SICK • 1250QXG3193

5354.
Grandpa
SICK • 1250QXG3196

5355.
Grandson
KLIN • 1000QXG2993

5356.
Grinchy Claus
WILL • 1500QXI6183

5357.
Happiness Is…
1250QXI6163

5358.
Happy Haulers
CROW • 3200QLX7613
MAGIC

5359.
Harley-Davidson®
Motorcycle Milestones 8:
1994 FLHR Road King®
PALM • 1500QX2333

5360.
Harry Potter™ –
Danger in the Hallways
FEUR • 1500QXI6156

5361.
Hello Ricky? – I Love Lucy®
1650QXI6366
MAGIC

5362.
Holiday Angels 1:
The Gift of Love
FORS/KEGR • 1650QX2142

5363.
A Holiday for Two
1500QXG3016

5364.
Home Improvement Pro
PALM • 1250QXG2303

5365.
Imperial AT-AT™ and
Rebel Snowspeeder™
HURL • 2800QXI6193
MAGIC

5366.
Jack Sparrow –
Pirates of the Caribbean
1500QXD6376
MAGIC

5367.
Jack-in-the-Box Memories 4:
Pop! Goes the Teddy Bear
VISK • 1500QX2493
MAGIC,/I>

5368.
The Jingle Ball
TAGU • 1000QXG2616

5369.
Joe Coolest
LARS • 1250QXI3203

5370.
Keeping It "Reel"
KEGR • 1000QXG2636

5371.
Keepsake Kids:
"Santa's Workshop"
Countdown Calendar
4000QKK3066
Set/31

5372.
Keepsake Kids:
A Gift for Jesus
2500QKK3053

5373.
Keepsake Kids:
Home Sweet Home
2500QKK3056

5374.
Keepsake Kids: My Very
Own Christmas Tree
1495QKK3004
Re-issued from 2004 and 2005.

5375.
Keepsake Kids:
Three Kings From Afar
2495QKK3002
Set/6 • Re-issued from 2005.

5376.
Kiddie Car Classics 13:
1964 1/2 Ford® Mustang™
PALM • 1400QX2343

5377.
A Kitty for Christmas!
AUBE • 1500QXG2793

5378.
Letters to Santa
LARS • 3200QLX7606
MAGIC

5379.
Lifesavers
1000QXG3183

5380.
Lighthouse Greetings 10
FRAN • 2400QX2396
MAGIC

5381.
Lightning McQueen
and Mater – Cars
1500QXD8386
Set/2

5382.
LIONEL® Trains 2: 1950 Santa
Fe F3 Diesel Locomotive
1850QXE3233
Limited Edition – 2006

5383.
LIONEL® Trains 11:
Union Pacific Veranda
Turbine Locomotive
1850QX2323

5384.
LIONEL® Trains
Complement: Union Pacific
Veranda Stock Car
1250QXI6176

5385.
LIONEL® Trains
Complement: Union Pacific
Veranda Tender
1250QXI6173

5386.
Looking for Santa
LARS • 1250QXG2783

5387. Lots to Do –
Bob the Builder
1000QXI6326

5388. Love You a Latte
CHAD • 1500QXI6143

5389. Lucy and the Wardrobe –
Narnia
1500QXD8393

5390. Madame Alexander® 11:
Christmas Tea
FRAN • 1500QX2346

5391. The Man of Steel™ –
Superman™
FEUR • 1500QXI6323

5392. Mary's Angels 1: Angelica
CHAD/HAMI • 1000QXE4466
Limited Edition

5393. Mary's Angels 19: Veronica
CHAD • 850QX2556

5394. MegaRocketron 3000
WILL • 1650QLX7583
MAGIC

5395. Merry Bakers: Display
HADD/TAGU • 3000QP1773

5396. Merry Bakers: Dollop
TAGU • 1500QP1763

5397. Merry Bakers:
Dusty and Smidgen
HADD • 1500QP1746

5398. Merry Bakers:
Holiday Confections
HADD/TAGU • 1200QP1776
Set/4

5399. Merry Bakers: Hugh
HADD • 1250QP1756

5400. Merry Bakers:
Snicker and Doodle
TAGU • 1500QP1743

5401. Merry Bakers: Sprinkle
HADD • 1500QP1766

5402. Merry Bakers: Whisk
TAGU • 1250QP1753

5403. Merry Kitchen Magic
KEGR • 1000QXG2623

5404. Mischievous Kittens 8
AUBE • 1000QX2483

5405. Model 9620 Tractor –
John Deere
1500QXI6263

5406. Mom
KLIN • 1000QXG2913

5407. Mom and Daughter
VOTR • 1250QXG2983

5408. Mrs. Claus's Polarola
1650QXG2466
MAGIC

5409. Mumble Moves! –
Happy Feet
KLIN • 1000QXI3086

5410. Music
BEST • 1250QXG3356

5411. Nature's Sketchbook:
Nature's Sketchbook 4
BAST/FRAN • 1000QX2383

5412. New Home
FORS • 1250QXG3003

5413. Nick and Christopher 3:
Speedy Delivery
LARS • 1250QX2586

5414. Noah's Ark
CROW • 1800QXG2676
MAGIC

5415. Noelville 1: Sweet Shop
SICK • 1650QX2456

5416. North Pole Band Teddy
BRIC • 1650QXG3026

5417. Nose So Bright! – Rudolph
the Red-Nosed Reindeer®
CHAD • 1500QXG2756
MAGIC

5418. Nostalgic Houses & Shops
23: Corner Bank
PALM • 1500QX2576

5419. Nostalgic Houses & Shops
Complement: Snow Globe
PALM • 4800QXE3323

5420. NP3 Player
WILL • 1650QXG2476
MAGIC

5421. Oh, So Sweet!
HADD • 1000QXG2273

167

5422.
Oh, What a Grill!
1250QXG2443

5423.
Our Christmas Together
HADD • 1500QXG2726

5424.
Our Family
BEST/HURL • 1250QXG2943

5425.
Parents-to-Be
FRAN • 1000QXG2853

5426.
Part of Your World –
The Little Mermaid
1500QXD8366
MAGIC

5427.
Peppermint Pals
TAGU • 1250QXE3263
Set/2 • Limited Edition – 2006

5428.
A Playful Pup
BRIC/KEGR • 1000QXG2263

5429.
The Polar Express™ –
A Christmas to Remember
WILL • 1500QXI6316
Set/2

5430.
A Pony for Christmas 9
SICK • 1250QX2496

5431.
Princess Aurora and Prince
Phillip – Sleeping Beauty
2400QXD8383
MAGIC

5432.
Princess BARBIE™
Ornament
1600QXI6213

5433.
The Princess Tower
1850QXD8373
MAGIC

5434.
The Proud and Brave
FRAN • 1000QXG2646

5435.
A Puppy for Christmas!
AUBE • 1500QXG2806

5436.
Puppy Love 16
RGRS • 1000QX2533

5437.
A Purring Friend
BRIC/KEGR • 1000QXG2266

5438.
Reflections of Love
1000QXG3216

5439.
Ringing In Christmas
1000QXD8303

5440.
Rock Candy Railroad
CROW • 4200QLX7616
MAGIC

5441.
Santa's Little Helper
295LPR3366

5442.
Saturday Morning Cartoons
FEUR • 2400QXI6136
MAGIC

5443.
Scarlett O'Hara™
and Rhett Butler™ –
Gone With the Wind™
1850QXI6116

5444.
School
BEST • 1250QXG3333

5445.
Shrek®, Donkey, and
Puss In Boots
CHAD/KLIN • 1500QXI6226
Set/2

5446.
Sing-Along Pals
3200QXD8316
MAGIC

5447.
Sisters
VISK • 1250QXG2963

5448.
Sky's the Limit 10:
Monocoupe 110 Special
NORT • 1500QX2363

5449.
The Sleeping Village
ESCH • 2000QXC6002

5450.
Sleigh Ride
1850QXD8313

5451.
Snow Buddies 9
HADD • 1000QX2473

5452.
Snow Buddies 9
HADD • GiftQXC2473

5453.
Snow Fort Fun
KLIN • 1500QXG2803

5454.
Snowball and Tuxedo 6:
It's Snowtime!
ESCH • 850QX2593

5455.
Snowtop Lodge 2:
Bluster B. Toboggan
ESCH • 1850QX2583

5456.
Son
KLIN • 1000QXG2923

5457.
Sooper Loop – Hot Wheels™
1250QXI6243

5458.
Special Cat
HADD • 1000QXG2973

5459.
Special Dog
HADD • 1000QXG2966

5460.
Speedy Style Christmas
RGRS • 1250QXI3093

5461.
Spiderman™
RGRS • 1500QXI6236

5462.
Spirit of St. Nick
WILL • 2000QXE3226
Limited Edition – 2006

5463.
Sports
BEST • 1250QXG3343

5464.
Spotlight on Snoopy® 9:
The Legal Beagle
LARS • 1000QX2316

5465.
Sprucing Up Sylvester™
1500QXI6126

5466.
St. Nick
AUBE • 1000PR3945

5467.
Star Wars™ 10: Luke
Skywalker™ and Yoda™
KLIN • 1500QX2366

5468.
Stars and Stripes for Santa
SICK • 1000QXE3266
Limited Edition – 2006

5469.
Stolen Magic™ BARBIE™
ANDR • 2500QXC6008

5470.
"Suited" for the Season
TAGU • 1250QXI6246

5471.
Sweet Memories – Raggedy
Ann and Raggedy Andy®
FRAN • 1500QXI6283
Set/2

5472.
Sweet Tooth Treats 5
AUBE • 1500QX2526
Set/4

5473.
Taz™ the Snowman Wizard
CHAD • 1500QXI6133

5474.
Teddy Bear Band
CROW • 2800QLX7603
MAGIC

5475.
That's What Christmas Is
About, Charlie Brown®
3400QFM3316
MAGIC

5476.
Time for a Party!
TAGU • 1250QXG2613

5477.
Tinker Bell
1500QXD6373

5478.
A Toast to Wine
BEST • 1250QXG2296
Set/2

5479.
A Toast to Wine
BEST • 1250QXG2296
Set/2

5480.
Toymaker Santa 7
CROW • 1250QX2573

5481.
Toymaker Santa 7
CROW • 1250QXG3206

5482.
The Transporter Chamber
RGRS • 2800QXI6296
MAGIC

5483.
Treasures and Dreams 5:
Jewelry Box Castle
2000QX2546
MAGIC

5484.
Twuthful Tweety™
FRAN • 1500QXI6123
MAGIC

5485.
U.S.S. Enterprise™ NCC-1701
NORT • 3200QXI6293
MAGIC

5486.
Video Games
BEST • 1250QXG3346

5487.
Winnie the Pooh 9:
Eeyore Loses a Tail
1500QXD8336

5488.
Winnie the Pooh: A Very
Friendly Christmas Tree
1650QXD8343

5489.
Winnie the Pooh:
Baby's First Christmas
1500QXG2433

5490.
Winnie the Pooh:
Bouncin' Buddies
1250QXD8326

5491.
Winnie the Pooh:
Cocoa for Two
1500QXD8333

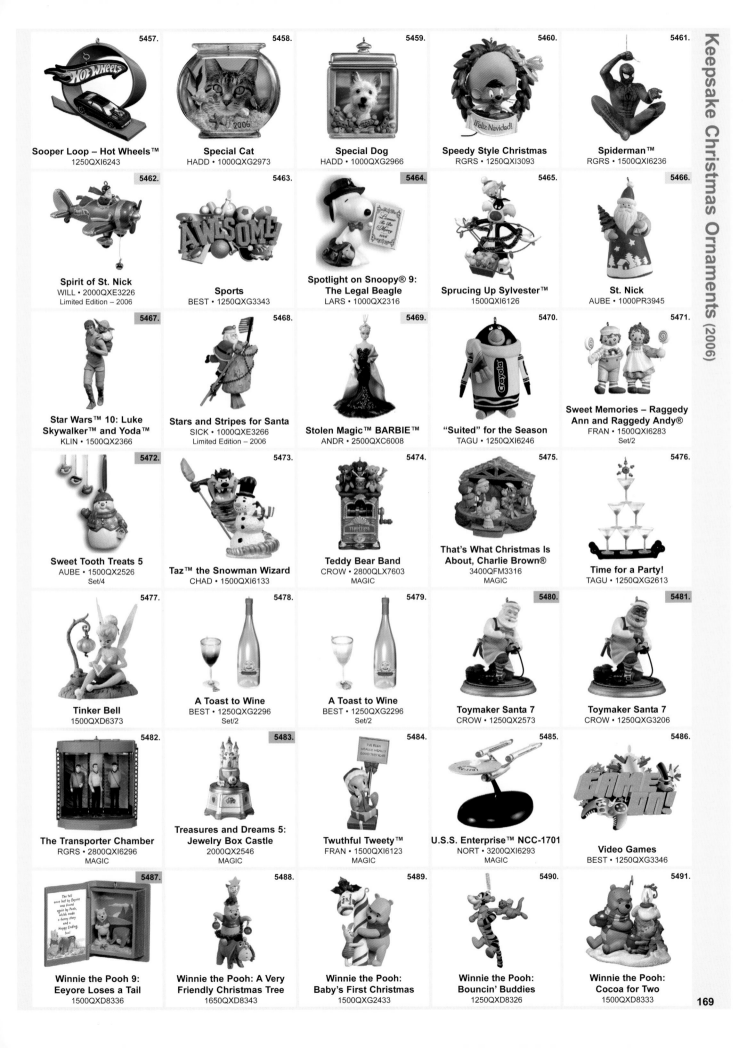

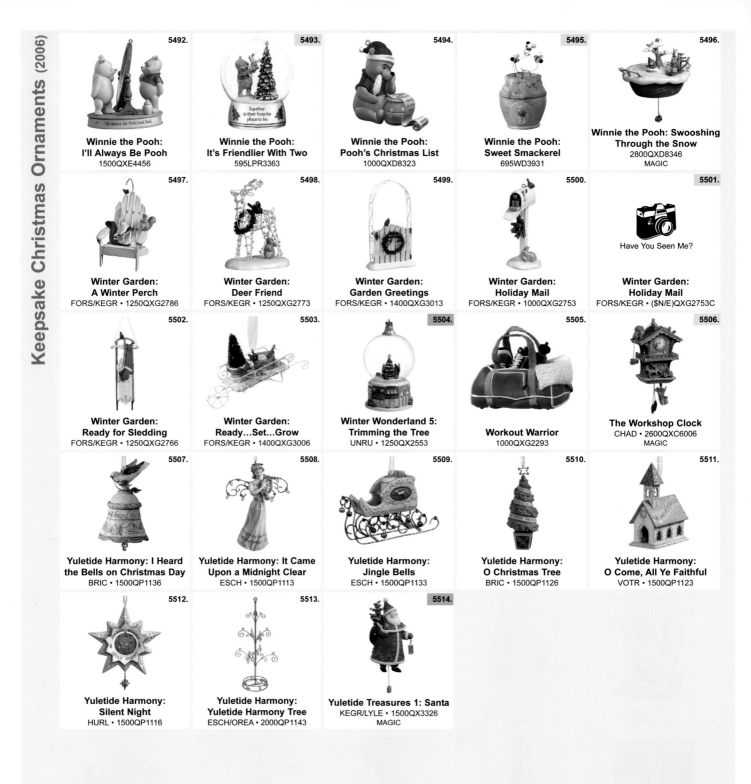

5492.
Winnie the Pooh:
I'll Always Be Pooh
1500QXE4456

5493.
Winnie the Pooh:
It's Friendlier With Two
595LPR3363

5494.
Winnie the Pooh:
Pooh's Christmas List
1000QXD8323

5495.
Winnie the Pooh:
Sweet Smackerel
695WD3931

5496.
Winnie the Pooh: Swooshing
Through the Snow
2800QXD8346
MAGIC

5497.
Winter Garden:
A Winter Perch
FORS/KEGR • 1250QXG2786

5498.
Winter Garden:
Deer Friend
FORS/KEGR • 1250QXG2773

5499.
Winter Garden:
Garden Greetings
FORS/KEGR • 1400QXG3013

5500.
Winter Garden:
Holiday Mail
FORS/KEGR • 1000QXG2753

5501.
Have You Seen Me?
Winter Garden:
Holiday Mail
FORS/KEGR • ($N/E)QXG2753C

5502.
Winter Garden:
Ready for Sledding
FORS/KEGR • 1250QXG2766

5503.
Winter Garden:
Ready...Set...Grow
FORS/KEGR • 1400QXG3006

5504.
Winter Wonderland 5:
Trimming the Tree
UNRU • 1250QX2553

5505.
Workout Warrior
1000QXG2293

5506.
The Workshop Clock
CHAD • 2600QXC6006
MAGIC

5507.
Yuletide Harmony: I Heard
the Bells on Christmas Day
BRIC • 1500QP1136

5508.
Yuletide Harmony: It Came
Upon a Midnight Clear
ESCH • 1500QP1113

5509.
Yuletide Harmony:
Jingle Bells
ESCH • 1500QP1133

5510.
Yuletide Harmony:
O Christmas Tree
BRIC • 1500QP1126

5511.
Yuletide Harmony:
O Come, All Ye Faithful
VOTR • 1500QP1123

5512.
Yuletide Harmony:
Silent Night
HURL • 1500QP1116

5513.
Yuletide Harmony:
Yuletide Harmony Tree
ESCH/OREA • 2000QP1143

5514.
Yuletide Treasures 1: Santa
KEGR/LYLE • 1500QX3326
MAGIC

Ambassador Holiday House Collection

The Holiday House Collection of ornaments was created by Hallmark for distribution through its subsidiary, Ambassador Cards, in F.W. Woolworth's, Ben Franklin, Card Shops, Super Markets and Drug Stores from 1979 through 1982. The VERY RARE Ambassador test ornaments distributed in 1979 were almost exclusively repackaged ornaments from Hallmark's regular ornament line.   The only way to tell that some of these ornaments are from the Ambassador line is if the ornament is still in the Ambassador box, otherwise they would be considered a no box Hallmark ornament. We have pictured these 1979 ornaments in their rare Ambassador packaging which greatly increases their value. Designs in 1980-82 were exclusive to the Ambassador line.

1979

5515.
Carousel Angel #2
649QX45G • $750
EXTREMELY RARE

5516.
Chickadee
350unknown • $250

5517.
A Christmas Treat
498QX42G • $200
VERY RARE

5518.
Colors of Christmas:
Partridge
($N/E)unknown • $100
RARE

5519.
Colors of Christmas:
Wreath
349QX35G • $100
RARE

5520.
Holiday Highlights:
Christmas Cheer
349QX38G • $75
RARE

5521.
Holiday Highlights:
Snowflake
349QX37G • $100
RARE

5522.
Matchless Christmas
398QX41G • $300
VERY RARE

5523.
Pink Panther™
349QX49G • $150
VERY RARE

5524.
Scooby-Doo™
349QX48G • $150
VERY RARE

5525.
Thimble Soldier
TAGU • 298QX40G • $400
VERY RARE

1980

5526.
Angel
649QX3H • $75

5527.
Angel Love
398QX14H • $35

5528.
Baby's First Christmas
398QX8H • $45

5529.
Beauty of Christmas
398QX15H • $35

5530.
Colors of Christmas: Joy
398QX19H • $45

5531.
Colors of Christmas:
Wreath
398QX18H • $45

5532.
Dove
398QX20H • $45

5533.
First Christmas Together
398QX9H • $45

5534.
Home
398QX16H • $40

5535.
Little Blessing
398QX17H • $35

5536.
Little Redbird
398QX4H • $35

5537.
Mickey Mouse
398QX6H • $50

5538.
Mouse and Candlestick
398QX21H • $45

5539.
Night Before Christmas
398QX11H • $35

5540.
PEANUTS®
398QX10H • $50

5541.
Pink Panther™
398QX13H • $100
RARE

5542.
Rocking Horse
549QX1H • $75

1981

5543.
Santa
398QX2H • $48
Re-issued in 1981.

5544.
Santa's Visit
398QX12H • $35

5545.
Train
649QX5H • $75

5546.
Winter's Gift
398QX7H • $40

5547.
Baby's First Christmas
449QX38E • $45

5548.
Baby's First Christmas
498QX48E • $200
VERY RARE

5549.
Birds of Winter
449QX41E • $45

5550.
Colors of Christmas: Cardinal
449QX33E • $100

5551.
Colors of Christmas: Merry Christmas
449QX34E • $100

5552.
Disney
449QX37E • $45

5553.
First Christmas Together
449QX45E • $40

5554.
Home
449QX45E • $35

5555.
Love Heart
498QX32E • $150
RARE

5556.
Mouse on Moon
698QX30E • $75

5557.
Nativity
498QX31E • $150
RARE

5558.
Night Before Christmas
449QX40E • $35

5559.
PEANUTS®
449QX35E • $50

5560.
Pink Panther™
449QX36E • $40

5561.
Raccoon on Candycane
698QX29E • $300
VERY RARE

5562.
Santa
398QX2H • $48
Re-issued from 1980.

5563.
Skating Redbird
498QX26E • $200

5564.
Soldier
498QX25E • $100

5565.
Together Times Friendship
449QX44E • $30

5566.
Twirl-About Santa
698QX27E • $175
RARE

5567.
White Mouse
449QX47E • $400
RARE

1982

5568.
Baby's First Christmas
($N/E)unknown • $400
EXTREMELY RARE

5569.
Dog in Stocking
499QX49F • $15

Hall Family Ornaments

Beginning in 1974, Joyce C. Hall and more recently his son, Donald Hall, have selected an artist from Hallmark to create an ornament which is attached to their annual family Christmas card. Only employees who have been with Hallmark for at least 25 years & the personal mailing list of the Hall Family are included in the distribution. Thus, these cards with ornaments are very rare and highly collectible.

5570.	5571.	5572.	5573.	5574.
1974 – Acrylic Disc Gift • $473 RARE	**1975 – Stained Glass Angel** Gift • $348 RARE	**1976 – Acrylic Star** Gift • $348 RARE	**1977 – Acrylic Dove** Gift • $263	**1978 – Tree & Birds** Gift • $105
5575.	5576.	5577.	5578.	5579.
1979 – Snowflake Gift • $110	**1980 – Acrylic Bell** Gift • $103	**1981 – Angel in Blue Star** Gift • $93	**1982 – Brass Nativity** Gift • $103	**1983 – Three Kings** Gift • $63
5580.	5581.	5582.	5583.	5584.
1984 – White Bisque Angel Gift • $110	**1985 – Mary & Joseph** Gift • $93	**1986 – Brass Nativity Tree** Gift • $63	**1987 – Angel with Harp** HAAS • Gift • $85	**1988 – Lion & Lamb** Gift • $88
5585.	5586.	5587.	5588.	5589.
1989 – Silver Angel Gift • $80	**1990 – Brass Star with Dove** FUNV • Gift • $113	**1991 – Nativity** Gift • $90	**1992 – Madonna & Child** HAAS • Gift • $160	**1993 – Mary Hamilton Angel** HAMI • Gift • $175
5590.	5591.	5592.	5593.	5594.
1994 – Acrylic Poinsettia FUNV • Gift • $93	**1995 – M. Bastin Birdhouse** BAST • Gift • $113	**1996 – Christmas Tree** FUNV • Gift • $150	**1997 – Brass Manger** FUNV • Gift • $135	**1998 – Laser Cut Wreath** GRIL • Gift • $150
5595.	5596.	5597.	5598.	5599.
1999 – Tiffany Angel HAAS • Gift • $175	**2000 – Silver Dove** FACC • Gift • $135	**2001 – Magi Scene** Gift • $135	**2002 – Mary with Lamb** GIUN • Gift • $175	**2003 – Brass Filigree Wreath** FACC • Gift • $135

5600.

**2004 – Brass Filigree
Stocking**
Gift • $145

5601.

2005 - Brass Baby Jesus
JOGO • Gift • $145

Mayor's Tree Ornaments

The annual Mayor's Christmas Tree Ornament is sold only at the Hallmark Crown Center Headquarters between Thanksgiving & Christmas each year, proceeds going to a charity fund. From 1981 through 1986, the Mayor's ornaments utilized designs from the Hallmark line, but revised the inscriptions. Since 1987, the ornament has been a unique design from Hallmark artist, Fayrol Unverferth, utilizing the wood from the previous year's 100 foot Christmas tree and have a very limited production.

5602.
1981 – Five Pointed Acrylic Star
550 • $195

5603.
1982 – Triangular Shape Acrylic Tree
SEAL • 550 • $395
RARE

5604.
1983 – Acrylic Stocking
($N/E) • $295

5605.
1984 – Acrylic Bear
JLEE • 600 • $245

5606.
1985 – Acrylic Mug
JLEE • 575 • $149

5607.
1986 – Wood Sleigh
VOTR • ($N/E) • $N/E

5608.
1987 – Oval Tree
FUNV • ($N/E) • $500
RARE

5609.
1988 – Triangular Tree
FUNV • 600 • $59

5610.
1989 – Shaped Tree
FUNV • 750 • $49

5611.
1990 – Tree on Round Disk
FUNV • 750 • $59

5612.
1991 – Holiday Pinecone
FUNV • ($N/E) • $468
RARE

5613.
1992 – Christmas Wreath
FUNV • 995 • $415
RARE

5614.
1993 – Toy Soldier
FUNV • 995 • $600
RARE

5615.
1994 – Rocking Horse
FUNV • 1000 • $300

5616.
1995 – Caroling Angel
FUNV • 1050 • $89

5617.
1996 – Locomotive
FUNV • 1200 • $67

5618.
1997 – Holiday Homestead
FUNV • 1200 • $313

5619.
1998 – Teddy Bear
FUNV • 1200 • $42

5620.
1999 – Snowflake
FUNV • 1200 • $40

5621.
2000 – Dove with Heart
FUNV • 1250 • $39

5622.
2001 – Glittery Reindeer
FUNV • 1250 • $38

5623.
2002 – Teddy Bear
FUNV • 1250 • $35

5624.
2003 – Nostalgic Sled
FUNV • 1250 • $39

5625.
2004 – Snowman
FUNV • 1250 • $39

5626.
2005 – Gingerbread Man
FUNV • 1250 • $34

Miniature Ornaments

Introduced in 1988, Miniature Ornaments are tiny, yet full of personality and amazing detail.   A tabletop tree full of these mini ornaments will fill the room with fun.

1988

5627.
Acrylic Snowflakes
400QXM5781 • $12
Set/10

5628.
Baby's First Christmas
DLEE • 600QXM5744 • $14

5629.
Brass Angel
LYLE • 150QXM5671 • $16

5630.
Brass Star
LYLE • 150QXM5664 • $14

5631.
Brass Tree
LYLE • 150QXM5674 • $10

5632.
Candy Cane Elf
SIED • 300QXM5701 • $17

5633.
Country Wreath
RGRS • 400QXM5731 • $9
Re-issued in 1989.

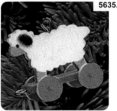
5634.
First Christmas Together
MCGE • 400QXM5741 • $12

5635.
Folk Art Lamb
PATT • 275QXM5681 • $18

5636.
Folk Art Reindeer
PATT • 300QXM5684 • $12

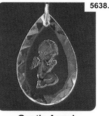
5637.
Friends Share Joy
PATT • 200QXM5764 • $14

5638.
Gentle Angel
VOTR • 200QXM5771 • $16

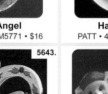
5639.
Happy Santa
PATT • 450QXM5614 • $16

5640.
Hold On Tight
SIED • GiftQXC5704 • $35

5641.
Holy Family
UNRU • 850QXM5611 • $12
Re-issued in 1989.

5642.
Jolly St. Nick
UNRU • 800QXM5721 • $19

5643.
Joyous Heart
MCGE • 350QXM5691 • $19

5644.
Kittens In Toyland 1
CROW • 500QXM5621 • $19

5645.
Little Drummer Boy
SIED • 450QXM5784 • $14

5646.
Love Is Forever
PATT • 200QXM5774 • $14

5647.
Miniature Rocking Horse 1
SICK • 450QXM5624 • $42

5648.
Mother
PIKE • 300QXM5724 • $13

5649.
**Old English Village 1:
Family Home**
DLEE • 850QXM5634 • $34

5650.
Penguin Pal 1
SIED • 375QXM5631 • $19

5651.
Skater's Waltz
UNRU • 700QXM5601 • $17

5652.
Sneaker Mouse
400QXM5711 • $15

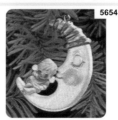
5653.
Snuggly Skater
SIED • 450QXM5714 • $15

5654.
Sweet Dreams
700QXM5604 • $17

5655.
Three Little Kitties
PIKE • 600QXM5694 • $16
Re-issued in 1989.

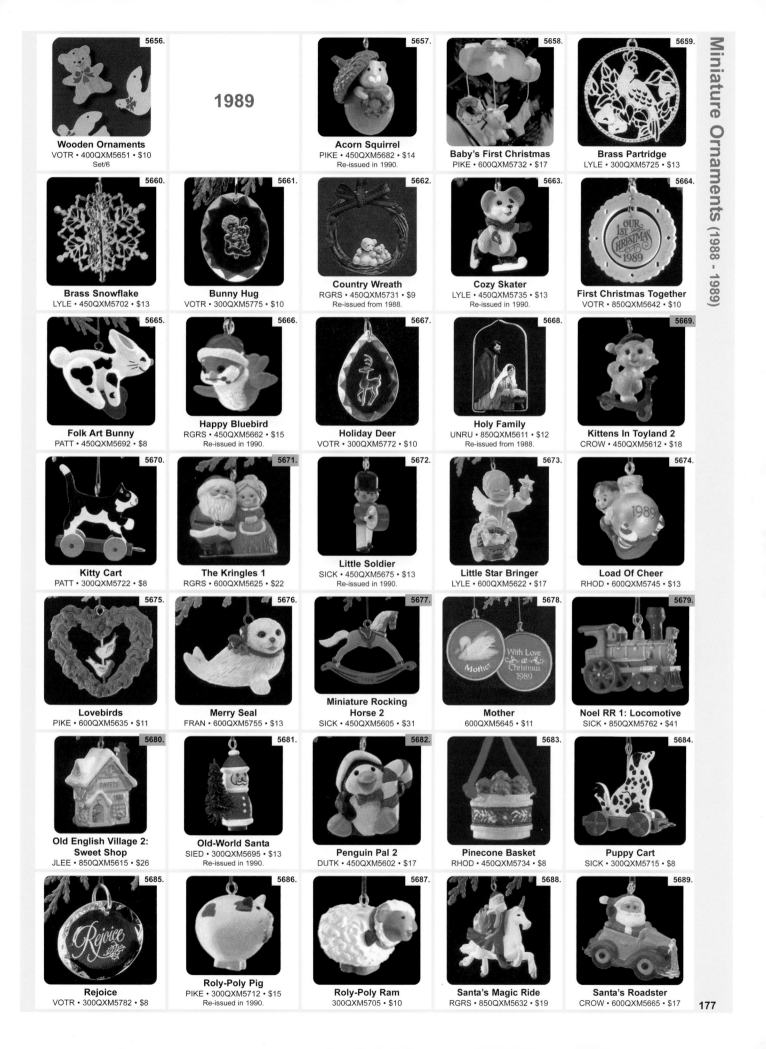

1989

5656.
Wooden Ornaments
VOTR • 400QXM5651 • $10
Set/6

5657.
Acorn Squirrel
PIKE • 450QXM5682 • $14
Re-issued in 1990.

5658.
Baby's First Christmas
PIKE • 600QXM5732 • $17

5659.
Brass Partridge
LYLE • 300QXM5725 • $13

5660.
Brass Snowflake
LYLE • 450QXM5702 • $13

5661.
Bunny Hug
VOTR • 300QXM5775 • $10

5662.
Country Wreath
RGRS • 450QXM5731 • $9
Re-issued from 1988.

5663.
Cozy Skater
LYLE • 450QXM5735 • $13
Re-issued in 1990.

5664.
First Christmas Together
VOTR • 850QXM5642 • $10

5665.
Folk Art Bunny
PATT • 450QXM5692 • $8

5666.
Happy Bluebird
RGRS • 450QXM5662 • $15
Re-issued in 1990.

5667.
Holiday Deer
VOTR • 300QXM5772 • $10

5668.
Holy Family
UNRU • 850QXM5611 • $12
Re-issued from 1988.

5669.
Kittens In Toyland 2
CROW • 450QXM5612 • $18

5670.
Kitty Cart
PATT • 300QXM5722 • $8

5671.
The Kringles 1
RGRS • 600QXM5625 • $22

5672.
Little Soldier
SICK • 450QXM5675 • $13
Re-issued in 1990.

5673.
Little Star Bringer
LYLE • 600QXM5622 • $17

5674.
Load Of Cheer
RHOD • 600QXM5745 • $13

5675.
Lovebirds
PIKE • 600QXM5635 • $11

5676.
Merry Seal
FRAN • 600QXM5755 • $13

5677.
Miniature Rocking Horse 2
SICK • 450QXM5605 • $31

5678.
Mother
600QXM5645 • $11

5679.
Noel RR 1: Locomotive
SICK • 850QXM5762 • $41

5680.
Old English Village 2: Sweet Shop
JLEE • 850QXM5615 • $26

5681.
Old-World Santa
SIED • 300QXM5695 • $13
Re-issued in 1990.

5682.
Penguin Pal 2
DUTK • 450QXM5602 • $17

5683.
Pinecone Basket
RHOD • 450QXM5734 • $8

5684.
Puppy Cart
SICK • 300QXM5715 • $8

5685.
Rejoice
VOTR • 300QXM5782 • $8

5686.
Roly-Poly Pig
PIKE • 300QXM5712 • $15
Re-issued in 1990.

5687.
Roly-Poly Ram
300QXM5705 • $10

5688.
Santa's Magic Ride
RGRS • 850QXM5632 • $19

5689.
Santa's Roadster
CROW • 600QXM5665 • $17

5690.	5691.	5692.	5693.	5694.
Scrimshaw Reindeer VOTR • 450QXM5685 • $11	**Sharing A Ride** DUTK • 850QXM5765 • $17	**Sitting Purrty** DUTK • ($N/E)QXC5812 • $12	**Slow Motion** SIED • 600QXM5752 • $17	**Special Friend** 450QXM5652 • $9

5695.	5696.	5697.	5698.	
Starlit Mouse RHOD • 450QXM5655 • $17	**Stocking Pal** JLEE • 450QXM5672 • $12 Re-issued in 1990.	**Strollin' Snowman** SIED • 450QXM5742 • $14	**Three Little Kitties** PIKE • 600QXM5694 • $16 Re-issued from 1988.	**1990**

5699.	5700.	5701.	5702.	5703.
Acorn Squirrel PIKE • 450QXM5682 • $14 Re-issued from 1989.	**Acorn Wreath** CROW • 600QXM5686 • $13	**Air Santa** 450QXM5656 • $17	**Baby's First Christmas** FRAN • 850QXM5703 • $13	**Basket Buddy** RGRS • 600QXM5696 • $17

5704.	5705.	5706.	5707.	5708.
Bear Hug PALM • 600QXM5633 • $12	**Brass Bouquet** LYLE • 600QXM5776 • $10	**Brass Horn** PATT • 300QXM5793 • $10	**Brass Peace** 300QXM5796 • $12	**Brass Santa** PATT • 300QXM5786 • $12

5709.	5710.	5711.	5712.	5713.
Brass Year 300QXM5833 • $10	**Busy Carver** CROW • 450QXM5673 • $12	**Christmas Dove** SIED • 450QXM5636 • $17	**Cloisonne Poinsettia** VOTR • 1050QXM5533 • $23	**Country Heart** RGRS • 450QXM5693 • $8

5714.	5715.	5716.	5717.	5718.
Cozy Skater LYLE • 450QXM5735 • $13 Re-issued from 1989.	**Crown Prince** RGRS • ($N/E)QXC5603 • $23	**First Christmas Together** ANDR • 600QXM5536 • $12	**Going Sledding** JLEE • 450QXM5683 • $14	**Grandchild's First Christmas** SIED • 600QXM5723 • $12

5719.	5720.	5721.	5722.	5723.
Happy Bluebird RGRS • 450QXM5662 • $15 Re-issued from 1989.	**Holiday Cardinal** FRAN • 300QXM5526 • $14	**Kittens In Toyland 3** CROW • 450QXM5736 • $18	**The Kringles 2** RGRS • 600QXM5753 • $19	**Lion and Lamb** SICK • 450QXM5676 • $14

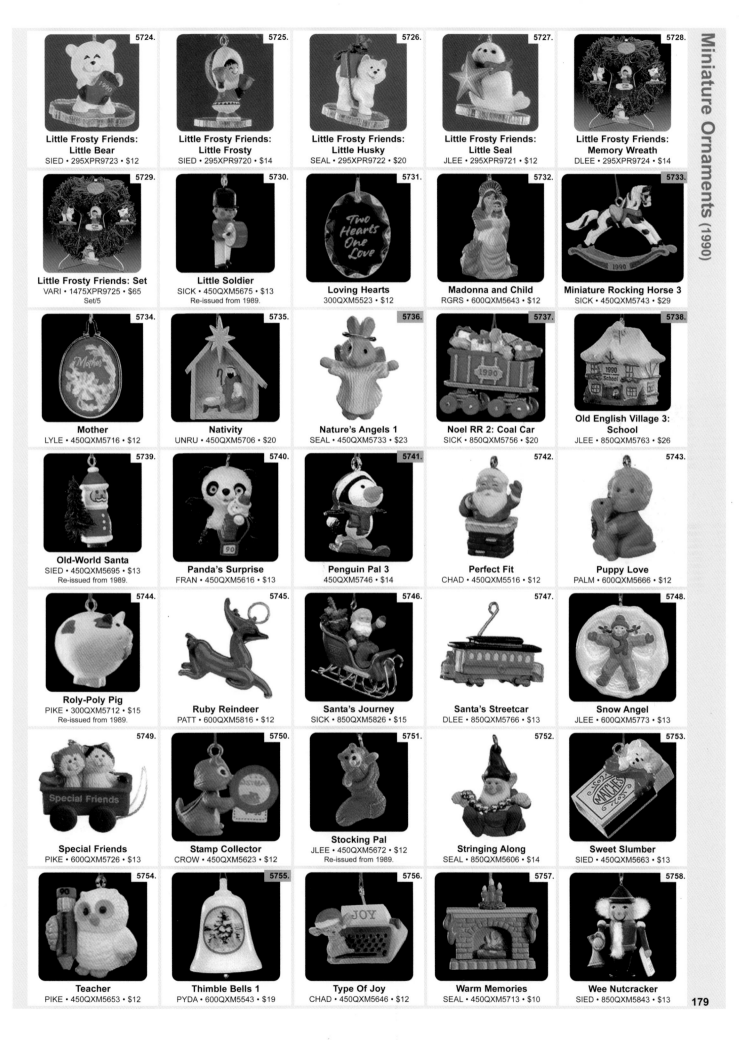

5724.
Little Frosty Friends:
Little Bear
SIED • 295XPR9723 • $12

5725.
Little Frosty Friends:
Little Frosty
SIED • 295XPR9720 • $14

5726.
Little Frosty Friends:
Little Husky
SEAL • 295XPR9722 • $20

5727.
Little Frosty Friends:
Little Seal
JLEE • 295XPR9721 • $12

5728.
Little Frosty Friends:
Memory Wreath
DLEE • 295XPR9724 • $14

5729.
Little Frosty Friends: Set
VARI • 1475XPR9725 • $65
Set/5

5730.
Little Soldier
SICK • 450QXM5675 • $13
Re-issued from 1989.

5731.
Loving Hearts
300QXM5523 • $12

5732.
Madonna and Child
RGRS • 600QXM5643 • $12

5733.
Miniature Rocking Horse 3
SICK • 450QXM5743 • $29

5734.
Mother
LYLE • 450QXM5716 • $12

5735.
Nativity
UNRU • 450QXM5706 • $20

5736.
Nature's Angels 1
SEAL • 450QXM5733 • $23

5737.
Noel RR 2: Coal Car
SICK • 850QXM5756 • $20

5738.
Old English Village 3:
School
JLEE • 850QXM5763 • $26

5739.
Old-World Santa
SIED • 450QXM5695 • $13
Re-issued from 1989.

5740.
Panda's Surprise
FRAN • 450QXM5616 • $13

5741.
Penguin Pal 3
450QXM5746 • $14

5742.
Perfect Fit
CHAD • 450QXM5516 • $12

5743.
Puppy Love
PALM • 600QXM5666 • $12

5744.
Roly-Poly Pig
PIKE • 300QXM5712 • $15
Re-issued from 1989.

5745.
Ruby Reindeer
PATT • 600QXM5816 • $12

5746.
Santa's Journey
SICK • 850QXM5826 • $15

5747.
Santa's Streetcar
DLEE • 850QXM5766 • $13

5748.
Snow Angel
JLEE • 600QXM5773 • $13

5749.
Special Friends
PIKE • 600QXM5726 • $13

5750.
Stamp Collector
CROW • 450QXM5623 • $12

5751.
Stocking Pal
JLEE • 450QXM5672 • $12
Re-issued from 1989.

5752.
Stringing Along
SEAL • 850QXM5606 • $14

5753.
Sweet Slumber
SIED • 450QXM5663 • $13

5754.
Teacher
PIKE • 450QXM5653 • $12

5755.
Thimble Bells 1
PYDA • 600QXM5543 • $19

5756.
Type Of Joy
CHAD • 450QXM5646 • $12

5757.
Warm Memories
SEAL • 450QXM5713 • $10

5758.
Wee Nutcracker
SIED • 850QXM5843 • $13

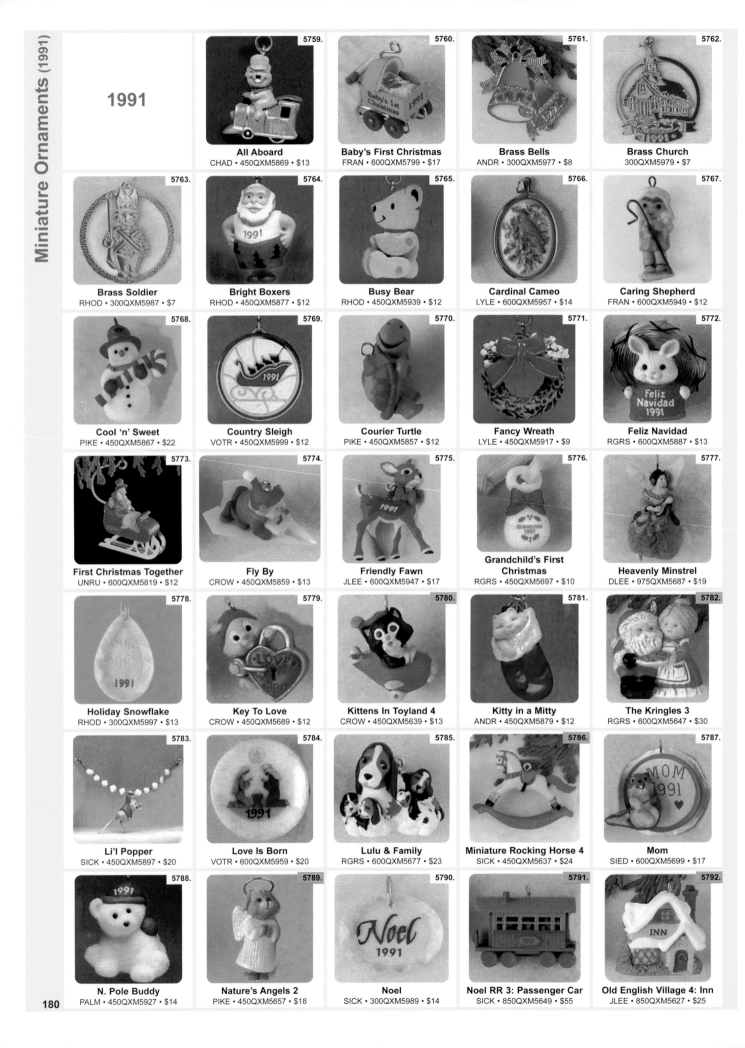

1991

5759.
All Aboard
CHAD • 450QXM5869 • $13

5760.
Baby's First Christmas
FRAN • 600QXM5799 • $17

5761.
Brass Bells
ANDR • 300QXM5977 • $8

5762.
Brass Church
300QXM5979 • $7

5763.
Brass Soldier
RHOD • 300QXM5987 • $7

5764.
Bright Boxers
RHOD • 450QXM5877 • $12

5765.
Busy Bear
RHOD • 450QXM5939 • $12

5766.
Cardinal Cameo
LYLE • 600QXM5957 • $14

5767.
Caring Shepherd
FRAN • 600QXM5949 • $12

5768.
Cool 'n' Sweet
PIKE • 450QXM5867 • $22

5769.
Country Sleigh
VOTR • 450QXM5999 • $12

5770.
Courier Turtle
PIKE • 450QXM5857 • $12

5771.
Fancy Wreath
LYLE • 450QXM5917 • $9

5772.
Feliz Navidad
RGRS • 600QXM5887 • $13

5773.
First Christmas Together
UNRU • 600QXM5819 • $12

5774.
Fly By
CROW • 450QXM5859 • $13

5775.
Friendly Fawn
JLEE • 600QXM5947 • $17

5776.
Grandchild's First
Christmas
RGRS • 450QXM5697 • $10

5777.
Heavenly Minstrel
DLEE • 975QXM5687 • $19

5778.
Holiday Snowflake
RHOD • 300QXM5997 • $13

5779.
Key To Love
CROW • 450QXM5689 • $12

5780.
Kittens In Toyland 4
CROW • 450QXM5639 • $13

5781.
Kitty in a Mitty
ANDR • 450QXM5879 • $12

5782.
The Kringles 3
RGRS • 600QXM5647 • $30

5783.
Li'l Popper
SICK • 450QXM5897 • $20

5784.
Love Is Born
VOTR • 600QXM5959 • $20

5785.
Lulu & Family
RGRS • 600QXM5677 • $23

5786.
Miniature Rocking Horse 4
SICK • 450QXM5637 • $24

5787.
Mom
SIED • 600QXM5699 • $17

5788.
N. Pole Buddy
PALM • 450QXM5927 • $14

5789.
Nature's Angels 2
PIKE • 450QXM5657 • $18

5790.
Noel
SICK • 300QXM5989 • $14

5791.
Noel RR 3: Passenger Car
SICK • 850QXM5649 • $55

5792.
Old English Village 4: Inn
JLEE • 850QXM5627 • $25

5793.
Penguin Pal 4
SIED • 450QXM5629 • $12

5794.
Ring-A-Ding Elf
CHAD • 850QXM5669 • $14

5795.
Seaside Otter
SIED • 450QXM5909 • $11

5796.
Silvery Santa
JLEE • 975QXM5679 • $16

5797.
Six Mice: Tiny Tea Party Set
SEAL • 2900QXM5827 • $130
Set/6

5798.
Special Friends
JLEE • 850QXM5797 • $17

5799.
Thimble Bells 2
PYDA • 600QXM5659 • $15

5800.
Top Hatter
SEAL • 600QXM5889 • $13

5801.
Treeland Trio
CHAD • 850QXM5899 • $12

5802.
Upbeat Bear
FRAN • 600QXM5907 • $14

5803.
Vision Of Santa
CHAD • 450QXM5937 • $11

5804.
Wee Toymaker
BISH • 850QXM5967 • $13

5805.
Woodland Babies 1
CROW • 600QXM5667 • $18

1992

5806.
A+ Teacher
UNRU • 375QXM5511 • $10

5807.
Angelic Harpist
LYLE • 450QXM5524 • $16

5808.
Baby's First Christmas
LYLE • 450QXM5494 • $22

5809.
The Bearymores 1
RGRS • 575QXM5544 • $13

5810.
Black-Capped Chickadee
FRAN • 300QXM5484 • $20

5811.
Bright Stringers
SEAL • 375QXM5841 • $23

5812.
Buck-A-Roo
CROW • 450QXM5814 • $14

5813.
Chipmunk Parcel Service
SEAL • GiftQXC5194 • $25

5814.
Christmas Bonus
PALM • 300QXM5811 • $13

5815.
Christmas Copter
FRAN • 575QXM5844 • $13

5816.
Christmas Treasures
CHAD • 2200QXC5464 • $145
Set/4 • Limited Edition – 15500

5817.
Coca-Cola® Santa
UNRU • 575QXM5884 • $15

5818.
Cool Uncle Sam
JLEE • 300QXM5561 • $17

5819.
Cozy Kayak
JLEE • 375QXM5551 • $13

5820.
Fast Finish
RHOD • 375QXM5301 • $13

5821.
Feeding Time
CROW • 575QXM5481 • $18

5822.
Friendly Tin Soldier
SICK • 450QXM5874 • $14

5823.
Friends Are Tops
CROW • 450QXM5521 • $13

5824.
Gerbil, Inc.
SIED • 375QXM5924 • $10

5825.
Going Places
ANDR • 375QXM5871 • $10

5826.
Grandchild's First
Christmas
FRAN • 575QXM5501 • $11

5827.
Grandma
UNRU • 450QXM5514 • $11

5828.
Harmony Trio
VOTR • 1175QXM5471 • $17
Set/3

5829.
Hickory, Dickory, Dock
CHAD • 375QXM5861 • $12

5830.
Holiday Holly
975QXM5364 • $13

5831.
Holiday Splash
FRAN • 575QXM5834 • $13

5832.
Hoop It Up
CROW • 450QXM5831 • $10

5833.
Inside Story
SEAL • 725QXM5881 • $14

5834.
Kittens In Toyland 5
CROW • 450QXM5391 • $14

5835.
The Kringles 4
RGRS • 600QXM5381 • $14

5836.
Little Town of Bethlehem
SICK • 300QXM5864 • $17

5837.
Miniature Rocking Horse 5
SICK • 450QXM5454 • $28

5838.
Minted for Santa
UNRU • 375QXM5854 • $10

5839.
Mom
ANDR • 450QXM5504 • $12

5840.
Nature's Angels 3
PIKE • 450QXM5451 • $17

5841.
The Night Before Christmas 1
UNRU • 1375QXM5541 • $25

5842.
Noel RR 4: Box Car
SICK • 700QXM5441 • $28

5843.
Old English Village 5: Church
JLEE • 700QXM5384 • $31

5844.
Perfect Balance
RGRS • 300QXM5571 • $12

5845.
Polar Polka
SEAL • 450QXM5534 • $12

5846.
Puppet Show
SIED • 300QXM5574 • $10

5847.
Six Mice: Sew, Sew Tiny
SEAL • 2900QXM5794 • $43
Set/6

5848.
Ski For Two
ANDR • 450QXM5821 • $12

5849.
Snowshoe Bunny
VOTR • 375QXM5564 • $12

5850.
Snug Kitty
PIKE • 375QXM5554 • $12

5851.
Spunky Monkey
CHAD • 300QXM5921 • $12

5852.
Thimble Bells 3
LYLE • 600QXM5461 • $15

5853.
Visions Of Acorns
ANDR • 450QXM5851 • $12

5854.
Wee Three Kings
PALM • 575QXM5531 • $17

5855.
Woodland Babies 2
PALM • 600QXM5444 • $12

1993

5856.
Baby's First Christmas
VOTR • 575QXM5145 • $12

5857.
The Bearymores 2
RGRS • 575QXM5125 • $14

5858.
Cheese Please
SIED • 375QXM4072 • $9

5859.
Christmas Castle
SEAL • 575QXM4085 • $11

5860.
Cloisonne Snowflake
VOTR • 975QXM4012 • $16

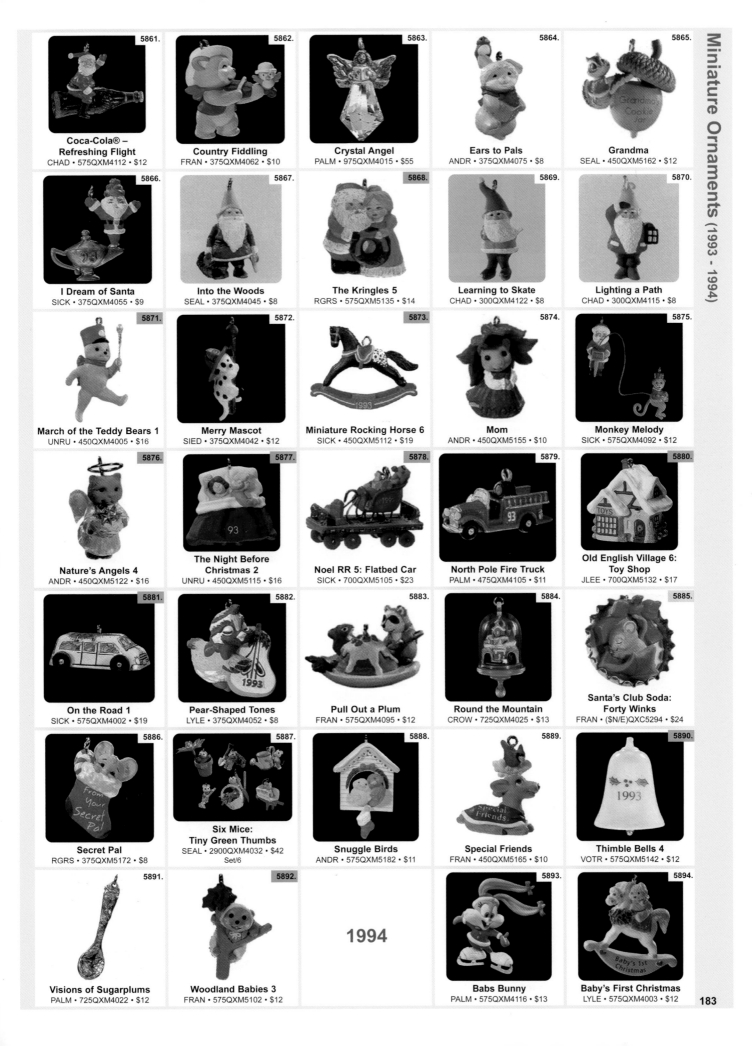

5861.
Coca-Cola® –
Refreshing Flight
CHAD • 575QXM4112 • $12

5862.
Country Fiddling
FRAN • 375QXM4062 • $10

5863.
Crystal Angel
PALM • 975QXM4015 • $55

5864.
Ears to Pals
ANDR • 375QXM4075 • $8

5865.
Grandma
SEAL • 450QXM5162 • $12

5866.
I Dream of Santa
SICK • 375QXM4055 • $9

5867.
Into the Woods
SEAL • 375QXM4045 • $8

5868.
The Kringles 5
RGRS • 575QXM5135 • $14

5869.
Learning to Skate
CHAD • 300QXM4122 • $8

5870.
Lighting a Path
CHAD • 300QXM4115 • $8

5871.
March of the Teddy Bears 1
UNRU • 450QXM4005 • $16

5872.
Merry Mascot
SIED • 375QXM4042 • $12

5873.
Miniature Rocking Horse 6
SICK • 450QXM5112 • $19

5874.
Mom
ANDR • 450QXM5155 • $10

5875.
Monkey Melody
SICK • 575QXM4092 • $12

5876.
Nature's Angels 4
ANDR • 450QXM5122 • $16

5877.
The Night Before
Christmas 2
UNRU • 450QXM5115 • $16

5878.
Noel RR 5: Flatbed Car
SICK • 700QXM5105 • $23

5879.
North Pole Fire Truck
PALM • 475QXM4105 • $11

5880.
Old English Village 6:
Toy Shop
JLEE • 700QXM5132 • $17

5881.
On the Road 1
SICK • 575QXM4002 • $19

5882.
Pear-Shaped Tones
LYLE • 375QXM4052 • $8

5883.
Pull Out a Plum
FRAN • 575QXM4095 • $12

5884.
Round the Mountain
CROW • 725QXM4025 • $13

5885.
Santa's Club Soda:
Forty Winks
FRAN • ($N/E)QXC5294 • $24

5886.
Secret Pal
RGRS • 375QXM5172 • $8

5887.
Six Mice:
Tiny Green Thumbs
SEAL • 2900QXM4032 • $42
Set/6

5888.
Snuggle Birds
ANDR • 575QXM5182 • $11

5889.
Special Friends
FRAN • 450QXM5165 • $10

5890.
Thimble Bells 4
VOTR • 575QXM5142 • $12

5891.
Visions of Sugarplums
PALM • 725QXM4022 • $12

5892.
Woodland Babies 3
FRAN • 575QXM5102 • $12

1994

5893.
Babs Bunny
PALM • 575QXM4116 • $13

5894.
Baby's First Christmas
LYLE • 575QXM4003 • $12

183

5895.
Beary Perfect Tree
BISH • 475QXM4076 • $11

5896.
The Bearymores 3
RGRS • 575QXM5133 • $12

5897.
Buster Bunny™
PALM • 575QXM5163 • $12

5898.
Centuries of Santa 1
SICK • 600QXM5153 • $28

5899.
Coca-Cola® –
Pour Some More
CHAD • 575QXM5156 • $13

5900.
Corny Elf
RHOD • 450QXM4063 • $12

5901.
Cute as a Button
CROW • 375QXM4103 • $13

5902.
Dazzling Reindeer
VOTR • 975QXM4026 • $16

5903.
Dizzy Devil
PALM • 575QXM4133 • $16

5904.
Friends Need Hugs
LYLE • 450QXM4016 • $13

5905.
Graceful Carousel Horse
BISH • 775QXM4056 • $16

5906.
Hamton™
PALM • 575QXM4126 • $12

5907.
Have a Cookie
DLEE • 575QXM5166 • $17

5908.
Hearts A-Sail
BISH • 575QXM4006 • $10

5909.
Holiday Express Train Base
SICK • 5000QXM5452 • $90
Re-issued in 1995.

5910.
Jolly Visitor
SICK • 575QXM4053 • $12

5911.
Jolly Wolly Snowman
VOTR • 375QXM4093 • $14

5912.
Journey to Bethlehem
LYLE • 575QXM4036 • $26

5913.
Just My Size
BISH • 375QXM4086 • $13

5914.
Love Was Born
SICK • 450QXM4043 • $17

5915.
March of the Teddy Bears 2
UNRU • 450QXM5106 • $16

5916.
Melodic Cherub
RGRS • 375QXM4066 • $17

5917.
A Merry Flight
CROW • 575QXM4073 • $13

5918.
Miniature Rocking Horse 7
SICK • 450QXM5116 • $20

5919.
Mom
RGRS • 450QXM4013 • $12

5920.
Nature's Angels 5
VOTR • 450QXM5126 • $12

5921.
The Night Before
Christmas 3
UNRU • 450QXM5123 • $10

5922.
Noah's Ark: Noah's Ark
SICK • 2450QXM4106 • $77
Set/3

5923.
Noel RR 6: Stock Car
SICK • 700QXM5113 • $22

5924.
Nutcracker Guild 1
SICK • 575QXM5146 • $26

5925.
Old English Village 7:
Hat Shop
ANDR • 700QXM5143 • $16

5926.
On the Road 2
SICK • 575QXM5103 • $16

5927.
Plucky Duck
PALM • 575QXM4123 • $13

5928.
Santa's Club Soda:
Sweet Bouquet
FRAN • GiftQXC4806 • $23

5929.
Scooting Along
FRAN • 675QXM5173 • $12

1995

5930.
Six Mice:
Baking Tiny Treats
SEAL • 2900QXM4033 • $70
Set/6

5931.
Sweet Dreams
CROW • 300QXM4096 • $17

5932.
Tea with Teddy
RGRS • 725QXM4046 • $13

5933.
Alice in Wonderland 1: Alice
ANDR • 675QXM4777 • $13

5934.
Baby's First Christmas
SEAL • 475QXM4027 • $13

5935.
Calamity Coyote
RGRS • 675QXM4467 • $11

5936.
Centuries of Santa 2
SICK • 575QXM4789 • $17

5937.
Christmas Bells 1
SEAL • 475QXM4007 • $35

5938.
Christmas Wishes
SEAL • 375QXM4087 • $14

5939.
Cloisonne Partridge
VOTR • 975QXM4017 • $14

5940.
Coca-Cola® – Cool Santa
FRAN • ($N/E)QXC4457 • $12

5941.
Downhill Double
PALM • 475QXM4837 • $10

5942.
Friendship Duet
UNRU • 475QXM4019 • $8

5943.
Furrball
RGRS • 575QXM4459 • $10

5944.
A Gift From Rodney
SICK • ($N/E)QXC4129 • $10

5945.
Grandpa's Gift
RGRS • 575QXM4829 • $11

5946.
Heavenly Praises
ANDR • 575QXM4037 • $10

5947.
Holiday Express Train Base
SICK • 5000QXM5452 • $90
Re-issued from 1994.

5948.
Joyful Santa
UNRU • 475QXM4089 • $10

5949.
Little Beeper
RGRS • 575QXM4469 • $11

5950.
March of the Teddy Bears 3
UNRU • 475QXM4799 • $12

5951.
Miniature Clothespin
Soldier 1: British
SICK • 375QXM4097 • $17

5952.
Miniature Kiddie Car
Classics 1:
Murray® Champion
PALM • 575QXM4079 • $15

5953.
Miniature Kiddie Car
Classics 1:
Murray® Champion
PALM • PrizeQXM4079C • $500
Edition Size – 64

5954.
Miniature Rocking Horse 8
SICK • 475QXM4827 • $16

5955.
A Moustershire Christmas
RHOD • 2450QXM4839 • $29
Set/4

5956.
Nature's Angels 6
ANDR • 475QXM4809 • $14

5957.
The Night Before
Christmas 4
UNRU • 475QXM4807 • $20

5958.
Noah's Ark: Merry Walruses
SICK • 575QXM4057 • $20

5959.
Noah's Ark:
Playful Penguins
SICK • 575QXM4059 • $34

5960.
Noel RR 7: Milk Tank Car
SICK • 675QXM4817 • $17

5961.
Nutcracker Guild 2
SICK • 575QXM4787 • $16

5962.
Old English Village 8:
Tudor House
JLEE • 675QXM4819 • $13

5963.
On the Road 3
SICK • 575QXM4797 • $13

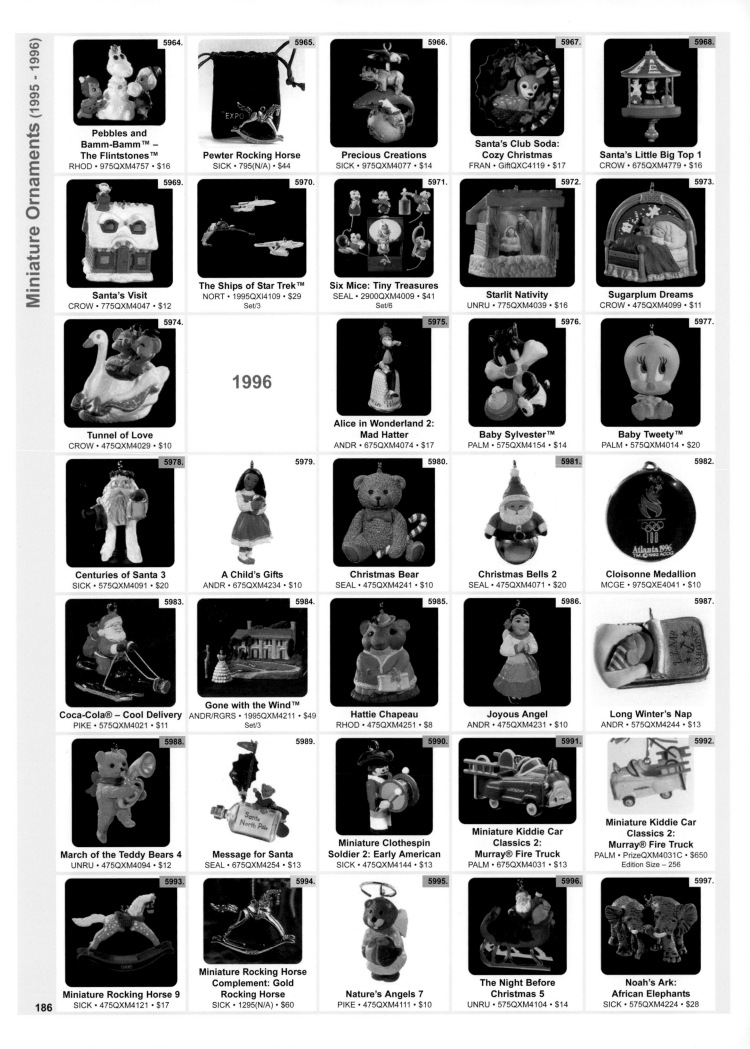

5964.
Pebbles and Bamm-Bamm™ – The Flintstones™
RHOD • 975QXM4757 • $16

5965.
Pewter Rocking Horse
SICK • 795(N/A) • $44

5966.
Precious Creations
SICK • 975QXM4077 • $14

5967.
Santa's Club Soda: Cozy Christmas
FRAN • GiftQXC4119 • $17

5968.
Santa's Little Big Top 1
CROW • 675QXM4779 • $16

5969.
Santa's Visit
CROW • 775QXM4047 • $12

5970.
The Ships of Star Trek™
NORT • 1995QXI4109 • $29
Set/3

5971.
Six Mice: Tiny Treasures
SEAL • 2900QXM4009 • $41
Set/6

5972.
Starlit Nativity
UNRU • 775QXM4039 • $16

5973.
Sugarplum Dreams
CROW • 475QXM4099 • $11

5974.
Tunnel of Love
CROW • 475QXM4029 • $10

1996

5975.
Alice in Wonderland 2: Mad Hatter
ANDR • 675QXM4074 • $17

5976.
Baby Sylvester™
PALM • 575QXM4154 • $14

5977.
Baby Tweety™
PALM • 575QXM4014 • $20

5978.
Centuries of Santa 3
SICK • 575QXM4091 • $20

5979.
A Child's Gifts
ANDR • 675QXM4234 • $10

5980.
Christmas Bear
SEAL • 475QXM4241 • $10

5981.
Christmas Bells 2
SEAL • 475QXM4071 • $20

5982.
Cloisonne Medallion
MCGE • 975QXE4041 • $10

5983.
Coca-Cola® – Cool Delivery
PIKE • 575QXM4021 • $11

5984.
Gone with the Wind™
ANDR/RGRS • 1995QXM4211 • $49
Set/3

5985.
Hattie Chapeau
RHOD • 475QXM4251 • $8

5986.
Joyous Angel
ANDR • 475QXM4231 • $10

5987.
Long Winter's Nap
ANDR • 575QXM4244 • $13

5988.
March of the Teddy Bears 4
UNRU • 475QXM4094 • $12

5989.
Message for Santa
SEAL • 675QXM4254 • $13

5990.
Miniature Clothespin Soldier 2: Early American
SICK • 475QXM4144 • $13

5991.
Miniature Kiddie Car Classics 2: Murray® Fire Truck
PALM • 675QXM4031 • $13

5992.
Miniature Kiddie Car Classics 2: Murray® Fire Truck
PALM • PrizeQXM4031C • $650
Edition Size – 256

5993.
Miniature Rocking Horse 9
SICK • 475QXM4121 • $17

5994.
Miniature Rocking Horse Complement: Gold Rocking Horse
SICK • 1295(N/A) • $60

5995.
Nature's Angels 7
PIKE • 475QXM4111 • $10

5996.
The Night Before Christmas 5
UNRU • 575QXM4104 • $14

5997.
Noah's Ark: African Elephants
SICK • 575QXM4224 • $28

5998.

Noel RR 8: Cookie Car
SICK • 675QXM4114 • $20

5999.

Nutcracker Ballet 1:
Nutcracker Ballet
VOTR • 1475QXM4064 • $25

6000.

Nutcracker Guild 3
SICK • 575QXM4084 • $20

6001.

O Holy Night
RHOD • 2450QXM4204 • $32
Set/4

6002.

Old English Village 9:
Village Mill
RHOD • 675QXM4124 • $23

6003.

On the Road 4
SICK • 575QXM4101 • $13

6004.

Peaceful Christmas
UNRU • 475QXM4214 • $12

6005.

Rudolph's Helper
SIED • ($N/E)QXC4171 • $10

6006.

Santa's Club Soda:
Holiday Bunny
FRAN • GiftQXC4191 • $12

6007.

Santa's Little Big Top 2
CROW • 675QXM4081 • $17

6008.

Six Mice:
Tiny Christmas Helpers
SEAL • 2900QXM4261 • $42
Set/6

6009.

Sparkling Crystal Angel
VOTR • 975QXM4264 • $18

6010.

A Tree for Woodstock®
SIED • 575QXM4767 • $17

6011.

The Vehicles of Star Wars™
RHOD • 1995QXM4024 • $42
Set/3

6012.

Winnie the Pooh
and Tigger
975QXM4044 • $20

1997

6013.

Alice in Wonderland 3:
White Rabbit
ANDR • 695QXM4142 • $12

6014.

Antique Tractors 1
SICK • 695QXM4185 • $17

6015.

C-3PO™ and R2-D2™
RHOD • 1295QXI4265 • $31
Set/2

6016.

Casablanca™
ANDR • 1995QXM4272 • $24
Set/3

6017.

Centuries of Santa 4
SICK • 595QXM4295 • $11

6018.

Christmas Bells 3
SEAL • 495QXM4162 • $19

6019.

Coca-Cola® –
Ice Cold Coca-Cola®
CHAD • 695QXM4252 • $11

6020.

Future Star
PIKE • 595QXM4232 • $8

6021.

He Is Born
VOTR • 795QXM4235 • $12

6022.

Heavenly Music
TAGU • 595QXM4292 • $8

6023.

Home Sweet Home
SEAL • 595QXM4222 • $11

6024.

Honey of a Gift
695QXD4255 • $13

6025.

Jolly Old Santa
WILL • ($N/E)QXC5145 • $8

6026.

King of the Forest
RGRS • 2400QXM4262 • $47
Set/4

6027.

Miniature 1997 Corvette®
PALM • 695QXI4322 • $8

6028.

Miniature Clothespin
Soldier 3: Canadian Mountie
SICK • 495QXM4155 • $10

6029.

Miniature Kiddie Car
Classics 3: Murray®
Pursuit Airplane
PALM • 695QXM4132 • $11

6030.

Miniature Kiddie Car
Classics 3: Murray®
Pursuit Airplane
PALM • PrizeQXM4132C • $650
Edition Size – 320

6031.

Miniature Rocking Horse 10
SICK • 495QXM4302 • $10

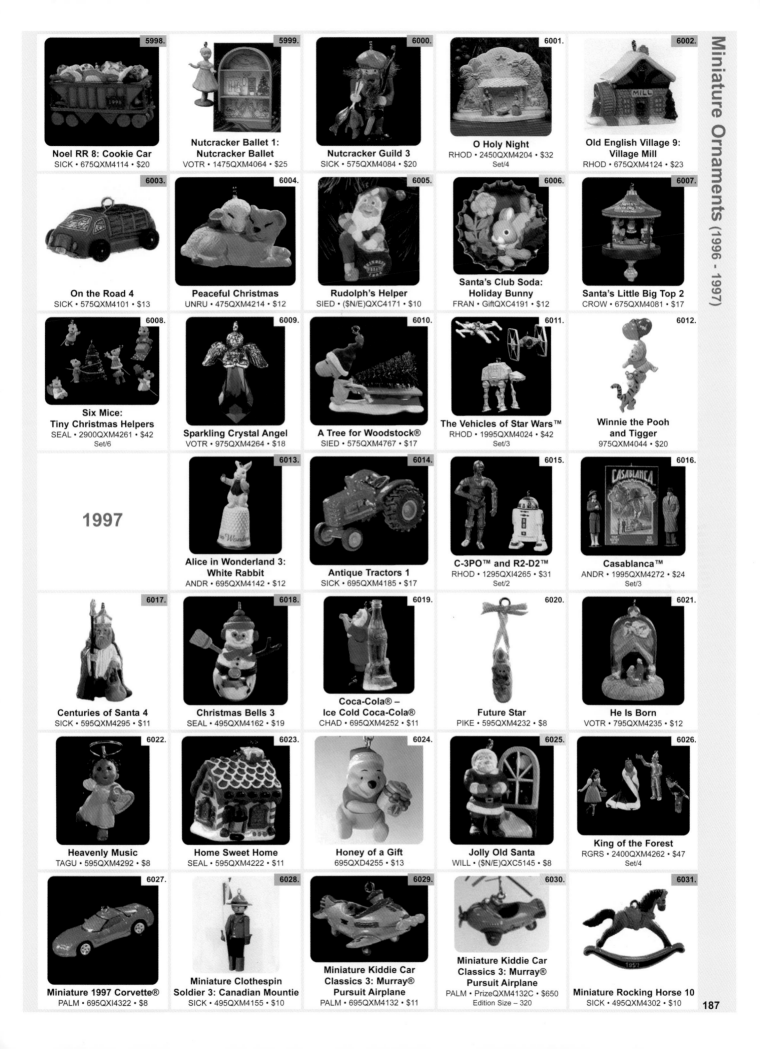

6032.
Noah's Ark: Gentle Giraffes
SICK • 595QXM4221 • $16

6033.
Noel RR 9: Candy Car
SICK • 695QXM4175 • $13

6034.
Nutcracker Ballet 2:
Herr Drosselmeyer
VOTR • 595QXM4135 • $13

6035.
Nutcracker Guild 4
SICK • 695QXM4165 • $12

6036.
Old English Village 10:
Village Depot
LARS • 695QXM4182 • $11

6037.
On the Road 5
SICK • 595QXM4172 • $10

6038.
Our Lady of Guadalupe
CHAD • 895QXM4275 • $9

6039.
Peppermint Painter
TAGU • 495QXM4312 • $10

6040.
Polar Buddies
FRAN • 495QXM4332 • $10

6041.
Ready for Santa
WILL • GiftQXC5142 • $7

6042.
Santa's Little Big Top 3
CROW • 695QXM4152 • $13

6043.
Seeds of Joy
TAGU • 695QXM4242 • $10

6044.
Sew Talented
SEAL • 595QXM4195 • $11

6045.
Shutterbug
TAGU • 595QXM4212 • $10

6046.
Six Mice:
Tiny Home Improvers
SEAL • 2900QXM4282 • $46
Set/6

6047.
Snowboard Bunny
TAGU • 495QXM4315 • $7

6048.
Snowflake Ballet 1
ANDR • 595QXM4192 • $17

6049.
Teddy-Bear Style 1
UNRU • 595QXM4215 • $11

6050.
Victorian Skater
UNRU • 595QXM4305 • $8

6051.
Welcome Friends 1
PIKE • 695QXM4205 • $14

1998

6052.
Alice in Wonderland 4:
Cheshire Cat
ANDR • 695QXM4186 • $13

6053.
Angel Chime
TAGU • 895QXM4283 • $16

6054.
Antique Tractors 2
SICK • 695QXM4166 • $20

6055.
Betsey's Prayer
KLIN • 495QXM4263 • $7

6056.
Centuries of Santa 5
SICK • 595QXM4206 • $17

6057.
Christmas Bells 4
SEAL • 495QXM4196 • $12

6058.
Coca-Cola® Time
UNRU • 695QXM4296 • $14

6059.
Ewoks™
BRIC • 1695QXI4223 • $25
Set/3

6060.
Fishy Surprise
ESCH • 695QXM4276 • $12

6061.
Glinda and the Wicked
Witch of the West™
LYLE • 1495QXM4233 • $30
Set/2

6062.
Holly-Jolly Jig
TAGU • 695QXM4266 • $12

6063.
Kansas City Angel
VOTR • GiftQXC4526 • $195
Edition Size – 3400

6064.
Kringle Bells
BRIC • GiftQXC4486 • $10

6065.
Miniature Clothespin
Soldier 4:
Scottish Highlander
SICK • 495QXM4193 • $13

6066.
Miniature Kiddie Car
Classics 4:
Murray® Dump Truck
PALM • 695QXM4183 • $12

6067.
Miniature Kiddie Car
Luxury Edition 1: 1937
Steelcraft Auburn
PALM • 695QXM4143 • $11

6068.
The Nativity 1
UNRU • 995QXM4156 • $33

6069.
Noah's Ark:
Peaceful Pandas
SICK • 595QXM4253 • $14

6070.
Noel RR 10: Caboose
SICK • 695QXM4216 • $16

6071.
Noel RR Complement: Noel
RR Locomotive 1989 – 1998
SICK • 1095QXM4286 • $19

6072.
Nutcracker Ballet 3:
Nutcracker
VOTR • 595QXM4146 • $14

6073.
Nutcracker Guild 5
SICK • 695QXM4203 • $16

6074.
On the Road 6
SICK • 595QXM4213 • $12

6075.
Pixie Parachute
ESCH • 495QXM4256 • $12

6076.
Sharing Joy
495QXM4273 • $13

6077.
Singin' in the Rain™
ANDR • 1095QXM4303 • $16
Set/2

6078.
Snowflake Ballet 2
ANDR • 595QXM4173 • $20

6079.
Superman™
CHAD • 1095QXM4313 • $20
Set/2

6080.
Teddy-Bear Style 2
UNRU • 595QXM4176 • $12

6081.
Tree Trimmin' Time
1995QXD4236 • $30
Set/3

6082.
Welcome Friends 2
PIKE • 695QXM4153 • $20

6083.
Winter Fun with Snoopy® 1
LARS • 695QXM4243 • $28

1999

6084.
Antique Tractors 3
SICK • 695QXM4567 • $16

6085.
Betsey's Perfect 10
KLIN • 495QXM4609 • $8

6086.
Celestial Kitty
AUBE • 695QXM4639 • $13

6087.
Centuries of Santa 6
SICK • 595QXM4589 • $12

6088.
Christmas Bells 5
SEAL • 495QXM4489 • $12

6089.
Classic Batman™
and Robin™
CHAD • 1295QXM4659 • $28
Set/2

6090.
Crystal Claus
VOTR • 995QXM4637 • $16

6091.
Girl Talk
1295QXD4069 • $19
Set/2

6092.
Gold Locomotive
SICK • 1095(N/A) • $31

6093.
Holiday Flurries 1
SICK • 695QXM4547 • $15

6094.
LIONEL® Norfolk and
Western 1:
Locomotive and Tender
SEAL • 1095QXM4549 • $25
Set/2

6095.
Love to Share
SICK • 695QXM4557 • $11

6096.
Marvin the Martian™
CHAD • 895QXM4657 • $14

6097.
Max Rebo Band™
BRIC • 1995QXI4597 • $26
Set/3

6098.
Merry Grinch-mas
WILL • 1995QXI4627 • $26
Set/3

6099.
Miniature Clothespin
Soldier 5: French Officer
SICK • 495QXM4579 • $10

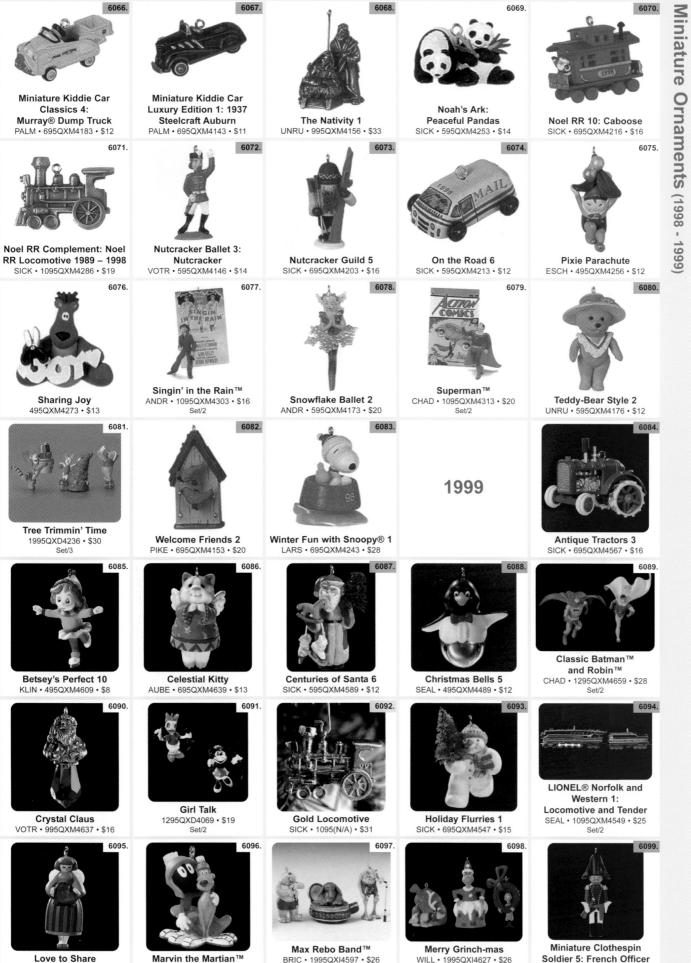

6100.
Miniature Harley-Davidson®
Motorcycles 1:
Electra-Glide®
PALM • 795QXI6137 • $20

6101.
Miniature Kiddie Car
Classics 5: Murray®
Tractor and Trailer
PALM • 695QXM4479 • $12

6102.
Miniature Kiddie Car
Luxury Edition 2:
1937 Steelcraft Airflow
PALM • 995QXM4477 • $12

6103.
The Nativity 2
UNRU • 995QXM4497 • $22

6104.
Noah's Ark: Trusty Reindeer
SICK • 595QXM4617 • $12

6105.
Nutcracker Ballet 4:
Mouse King
VOTR • 595QXM4487 • $12

6106.
Nutcracker Guild 6
SICK • 695QXM4587 • $12

6107.
Roll-A-Bear
SICK • 695QXM4629 • $10

6108.
Santa Time
UNRU • 795QXM4647 • $13

6109.
Seaside Scenes 1
SEAL • 795QXM4649 • $14

6110.
Skating with Pooh
695QXD4127 • $12

6111.
Snowflake Ballet 3
ANDR • 595QXM4569 • $12

6112.
Snowy Surprise
HADD • GiftQXC4529 • $10

6113.
Taz™ and the She-Devil
CHAD • 895QXM4619 • $13

6114.
Teddy-Bear Style 3
UNRU • 595QXM4499 • $12

6115.
Travel Case and
BARBIE™ Ornament
ANDR • 1295QXI6129 • $22
Set/2

6116.
Welcome Friends 3
PIKE • 695QXM4577 • $12

6117.
Winter Fun with Snoopy® 2
LARS • 695QXM4559 • $38

6118.
Wonders of Oz™ 1:
Dorothy's Ruby Slippers™
KLIN • 595QXM4599 • $84

2000

6119.
Antique Tractors 4
SICK • 695QXM5994 • $20

6120.
Bugs Bunny™ and
Elmer Fudd™
CHAD • 995QXM5934 • $12

6121.
Catwoman™
RGRS • 995QXM6021 • $11

6122.
Celestial Bunny
AUBE • 695QXM6641 • $10

6123.
Christmas Bells 6
SEAL • 495QXM5964 • $23

6124.
Christmas Bells 6
SEAL • GiftQXM5964C • $52

6125.
Devoted Donkey
SICK • 695QXM6044 • $12

6126.
A Friend Chimes In
TAGU • GiftQXC4491 • $17

6127.
Green Eggs and Ham™ –
Dr. Seuss®
WILL • 1995QXM6034 • $29
Set/3

6128.
Holiday Flurries 2
SICK • 695QXM5311 • $17

6129.
Ice Block Buddies 1
SICK • 595QXM6011 • $9

6130.
Jedi™ Council Members
BRIC • 1995QXI6744 • $26
Set/3

6131.
LIONEL® Norfolk and
Western 2: Horse Car
and Milk Car
SEAL • 1295QXM5971 • $18
Set/2

6132.
Little Frosty Friends: Husky
SEAL • GiftXPT1995 • $10

6133.
Loyal Elephant
SICK • 695QXM6041 • $13

6134.
Mickey and Minnie Mouse
1295QXD4041 • $19
Set/2

6135.
Miniature Clothespin
Soldier 6: Sailor
SICK • 495QXM5334 • $13

6136.
Miniature Harley-Davidson®
Motorcycles 2:
1962 Duo-Glide®
PALM • 795QXI6001 • $17

6137.
Miniature Kiddie Car
Classics 6: 1968 Jolly
Roger Flagship
WEBB • 695QXM5944 • $12

6138.
Miniature Kiddie Car
Luxury Edition 3: 1935
Steelcraft by Murray®
WEBB • 695QXM5951 • $13

6139.
Monopoly™: Advance
to Go 1: Sack of Money
PIKE • 895QXM5341 • $12

6140.
Mr. Potato Head®
SIED • 595QXM6014 • $13

6141.
The Nativity 3
UNRU • 695QXM5961 • $16

6142.
Noah's Ark: Kindly Lions
SICK • 595QXM5314 • $12

6143.
Nutcracker Ballet 5:
Sugarplum Fairy
VOTR • 595QXM5984 • $32

6144.
Nutcracker Guild 7
SICK • 695QXM5991 • $12

6145.
Precious Penguin
VOTR • 995QXM6104 • $16

6146.
Santa's Journey Begins
CROW • 995QXM6004 • $14

6147.
Seaside Scenes 2
SEAL • 795QXM5974 • $13

6148.
Silken Flame BARBIE™
Ornament and Travel Case
ANDR • 1295QXM6031 • $20
Set/2

6149.
Star Fairy
ESCH • 495QXM6101 • $20

6150.
Teddy-Bear Style 4
UNRU • 595QXM5954 • $10

6151.
Welcoming Angel
ESCH • 595QXM5321 • $17

6152.
Winnie the Pooh:
Tigger-ific Tidings to Pooh
895QXD4014 • $14

6153.
Winter Fun with Snoopy® 3
LARS • 695QXM5324 • $17

6154.
Wonders of Oz™ 2:
The Tin Man's Heart™
RGRS • 595QXM5981 • $10

2001

6155.
Antique Tractors 5
SICK • 695QXM5252 • $18

6156.
Antique Tractors 5
SICK • 695QXM5252C • $38

6157.
Battle of Naboo™
RHOD/WEBB • 1495QXM5212 • $26
Set/3

6158.
Celebration Wreath
VARI • 6500QXC4572 • $127

6159.
Christmas Bells 7
SEAL • 495QXM5245 • $10

6160.
Christmas Bells 7
SEAL • GiftQXM5245C • $35
Edition Size – 15000

6161.
Cooking for Christmas:
Sweet Contribution
LARS • 495QXM4492 • $13

6162.
Cooking for Christmas:
Sweet Contribution
LARS • PrizeQXM4492C • $50
Edition Size – 5000

6163.
Dashing Through the Snow
CROW • 695QXM5335 • $10

6164.
Disney Birthday Bash –
Fantasia
1495QXD4205 • $20
Set/6

6165.
Gearing Up For Christmas
CROW • 695QXM5352 • $8

6166.
The Glass Slipper –
Cinderella
795QXD4182 • $13

6167.
Holiday Flurries 3
SICK • 695QXM5272 • $12

6168.
Holiday Shoe
ESCH • 495QXM5365 • $7

6169.
Ice Block Buddies 2
SICK • 595QXM5295 • $16

6170.
Jiminy Cricket – Pinocchio
795QXD4185 • $12

6171.
LIONEL® Norfolk and Western 3: Car Carrier and Caboose
1295QXM5265 • $24
Set/2

6172.
Miniature Harley-Davidson® Motorcycles 3: 1947 Servi-Car®
PALM • 795QXI5282 • $24

6173.
Miniature Kiddie Car Classics 7: 1924 Toledo Fire Engine #6
WEBB • 695QXM5192 • $34

6174.
Miniature Kiddie Car Luxury Edition 4: 1937 Garton Ford®
WEBB • 695QXM5195 • $14

6175.
Miniature Rocking Horse Complement
SICK • GiftQC4592 • $10

6176.
Miniature Sky's the Limit 1: The Flight at Kitty Hawk
NORT • 695QXM5215 • $22

6177.
Monopoly™: Advance to Go 2: Race Car
PIKE • 895QXM5292 • $13

6178.
The Nativity 4
UNRU • 995QXM5255 • $17

6179.
Noah's Ark: Bouncy Kangaroos
SICK • 595QXM5332 • $11

6180.
Radiant Christmas
VOTR • 795QXM5342 • $11

6181.
Ready for a Ride
AUBE • 695QXM5302 • $16

6182.
Santa-in-a-Box
FRAN • 695QXM5355 • $10

6183.
Scooby-Doo™
CHAD • 695QXM5322 • $12

6184.
Seaside Scenes 3
SEAL • 795QXM5275 • $12

6185.
Solo in the Spotlight Case and BARBIE™ Ornament
ANDR • 1295QXM5312 • $19
Set/2

6186.
Starfleet™ Legends
NORT • 1495QXM5325 • $39
Set/3

6187.
Sweet Slipper Dream
AUBE • 495QXM5345 • $11

6188.
Thing One and Thing Two!™ – The Cat in the Hat™
WILL • 1495QXM5315 • $22
Set/3

6189.
Tweety™
CHAD • 695QXM5305 • $11

6190.
Winter Fun with Snoopy® 4
LARS • 695QXM5262 • $16

6191.
Wonders of Oz™ 3: Toto™
LYLE • 595QXM5285 • $19

2002

6192.
Angel in Training
VOTR • 695QXM4403 • $17

6193.
Antique Tractors 6
SICK • 695QXM4336 • $16

6194.
Antique Tractors 6
SICK • PrizeQXM4336C • $35
Edition Size – 5000

6195.
Christmas Angel Display
TAGU • 1695QXM4573 • $26

6196.
Christmas Bells 8
SEAL • 495QXM4326 • $17

6197.
Enchanted Evening Case and BARBIE™ Ornament
ANDR • 1295QXM4383 • $26
Set/2

6198.
Gift For Gardening
SEAL • 495QXM4463 • $15

6199.
Gifts of the Season
TAGU • 2800QXM4576 • $53
Set/6

6200.
Ice Block Buddies 3
SICK • 495QXM4356 • $17

6201.
Jingle Belle
TAGU • 595QXM4483 • $16

6202.
Lighted Display Tree
1495QXM4536 • $26
Re-issued in 2003.

6203.
Steam Locomotive & Tender –
LIONEL®, The General
1295QXM4366 • $26
Set/2

6204.
Miniature Harley-Davidson®
Motorcycles 4:
1958 FL Duo Glide®
PALM • 795QXI4346 • $24

6205.
Miniature Kiddie Car
Classics 8:
1930 Custom Biplane
WEBB • 695QXM4333 • $17

6206.
Miniature Kiddie Car
Classics 8:
1930 Custom Biplane
WEBB • PrizeQXM4333C • $35
Edition Size – 5000

6207.
Miniature Sky's the Limit 2:
1917 Curtiss JN-4D "Jenny"
NORT • 695QXM4363 • $14

6208.
Mistletoad
AUBE • 495QXM4563 • $17

6209.
Monopoly™: Advance
to Go 3: Locomotive
PIKE • 895QXM4353 • $22

6210.
Paintbox Pixies 1: Dream
SICK • 695QXM4543 • $12
Set/2

6211.
Raggedy Ann and Andy®
FRAN • 995QXM4496 • $17
Set/2

6212.
Santa Jumping Jack
VISK • 595QXM4473 • $23

6213.
Santa's Big Night:
Five Tiny Favorites
GiftQXM4566 • $20
Set/5

6214.
Snow Cozy 1
KLIN • 495QXM4546 • $17

6215.
Sugar Plum Fairies
SICK • 1495QXM4513 • $27
Set/6

6216.
Sugar Plum Tabletop
Topiary
SICK • 1995QXM4506 • $36

6217.
Tin Man™
RGRS • 695QXM4556 • $11

6218.
Two Tiny Penguins
VISK • 995QXM4413 • $18
Set/3

6219.
Up to the Tweetop –
Tweety™
PALM • 595QXM4396 • $26

6220.
Winnie the Pooh:
On the Slopes
695QXD4553 • $12

6221.
Winter Fun with Snoopy® 5
LARS • 695QXM4343 • $17

6222.
Winter's Here!
PIKE • 695QXM4423 • $14

2003

6223.
Afternoon Tea 1
VOTR • 695QXM4937 • $28

6224.
Antique Tractors 7
SICK • 695QXM4889 • $16

6225.
Antique Tractors 7
SICK • 695QXM4889C • $34

6226.
Bunny Skates – Maxine
SIED/WAGN • 595QXM4957 • $10

6227.
Charming Hearts 1
RHOD • 995QXM4939 • $13

6228.
Charming Hearts 1
RHOD • PrizeQXM4939C • $49

6229.
Christmas Bells 9
SEAL • 495QXM4927 • $10

6230.
The Christmas Pageant
LYLE • 995QXM4406 • $17
Set/3

6231.
Clever Cardinal
FRAN • 695QXM5019 • $12

6232.
Clone Troopers™
WILL • 995QXM5127 • $26
Set/2

6233.
The Cowardly Lion™
RGRS • 695QXM4219 • $11

6234.
Here Comes Santa
Complement
VARI • 1495QXM4929 • $25
Set/3

6235.
Ice Block Buddies 4
SICK • 495QXM4899 • $12

193

6236.
Join the Caravan! –
Corvette® 50th Anniversary
PALM • 3000QXM4977 • $32
Set/5

6237.
Jolly Li'l Santa
VISK • 495QXM4433 • $10

6238.
Joy to the Birds! –
Woodstock®
595QXM4967 • $11

6239.
Keepsake Ornament
Gallery Collection
VARI • 7500QXC4609 • $95

6240.
Kitchen Angels
TAGU • 995QXM5029 • $22
Set/3

6241.
Kitchen Angels Spoon Tree
TAGU • 1995QXM5027 • $29
Set/7

6242.
Kitty Catch
KLIN • 495QXM4997 • $12

6243.
Lawn Patrol
SICK • 595QXM4979 • $12

6244.
Lighted Display Tree
1495QXM4536 • $26
Re-issued from 2002.

6245.
LIONEL® Blue Comet Steam
Locomotive and Tender
1295QXM4887 • $20
Set/2

6246.
Merrier by the Dozen
VISK • 1495QXM5049 • $23
Set/12

6247.
Miniature Harley-Davidson®
Motorcycles 5:
1948 Panhead
PALM • 795QXM4879 • $16

6248.
Miniature Kiddie Car
Classics 9:
Jingle Bell Express
WEBB • 695QXM4867 • $12

6249.
Miniature Ornament
Display Window
FORS • 1495QXC4687 • $28

6250.
Miniature Sky's the Limit 3:
Curtiss R3C-2 Racer
NORT • 695QXM4877 • $18

6251.
Miniature Sky's the Limit 3:
Curtiss R3C-2 Racer
NORT • PrizeQXM4877C • $35

6252.
Mouse-Warming Gift
BRIC • 695QXM4999 • $12
Set/3

6253.
Paintbox Pixies 2: Believe
SICK • 695QXM4919 • $12
Set/2

6254.
Presents of Angels
GiftWD2845 • $10
Set/7

6255.
Puppies on the Doorstep
CHAD • 695QXM4989 • $14

6256.
Shopping for Shoes
BARBIE™
1495QXM4949 • $20
Set/7

6257.
Snow Cozy 2
KLIN • 495QXM4917 • $16

6258.
Snow Cozy 2
KLIN • 495QXM4917C • $32

6259.
The Snowmen of Mitford
1295QXM4959 • $22
Set/3

6260.
A Sweet for Tweety™
DIRH • 595QXM5057 • $10

6261.
Symbols of Christmas
FORS/KLIN • 1995QXC4597 • $34
Set/6

6262.
Tinker Bell – Peter Pan
695QXM5097 • $20

6263.
'Tis the Season!
MMOL/VISK • 1495QXM5047 • $20
Re-issued in 2004.

6264.
Winnie the Pooh:
Ring-a-ling Pals
1295QXM5077 • $15
Set/3

6265.
Winter Fun with Snoopy® 6
LARS • 695QXM4869 • $12

2004

6266.
Adding the Right Touch
BARBIE™ Ornaments
ANDR • 1495QXM5214 • $25
Set/9

6267.
Afternoon Tea 2
VOTR • 695QXM5171 • $13

6268.
Antique Tractors 8
SICK • 695QXM5154 • $13

6269.
Candy Cane Trio – Winnie
the Pooh & Friends
1295QXM5114 • $19
Set/3

6270.

Charming Hearts 2
RHOD • 995QXM5194 • $14

6271.
Charming Hearts 2
RHOD • PrizeQXM5194C • $40

6272.
Christmas Bells 10
495QXM5134 • $13

6273.
Classic Red Riding Hood
FRAN • 795QXM5201 • $13

6274.
Cookies, Anyone?
RHOD • GiftWD3037 • $13

6275.
Display Tree
1695QXM5254 • $30

6276.
Forever Friends 1: Santa Wanna-Be
TAGU • 595QXM5151 • $12

6277.
Holiday Bouquet
VOTR • 1995QXM5244 • $30
Set/5

6278.
Ice Block Buddies 5
SICK • 495QXM5141 • $13

6279.
Just for Santa
RGRS • GiftWD3036 • $13

6280.
Let It Snow, Man!
SICK • 695QXM5234 • $15

6281.
LIONEL® Southern Pacific Daylight – Steam Locomotive and Tender
1295QXM5131 • $24
Set/2

6282.
Miniature Fire Brigade 1: 1929 Chevrolet® Fire Engine
WEBB • 995QXM5164 • $19

6283.
Miniature Harley-Davidson® Motorcycles 6: 1933 Flathead Model VLD
PALM • 795QXM5191 • $13

6284.
Miniature Kiddie Car Classics 10: 1949 Gillham™ Sport Miniature
PALM • 695QXM5161 • $13

6285.
Miniature Sky's the Limit 4: Spirit of St. Louis
NORT • 695QXM5181 • $19

6286.
Paintbox Pixies 3: Wish
SICK • 695QXM5174 • $12
Set/2

6287.
Pinocchio Marionette
795QXM5121 • $18

6288.
Prince Charming
TAGU • 595QXM5224 • $16

6289.
Purr-Fectly Contented
SICK • 995QXM5241 • $19
Set/3

6290.
Putting On The Glitz – Tweety™
995QXM5111 • $16

6291.
Santa's Balloon Tree
BRIC • 595QXM5221 • $11

6292.
Scarecrow™
RGRS • 695QXM5091 • $12

6293.
Snow Cozy 3
KLIN • 495QXM5144 • $11

6294.
Star Trek™ Insignias
NORT • 1295QXM5211 • $20
Set/3

6295.
Star-Spangled Banner
895QXM5204 • $13

6296.
Sweeter By The Dozen
1495QXM5274 • $23
Set/12

6297.
'Tis the Season!
MMOL/VISK • 1495QXM5047 • $20
Re-issued from 2003.

6298.
Welcome Sound – Mickey Mouse
595QXM5231 • $12

6299.
Who Goes There!
595QXM5094 • $10

6300.
Winter Fun with Snoopy® 7
LARS • 695QXM5184 • $16

2005

6301.
Afternoon Tea 3
VOTR • 695QXM8955 • $12

6302.
Amazing No. 53 – Herbie, the Love Bug
695QXM8175 • $9

6303.
Angelic Trio
HADD/HAMI • 1295QXM8162 • $19
Set/3

6304. Antique Tractors 9
SICK • 695QXM8992 • $18

6305. Antique Tractors 9
SICK • 695QXM8992C • $40

6306. Candy Cane Tweat –
Tweety™
FEUR • 695QXM8752 • $10

6307. Charming Hearts 3
RHOD • 995QXM8962 • $14

6308. Christmas Bells 11
495QXM8975 • $12

6309. Christmas Stocking Display
2495QXM8182 • $25

6310. Dancing Santa
VISK • 595QXM8132 • $14

6311. Dorothy –
The Wizard of Oz™
RGRS • 695QXM8922 • $19

6312. Forever Friends 2:
Love to Shop!
TAGU • 595QXM8935 • $10

6313. Holiday Headliner –
Mickey Mouse
995QXM8942 • $12

6314. Ice Block Buddies 6
SICK • 495QXM8972 • $12

6315. LIONEL® 1939 Hiawatha
Steam Locomotive
and Tender
1295QXM2075 • $19
Set/2

6316. Lucky Slot Machine
SICK • 795QXM8135 • $12

6317. Madame Alexander®
Complement: Rosette
Dreams Bride and Groom
LYLE • 1295QXM2082 • $20
Set/2

6318. Miniature Fire Brigade 2:
American LaFrance 700
Series Pumper
WEBB • 995QXM2062 • $16

6319. Miniature Harley-Davidson®
Motorcycles 7: 1994 FLHR
ROAD KING®
PALM • 795QXM2065 • $16

6320. Miniature Kiddie Car
Classics 11:
1935 Timmy Racer
WEBB • 695QXM8985 • $14

6321. Miniature Sky's the Limit 5:
GeeBee R-1
Super Sportster®
NORT • 695QXM2072 • $18

6322. Peace, Hope and Joy –
The Gifts of Christmas
FORS/TAGU • 1295QXM8172 • $16
Set/3

6323. Penguin Races
KLIN • 1295QXM8155 • $24
Set/3

6324. Penguin Races
KLIN • PrizeQXM8155C • $395
Set/3 • Edition Size – 96

6325. The Polar Express™ –
The Conductor's Watch
FEUR • 795QXM6472 • $14

6326. The Polar Express™ –
Train Set
WILL • 2400QXM6475 • $29
Set/7

6327. Road Trip BARBIE™
Ornament Set
1495QXM8982 • $19
Set/4

6328. The Royal Princesses
1995QXM8952 • $24
Set/4

6329. Rudolph the Red-Nosed
Reindeer®
CHAD • 795QXM8995 • $10

6330. See No Humbug!
SICK • 1295QXM8152 • $18
Set/3

6331. See No Humbug!
SICK • PrizeQXM8152C • $45
Set/3

6332. Sleepy-Time Mouse
VOTR • 695QXM8145 • $10

6333. Snow Cozy 4
KLIN • 495QXM8965 • $16

6334. TIE Advanced x1™ and
Millennium Falcon™
NORT/RHOD • 1495QXM2085 • $19
Set/2

6335. Tiny Ballerina
TAGU • 595QXM8142 • $16

6336. Winnie the Pooh: Up
for Adventure – Winnie
the Pooh® and Tigger
1295QXM8945 • $29
Set/2

6337. Winter Friends
BAST/SICK • 2800QXM8165 • $28
Set/5

6338. Winter Fun with Snoopy® 8
LARS • 695QXM2092 • $29

2006

6339.
Antique Tractors 10
SICK • 650QXM2143 • $14

6340.
Asajj Ventress™, Anakin
Skywalker™ and Yoda™
FEUR • 1500QXM2113
Set/3

6341.
BARBIE™ Fashion Minis
FORS/KLIN • 2000QXM3156
Set/6

6342.
Disney Ladies
2000QXM3153
Set/6

6343.
"A Happy Life Together"
Ornament Collection
FORS • 2400QXM2206
Set/12

6344.
Jolly Snowmen
KLIN • 2000QXM3176
Set/6

6345.
Jumping for Joy
1250QXM2116
Set/2

6346.
LIONEL® Pennsylvania
B6 Steam Locomotive
and Tender
1250QXM2096
Set/2

6347.
The Magic of Glinda –
The Wizard of Oz™
RGRS • 1500QXM2043
Set/3

6348.
Merry and Bright
Miniature Collection
VISK • 2500QXM2183
Set/6

6349.
Miniature Fire Brigade 3:
Firehouse No. 2006
PALM • 1000QXM3096

6350.
Miniature Glass Ball
Ornaments
400QXM3243
Set/15

6351.
Miniature Harley-Davidson®
Motorcyles 8:
1986 Heritage Softail®
PALM • 800QXM2093

6352.
The Mini-Tree Miniature
Christmas Ornament Display
2500QXM2173

6353.
A New Breed of
Super Heroes
2400QXM2233
Set/6

6354.
New York Yorkie™
BARBIE™ Ornament
1500QXM6336
Set/4

6355.
PEANUTS® Nativity
2000QXM3146
Set/6

6356.
The Perfect Evening Out
FORS • 3500QFM4483
Set/10

6357.
Precocious Tink
650QXM2126

6358.
Santa's From Around
the World
BRIC • 2000QXM3143
Set/6

6359.
Santa's Wittle Helper
RGRS • 650QXM3163

6360.
Winter Fun with Snoopy® 9
LARS • 650QXM2066

6361.
Yankee Doodle and
Celebrating America
LYLE • 1250QXM2103
Set/2

Easter/Spring Ornaments

Designed to brighten your spring, Easter/Spring ornaments are colorful and simply delightful. The Spring Ornament Line, first offered in 1991, offers variety ranging from religious to whimsical; there is something for everyone.

1991

6362.
Baby's First Easter
875QEO5189 • $25

6363.
Daughter
575QEO5179 • $30

6364.
Easter Memories
775QEO5137 • $13

6365.
Full Of Love
775QEO5149 • $45

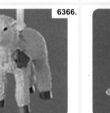
6366.
Gentle Lamb
675QEO5159 • $19

6367.
Grandchild
675QEO5177 • $22

6368.
Li'l Dipper
675QEO5147 • $25

6369.
Lily Egg
UNRU • 975QEO5139 • $17

6370.
Son
575QEO5187 • $25

6371.
Spirit Of Easter
775QEO5169 • $29

6372.
Springtime Stroll
675QEO5167 • $20

1992

6373.
Baby's First Easter
FRAN • 675QEO9271 • $20

6374.
Belle Bunny
VOTR • 975QEO9354 • $32

6375.
Bless You
FRAN • 675QEO9291 • $20

6376.
Cosmic Rabbit
SIED • 775QEO9364 • $19

6377.
Crayola® Bunny
RGRS • 775QEO9304 • $35

6378.
Cultivated Gardener
SIED • 575QEO9351 • $16

6379.
Daughter
RGRS • 575QEO9284 • $17

6380.
Easter Parade 1
CROW • 675QEO9301 • $22

6381.
Eggs in Sports 1
SIED • 675QEO9341 • $30

6382.
Eggspert Painter
SIED • 675QEO9361 • $22

6383.
Everything's Ducky
PIKE • 675QEO9331 • $22

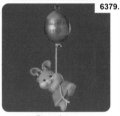
6384.
Grandchild
CROW • 675QEO9274 • $17

6385.
Joy Bearer
PALM • 875QEO9334 • $22

6386.
Promise Of Easter
LYLE • 875QEO9314 • $23

6387.
Rocking Bunny
VOTR • 975QEO9324 • $22

6388.
Somebunny Loves You
FRAN • 675QEO9294 • $37

6389.
Son
RGRS • 575QEO9281 • $17

1993

6390.
Springtime Egg
JLEE • 875QEO9321 • $20

6391.
Sunny Wisher
PIKE • 575QEO9344 • $17

6392.
Warm Memories
VOTR • 775QEO9311 • $13

6393.
Baby's First Easter
PALM • 675QEO8345 • $14

6394.
Backyard Bunny
SICK • 675QEO8405 • $16

6395.
Barrow of Giggles
ANDR • 875QEO8402 • $22

6396.
Beautiful Memories
UNRU • 675QEO8362 • $16

6397.
Best-dressed Turtle
JLEE • 575QEO8392 • $18

6398.
Daughter
ANDR • 575QEO8342 • $16

6399.
Easter Parade 2
JLEE • 675QEO8325 • $18

6400.
Eggs in Sports 2
SIED • 675QEO8332 • $14

6401.
Grandchild
SIED • 675QEO8352 • $14

6402.
Li'l Peeper
JLEE • 775QEO8312 • $20

6403.
Lop-Eared Bunny
SICK • 575QEO8315 • $18

6404.
Lovely Lamb
VOTR • 975QEO8372 • $20

6405.
Maypole Stroll
CHAD/FRAN • 2800QEO8395 • $34
Set/4

6406.
Nutty Eggs
JLEE • 675QEO8382 • $13

6407.
Radiant Window
UNRU • 775QEO8365 • $13

6408.
Son
ANDR • 575QEO8335 • $16

6409.
Springtime Bonnets 1
DLEE • 775QEO8322 • $25

6410.
Time for Easter
CHAD • 875QEO8385 • $18

6411.
**Twirl-About –
Chicks-on-a-Twirl**
LYLE • 775QEO8375 • $14

1994

6412.
Baby's First Easter
FRAN • 675QEO8153 • $19

6413.
**Collector's Plate – Easter 1:
Gathering Sunny Memories**
VOTR • 775QEO8233 • $28

6414.
Colorful Spring
CROW • 775QEO8166 • $30

6415.
Daughter
ANDR • 575QEO8156 • $14

6416.
Divine Duet
VOTR • 675QEO8183 • $17

6417.
Easter Art Show
VOTR • 775QEO8193 • $17

6418.
Easter Parade 3
RHOD • 675QEO8136 • $23

6419.
Eggs in Sports 3
SIED • 675QEO8133 • $17

6420.
First Hello
RGRS • GiftQXC4846 • $40

6421.
Here Comes Easter 1
CROW • 775QEO8093 • $34

6422.
Joyful Lamb
UNRU • 575QEO8206 • $23

6423.
PEANUTS®
UNRU • 775QEO8176 • $30

6424.
Peeping Out
UNRU • 675QEO8203 • $16

6425.
Riding a Breeze
PALM • 575QEO8213 • $16

6426.
Son
ANDR • 575QEO8163 • $12

6427.
Springtime Bonnets 2
BISH • 775QEO8096 • $32

6428.
Sunny Bunny Garden
SEAL • 1500QEO8146 • $24
Set/3

6429.
Sweet As Sugar
RGRS • 875QEO8086 • $17

6430.
Tender Touches:
Sweet Easter Wishes
SEAL • 875QEO8196 • $26

6431.
Tilling Time
SEAL • GiftQXC8256 • $22

6432.
Treetop Cottage
SICK • 975QEO8186 • $17

6433.
Yummy Recipe
RGRS • 775QEO8143 • $17

1995

6434.
Apple Blossom Lane 1
FRAN • 895QEO8207 • $18

6435.
April Shower
SIED • 695QEO8253 • $10

6436.
Baby's First Easter
PALM • 795QEO8237 • $13

6437.
Bugs Bunny™
CHAD • 895QEO8279 • $16

6438.
Collector's Plate – Easter 2:
Catching the Breeze
VOTR • 795QEO8219 • $14

6439.
Crayola®: Picture Perfect
CROW • 795QEO8249 • $16

6440.
Daughter
RGRS • 595QEO8239 • $12

6441.
Easter Beagle
RHOD • 795QEO8257 • $26

6442.
Easter Eggspress
SIED • 495QEO8269 • $11

6443.
Elegant Lily
VOTR • 695QEO8267 • $8

6444.
Flowerpot Friends
ANDR • 1495QEO8229 • $23
Set/4

6445.
Garden Club 1
SICK • 795QEO8209 • $18

6446.
Ham 'n Eggs
CHAD • 795QEO8277 • $11

6447.
Here Comes Easter 2
CROW • 795QEO8217 • $19

6448.
May Flower
SIED • GiftQXC8246 • $36

6449.
Son
RGRS • 595QEO8247 • $15

6450.
Springtime BARBIE™ 1
ANDR • 1295QEO8069 • $24

6451.
Springtime Bonnets 3
UNRU • 795QEO8227 • $14

6452.
Tender Touches: High Hopes
SEAL • 895QEO8259 • $17

1996

6453.
Apple Blossom Lane 2
FRAN • 895QEO8084 • $13

6454.
Beatrix Potter™ 1:
Peter Rabbit
VOTR • 895QEO8071 • $78

6455.
Collector's Plate – Easter 3:
Keeping a Secret
VOTR • 795QEO8221 • $14

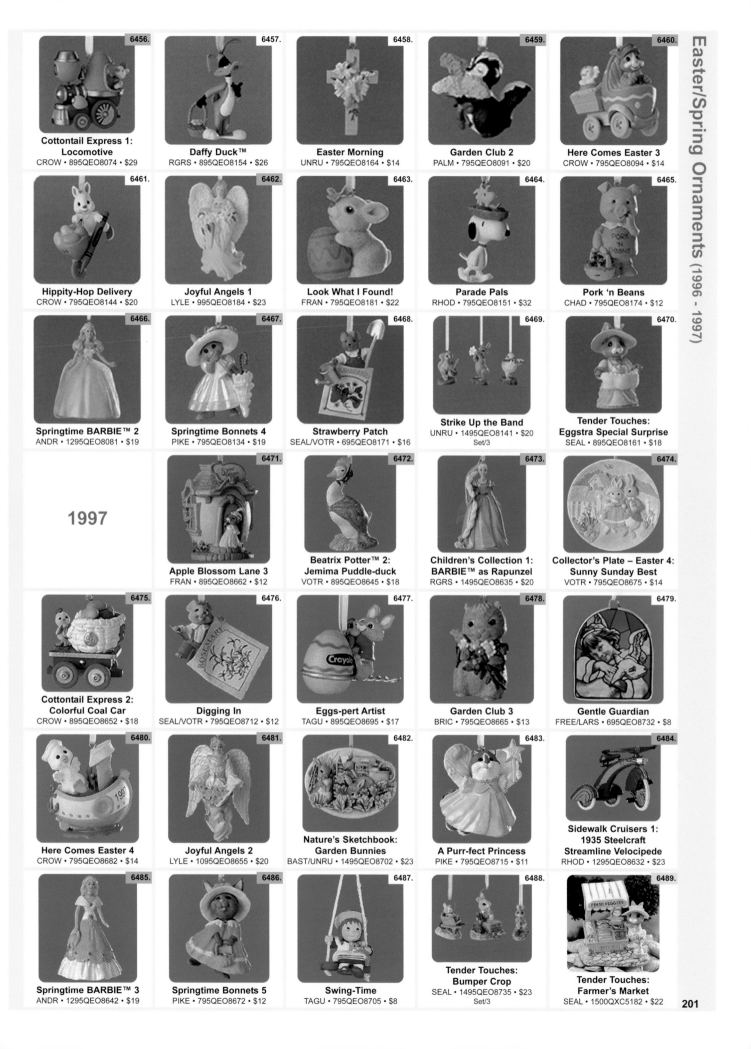

6456.
Cottontail Express 1:
Locomotive
CROW • 895QEO8074 • $29

6457.
Daffy Duck™
RGRS • 895QEO8154 • $26

6458.
Easter Morning
UNRU • 795QEO8164 • $14

6459.
Garden Club 2
PALM • 795QEO8091 • $20

6460.
Here Comes Easter 3
CROW • 795QEO8094 • $14

6461.
Hippity-Hop Delivery
CROW • 795QEO8144 • $20

6462.
Joyful Angels 1
LYLE • 995QEO8184 • $23

6463.
Look What I Found!
FRAN • 795QEO8181 • $22

6464.
Parade Pals
RHOD • 795QEO8151 • $32

6465.
Pork 'n Beans
CHAD • 795QEO8174 • $12

6466.
Springtime BARBIE™ 2
ANDR • 1295QEO8081 • $19

6467.
Springtime Bonnets 4
PIKE • 795QEO8134 • $19

6468.
Strawberry Patch
SEAL/VOTR • 695QEO8171 • $16

6469.
Strike Up the Band
UNRU • 1495QEO8141 • $20
Set/3

6470.
Tender Touches:
Eggstra Special Surprise
SEAL • 895QEO8161 • $18

1997

6471.
Apple Blossom Lane 3
FRAN • 895QEO8662 • $12

6472.
Beatrix Potter™ 2:
Jemima Puddle-duck
VOTR • 895QEO8645 • $18

6473.
Children's Collection 1:
BARBIE™ as Rapunzel
RGRS • 1495QEO8635 • $20

6474.
Collector's Plate – Easter 4:
Sunny Sunday Best
VOTR • 795QEO8675 • $14

6475.
Cottontail Express 2:
Colorful Coal Car
CROW • 895QEO8652 • $18

6476.
Digging In
SEAL/VOTR • 795QEO8712 • $12

6477.
Eggs-pert Artist
TAGU • 895QEO8695 • $17

6478.
Garden Club 3
BRIC • 795QEO8665 • $13

6479.
Gentle Guardian
FREE/LARS • 695QEO8732 • $8

6480.
Here Comes Easter 4
CROW • 795QEO8682 • $14

6481.
Joyful Angels 2
LYLE • 1095QEO8655 • $20

6482.
Nature's Sketchbook:
Garden Bunnies
BAST/UNRU • 1495QEO8702 • $23

6483.
A Purr-fect Princess
PIKE • 795QEO8715 • $11

6484.
Sidewalk Cruisers 1:
1935 Steelcraft
Streamline Velocipede
RHOD • 1295QEO8632 • $23

6485.
Springtime BARBIE™ 3
ANDR • 1295QEO8642 • $19

6486.
Springtime Bonnets 5
PIKE • 795QEO8672 • $12

6487.
Swing-Time
TAGU • 795QEO8705 • $8

6488.
Tender Touches:
Bumper Crop
SEAL • 1495QEO8735 • $23
Set/3

6489.
Tender Touches:
Farmer's Market
SEAL • 1500QXC5182 • $22

6490.
Victorian Cross
895QEO8725 • $12

1998

6491.
Bashful Gift
AUBE • 1195QEO8446 • $18
Set/2

6492.
Beatrix Potter™ 3:
Benjamin Bunny
VOTR • 895QEO8383 • $19

6493.
Bouquet of Memories
TAGU • 795QEO8456 • $12

6494.
Children's Collection 2:
BARBIE™ as Little Bo Peep
RGRS • 1495QEO8373 • $22

6495.
Cottontail Express 3:
Passenger Car
CROW • 995QEO8376 • $17

6496.
Forever Friends
BRWN/PIKE • 995QEO8423 • $16

6497.
Garden Club 4
PIKE • 795QEO8426 • $12

6498.
The Garden of Piglet
and Pooh
1295QEO8403 • $19
Set/2

6499.
Going Up? Charlie Brown®
PIKE • 995QEO8433 • $19

6500.
Happy Diploma Day!
HADD • 795QEO8476 • $13

6501.
Joyful Angels 3
LYLE • 1095QEO8386 • $17

6502.
Midge™ – 35th Anniversary
ANDR • 1495QEO8413 • $20

6503.
Practice Swing –
Donald Duck
1095QEO8396 • $16

6504.
Precious Baby
TAGU • 995QEO8463 • $14

6505.
Sidewalk Cruisers 2:
1939 Mobo Horse
1295QEO8393 • $22

6506.
Special Friends
KELL/VOTR • 1295QEO8523 • $17

6507.
Star Wars™
GOSL • 1295QEO8406 • $20

6508.
Sweet Birthday
KLIN • 795QEO8473 • $13

6509.
Tigger in the Garden
995QEO8436 • $17

6510.
Victorian Cross
UNRU • 895QEO8453 • $16

6511.
Vintage Roadsters 1: 1931
Ford® Model A Roadster™
PALM • 1495QEO8416 • $20

6512.
Wedding Memories
VOTR • 995QEO8466 • $14

6513.
What's Your Name?
KLIN • 795QEO8443 • $14

1999

6514.
40th Anniversary Edition
- BARBIE™ Lunchbox
1295QEO8399 • $20

6515.
Batter Up! Charlie
Brown® and Snoopy®
RHOD • 1295QEO8389 • $22
Set/2

6516.
Beatrix Potter™ 4:
Tom Kitten
VOTR • 895QEO8329 • $14

6517.
Birthday Celebraton
AUBE • 895QEO8409 • $9

6518.
Children's Collection 3:
BARBIE™ as Cinderella
RGRS • 1495QEO8327 • $24

6519.
Cottontail Express 4:
Flatbed Car
CROW • 995QEO8387 • $14

6520.
Cross of Faith
VOTR • 1395QEO8467 • $23

6521.
Easter Egg Nest
SICK • 795QEO8427 • $12

6522.
Easter Egg Surprise 1: Duck
VOTR • 1495QEO8377 • $18

6523.
Fairy Berry Bears 1:
Strawberry
TAGU • 1495QEO8369 • $15

6524.
Final Putt, Minnie Mouse
1095QEO8349 • $14

6525.
Friendly Delivery, Mary's
Bears
HAMI/KLIN • 1295QEO8419 • $18

6526.
Happy Bubble Blower
TAGU • 795QEO8437 • $10

6527.
Happy Diploma Day!
1095QEO8357 • $13

6528.
Inspirational Angel
LYLE • 1295QEO8347 • $22

6529.
Mop Top Billy
FRAN • 1495QEO8337 • $29

6530.
Precious Baby
LYLE • 995QEO8417 • $13

6531.
Sidewalk Cruisers 3:
1950 Garton® Delivery Cycle
1295QEO8367 • $24

6532.
Spring Chick
AUBE • 2200QEO8469 • $23

6533.
Springtime Harvest
SICK • 795QEO8429 • $11

6534.
The Tale of Peter Rabbit
- Beatrix Potter™
VOTR • 1995QEO8397 • $28
Set/3

6535.
Tiggerific Easter Delivery
1095QEO8359 • $14

6536.
Vintage Roadsters 2: 1932
Chevrolet® Sports Roadster
PALM • 1495QEO8379 • $23

6537.
Wedding Memories
UNRU • 995QEO8407 • $10

6538.
Winner's Circle 1: 1956
Garton® Hot Rod Racer
UNRU • 1395QEO8479 • $20

2000

6539.
Alice in Wonderland
FRAN • 1495QEO8421 • $35

6540.
Ballerina BARBIE™
ANDR • 1295QEO8471 • $32

6541.
Bar and Shield
Harley-Davidson®
RHOD • 1395QEO8544 • $35

6542.
Beatrix Potter™ 5:
Mr. Jeremy Fisher
VOTR • 895QEO8441 • $17

6543.
Bugs Bunny™
CHAD • 1095QEO8524 • $16

6544.
Cottontail Express 5:
Caboose
CROW • 995QEO8464 • $17

6545.
Easter Egg Surprise 2:
Rabbit
VOTR • 1495QEO8461 • $26

6546.
Fairy Berry Bears 2:
Blueberry
TAGU • 995QEO8454 • $17

6547.
Frolicking Friends – Bambi®,
Thumper, and Flower
1495QEO8434 • $25
Set/3

6548.
Happy Diploma Day!
1095QEO8431 • $13

6549.
PEANUTS® Lunchbox Set
1495QEO8444 • $26
Set/2

6550.
Sidewalk Cruisers 4:
Hopalong Cassidy
Velocipede
1295QEO8411 • $45

6551.
A Snug Hug
PIKE • 995QEO8424 • $28

6552.
Spring is in the Air 1:
Eastern Bluebird
CROW • 995QEO8451 • $28

6553.
A Swing With Friends
1495QEO8414 • $26

6554.
Time in the Garden
SEAL • 1095QEO8511 • $17

6555.
Vintage Roadsters 3:
1935 Auburn Speedster
PALM • 1495QEO8401 • $40

6556.
Winner's Circle 2: 1940
Garton® Red Hot Roadster
PALM • 1395QEO8404 • $22

2001

6557.
Bashful Bunny
FRAN • 595QEO8502 • $10

6558.
Birthday Wishes BARBIE™ 1
RGRS • 1495QEO8575 • $25

6559.
Charming Chick
VOTR • 595QEO8515 • $10

6560.
Easter Egg Surprise 3: Chick
VOTR • 1495QEO8532 • $19

6561.
The Empire Strikes Back™ Lunchbox Set
LAPR • 1495QEO8585 • $24
Set/2

6562.
Fairy Berry Bears 3: Raspberry
TAGU • 995QEO8565 • $12

6563.
Happy Hopper
AUBE • 595QEO8505 • $10

6564.
Lovey Lamb
HADD • 595QEO8512 • $10

6565.
Peter Rabbit – Beatrix Potter™
VOTR • 895QEO8545 • $12

6566.
Riding on the Breeze
1095QEO8612 • $18

6567.
Sidewalk Cruisers 5: 1934 Mickey Mouse Velocipede
1295QEO8552 • $30

6568.
Spring is in the Air 2: American Goldfinch
CROW • 995QEO8535 • $17

6569.
Taz™ Paint Egg!
CHAD • 1095QEO8572 • $16

6570.
Vintage Roadsters 4: 1930 Cadillac®
PALM • 1495QEO8555 • $28

6571.
Winner's Circle 3: 1960 Eight Ball Racer
PALM • 1395QEO8562 • $23

2002

6572.
Birthday Wishes BARBIE™ 2
1495QEO8513 • $26

6573.
Peek-a-Boo Egg: Bunny Business
995QEO8546 • $23

6574.
Peek-a-Boo Egg: Easter Egg-spress
995QEO8536 • $26

6575.
Peek-a-Boo Egg: Spring Peepers
995QEO8543 • $23

6576.
Sculpted Bunny Spring Ornament Tree
1495QEO8556 • $28
Re-issued in 2003.

6577.
Shimmering Carrot Trimmers
595QEO8563 • $10
Set/8 • Re-issued in 2003.

6578.
Shimmering Easter Eggs
1495QEO8553 • $19
Set/4

6579.
Sidewalk Cruisers 6: 1937 Mickey Mouse® Streamline Express Coaster Wagon
1295QEO8516 • $28

6580.
Spring is in the Air 3: American Robin
CROW • 995QEO8506 • $26

6581.
Vintage Roadsters 5: 1954 Buick® Wildcat II
WEBB • 1495QEO8526 • $36

6582.
Winner's Circle 4: 1941 Garton® Speed Demon
PALM • 1395QEO8503 • $26

2003

6583.
Birdhouse Row
1295QEO8529 • $17
Set/4

6584.
Birthday Wishes BARBIE™ 3
RGRS • 1495QEO8549 • $32

6585.
Buzz-A-Dee Bugs
795QEO8537 • $14
Set/3

6586.
Keepsake Ornament Tree
WEBB • 1495QEO8547 • $22

6587.
Nature's Sketchbook: A Place in the Sun
VARI • 1295QEO8019 • $22

6588.
Nature's Sketchbook: Around the Home
BAST/FRAN • 1295QEO8017 • $26

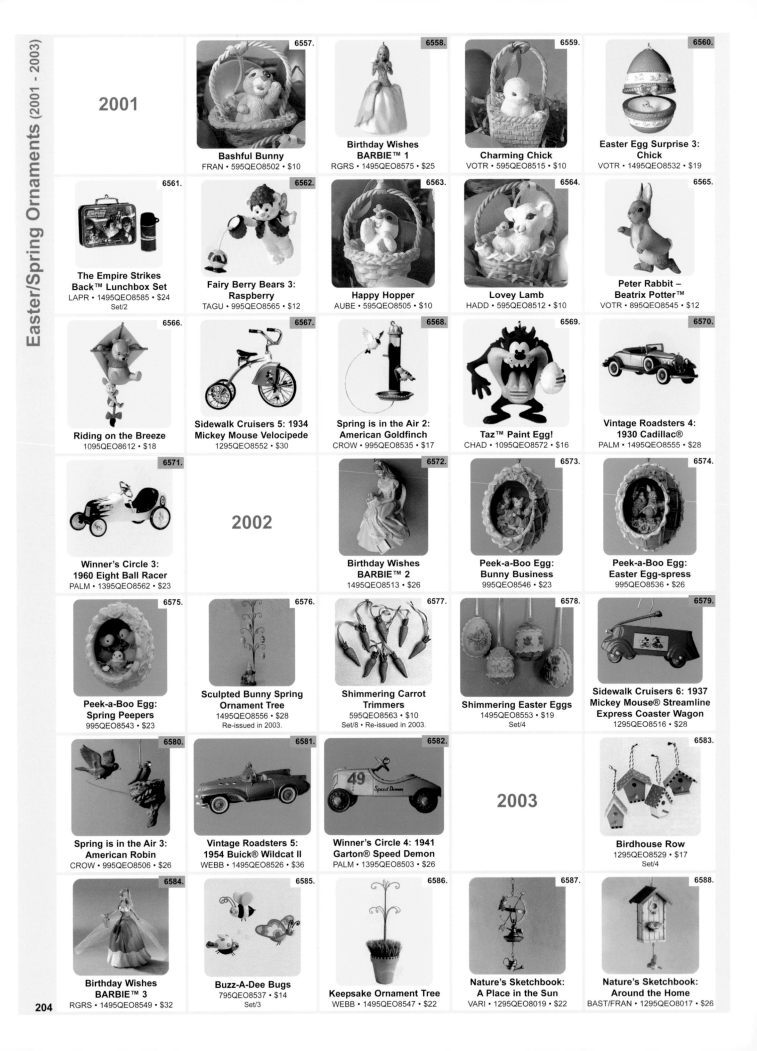

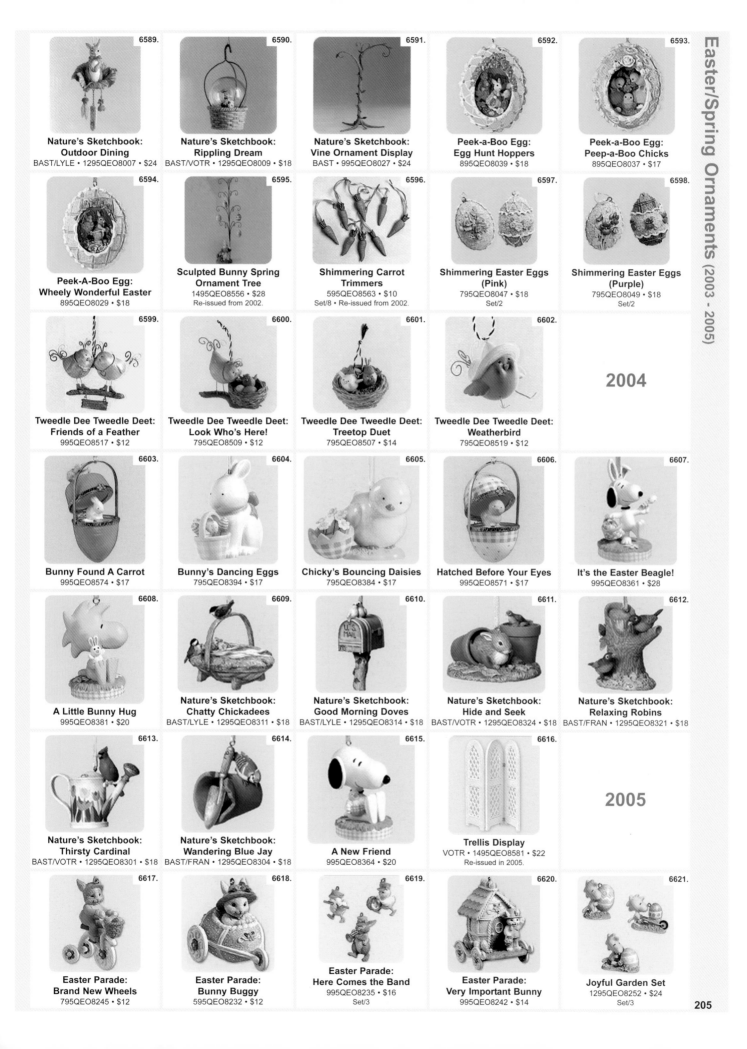

6589.
Nature's Sketchbook:
Outdoor Dining
BAST/LYLE • 1295QEO8007 • $24

6590.
Nature's Sketchbook:
Rippling Dream
BAST/VOTR • 1295QEO8009 • $18

6591.
Nature's Sketchbook:
Vine Ornament Display
BAST • 995QEO8027 • $24

6592.
Peek-a-Boo Egg:
Egg Hunt Hoppers
895QEO8039 • $18

6593.
Peek-a-Boo Egg:
Peep-a-Boo Chicks
895QEO8037 • $17

6594.
Peek-A-Boo Egg:
Wheely Wonderful Easter
895QEO8029 • $18

6595.
Sculpted Bunny Spring
Ornament Tree
1495QEO8556 • $28
Re-issued from 2002.

6596.
Shimmering Carrot
Trimmers
595QEO8563 • $10
Set/8 • Re-issued from 2002.

6597.
Shimmering Easter Eggs
(Pink)
795QEO8047 • $18
Set/2

6598.
Shimmering Easter Eggs
(Purple)
795QEO8049 • $18
Set/2

6599.
Tweedle Dee Tweedle Deet:
Friends of a Feather
995QEO8517 • $12

6600.
Tweedle Dee Tweedle Deet:
Look Who's Here!
795QEO8509 • $12

6601.
Tweedle Dee Tweedle Deet:
Treetop Duet
795QEO8507 • $14

6602.
Tweedle Dee Tweedle Deet:
Weatherbird
795QEO8519 • $12

2004

6603.
Bunny Found A Carrot
995QEO8574 • $17

6604.
Bunny's Dancing Eggs
795QEO8394 • $17

6605.
Chicky's Bouncing Daisies
795QEO8384 • $17

6606.
Hatched Before Your Eyes
995QEO8571 • $17

6607.
It's the Easter Beagle!
995QEO8361 • $28

6608.
A Little Bunny Hug
995QEO8381 • $20

6609.
Nature's Sketchbook:
Chatty Chickadees
BAST/LYLE • 1295QEO8311 • $18

6610.
Nature's Sketchbook:
Good Morning Doves
BAST/LYLE • 1295QEO8314 • $18

6611.
Nature's Sketchbook:
Hide and Seek
BAST/VOTR • 1295QEO8324 • $18

6612.
Nature's Sketchbook:
Relaxing Robins
BAST/FRAN • 1295QEO8321 • $18

6613.
Nature's Sketchbook:
Thirsty Cardinal
BAST/VOTR • 1295QEO8301 • $18

6614.
Nature's Sketchbook:
Wandering Blue Jay
BAST/FRAN • 1295QEO8304 • $18

6615.
A New Friend
995QEO8364 • $20

6616.
Trellis Display
VOTR • 1495QEO8581 • $22
Re-issued in 2005.

2005

6617.
Easter Parade:
Brand New Wheels
795QEO8245 • $12

6618.
Easter Parade:
Bunny Buggy
595QEO8232 • $12

6619.
Easter Parade:
Here Comes the Band
995QEO8235 • $16
Set/3

6620.
Easter Parade:
Very Important Bunny
995QEO8242 • $14

6621.
Joyful Garden Set
1295QEO8252 • $24
Set/3

6622.
Nature's Sketchbook:
A New Address
BAST/FRAN • 1295QEO8275 • $18

6623.
Nature's Sketchbook:
First Bouquet
BAST/HADD • 1295QEO8282 • $18

6624.
Nature's Sketchbook:
Nature's Secret Artist
BAST/VOTR • 995QEO8272 • $16

6625.
Nature's Sketchbook:
New Joys
BAST/VOTR • 995QEO8265 • $14

6626.
Nature's Sketchbook:
Spring's Peaceful Promise
BAST/LYLE • 995QEO8262 • $16

6627.
Nature's Sketchbook:
The Garden Awakens
BAST/LYLE • 1495QEO8285 • $24
Set/3

6628.
Springtime Inspirations
995QEO8255 • $24

6629.
Trellis Display
VOTR • 1495QEO8581 • $22
Re-issued from 2004.

2006

6630.
Nature's Sketchbook:
Find Yourself in the Garden
BAST/LYLE • 1295QEO8286

6631.
Nature's Sketchbook:
Gardens Grow Happiness
BAST/LYLE • 995QEO8283

6632.
Nature's Sketchbook:
Spring Daydreams
BAST/LYLE • 995QEO8273

6633.
Nature's Sketchbook:
Sprinkle Sunshine
BAST/LYLE • 995QEO8266

6634.
Nature's Sketchbook:
The First Spring Songs
BAST/LYLE • 995QEO8276

6635.
Nature's Sketchbook:
The Garden Is Calling
BAST • 1295QEO8263

6636.
Spring Ornament Display
1495QEO8256

Halloween Ornaments

Halloween is now the number two decorating holiday. The new Hallmark Halloween Line of ornaments and "haunted village" pieces make decorating quick and easy. They are fast becoming spook-tacular family favorites!

2002

6637.
Bat
($N/E)(N/A) • $15

6638.
Candy Corn
($N/E)(N/A) • $15

6639.
Cat
($N/E)(N/A) • $15

6640.
Ghost
($N/E)(N/A) • $15

6641.
Jack O'Lantern
($N/E)(N/A) • $15

6642.
Spider
($N/E)(N/A) • $15

6643.
Witch
($N/E)(N/A) • $15

2003

6644.
1300 Old Oak Road
ANDR/MCGE • 1295QFO6037 • $32

6645.
The Acrobats
495QFO6029 • $28
Set/6

6646.
Dots & Stripes Glass Balls
($N/E)HTF1571 • $30
Set/6

6647.
Fall Assortment Blown Glass Set
995FALL3836 • $30
Set/6

6648.
Halloween Candy Blown Glass Set
($N/E)HTF1558 • $30
Set/6

6649.
Mesmerelda
ANDR • 995QFO6039 • $18

6650.
Midnight Serenade
RHOD • 695QFO6047 • $20

6651.
Mr. Tap Happy
SIED • 695QFO6017 • $28

6652.
Sneakaboo
ANDR • 695QFO6009 • $20

6653.
Stack O'Lanterns
FRAN • 695QFO6049 • $12

6654.
Van Ghoul
ANDR • 695QFO6007 • $20

6655.
Zephyr
FRAN • 695QFO6019 • $12

2004

6656.
Bateson, The Butler
795QFO6054 • $14

6657.
Frederick O'Ghastly and Friends
1295QFO6061 • $26
Set/3

6658.
Hugo, The Handyman
WILL • 1295QFO6044 • $19

6659.
The Mansion on Ravenwood Lane
LARS/WEBB • 3995QFO6024 • $50

6660.
The Master
WILL • 1295QFO6031 • $19

6661.
Matilda, The Cook
LARS • 1295QFO6041 • $19

6662.
Old Ned, The Musician
WEBB • 1295QFO6034 • $19

6663.
Trick or Treat!
995QFO6051 • $26

2005

6664.
Hauntington:
Bartholomew Hauntswell
WILL • 1295QFO6322 • $14

6665.
Hauntington: Cass Taspell
LARS • 795QFO6302 • $12

6666.
Hauntington:
Deadwood Street Shops
BEST • 3995QFO6325 • $65
MAGIC

6667.
Hauntington:
Grandma Tillie and Willie
VISK • 1295QFO6335 • $20
Set/2

6668.
Hauntington:
Hauntington Town Hall
BEST • 3995QFO6332 • $55
MAGIC

6669.
Hauntington:
Ivana Hacketoff
VISK • 795QFO6305 • $18

6670.
Hauntington:
Ms. Bonnie and Bones
VISK • 1295QFO6342 • $22
Set/2

6671.
Hauntington:
Officer Rob Graver
VISK • 795QFO6315 • $12

6672.
Hauntington:
Scoops McGore
LARS • 795QFO6312 • $12

6673.
Hauntington: The Old Oak
VISK • 1495QFO6345 • $34

2006

6674.
It's the Great Pumpkin,
Charlie Brown®:
Charlie Brown®
800QFO6066

6675.
It's the Great Pumpkin,
Charlie Brown®:
Linus and Base
2500QFO6076
Set/2

6676.
It's the Great Pumpkin,
Charlie Brown®: Lucy
800QFO6073

6677.
It's the Great Pumpkin,
Charlie Brown®: Sally
800QFO6056

6678.
It's the Great Pumpkin,
Charlie Brown®: Snoopy®
1250QFO6063

Tree Toppers

The perfect way to top your Hallmark Ornament tree is with a Hallmark Tree Topper. With many different styles and materials from which to choose, there is one that would be perfect for any style or size tree.

Full Size

6679.
Angel
900HSD2302 • $168
1977

6680.
Angel
ESCH • 4800QFM3276
2006

6681.
Angel
2450QTT7101 • $46
1984 & 1985

6682.
Angel
($N/E)XXA9155 • $45

6683.
Angel Baby
($N/E)unknown • $45

6684.
Angel of Light
RGRS • 3000QLT7239 • $48
1991 & 1992

6685.
Angel Snowman
($N/E)XBH4315 • $30

6686.
Brass Angel
($N/E)unknown • $75

6687.
Brass Star
2500QX7054 • $80
1980

6688.
Chris Mouse
1295XKC3389 • $35
1999

6689.
Christmas Star
750QX7023 • $42
1978

6690.
Christmas Star
695XXA9149 • $55
1991

6691.
Country Holiday Goose
1400QTT7123 • $35
1986

6692.
Frostlight Faeries: Queen Aurora
ESCH • 3500QP1662 • $56
2001

6693.
Gentle Angel
1400QTT7126 • $28
1987

6694.
Homespun Angel
1600QTT6252 • $29
1985

6695.
Illuminations: Starlight
5500QLM7972 • $55
2005

6696.
Mary Engelbreit
($N/E)unknown • $35

6697.
Mary's Angel
VARI • 3000QXE3303
2006

6698.
Maxine
1695ZXS6002 • $26
1997

6699.
Mitford Snowman
($N/E)unknown • $35
2000

6700.
Santa
1800QTO7006 • $29
1986

6701.
Santa
995XPF4253 • $24
1988

6702.
Santa Bear
1600XXA8259 • $24
1991 & 1992

6703.
Santa with North Pole
($N/E)XXA4152 • $24
1994

6704.
Shining Star
1750QLT7096 • $50
1986

6705.
Snowman
($N/E)XPF3209 • $35

6706.
Star
STGR • 3800QFM3273
2006

6707.
Star
3500XXA7139 • $40
1991 & 1992

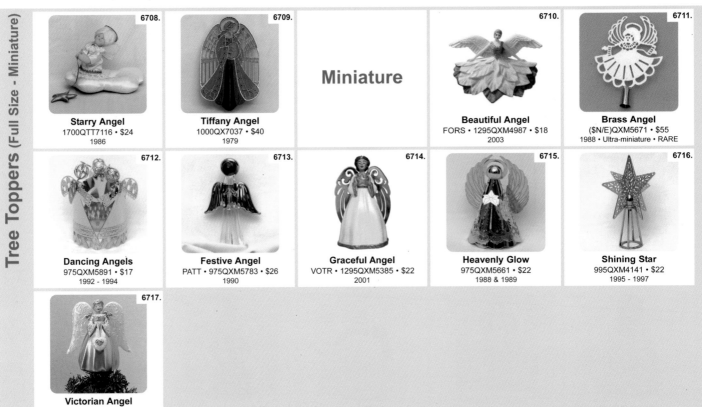

Miniature

6708.
Starry Angel
1700QTT7116 • $24
1986

6709.
Tiffany Angel
1000QX7037 • $40
1979

6710.
Beautiful Angel
FORS • 1295QXM4987 • $18
2003

6711.
Brass Angel
($N/E)QXM5671 • $55
1988 • Ultra-miniature • RARE

6712.
Dancing Angels
975QXM5891 • $17
1992 - 1994

6713.
Festive Angel
PATT • 975QXM5783 • $26
1990

6714.
Graceful Angel
VOTR • 1295QXM5385 • $22
2001

6715.
Heavenly Glow
975QXM5661 • $22
1988 & 1989

6716.
Shining Star
995QXM4141 • $22
1995 - 1997

6717.
Victorian Angel
LYLE • 1295QXM4293 • $19
1998 - 2000

Merry Miniatures

First issued as party favors, Merry Miniature figurines made their debut in 1974. Early issues are much larger than the smaller figures produced in the 90s. In 1996 Hallmark began selling Merry Miniatures in boxes and often as sets of 2 to 5. Packaging was again changed in 2000 to clear plastic and the last issues produced in 2002. They remain one of the most popular Hallmark collectibles today.

1974

Angel
125XPF506 • $350

Bunny
059EPF186 • $450

Chick
SICK • 159EPF206 • $400

Child
TAGU • 050EPF193 • $300

Jack-O-Lantern
075HPF502 • $40

Pilgrims
100TPF13 • $165

Raggedy Andy®
125PF1433 • $110

Raggedy Ann®
125PF1432 • $100

Reindeer
SICK • 125XPF493 • $400

Santa
SICK • 125XPF486 • $250

Scarecrow
100HPF • $235

Snowman
125XPF473 • $95

Turkey
SICK • 075TPF13 • $250

1975

Bunny
SICK • 125EPF49 • $500
RARE

Devil
125HPF29 • $220

Duck
SICK • 125EPF69 • $475

Girl
125EPF57 • $250

Indian
125TPF29 • $50

1976

Santa
TAGU • 125XPF49 • $175

Betsey Clark
125XPF151 • $175

Drummer Boy
125XPF144 • $150

Owl
100HPF515 • $160

Pilgrims
TAGU • 100TPF502 • $125

Pipe
089SPF266 • $125

Santa
125XPF131 • $60

Scarecrow
100HPF522 • $125

Snowman
125XPF44 • $50

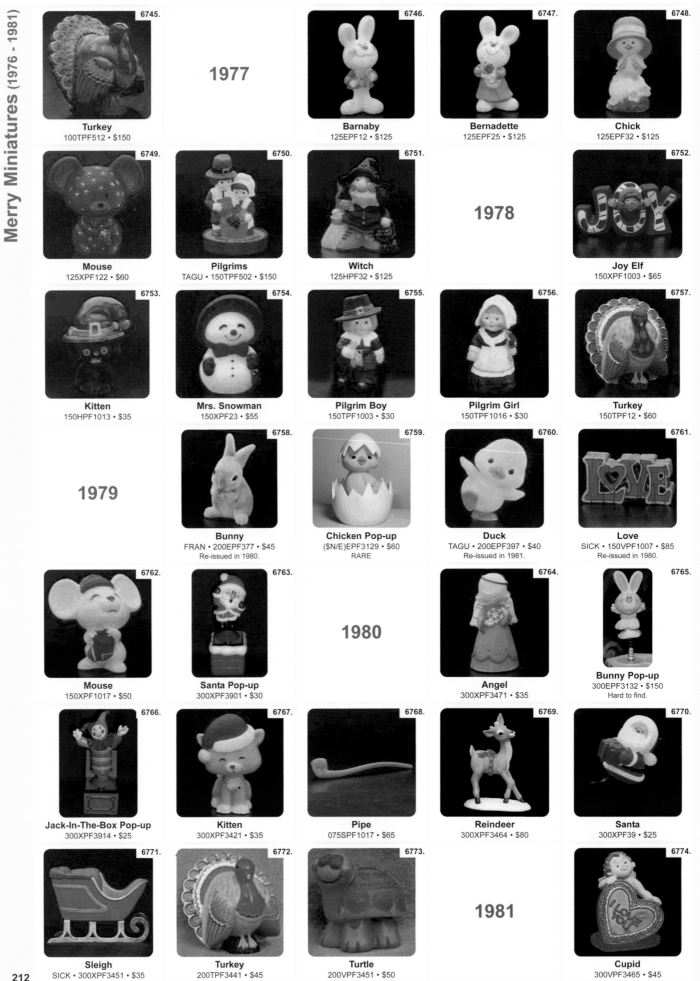

6745.
Turkey
100TPF512 • $150

1977

6746.
Barnaby
125EPF12 • $125

6747.
Bernadette
125EPF25 • $125

6748.
Chick
125EPF32 • $125

6749.
Mouse
125XPF122 • $60

6750.
Pilgrims
TAGU • 150TPF502 • $150

6751.
Witch
125HPF32 • $125

1978

6752.
Joy Elf
150XPF1003 • $65

6753.
Kitten
150HPF1013 • $35

6754.
Mrs. Snowman
150XPF23 • $55

6755.
Pilgrim Boy
150TPF1003 • $30

6756.
Pilgrim Girl
150TPF1016 • $30

6757.
Turkey
150TPF12 • $60

1979

6758.
Bunny
FRAN • 200EPF377 • $45
Re-issued in 1980.

6759.
Chicken Pop-up
($N/E)EPF3129 • $60
RARE

6760.
Duck
TAGU • 200EPF397 • $40
Re-issued in 1981.

6761.
Love
SICK • 150VPF1007 • $85
Re-issued in 1980.

6762.
Mouse
150XPF1017 • $50

6763.
Santa Pop-up
300XPF3901 • $30

1980

6764.
Angel
300XPF3471 • $35

6765.
Bunny Pop-up
300EPF3132 • $150
Hard to find.

6766.
Jack-In-The-Box Pop-up
300XPF3914 • $25

6767.
Kitten
300XPF3421 • $35

6768.
Pipe
075SPF1017 • $65

6769.
Reindeer
300XPF3464 • $80

6770.
Santa
300XPF39 • $25

6771.
Sleigh
SICK • 300XPF3451 • $35

6772.
Turkey
200TPF3441 • $45

6773.
Turtle
200VPF3451 • $50

1981

6774.
Cupid
300VPF3465 • $45

6775.
Ghost
300HHA3402 • $150

6776.
Ghost Pop-up
200HPF3911 • $45

6777.
Hug Bug Pop-up
250VPF4507 • $45

6778.
Lamb
FRAN • 300EPF402 • $25
Re-issued in 1982.

6779.
Leprechaun
300SHA3415 • $40

6780.
Penguin
300XHA3412 • $60

6781.
Raccoon Pilgrim
FRAN • 300THA3402 • $35

6782.
Redbird
300XHA3405 • $35

6783.
Squirrel Indian
FRAN • 300THA3415 • $40

6784.
Table Trimmer – Kitten
695HA4906 • $160

6785.
Table Trimmer – Mouse
695HA4905 • $120

6786.
Table Trimmer – Puppy
695HA4902 • $150

6787.
Table Trimmer – Squirrel
695HA4901 • $120

6788.
Turkey
300THA22 • $40

1982

6789.
Cake Topper – Circus
500CDB8678 • $195

6790.
Cake Topper – Dragon
750CDB8820 • $120

6791.
Cake Topper – Little Bo Peep
TAGU • 750CDB8818 • $50

6792.
Cake Topper – Mickey Mouse
750CDB8821 • $95

6793.
Cake Topper – Snoopy®
1250CDB8611 • $150

6794.
Cake Topper – Soldier Boy
TAGU • 750CDB8819 • $45

6795.
Ceramic Bunny
300EPF3702 • $30

6796.
Container – Jack-O-Lantern
FRAN • 395HHA3446 • $85

6797.
**Container –
Teddy Bear on Drum**
450XHA5013 • $30

6798.
Duck
300EHA3403 • $30

6799.
Kermit™
395VHA3403 • $35

6800.
Kitten
395HHA3466 • $50

6801.
Miss Piggy™
395VHA3416 • $35

6802.
Mouse
FRAN • 450XHA5023 • $50

6803.
Pilgrim Mouse
295THA3433 • $125

6804.
Rocking Horse
450XHA5003 • $70

6805.
Santa
450XHA5016 • $100

6806.
Tree
450XHA5006 • $95

6807.

Witch
TAGU • 395HHA3456 • $325
RARE

213

1983

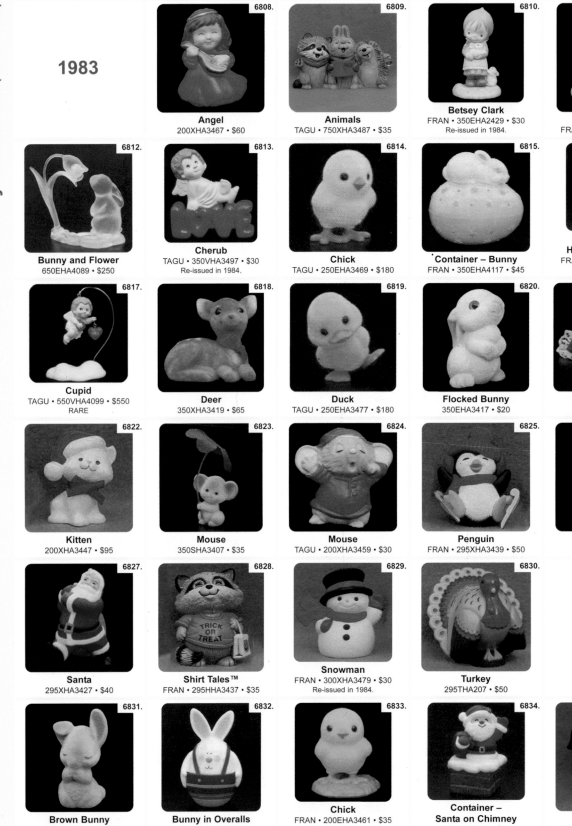

6808.
Angel
200XHA3467 • $60

6809.
Animals
TAGU • 750XHA3487 • $35

6810.
Betsey Clark
FRAN • 350EHA2429 • $30
Re-issued in 1984.

6811.
Bunny
FRAN • 250EHA3457 • $20

6812.
Bunny and Flower
650EHA4089 • $250

6813.
Cherub
TAGU • 350VHA3497 • $30
Re-issued in 1984.

6814.
Chick
TAGU • 250EHA3469 • $180

6815.
Container – Bunny
FRAN • 350EHA4117 • $45

6816.
**Container –
Hedgehog on Heart**
FRAN • 350VHA4107 • $85
Re-issued in 1984.

6817.
Cupid
TAGU • 550VHA4099 • $550
RARE

6818.
Deer
350XHA3419 • $65

6819.
Duck
TAGU • 250EHA3477 • $180

6820.
Flocked Bunny
350EHA3417 • $20

6821.
Kitten
350VHA3489 • $35

6822.
Kitten
200XHA3447 • $95

6823.
Mouse
350SHA3407 • $35

6824.
Mouse
TAGU • 200XHA3459 • $30

6825.
Penguin
FRAN • 295XHA3439 • $50

6826.
Polar Bear
350XHA3407 • $120

6827.
Santa
295XHA3427 • $40

6828.
Shirt Tales™
FRAN • 295HHA3437 • $35

6829.
Snowman
FRAN • 300XHA3479 • $30
Re-issued in 1984.

6830.
Turkey
295THA207 • $50

1984

6831.
Brown Bunny
350EHA3401 • $12

6832.
Bunny in Overalls
350EHA4121 • $30

6833.
Chick
FRAN • 200EHA3461 • $35
Re-issued in 1985.

6834.
**Container –
Santa on Chimney**
450XHA3451 • $25

6835.
Dog
FRAN • 200VHA3451 • $40

6836.
Duck
350EHA3434 • $20

6837.
Duck
FRAN • 200EHA3474 • $35

6838.
Greetings: Bear
FRAN • 395HA4204 • $120

6839.
Greetings: Bluebird
395HA4303 • $40

6840.
Greetings: Dog
395HA4202 • $90

6841.
Greetings: Duck
395HA4301 • $35

6842.
Greetings: Kitten
395HA4201 • $90

6843.
Greetings: Lamb
FRAN • 395HA4304 • $50

6844.
Greetings: Mouse
FRAN • 395HA4203 • $120

6845.
Greetings: Rabbit
FRAN • 395HA4302 • $100

6846.
Hedgehog
ESCH • 200THA3444 • $15
Re-issued in 1985.

6847.
Hugga Bunch: Bubbles
325HA3731 • $80

6848.
Hugga Bunch: Huggins
325HA3733 • $50

6849.
Hugga Bunch: Hugsy
325HA3728 • $25

6850.
Hugga Bunch: Impkins
325HA3734 • $20

6851.
Hugga Bunch: Patootie
325HA3721 • $50

6852.
Hugga Bunch: Precious
325HA3729 • $15

6853.
Hugga Bunch: Tickles
325HA3735 • $50

6854.
Hugga Bunch: Tweaker
325HA3727 • $95

6855.
Jack-O-Lantern
200HHA3454 • $20

6856.
Kitten
ESCH • 200HHA3441 • $25
Re-issued in 1985.

6857.
Koala
FRAN • 295XHA3401 • $20
Re-issued in 1985.

6858.
Mouse
FRAN • 200THA3451 • $45

6859.
Mouse in Matchbox
FRAN • 450XHA3464 • $40
Re-issued in 1985.

6860.
Panda
200VHA3471 • $20

6861.
Penguin
200VHA3464 • $25

6862.
Puppy
FRAN • 200XHA3494 • $30
Re-issued in 1985.

6863.
Redbird
200XHA3501 • $35

6864.
Rodney
FRAN • 295XHA3391 • $35
Re-issued in 1985.

6865.
Soldier
FRAN • 200XHA3481 • $25
Re-issued in 1985.

1985

6866.
Basket
FRAN • 200EHA3495 • $30
Re-issued in 1987.

6867.
Bears
450XHA3392 • $30

6868.
Bunny
ESCH • 200EHA3482 • $30

6869.
Cat
AUBE • 200XHA3482 • $35
Re-issued in 1987.

6870.
Ceramic Bunny
FORS • ($N/E)EPR3701 • $10

6871.
Container – Duck
FRAN • 350EHA4132 • $30
Re-issued in 1986.

6872.
Container – Elf
450XHA3452 • $25

6873.
Container – Haunted House
450HHA3462 • $25

6874.
Container – Soldier on Drum
TAGU • 450XHA3465 • $15

6875.

Container –
Teddy Bear on Red Heart
FRAN • 350VHA4112 • $20

6876.

Goose
250XHA3522 • $15

6877.

Horse
350XHA3412 • $15

6878.

Kitten
FRAN • 200VHA3495 • $20
Re-issued in 1986.

6879.

Lamb
350EHA3442 • $20

6880.

Mouse
350EHA3455 • $35

6881.

Mouse
350XHA3405 • $30

6882.

Mr. Santa
FRAN • 200XHA3495 • $25
Re-issued in 1986.

6883.

Mrs. Santa
FRAN • 200XHA3502 • $25
Re-issued in 1986.

6884.
Rocking Horse
200XHA3515 • $30
2 issues – dated.

6885.

Shamrock
200SHA3452 • $20

6886.

Skunk
FRAN • 200VHA3482 • $15
Re-issued in 1987.

6887.

Turkey
295THA3395 • $20

1986

6888.

Boy Bunny
295EPF4133 • $25

6889.

Bunny
AUBE • 350EHA3476 • $25

6890.

Bunny Girl
FRAN • 295EPF4106 • $25
Re-issued in 1987.

6891.

Cat
AUBE • 200HHA3486 • $15
Re-issued in 1987.

6892.

Container – Basket
225EHA4143 • $15

6893.

Container – Blue Star
295EPF4486 • $35

6894.
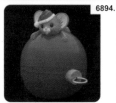
Container –
Mouse on Ornament
450XHA3473 • $25

6895.

Container – Penguin on Igloo
450XHA3486 • $25
Re-issued in 1987.

6896.

Container – Pink Heart
295EPF4473 • $50

6897.

Container – Rodney
($N/E)EPF4466 • $60

6898.

Duck
FRAN • 295EHA3463 • $15
Re-issued in 1987

6899.

Duck Sailor
FRAN • 295EPF4113 • $15
Re-issued in 1987

6900.
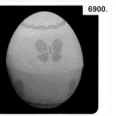
Egg Container – Butterfly
225EPF4203 • $25

6901.
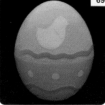
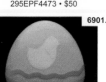
Egg Container – Chick
225EPF4163 • $35

6902.
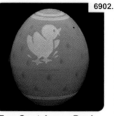
Egg Container – Ducks
225EPF4246 • $90

6903.
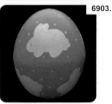
Egg Container –
Egg & Rabbits
225EPF4183 • $30

6904.
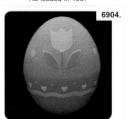
Egg Container – Flower
225EPF4216 • $30

6905.

Egg Container –
Geese and Tulips
350EHA4156 • $30

6906.

Egg Container –
Happy Easter
225EPF4143 • $18

6907.
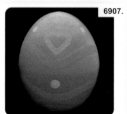
Egg Container – Hearts
225EPF4196 • $40

6908.

Egg Container – Lambs
225EPF4176 • $40

6909.
Egg Container – Polka Dot
225EPF4253 • $40

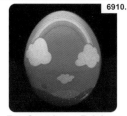
6910.
Egg Container – Rainbow
225EPF4223 • $35

6911.
Egg Container – Striped
225EPF4156 • $30

6912.
Egg Container – Teddy Bear
225EPF4233 • $90

6913.
Girl Bunny
FRAN • 200EHA3503 • $25
Re-issued in 1987

6914.
Goose
ESCH • 200EHA3516 • $15
Re-issued in 1987

6915.
Katybeth
FRAN • 200XHA3666 • $40

6916.
Mouse
FRAN • 200XHA3533 • $50
Re-issued in 1987

6917.
Mr. Mouse
FRAN • 200XHA3573 • $25
Re-issued in 1987

6918.
Mr. Squirrel
FRAN • 200THA3403 • $25

6919.
Mrs. Mouse
FRAN • 200XHA3653 • $25
Re-issued in 1987

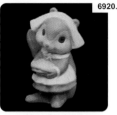
6920.
Mrs. Squirrel
FRAN • 200THA3416 • $20

6921.
Owl
TAGU • 200GHA3456 • $12

6922.
Pandas
AUBE • 350VHA3523 • $20
Re-issued in 1987

6923.
Penguin
AUBE • 295XHA4413 • $18
Re-issued in 1987

6924.
Rhonda
350XHA3553 • $30
Re-issued in 1987

6925.
Rodney
350XHA3546 • $20
Re-issued in 1987

6926.
Santa
350XHA3673 • $40

6927.
Sebastian
ESCH • 200VHA3516 • $65
Re-issued in 1987

6928.
Sebastian
ESCH • 200XHA3566 • $60
Re-issued in 1987

6929.
Sheep & Bell
295EPF4126 • $15

6930.
Unicorn
FRAN • 200VHA3503 • $15
4 colors • Re-issued in 1987

6931.
Witch
300HHA3473 • $75

1987

6932.
Bear
FRAN • 450XHA3709 • $25

6933.
Boy Lamb
FRAN • 295EHA4197 • $20

6934.
Bunny
FRAN • 200EHA4179 • $20

6935.
Bunny
250XHA3729 • $90

6936.
Bunny Boy
FRAN • 250XHA3737 • $20

6937.
Bunny Girl
FRAN • 250XHA3749 • $20

6938.
Chick In Egg
AUBE • 350EHA4199 • $15

6939.
Clown Teddy
FRAN • 200VHA3507 • $12

6940.
Container – Apple with Owl
AUBE • 450XHA3687 • $18

6941.
**Container –
Gingerbread House**
450XHA3699 • $30

6942.
Fawn
FRAN • 200XHA3757 • $30

6943.

Ginger Bear
200XHA207 • $28

6944.

Giraffe
FRAN • 350VHA3519 • $75

6945.

Girl Lamb
FRAN • 295EHA4187 • $22

6946.

Mouse
TAGU • 200SHA3467 • $30

6947.

Mouse
FRAN • 295VHA3527 • $15

6948.

Puppy
200XHA3769 • $20

6949.

Purrrsonality Cats: Calvin
AUBE • 295PF3847 • $55

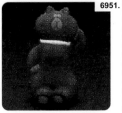

6950.

Purrrsonality Cats: Chuck
AUBE • 295PF3859 • $40

6951.

Purrrsonality Cats: Electra
AUBE • 295PF3827 • $80

6952.

Purrrsonality Cats: Felina
FRAN • 295PF3839 • $80

6953.

Purrrsonality Cats: Franklin
AUBE • 295PF3807 • $160

6954.

Purrrsonality Cats: Josh
AUBE • 295PF3879 • $40

6955.

Purrrsonality Cats: Lester
AUBE • 295PF3887 • $150

6956.

Purrrsonality Cats: Maude
295PF3819 • $150

6957.

Purrrsonality Cats: Taffi
295PF3867 • $40

6958.

Raccoon Witch
ESCH • 200HHA3487 • $20

6959.

Santa
FRAN • 350XHA3717 • $35

6960.

Sebastian
ESCH • 200EHA4167 • $50

6961.

Turkey
375THA49 • $15

1988

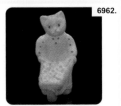

6962.

**Cosmopolitan Cats:
Boy Kitten**
650GCT1098 • $15

6963.

**Cosmopolitan Cats:
Exercise Kitten**
600GCT1099 • $20

6964.

**Cosmopolitan Cats:
Girl Kitten**
FORS • 650GCT1095 • $30

6965.

**Cosmopolitan Cats:
Girl Kitten**
FORS • 750GCT1096 • $30

6966.

**Cosmopolitan Cats:
Girl Kitten**
FORS • 750GCT1097 • $20

6967.

**Cosmopolitan Cats:
Kitten in Hat**
600GCT1102 • $15

6968.

**Cosmopolitan Cats:
Kitten with Gift**
600GCT1100 • $15

6969.

**Cosmopolitan Cats:
Kitten with Plant**
600GCT1101 • $15

6970.

Dog
FRAN • 200GHA3524 • $10

6971.

Easter Bunny
295EBO3215 • $18
Re-issued in 1989.

6972.

Egg Container – Bunnies
195EBO2384 • $10

6973.

Egg Container – Chick
195EBO2371 • $10

6974.

Egg Container – Goose
195EBO2381 • $10

6975.

Egg Container – Lamb
195EBO2374 • $10

6976.

Indian Bear
325QFM1511 • $10

6977.
Kitten In Slipper
RGRS • 250QFM1544 • $10

6978.
Koala & Hearts
AUBE • 200VHA3531 • $20

6979.
Koala & Lollipop
FORS • 200VHA3651 • $25

6980.
Koala & Ruffled Heart
200VHA3631 • $50

6981.
Koala With Bow & Arrow
FORS • 200VHA3624 • $20

6982.
Mechanical – Chick
350EBO2591 • $50

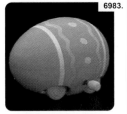
6983.
Mechanical – Egg
350EBO2594 • $15

6984.
**Mechanical –
Rabbit on Wheels**
350EBO2604 • $15

6985.
Mouse Angel
250QFM1551 • $25

6986.
Mouse In Cornucopia
225QFM1514 • $15
Re-issued in 1989

6987.
Mouse in Pumpkin
225QFM1501 • $30

6988.
Nativity Set
SIED • 3550QFM1685 • $110
Set/10 • Re-issued in 1989

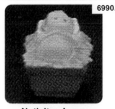
6989.
Nativity: Donkey
SIED • 225QFM1581 • $10
Re-issued in 1989

6990.
Nativity: Jesus
SIED • 250QFM1564 • $25
Re-issued in 1989

6991.
Nativity: Joseph
SIED • 250QFM1561 • $15
Re-issued in 1989

6992.
Nativity: Lamb
SIED • 225QFM1574 • $25
Re-issued in 1989

6993.
Nativity: Mary
SIED • 250QFM1554 • $20
Re-issued in 1989

6994.
Nativity: Shepherd
SIED • 250QFM1571 • $10
Re-issued in 1989

6995.
Nativity: Stable
SIED • 1400QFM1584 • $35
Re-issued in 1989

6996.
Owl
225QFM1504 • $10

6997.
Penguin
375QFM1541 • $10

6998.
Santa
TAGU • 375QFM1521 • $25

6999.
Seal Of Friendship
VOTR • GiftQXC5104 • $35

7000.
Snowman
350QFM1534 • $10

7001.
Tank Car
300QFM1591 • $25

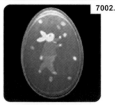
7002.
**Tin Egg Container –
Boy Bunny**
295EBO2314 • $10

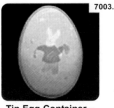
7003.
**Tin Egg Container –
Bunny and Carrot**
295EBO2321 • $15

7004.
**Tin Egg Container –
Girl Bunny**
295EBO2311 • $15

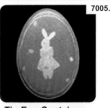
7005.
**Tin Egg Container –
Girl Bunny**
295EBO2311 • $20

7006.
Train Engine
300QFM1531 • $10

7007.
Unicorn
RGRS • 350QFM1524 • $25

1989

7008.
Baby Boy
AUBE • 300QFM1585 • $10

7009.
Baby Girl
AUBE • 300QFM1592 • $10

7010.
Baby's First Christmas
JLEE • 300QFM1615 • $5

7011.

Bear
250QSM1525 • $15

7012.

Bear Baker
350QSM1522 • $10

7013.

Bunny
TAGU • 300QFM1565 • $15

7014.

Bunny
CHAD • 250QSM1512 • $15

7015.

Bunny
CHAD • 350QSM1552 • $10

7016.

Bunny & Skateboard
ESCH • 350EBO3092 • $20

7017.

Bunny Caroler
TAGU • 300QFM1662 • $10

7018.
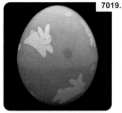
Dog & Kitten
RGRS • 350QSM1515 • $25

7019.

Egg Container – Bunnies
195EBO3025 • $10

7020.

Egg Container – Flowers
195EBO3032 • $10

7021.

Egg Container – Happy Easter
195EBO3035 • $15

7022.

Elf
JLEE • 300QFM1622 • $5

7023.

Grey Mouse
LYLE • 250QSM1502 • $15

7024.

Joy Elf
300QFM1605 • $10

7025.

Kitten
250QSM1505 • $15

7026.

Lamb
PALM • 350QSM1545 • $10

7027.

Momma Bear
AUBE • 350QFM1582 • $10

7028.

Mouse
TAGU • 250QFM1572 • $10

7029.

Mouse Caroler
TAGU • 250QFM1655 • $10

7030.

Mr. Claus
PALM • 350QFM1595 • $10

7031.

Mrs. Claus
PALM • 350QFM1602 • $10

7032.

Nativity: Blue King
FORS • 300QFM1632 • $15

7033.

Nativity: Pink King
FORS • 300QFM1642 • $12

7034.

Nativity: Yellow King
FORS • 300QFM1635 • $12

7035.

Owl
SIED • 250QSM1555 • $10

7036.

Raccoon
TAGU • 350QFM1575 • $8

7037.

Raccoon Caroler
TAGU • 350QFM1652 • $8

7038.

Teacher Elf
JLEE • 300QFM1612 • $5

7039.

Train Car
PALM • 350QFM1562 • $15

1990

7040.

Alligator
RHOD • 300QSM1573 • $6

7041.

Artist Raccoon
AUBE • 350QSM1543 • $6

7042.

Baby's First Christmas
SIED • 250QFM1683 • $6

7043.

Baby's First Easter
RHOD • 300QSM1536 • $6

7044.

Baseball Bunny
250QSM1576 • $6

Bear & Balloon
RHOD • 300QFM1716 • $5

7045.

Birthday Clowns 1
ANDR • 350QFM1706 • $8

7046.

Boy Bunny
RHOD • 350QSM1682 • $8

7047.

Bunny
TAGU • 300QSM1593 • $5

7048.

Bunny In Tux
300QFM1713 • $6

7049.

Candy Caboose
350QFM1693 • $20

7050.

E-Bunny
ESCH • 300QSM1726 • $11
Similar to 1988 Easter Bunny.

7051.

Elephant
SIED • 350QSM1566 • $5

7052.

First Christmas Together
FRAN • 350QFM1686 • $8

7053.

Gentle Pals 1
RGRS • 350QFM1656 • $6

7054.

Get Well Puppy
300QFM1703 • $5

7055.

Girl Bunny
RHOD • 350QSM1675 • $5

7056.

Green Monster
CHAD • 350QFM1613 • $8
Re-issued in 1991.

7057.

Grey Mouse
SIED • 250QSM1533 • $10

7058.

Hippo Cupid
SIED • 350QSM1513 • $10

7059.

Indian Chipmunk
VOTR • 300QFM1626 • $10

7060.

Jingle Bell Santa 1
CROW • 350QFM1663 • $13

7061.

Kangaroo
350QFM1653 • $6

7062.

Kitten
RGRS • 300QSM1516 • $10

7063.

Mama Polar Bear
SIED • 300QFM1666 • $6
Re-issued in 1991.

7064.

Mouse
TAGU • 250QSM1603 • $10

7065.

Mouse & Bunny
AUBE • 350QSM1546 • $15

7066.

Owl
300QSM1563 • $10

7067.

Papa Polar Bear & Child
SIED • 350QFM1673 • $6
Re-issued in 1991.

7068.

Pig
CROW • 300QSM1526 • $8

7069.

Pilgrim Mouse
RGRS • 250QFM1636 • $8

7070.

Pilgrim Squirrel
RGRS • 300QFM1633 • $8

7071.

Puppy
RHOD • 250QSM1583 • $5

7072.

Raccoon
TAGU • 350QSM1586 • $6

7073.

Scarecrow
350QFM1616 • $10

7074.

Snowman
PALM • 250QFM1646 • $11

7075.

Squirrel
AUBE • 250QSM1553 • $11

7076.

Squirrel Caroler
CHAD • 300QFM1696 • $10

7077.

Squirrel Hobo
CHAD • 300QFM1606 • $8

7078.

Stitched Teddy
PIKE • 350QSM1506 • $19

7079.

221

1991

7080.
Teacher Mouse
LYLE • 300QFM1676 • $4

7081.
Thankful Turkey 1
RGRS • 350QFM1623 • $17

7082.
Walrus
PALM • 250QFM1643 • $8

7083.
Aerobic Bunny
PIKE • 250QFM1817 • $10

7084.
Artist Mouse
AUBE • 250QSM1519 • $7

7085.
Baby Bunny
SIED • 350QSM1619 • $7

7086.
Baby's First Christmas
AUBE • 300QFM1797 • $7

7087.
Baby's First Easter
RGRS • 300QSM1557 • $8

7088.
Backpack Chipmunk
250QFM1809 • $7

7089.
Baseball Bear
SIED • 300QFM1827 • $10

7090.
Bear
AUBE • 250QFM1669 • $20

7091.
Birthday Clowns 2
CHAD • 350QSM1617 • $8

7092.
Bunny
300QSM1537 • $10
Re-issued in 1992.

7093.
Bunny Praying
RGRS • 250QSM1597 • $11

7094.
Carousel Set
JLEE • 1700QSM1667 • $50
Set/6

7095.
Carousel: Bear
JLEE • 300QSM1637 • $10

7096.
Carousel: Camel
JLEE • 300QSM1629 • $7

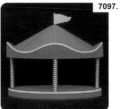

7097.
Carousel: Display
JLEE • 500QSM1627 • $19

7098.
Carousel: Elephant
JLEE • 300QSM1647 • $6

7099.
Carousel: Horse
JLEE • 300QSM1649 • $19

7100.
Carousel: Lion
JLEE • 300QSM1639 • $10

7101.
Cat Witch
AUBE • 300QFM1677 • $10
Re-issued in 1992.

7102.
Cookie Elf
RHOD • 300QFM1769 • $6

7103.
Cookie Reindeer
RHOD • 300QFM1777 • $6

7104.
Cookie Santa
RHOD • 300QFM1767 • $7

7105.
Daughter Bunny
RGRS • 250QSM1587 • $7
Re-issued in 1992.

7106.
Dog
PIKE • 250QSM1607 • $6

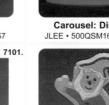

7107.
Duck
AUBE • 300QSM1549 • $11

7108.
First Christmas Together
FRAN • 350QFM1799 • $8

7109.
Football Beaver
350QFM1829 • $12

7110.
Fox
AUBE • 350QFM1689 • $7
Re-issued in 1992.

7111.
Gentle Pals 2
RGRS • 350QFM1709 • $11

7112.
Gift Bringer: Bunny
SIED • 300QFM1719 • $6

7113.
Gift Bringer: Frog
SIED • 300QFM1729 • $15

Gift Bringer: Kitten
SIED • 300QFM1737 • $7

Gift Bringer: Pig
SIED • 300QFM1739 • $10

Gift Bringer: Puppy
SIED • 300QFM1727 • $6

Gift Bringer: Turtle
SIED • 300QFM1747 • $7

Hugs and Kisses 1
SIED • 350QSM1609 • $17

I Love Dad
SIED • 250QSM1657 • $12

I Love Mom
SIED • 250QSM1659 • $12

Indian Maiden
AUBE • 250QFM1687 • $10
Re-issued in 1992.

Irish Frog
CHAD • 350QSM1539 • $10
Re-issued in 1992.

Jingle Bell Santa 2
CROW • 350QFM1717 • $13

Lamb & Duck
350QSM1569 • $8

Mother Bunny
RGRS • 300QSM1577 • $7
Re-issued in 1992.

Mouse
AUBE • 250QFM1789 • $7
Re-issued in 1992.

Mummy
RGRS • 250QFM1679 • $8
Re-issued in 1992.

Music Makers 1
FRAN • 300QFM1779 • $12

Puppy
AUBE • 300QFM1787 • $10

Puppy
AUBE • 300QSM1529 • $16

Raccoon Thief
AUBE • 350QSM1517 • $6

Skating Raccoon
350QFM1837 • $10

Snow Bunny
ANDR • 250QFM1749 • $7

Snow Lamb
ANDR • 250QFM1759 • $6

Snow Mice
ANDR • 250QFM1757 • $15

Soccer Skunk
SIED • 300QFM1819 • $10

Sweet Valentines 1
350QSM1509 • $13

Teacher Raccoon
AUBE • 350QFM1807 • $6

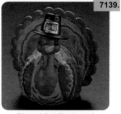
Thankful Turkey 2
RGRS • 350QFM1697 • $14

1992

Baby's First Easter
AUBE • 350QSM9777 • $10

Ballet Pig
AUBE • 250QSM9759 • $15

Barnyard: Cow
LYLE • 300QFM9034 • $15

Barnyard: Horse
LYLE • 300QFM9051 • $11

Barnyard: Lamb
LYLE • 250QFM9044 • $10

Barnyard: Pig
LYLE • 250QFM9041 • $20

Birthday Clowns 3
SIED • 350QSM9819 • $7

Bunny & Carrot
AUBE • 250QSM9799 • $15

Cat in PJs
LYLE • 350QFM9084 • $6

Chipmunk
CROW • 250QFM9144 • $8

Clown Mouse
PIKE • 250QFM9031 • $8

Crab
RGRS • 300QFM9174 • $6

Dog
AUBE • 300QSM9847 • $8

Dog in PJs
LYLE • 350QFM9081 • $8

Gentle Pals 3
RGRS • 350QFM9094 • $7

Ghost with Candy Corn
RGRS • 300QFM9014 • $15

Giraffe as Tree
VOTR • 300QFM9141 • $8

Goldfish
RGRS • 300QFM9181 • $8

Goose In Bonnet
UNRU • 300QSM9789 • $8

Grad Dog
PIKE • 250QSM9817 • $5

Haunted House
PALM • 350QFM9024 • $15

Hedgehog
AUBE • 250QSM9859 • $15

Hugs and Kisses 2
RGRS • 350QSM9827 • $12

Indian Bunnies
UNRU • 350QFM9004 • $15

Jingle Bell Santa 3
CROW • 350QFM9131 • $10

Kitten For Dad
AUBE • 350QSM9839 • $10

Kitten For Mom
AUBE • 350QSM9837 • $10

Kitten in Bib
AUBE • 350QSM9829 • $7

Lamb
PIKE • 350QSM9787 • $7

Lion
AUBE • 350QSM9719 • $7

Mouse
300QSM9769 • $10

Mouse in Peanut Car
FRAN • 300QFM9114 • $10

Music Makers 2
FRAN • 350QFM9134 • $8

Nina Ship
PALM • 350QFM9154 • $5

Octopus
RGRS • 300QFM9171 • $5

Party Dog
SICK • 300QFM9191 • $7

Penguin In Tux
AUBE • 300QSM9757 • $11

Penguin Skating
CROW • 350QFM9091 • $15

Pilgrim Beaver
PIKE • 300QFM9011 • $10

Pinta Ship
PALM • 350QFM9161 • $5

Praying Chipmunk
AUBE • 300QSM9797 • $15

Pumpkin
RGRS • 300QFM9021 • $15

Puppy
AUBE • 250QSM9767 • $25

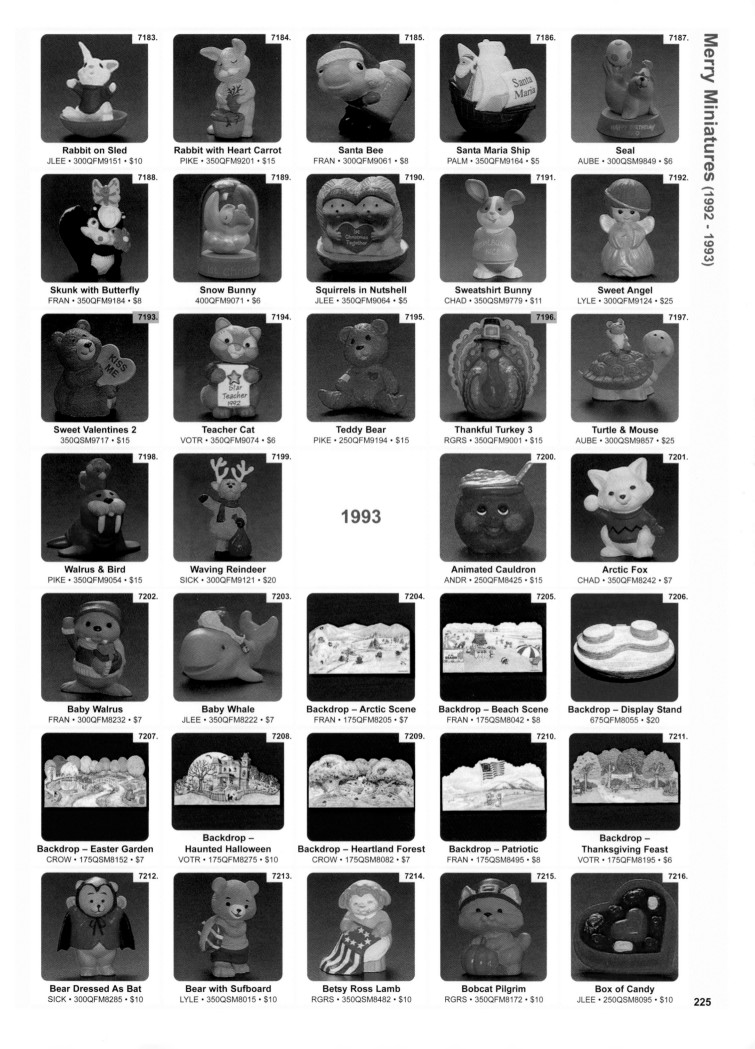

7183.
Rabbit on Sled
JLEE • 300QFM9151 • $10

7184.
Rabbit with Heart Carrot
PIKE • 350QFM9201 • $15

7185.
Santa Bee
FRAN • 300QFM9061 • $8

7186.
Santa Maria Ship
PALM • 350QFM9164 • $5

7187.
Seal
AUBE • 300QSM9849 • $6

7188.
Skunk with Butterfly
FRAN • 350QFM9184 • $8

7189.
Snow Bunny
400QFM9071 • $6

7190.
Squirrels in Nutshell
JLEE • 350QFM9064 • $5

7191.
Sweatshirt Bunny
CHAD • 350QSM9779 • $11

7192.
Sweet Angel
LYLE • 300QFM9124 • $25

7193.
Sweet Valentines 2
350QSM9717 • $15

7194.
Teacher Cat
VOTR • 350QFM9074 • $6

7195.
Teddy Bear
PIKE • 250QFM9194 • $15

7196.
Thankful Turkey 3
RGRS • 350QFM9001 • $15

7197.
Turtle & Mouse
AUBE • 300QSM9857 • $25

7198.
Walrus & Bird
PIKE • 350QFM9054 • $15

7199.
Waving Reindeer
SICK • 300QFM9121 • $20

1993

7200.
Animated Cauldron
ANDR • 250QFM8425 • $15

7201.
Arctic Fox
CHAD • 350QFM8242 • $7

7202.
Baby Walrus
FRAN • 300QFM8232 • $7

7203.
Baby Whale
JLEE • 350QFM8222 • $7

7204.
Backdrop – Arctic Scene
FRAN • 175QFM8205 • $7

7205.
Backdrop – Beach Scene
FRAN • 175QSM8042 • $8

7206.
Backdrop – Display Stand
675QFM8055 • $20

7207.
Backdrop – Easter Garden
CROW • 175QSM8152 • $7

7208.
**Backdrop –
Haunted Halloween**
VOTR • 175QFM8275 • $10

7209.
Backdrop – Heartland Forest
CROW • 175QSM8082 • $7

7210.
Backdrop – Patriotic
FRAN • 175QSM8495 • $8

7211.
**Backdrop –
Thanksgiving Feast**
VOTR • 175QFM8195 • $6

7212.
Bear Dressed As Bat
SICK • 300QFM8285 • $10

7213.
Bear with Sufboard
LYLE • 350QSM8015 • $10

7214.
Betsy Ross Lamb
RGRS • 350QSM8482 • $10

7215.
Bobcat Pilgrim
RGRS • 350QFM8172 • $10

7216.
Box of Candy
JLEE • 250QSM8095 • $10

7217.
Bunny Painting Egg
SEAL • 350QSM8115 • $10

7218.
Bunny with Basket
CROW • 250QSM8142 • $15

7219.
Bunny with Egg
VOTR • 300QSM8125 • $6

7220.
Bunny with Scarf
JLEE • 250QFM8235 • $10

7221.
Bunny with Shell
FRAN • 350QSM8005 • $10

7222.
Chipmunk
LYLE • 350QSM8002 • $10

7223.
Dog with Balloon
SIED • 250QSM8092 • $10

7224.
Dragon Dog
SICK • 300QFM8295 • $10

7225.
Duck with Egg
ANDR • 300QSM8135 • $5

7226.
Easter Basket
SEAL • 250QSM8145 • $10

7227.
Eskimo Child
CHAD • 300QFM8215 • $10

7228.
Fox on Skates
VOTR • 375QFM8303 • $10

7229.
Fox with Heart
UNRU • 350QSM8065 • $5

7230.
Ghost on Tombstone
SIED • 250QFM8282 • $10
Re-issued in 1994.

7231.
Goat Uncle Sam
JLEE • 300QSM8472 • $10

7232.
Hedgehog
SICK • 300QSM8026 • $10

7233.
Hedgehog Patriot
JLEE • 350QSM8492 • $10

7234.
Hippo
RGRS • 300QSM8032 • $15

7235.
Hugs and Kisses 3
UNRU • 350QSM8102 • $15

7236.
Husky Puppy
JLEE • 350QFM8245 • $6

7237.
Igloo
300QFM8252 • $15

7238.
Indian Bear
RGRS • 350QFM8162 • $10

7239.
Indian Squirrel
RGRS • 300QFM8182 • $6

7240.
Indian Turkey
RGRS • 350QFM8165 • $10

7241.
Lamb
PALM • 350QSM8112 • $8

7242.
Liberty Bell
JLEE • 250QSM8465 • $15

7243.
Liberty Mouse
JLEE • 300QSM8475 • $7

7244.
Mouse in Sunglasses
250QSM8035 • $10

7245.
Mouse Witch
SICK • 300QFM8292 • $8

7246.
Music Makers 3
FRAN • 350QFM8265 • $8

7247.
Owl and Pumpkin
SICK • 300QFM8302 • $15

7248.
Penguin in Hat
CHAD • 300QFM8212 • $10

7249.
Pig in Blanket
RGRS • 300QSM8022 • $15

7250.
Pilgrim Chipmunk
RGRS • 300QFM8185 • $10

7251.
Pilgrim Mouse
RGRS • 300QFM8175 • $15

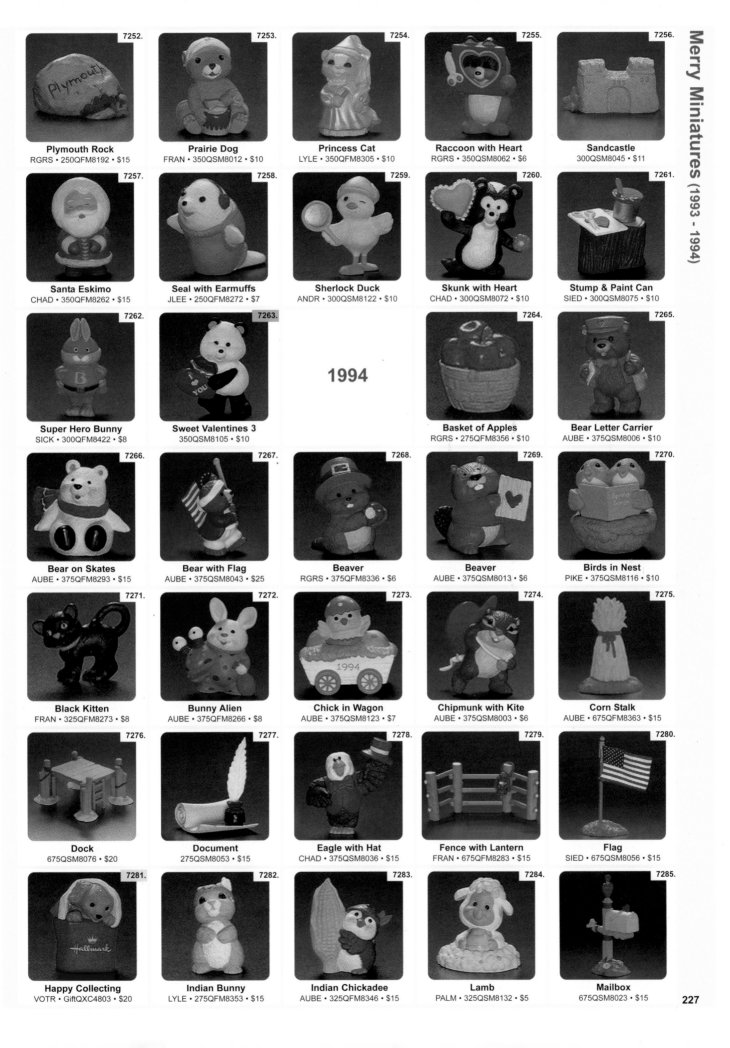

7252. Plymouth Rock
RGRS • 250QFM8192 • $15

7253. Prairie Dog
FRAN • 350QSM8012 • $10

7254. Princess Cat
LYLE • 350QFM8305 • $10

7255. Raccoon with Heart
RGRS • 350QSM8062 • $6

7256. Sandcastle
300QSM8045 • $11

7257. Santa Eskimo
CHAD • 350QFM8262 • $15

7258. Seal with Earmuffs
JLEE • 250QFM8272 • $7

7259. Sherlock Duck
ANDR • 300QSM8122 • $10

7260. Skunk with Heart
CHAD • 300QSM8072 • $10

7261. Stump & Paint Can
SIED • 300QSM8075 • $10

7262. Super Hero Bunny
SICK • 300QFM8422 • $8

7263. Sweet Valentines 3
350QSM8105 • $10

1994

7264. Basket of Apples
RGRS • 275QFM8356 • $10

7265. Bear Letter Carrier
AUBE • 375QSM8006 • $10

7266. Bear on Skates
AUBE • 375QFM8293 • $15

7267. Bear with Flag
AUBE • 375QSM8043 • $25

7268. Beaver
RGRS • 375QFM8336 • $6

7269. Beaver
AUBE • 375QSM8013 • $6

7270. Birds in Nest
PIKE • 375QSM8116 • $10

7271. Black Kitten
FRAN • 325QFM8273 • $8

7272. Bunny Alien
AUBE • 375QFM8266 • $8

7273. Chick in Wagon
AUBE • 375QSM8123 • $7

7274. Chipmunk with Kite
AUBE • 375QSM8003 • $6

7275. Corn Stalk
AUBE • 675QFM8363 • $15

7276. Dock
675QSM8076 • $20

7277. Document
275QSM8053 • $15

7278. Eagle with Hat
CHAD • 375QSM8036 • $15

7279. Fence with Lantern
FRAN • 675QFM8283 • $15

7280. Flag
SIED • 675QSM8056 • $15

7281. Happy Collecting
VOTR • GiftQXC4803 • $20

7282. Indian Bunny
LYLE • 275QFM8353 • $15

7283. Indian Chickadee
AUBE • 325QFM8346 • $15

7284. Lamb
PALM • 325QSM8132 • $5

7285. Mailbox
675QSM8023 • $15

7286.

Mouse with Flower
AUBE • 275QSM8243 • $15

7287.

Mrs. Claus
CHAD • 375QFM8286 • $10

7288.

North Pole Sign
675QFM8333 • $15

7289.

Owl in Stump
275QSM8085 • $10

7290.

Pail of Seashells
SICK • 275QSM8052 • $20

7291.

Penguin
275QFM8313 • $15

7292.

Pilgrim Bunny
375QFM8343 • $15

7293.

Polar Bears
325QFM8323 • $15

7294.

Pumpkin with Hat
CHAD • 325QFM8276 • $10

7295.

Rabbit
AUBE • 325QSM8016 • $10

7296.

Rabbit
AUBE • 275QSM8066 • $10

7297.

Rabbit with Can
AUBE • 325QSM8083 • $15

7298.

Rabbit with Croquet
AUBE • 375QSM8113 • $10

7299.

Raccoon
AUBE • 375QSM8063 • $25

7300.

Sled Dog
VOTR • 325QFM8306 • $6

7301.

Snowman
RGRS • 275QFM8316 • $15

7302.

Squirrel As Clown
VOTR • 375QFM8263 • $10

7303.

Tree
RGRS • 275QFM8326 • $10

7304.

Wishing Well
CHAD • 675QSM8033 • $10

1995

7305.

Bashful Boy
AUBE • 300QSM8107 • $15

7306.

Bashful Girl
AUBE • 300QSM8109 • $15

7307.

Bride and Groom
375QSM8067 • $7

7308.

Cameron (Bunny)
375QSM8029 • $12

7309.

Cameron (Camera)
375QSM8077 • $10

7310.

Cameron (Heart)
375QSM8009 • $10

7311.

Cameron (Pilgrim)
375QFM8169 • $10

7312.

Cameron (Pumpkin Costume)
375QFM8147 • $12

7313.

Cameron (Sled)
375QFM8199 • $8

7314.

Caroling Bear
AUBE • 325QFM8307 • $10

7315.

Caroling Bunny
AUBE • 325QFM8309 • $10

7316.

Caroling Mouse
PIKE • 300QFM8317 • $10

7317.

Chipmunk with Corn
UNRU • 375QFM8179 • $15

7318.

Christmas Tree
675QFM8197 • $15

7319.

Cinderella
LYLE • 400QSM8117 • $20

7320.
Cinderella's Stepsisters
PIKE • 375QXC4159 • $25

7321.
Cottage
AUBE • 675QSM8027 • $10

7322.
Cute Witch
AUBE • 300QFM8157 • $15

7323.
Fairy Godmother
LYLE • 400QSM8089 • $15

7324.
Feast Table
475QFM8167 • $15

7325.
Friendly Monster
AUBE • 300QFM8159 • $10

7326.
Groundhog
AUBE • 300QSM8079 • $10

7327.
Hamster with Cookie
AUBE • 325QFM8319 • $10

7328.
Happy Birthday Clowns 1
ESCH • 375QSM8057 • $8

7329.
Haunted House
675QFM8139 • $15

7330.
Koala Bear
375QSM8019 • $10

7331.
Leprechaun
AUBE • 350QSM8119 • $10

7332.
Lion and Lamb
AUBE • 400QFM8287 • $8

7333.
Mouse with Cranberries
AUBE • 300QFM8189 • $7

7334.
Mouse with Pumpkin
AUBE • 300QFM8187 • $7

7335.
Nutcracker
AUBE • 375QFM8297 • $6

7336.
Prince Charming
LYLE • 400QSM8049 • $15

7337.
Pumpkin Carriage
LYLE • 500QSM8127 • $10

7338.
Raccoon and Flower
AUBE • 300QSM8087 • $6

7339.
Rhino Mummy
AUBE • 375QFM8149 • $10

7340.
Santa
PIKE • 375QFM8299 • $7

7341.
Selby
RGRS • 300QSM8039 • $10

7342.
St. Bernard
AUBE • 375QSM8017 • $6

7343.
Stepmother
LYLE • 400QSM8099 • $10

7344.
Stylish Rabbit
375QSM8037 • $7

7345.
Toymaker Beaver
PIKE • 375QFM8289 • $6

7346.
Tree
AUBE • 675QSM8007 • $15

7347.
Turkey
AUBE • 375QFM8177 • $15

1996

7348.
Alice in Wonderland
AUBE • 1995QSM8014 • $20
Set/5

7349.
Bashful Mistletoe
AUBE • 1295QFM8054 • $16
Set/3

7350.
Blue-Ribbon Bunny
495QSM8064 • $10

7351.
Busy Bakers
795QFM8121 • $12
Set/2

7352.
Cowboy Cameron
1295QFM8041 • $18
Set/3

7353.
Easter Egg Hunt
495QSM8024 • $10

229

7354.

Giving Thanks
FRAN • 1295QFM8134 • $16
Set/3

7355.

Happy Birthday Clowns 2
ESCH • 795QSM8114 • $11
Set/2

7356.

Happy Haunting
TAGU • 1295QFM8124 • $22
Set/2

7357.

Lucky Cameron
795QSM8021 • $11
Set/2

7358.

Mr. and Mrs. Claus Bears
795QFM8044 • $11
Set/2

7359.

Noah and Friends
ESCH • 1995QSM8111 • $20
Set/5

7360.

PEANUTS® Pumpkin Patch
FRAN • 1995QFM8131 • $40
Set/5

7361.

Penda Kids
795QSM8011 • $8
Set/2

7362.

Santa's Helpers
AUBE • 1295QFM8051 • $17
Set/3

7363.

The Sewing Club
1295QFM8061 • $19
Set/3

7364.

Sweetheart Cruise
1295QSM8004 • $13
Set/3

1997

7365.

Apple Harvest – Mary's Bears
HAMI • 1295QFM8585 • $20
Set/3

7366.

Bashful Visitor
AUBE • 1295QFM8582 • $22
Set/3

7367.

Cupid Cameron
495QSM8552 • $10

7368.

Easter Parade
TAGU • 795QSM8562 • $12
Set/2

7369.

Getting Ready for Spring
TAGU • 1295QSM8575 • $14
Set/3

7370.

Happy Birthday Clowns 3
495QSM8565 • $8

7371.

Hershey's™ 1
BRIC • 1295QFM8625 • $19
Set/2

7372.

Holiday Harmony
TAGU • 1295QFM8612 • $16
Set/3

7373.

Making a Wish
TAGU • 795QFM8592 • $10
Set/2

7374.

The Nativity
HADD • 795QFM8615 • $16
Set/2

7375.

Noah's Friends
ESCH • 795QSM8572 • $12
Set/2

7376.

Peter Pan
TAGU • 1995QSM8605 • $30
Set/5

7377.

Santa Cameron
495QFM8622 • $10

7378.

Six Dwarfs
ESCH • 1295QFM8685 • $18
Set/3

7379.

Snow White and Dancing Dwarf
ESCH • 795QFM8535 • $10
Set/2

7380.

Snowbear Season
ESCH • 1295QFM8602 • $17
Set/3

7381.

Sule and Sara – PendaKids
HADD/JOHN • 795QSM8545 • $11
Set/2

7382.

Tea Time – Mary's Bears
HAMI • 1295QSM8542 • $18
Set/3

7383.

Three Wee Kings
HADD • 1295QFM8692 • $18
Set/3

1998

7384.

Bride and Groom – 1996
FRAN • 1295QFM8486 • $28
Set/2

7385.

Hershey's™ 2
BRIC • 1095QFM8493 • $16
Set/2

7386.

**Mickey's Express:
Donald's Passenger Car**
595QRP8513 • $8

7387.
Mickey's Express: Goofy®'s Caboose
595QRP8516 • $8

7388.
Mickey's Express: Mickey's Locomotive
595QRP8496 • $12

7389.
Mickey's Express: Minnie's Luggage Car
595QRP8506 • $8

7390.
Mickey's Express: Pluto®'s Coal Car
595QRP8503 • $8

7391.
Rapunzel
TAGU • 1295QSM8483 • $18
Set/2

1999

7392.
Anniversary Edition
HADD • 1295QFM8529 • $16
Set/2

7393.
Bashful Friends
AUBE • 1295QSM8459 • $14
Set/3

7394.
Christmas at Pooh's House: Eeyore®
495QRP8519 • $8

7395.
Christmas at Pooh's House: Piglet® on Base
495QRP8507 • $8

7396.
Christmas at Pooh's House: Tigger®
495QRP8527 • $10

7397.
Christmas at Pooh's House: Winnie the Pooh®
495QRP8509 • $10

7398.
Favorite Friends
KLIN • 895QFM8537 • $14
Set/2

7399.
Hershey's™ 3
BRIC • 1295QFM8497 • $17
Set/3

7400.
Park Avenue Wendy and Alex the Bellhop
FRAN • 1295QFM8499 • $23
Set/2

2000

7401.
Happy Hatters: B.B. Capps (June)
TAGU • 495QMM7008 • $7

7402.
Happy Hatters: Bonnie Bonnet (April)
TAGU • 495QMM7006 • $7

7403.
Happy Hatters: Bookie Beanie (September)
TAGU • 495QMM7017 • $7

7404.
Happy Hatters: Candy Capper (October)
TAGU • 495QMM7022 • $15

7405.
Happy Hatters: Cora Copia (November)
TAGU • 495QMM7023 • $7

7406.
Happy Hatters: Display Base
495QMM7003 • $7

7407.
Happy Hatters: Hattie Boxx (December)
TAGU • 495QMM7024 • $7

7408.
Happy Hatters: Libby Crown (July)
TAGU • 495QMM7015 • $7

7409.
Happy Hatters: Missy Milliner (May)
TAGU • 495QMM7007 • $7

7410.
Happy Hatters: Paddy O'Hatty (March)
TAGU • 495QMM7002 • $10

7411.
Happy Hatters: Panama Pete (August)
TAGU • 495QMM7016 • $7

7412.
Happy Hatters: Rosie Chapeauzie (February)
TAGU • 495QMM7001 • $8

7413.
Happy Hatters: Tiny Topper (January)
TAGU • 495QMM7000 • $8

7414.
Madame Alexander®: Fire Fighter Wendy (1997)
FORS • 695QMM7010 • $10

7415.
Madame Alexander®: Little Red Riding Hood (1991)
FORS • 695QMM7062 • $20

7416.
Madame Alexander®: Mary Had a Little Lamb (1996)
FORS • 695QMM7014 • $11

7417.
Madame Alexander®: Mop Top Billy (1996)
FRAN • 695QMM7005 • $20

7418.
Madame Alexander®: Mop Top Wendy (1996)
FRAN • 695QMM7004 • $20

7419.
Madame Alexander®: Mother Goose (1997)
FORS • 695QMM7013 • $10

2001

7420.

Madame Alexander®:
Pink Pristine Angel (1997)
FORS • 695QMM7020 • $12

7421.
Madame Alexander®:
Santa's Little Helper (1998)
FORS • 695QMM7021 • $10

7422.
Madame Alexander®:
Artiste Wendy (1997)
FORS • 695QMM7032 • $13

7423.
Madame Alexander®:
Christmas Holly (1998)
FRAN • 695QMM7031 • $16

7424.
Madame Alexander®:
Display Base
FORS • 895QMM7060 • $N/E

7425.
Madame Alexander®:
Empire Bride (1998)
FORS • 695QMM7027 • $12

7426.
Madame Alexander®:
Glistening Angel (1998)
FORS • 695QMM7030 • $14

7427.
Madame Alexander®:
Little Miss Muffet (1998)
FORS • 695QMM7029 • $13

7428.
Madame Alexander®:
Sleeping Beauty (1997)
FORS • 695QMM7034 • $13

7429.
Madame Alexander®:
Sleeping Beauty's Prince
(1999)
FORS • 695QMM7033 • $13

7430.
Madame Alexander®:
Tooth Fairy (1999)
FORS • 695QMM7028 • $17

7431.
Magic of Childhood: Blade
HADD • 495QMM7056 • $6

7432.
Magic of Childhood: Champ
HADD • 495QMM7043 • $5

7433.
Magic of Childhood: Cheer
HADD • 495QMM7059 • $5

7434.
Magic of Childhood: Glitter
HADD • 495QMM7057 • $5

7435.
Magic of Childhood: Hooper
HADD • 495QMM7055 • $6

7436.
Magic of Childhood: Hotshot
HADD • 495QMM7054 • $7

7437.
Magic of Childhood: Lucky
HADD • 495QMM7050 • $5

7438.
Magic of Childhood: Scout
HADD • 495QMM7049 • $5

7439.
Magic of Childhood: Slugger
HADD • 495QMM7045 • $7

7440.
Magic of Childhood: Speedy
HADD • 495QMM7042 • $5

7441.
Magic of Childhood: Star
HADD • 495QMM7044 • $6

7442.
Magic of Childhood: Trooper
HADD • 495QMM7058 • $5

7443.
Way to Bees:
Bee Bright (September)
TAGU • 495QMM7048 • $10

7444.
Way to Bees:
Bee Busy (June)
TAGU • 495QMM7041 • $10

7445.
Way to Bees:
Bee Caring (May)
TAGU • 495QMM7040 • $10

7446.
Way to Bees:
Bee Irish (March)
TAGU • 495QMM7037 • $10

7447.
Way to Bees:
Bee Joyful (January)
TAGU • 495QMM7035 • $10

7448.
Way to Bees:
Bee Loving (February)
TAGU • 495QMM7036 • $13

7449.
Way to Bees:
Bee Merry (December)
TAGU • 495QMM7053 • $12

7450.
Way to Bees:
Bee Playful (August)
TAGU • 495QMM7047 • $10

7451.
Way to Bees:
Bee Proud (July)
TAGU • 495QMM7046 • $10

7452.
Way to Bees:
Bee Scary (October)
TAGU • 495QMM7051 • $15

7453.
Way to Bees:
Bee Sweet (April)
TAGU • 495QMM7039 • $15

7454.

Way to Bees:
Bee Thankful (November)
TAGU • 495QMM7052 • $15

7455.

Way to Bees: Display Base
TAGU • 495QMM7038 • $10

2002

7456.

Itty Bitty Bears:
Blessing (November)
TAGU • 595QMM7085 • $10

7457.

Itty Bitty Bears:
Blossom (May)
TAGU • 595QMM7079 • $10

7458.

Itty Bitty Bears:
Booker (September)
TAGU • 595QMM7083 • $11

7459.

Itty Bitty Bears:
Candy (February)
TAGU • 595QMM7075 • $10

7460.

Itty Bitty Bears:
Dandy (July)
TAGU • 595QMM7081 • $25

7461.

Itty Bitty Bears:
Display Base
TAGU • 995QMM7077 • $12

7462.

Itty Bitty Bears:
Fisher (June)
TAGU • 595QMM7080 • $10

7463.

Itty Bitty Bears:
Peppermint (December)
TAGU • 595QMM7086 • $11

7464.

Itty Bitty Bears:
Raindrop (April)
TAGU • 595QMM7078 • $10

7465.

Itty Bitty Bears:
Snowflake (January)
TAGU • 595QMM7074 • $10

7466.

Itty Bitty Bears:
Treat (October)
TAGU • 595QMM7084 • $15

7467.

Itty Bitty Bears:
Trippy (August)
TAGU • 595QMM7082 • $10

7468.

Itty Bitty Bears:
Windy (March)
TAGU • 595QMM7076 • $10

Kiddie Car Classics

The popular Kiddie Car Classic Collection began in 1992. In 2001, the last eight cars were issued and all "active issue" cars were retired in 2001. These limited or numbered edition vehicles began as die cast replicas of the vintage Pedal Cars of yesteryear. Throughout the years of issue Hallmark expanded the line to include other small vehicles of childhood; such as those issued in the Sidewalk Cruisers line - and Custom Kiddie Cars created in the minds of the Hallmark artists. In 1997 nostalgic settings were added to the collection to offer avid fans creative display settings. Produced in two sizes - regular size and miniature. Average for regular size Kiddie Cars is approximately 4" H x 7" L x 3" W. Average for miniature Kiddie Cars is 2" H x 4" L x 1½" W.

1992

7469.

1941 Murray® Airplane
PALM • 5000QHG9003 • $185
LE 14500 • Retired 1993

7470.

1953 Murray® Dump Truck
PALM • 4800QHG9012 • $107
LE 14500 • Retired 1993

7471.

1955 Murray® Champion
PALM • 4500QHG9008 • $183
LE 14500 • Retired 1993

7472.

1955 Murray® Fire Truck
PALM • 5000QHG9001 • $272
LE 14500 • Retired 1993

7473.

1955 Murray® Tractor and Trailer
PALM • 5500QHG9004 • $300
LE 14500 • Retired 1993

1993

7474.

1955 Murray® Fire Chief
PALM • 4500QHG9006 • $175
LE 19500 • Retired 1996

7475.
1968 Murray® Boat Jolly Roger
PALM • 5000QHG9005 • $108
LE 19500 • Retired 1996

1994

7476.

1939 Steelcraft Lincoln Zephyr by Murray®
PALM • 5000QHG9015 • $128
LE 24500 • Retired 1996

7477.

1941 Steelcraft Spitfire Airplane by Murray®
PALM • 5000QHG9009 • $212
LE 19500 • Retired 1996

7478.

1955 Murray® Dump Truck
PALM • 4800QHG9011 • $139
LE 19500 • Retired 1996

7479.

1955 Murray® Fire Truck
PALM • 5000QHG9010 • $368
LE 19500 • Retired 1996

7480.

1955 Murray® Ranch Wagon
PALM • 4800QHG9007 • $145
LE 19500 • Retired 1996

7481.

1955 Murray® Red Champion
PALM • 4500QHG9002 • $142
LE 19500 • Retired 1996

7482.

1956 Garton Dragnet® Police Car
PALM • 5000QHG9016 • $89
LE 24500 • Retired 1997

7483.

1956 Garton® Kidillac
PALM • 5000QHG9094 • $80
Retired 1994

7484.

1956 Garton® Mark V
PALM • 4500QHG9022 • $79
LE 24500 • Retired 1997

7485.

1958 Murray® Atomic Missile
PALM • 5500QHG9018 • $96
LE 24500 • Retired 1997

7486.

1961 Murray® Circus Car
PALM • 4800QHG9014 • $85
LE 24500 • Retired 1997

7487.
1961 Murray® Speedway Pace Car
PALM • 4500QHG9013 • $84
LE 24500 • Retired 1997

1995

7488.

1937 Steelcraft Airflow by Murray®
PALM • 6500QHG9024 • $136
LE 24500 • Retired 1996

7489.

1937 Steelcraft Auburn
PALM • 6500QHG9021 • $164
LE 24500 • Retired 1996

7490.

1937 Steelcraft Auburn
PALM • PrizeQHG9021C • $1500
Edition Size – 8

7491.

1948 Murray® Pontiac®
PALM • 5000QHG9026 • $78
Retired 1998

7492.

1950 Murray® Torpedo
PALM • 5000QHG9020 • $170
Retired 1996

7493.

1955 Murray® Royal Deluxe
PALM • 5500QHG9025 • $88
LE 29500 • Retired 1999

7494.

1959 Garton® Deluxe Kidillac
PALM • 5500QHG9017 • $114
Retired 1996

7495.

1961 Garton® Casey Jones Locomotive
PALM • 5500QHG9019 • $140
Retired 1996

7496.
1962 Murray® Super Deluxe Fire Truck
PALM • 5500QHG9095 • $97
Retired 1995

7497.
1964 Garton® Tin Lizzie
PALM • 5000QHG9023 • $89
Retired 1997

1996

7498.
1935 Steelcraft Airplane by Murray®
PALM • 5000QHG9032 • $108
LE 29500 • Retired 1997

7499.
1935 Steelcraft by Murray®
PALM • 6500QHG9029 • $140
LE 24500 • Retired 1996

7500.
Have You Seen Me?
1937 Steelcraft Airflow by Murray®
PALM • PrizeQHG9024C • $N/E
Edition Size – 8

7501.
1941 Keystone Locomotive
PALM • 4500QHG6312 • $64
Retired 1998

7502.
1961 Murray® Super Deluxe Tractor with Trailer
PALM • 5500QHG9027 • $85
Retired 1998

7503.
1964-1/2 Ford® Mustang™
PALM • 5500QHG9030 • $84
Retired 1999

7504.
Winner's Circle Collectors 1
PALM • 5500QHG9028 • $91
Retired 1999

1997

7505.
1937 Garton Ford®
PALM • 6500QHG9035 • $140
LE 24500 • Retired 1997

7506.
1938 Garton® Lincoln Zephyr
PALM • 6500QHG9038 • $149
LE 24500 • Retired 1997

7507.
1939 Garton Ford® Station Wagon
PALM • 5500QHG9034 • $86
Retired 1999

7508.
1939 Garton Ford® Station Wagon
PALM • PrizeQHG9034C • $N/E
Edition Size – 10

7509.
1941 Murray® Junior Service Truck
PALM • 5500QHG9031 • $89
Retired 1999

7510.
1941 Steelcraft Oldsmobile® by Murray®
PALM • 5500QHG9036 • $90
Retired 1999

7511.
1956 Murray® Golden Eagle
PALM • 5000QHG9033 • $100
LE 29500 • Retired 1997

7512.
Winner's Circle Collectors 2
PALM • 5500QHG9037 • $75
Retired 1999

1998

7513.
1929 Steelcraft Roadster by Murray®
PALM • 7000QHG9040 • $94
LE 39500 • Retired 1998

7514.
1930 Custom Biplane
PALM • 5500QHG7104 • $89
Retired 2000

7515.
1930 Spirit of Christmas Custom Biplane
PALM • 6000QHG7105 • $92
Retired 1999

7516.
1932 Keystone Coast-to-Coast Bus
PALM • 4500QHG6320 • $45
LE 29500 • Retired 2000

7517.
1940 Custom Roadster with Trailer
PALM • 7500QHG7106 • $95
LE 39500 • Retired 2000

7518.
1941 Steelcraft Chrysler by Murray®
PALM • 5500QHG9044 • $70
Retired 2000

7519.
1941 Steelcraft Fire Truck by Murray®
PALM • 6000QHG9042 • $85
Retired 2000

7520.
1941 Steelcraft Fire Truck by Murray®
PALM • PrizeQHG9042C • $N/E
Edition Size – 25

7521.
1950s Custom Convertible
PALM • 6000QHG7101 • $79
Retired 1999

7522.
1955 Custom Chevy®
PALM • 5000QHG7103 • $78
Retired 2000

7523.
1958 Murray® Champion
PALM • 5500QHG9041 • $62
Retired 2000

7524.
1960s Sealtest Milk Truck
PALM • 4000QHG6315 • $49
Retired 2002

7525.
1998 NASCAR® 50th Anniversary Custom Champion
PALM • 6000QHG7110 • $70
Retired 2000

7526.
Don's Street Rod
PALM • 5500QHG7102 • $58
Retired 1999

7527.
Vintage Speedster 1
PALM • 9000QHG9045 • $151
LE 29500 • Retired 1998

7528.
Winner's Circle Collectors 3
PALM • 5500QHG9039 • $79
Retired 2000

1999

7529.
1934 Garton® Chrysler Airflow
PALM • 5000QHG9056 • $65
Retired 2000

7530.
1937 Steelcraft Junior Streamliner
PALM • 7000QHG9047 • $70
LE 39500 • Retired 2000

7531.
1941 Garton® Field Ambulance
WEBB • 6500QHG9049 • $95
LE 39500 • Retired 2000

7532.
1941 Garton® Roadster
PALM • 7000QHG9050 • $92
LE 39500 • Retired 2000

7533.
1949 Gillham™ Special
PALM • 5000QHG7108 • $70
Retired 2000

7534.
1949 Gillham™ Sport
PALM • 6000QHG7109 • $80
Retired 2000

7535.
1949 Gillham™ Sport
PALM • PrizeQHG7109C • $N/E
Edition Size – 6

7536.
1950 Holiday Murray® General
WEBB • 6000QHG9054 • $67
Retired 1999

7537.
1950 Murray® General
PALM • 5000QHG9051 • $91
Retired 2000

7538.
Vintage Speedster 2
PALM • 9000QHG9048 • $100
LE 29500 • Retired 2000

7539.
Winner's Circle Collectors 4
PALM • 5500QHG9046 • $75
Retired 2000

2000

7540.
1924 Toledo Fire Engine #6
PALM • 6500QHG9053 • $99
Retired 2002

7541.
1927 Gillham™ Honeymoon Special
WEBB • 6000QHG7111 • $85
Retired 2000

7542.
1934 Christmas Classic
5000QHG9061 • $68
Retired 2000

7543.
1935 American Tandem
PALM • 10000QHG9058 • $169
LE 24500 • Retired 2000

7544.
1938 American Graham Roadster
7500QHG9060 • $79
LE 29500 • Retired 2000

7545.
1938 Toledo Air King Airplane
5000QHG9052 • $89
Retired 2000

7546.
1938 Toledo Air King Airplane
PrizeQHG9052C • $N/E

7547.
1958 Custom Corvette®
PALM • 6500QHG7112 • $140
LE 29500 • Retired 2000

7548.
Vintage Speedster 3
PALM • 9000QHG9059 • $130
LE 24500 • Retired 2000

7549.
Winner's Circle Collectors 5
9000QHG9057 • $100
Retired 2000

2001

7550.
1928 Jingle Bell Express
6000QHG9065 • $62
LE 14500 • Retired 2002

7551.
1935 American-National Fire Tower
7500QHG9064 • $125
LE 14500 • Retired 2002

7552.
1935 Timmy Racer
WEBB • 5000QHG7118 • $65
LE 14500 • Retired 2002

7553.
1936 Gillham™ Birthday Special
WEBB • 2000QHG7115 • $55
LE 14500 • Retired 2002

7554.
1950s Red Baron Airplane
6500QHG7114 • $99
LE 14500 • Retired 2002

7555.
1957 Custom Chevy® Bel Air
WEBB • 5500QHG7117 • $56
LE 14500 • Retired 2002

7556.
Vintage Speedster 4
PALM • 9000QHG7116 • $116
LE 14500 • Retired 2002

2002

7557.
1933 Steelcraft Roadster
PALM • 7000QHG9062 • $95
LE 14500 • Retired 2002

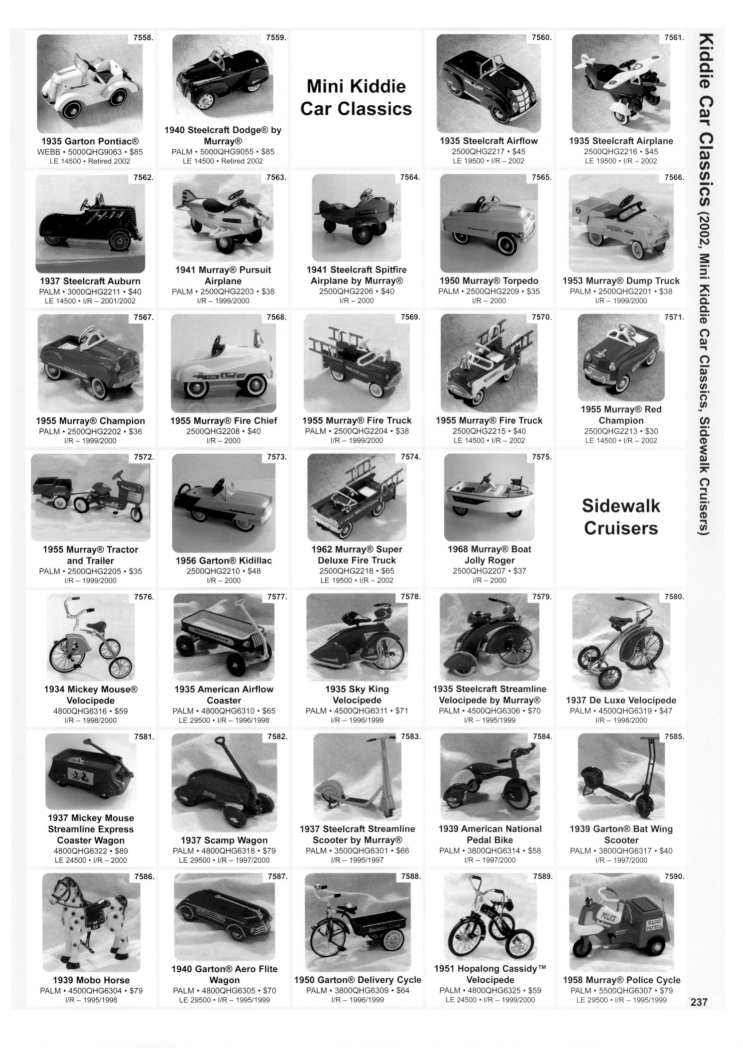

7558.
1935 Garton Pontiac®
WEBB • 5000QHG9063 • $85
LE 14500 • Retired 2002

7559.
1940 Steelcraft Dodge® by Murray®
PALM • 5000QHG9055 • $85
LE 14500 • Retired 2002

Mini Kiddie Car Classics

7560.
1935 Steelcraft Airflow
2500QHG2217 • $45
LE 19500 • I/R – 2002

7561.
1935 Steelcraft Airplane
2500QHG2216 • $45
LE 19500 • I/R – 2002

7562.
1937 Steelcraft Auburn
PALM • 3000QHG2211 • $40
LE 14500 • I/R – 2001/2002

7563.
1941 Murray® Pursuit Airplane
PALM • 2500QHG2203 • $38
I/R – 1999/2000

7564.
1941 Steelcraft Spitfire Airplane by Murray®
2500QHG2206 • $40
I/R – 2000

7565.
1950 Murray® Torpedo
PALM • 2500QHG2209 • $35
I/R – 2000

7566.
1953 Murray® Dump Truck
PALM • 2500QHG2201 • $38
I/R – 1999/2000

7567.
1955 Murray® Champion
PALM • 2500QHG2202 • $36
I/R – 1999/2000

7568.
1955 Murray® Fire Chief
2500QHG2208 • $40
I/R – 2000

7569.
1955 Murray® Fire Truck
PALM • 2500QHG2204 • $38
I/R – 1999/2000

7570.
1955 Murray® Fire Truck
2500QHG2215 • $40
LE 14500 • I/R – 2002

7571.
1955 Murray® Red Champion
2500QHG2213 • $30
LE 14500 • I/R – 2002

7572.
1955 Murray® Tractor and Trailer
PALM • 2500QHG2205 • $35
I/R – 1999/2000

7573.
1956 Garton® Kidillac
2500QHG2210 • $48
I/R – 2000

7574.
1962 Murray® Super Deluxe Fire Truck
2500QHG2218 • $65
LE 19500 • I/R – 2002

7575.
1968 Murray® Boat Jolly Roger
2500QHG2207 • $37
I/R – 2000

Sidewalk Cruisers

7576.
1934 Mickey Mouse® Velocipede
4800QHG6316 • $59
I/R – 1998/2000

7577.
1935 American Airflow Coaster
PALM • 4800QHG6310 • $65
LE 29500 • I/R – 1996/1998

7578.
1935 Sky King Velocipede
PALM • 4500QHG6311 • $71
I/R – 1996/1999

7579.
1935 Steelcraft Streamline Velocipede by Murray®
PALM • 4500QHG6306 • $70
I/R – 1995/1999

7580.
1937 De Luxe Velocipede
PALM • 4500QHG6319 • $47
I/R – 1998/2000

7581.
1937 Mickey Mouse Streamline Express Coaster Wagon
4800QHG6322 • $89
LE 24500 • I/R – 2000

7582.
1937 Scamp Wagon
PALM • 4800QHG6318 • $79
LE 29500 • I/R – 1997/2000

7583.
1937 Steelcraft Streamline Scooter by Murray®
PALM • 3500QHG6301 • $66
I/R – 1995/1997

7584.
1939 American National Pedal Bike
PALM • 3800QHG6314 • $58
I/R – 1997/2000

7585.
1939 Garton® Bat Wing Scooter
PALM • 3800QHG6317 • $40
I/R – 1997/2000

7586.
1939 Mobo Horse
PALM • 4500QHG6304 • $79
I/R – 1995/1998

7587.
1940 Garton® Aero Flite Wagon
PALM • 4800QHG6305 • $70
LE 29500 • I/R – 1995/1999

7588.
1950 Garton® Delivery Cycle
PALM • 3800QHG6309 • $64
I/R – 1996/1999

7589.
1951 Hopalong Cassidy™ Velocipede
PALM • 4800QHG6325 • $59
LE 24500 • I/R – 1999/2000

7590.
1958 Murray® Police Cycle
PALM • 5500QHG6307 • $79
LE 29500 • I/R – 1995/1999

7591.
1960 Murray® Blaz-O-Jet
Tricycle
PALM • 4500QHG6313 • $59
I/R – 1997/2000

7592.
1963 Garton® Speedster
PALM • 3800QHG6303 • $72
I/R – 1995/1999

7593.
1966 Garton® Super-Sonda
PALM • 4500QHG6302 • $71
I/R – 1995/1997

7594.
Late 1940s Mobo Sulky
PALM • 4800QHG6308 • $65
LE 29500 • I/R – 1996/1999

Kiddie Car Classics Accessories

7595.
Have You Seen Me?
1926 Steelcraft Catalog
Cover Tin Sign
795QHG5601 • $8
I/R – 2000

7596.
1943 Aviator Coloring
Book Cover Tin Sign
995QHG5602 • $10
I/R – 2000

7597.
Asking for Directions
Tin Sign
600QHG5603 • $8
I/R – 2000

7598.
Bill's Boards 1
SICK • 3000QHG3606 • $48
I/R – 1997/1999

7599.
Bill's Boards 2
SICK • 3000QHG3614 • $30
I/R – 1998/2000

7600.
Bill's Boards 3
SICK • 3000QHG3621 • $30
I/R – 1999/2000

7601.
Call Box & Fire Hydrant
SICK • 2500QHG3618 • $29
Set/2 • I/R – 1999/2000

7602.
Car Lift and Tool Box
2500QHG3608 • $26
I/R – 1998/2000

7603.
Cinder & Ella Dalmatians
SICK • 1500QHG3619 • $37
Set/2 • I/R – 1999/2000

7604.
Collector Pins
3000QHG5103 • $35
Set/5 • Also sold separately

7605.
Corner Drive-In
SICK • 7000QHG3610 • $70
LE 39500 • I/R – 1998/2000

7606.
Corner Drive-In Sidewalk
Signs
SICK • 1500QHG3616 • $31
Set/2 • I/R – 1999/2000

7607.
Don's Sign
UNRU • 1600QHG3623 • $N/E
I/R – 2000

7608.
Image shows -
Fire Station - QH03617
Flagpole - QH03620
Call Box & Fire Hydrant - QH03618
Cinder & Ella Dalmatians - QH03619
all items sold separately
Fire Station #1
SICK • 7000QHG3617 • $72
LE 39500 • I/R – 1999/2000

7609.
Flagpole
SICK • 2000QHG3620 • $40
I/R – 1999/2000

7610.
A - KC's Garage
B - Pedal Petroleum Gas Pump
C - Pedal Power Premium Gas Pump
D - Sidewalk Service Signs
E - Sidewalk Sales Signs
KC's Garage
SICK • 7000QHG3601 • $113
LE 29500 • I/R – 1997

7611.
KC's Motor Oil
1500QHG3609 • $17
I/R – 1998/2000

7612.
Menu Station with
Food Trays
SICK • 3000QHG3611 • $30
Set/3 • I/R – 1998/2000

7613.
Newspaper Box &
Trash Can Set
2000QHG3613 • $20
Set/2 • I/R – 1998/2000

7614.
Parking Sign
UNRU • 800QHG3630 • $10
I/R – 2000

7615.
Pedal Petroleum Gas Pump
SICK • 2500QHG3602 • $25
I/R – 1997/1999

7616.
Pedal Power Premium
Lighted Gas Pump
SICK • 3000QHG3603 • $49
I/R – 1997/1999

7617.
Sidewalk Sales Signs
SICK • 1500QHG3605 • $23
Set/2 • I/R – 1997/1999

7618.
Sidewalk Service Signs
SICK • 1500QHG3604 • $23
Set/2 • I/R – 1997/1999

7619.
Stop Sign
UNRU • 1000QHG3622 • $19
I/R – 2000

7620.
Street Signs
UNRU • 1000QHG3629 • $20
Set/2 • I/R – 2000

7621.
Streetlamp
UNRU • 1500QHG3624 • $39
I/R – 2000

7622.
Table and Benches
SICK • 2000QHG3615 • $31
Set/3 • I/R – 1999/2000

Legends in Flight

The Legends in Flight collection was produced by Hallmark Cards, Inc from 1999 through 2001. This collection features die cast scale replicas of famous planes from the Wright Flyer to modern day jets.   The scale of these numbered editions ranges from 1:48 to 1:72.

7623.

Bleriot XI
2500QHA1009 • $35
2000

7624.

Curtiss P-40 Warhawk
3000QHA1000 • $59
1999

7625.

Curtiss R3C-2 Seaplane
3200QHA1002 • $59
2000

7626.

F-14A Tomcat
4800QHA1006 • $50
1999 • Limited Edition – 24500

7627.

F4U-ID Corsair
3200QHA1008 • $349
2000

7628.

F-86F Sabre
2700QHA1010 • $59
2000

7629.

Fokker Dr.I "Red Baron"
3500QHA1005 • $99
1999

7630.

Gee-Bee R1 Sportster
3000QHA1015 • $125
2001

7631.

Jasta 6 Fokker
3000QHA1021 • $95
Limited Edition – 12500

7632.

P-38 Lightning Marge
3000QHA1017 • $65
2001

7633.

P-51 Mustang Big Beautiful Doll
3000QHA1016 • $99
2001 • Limited Edition – 12500

7634.

Ryan NYP Spirit of St. Louis
3000QHA1004 • $129
2000

7635.

SPAD XIII "Smith IV"
3200QHA1003 • $55
2000

7636.

SPAD XIII Escadrille SPA 3
2800QHA1014 • $55
2001 • Limited Edition – 12500

7637.

Vega 5B
3000QHA1007 • $55
2000

7638.

VX-9 F-14 Blackcat
3200QHA1020 • $55
2001 • Limited Edition – 12500

7639.

The Wright Flyer
3500QHA1001 • $49
1999 & 2001 Limited Edition – 12500

ALPHABETICAL INDEX

Below is an alphabetical listing of all the Ornaments and Tree Toppers featured in this Value Guide. Series, Series Complements, and Collections are in bold type with all their items listed alphabetically beneath the title.

Keepsake Christmas Ornaments

#

A

M

Z

Kiddie Car Classics

Accessories

Tree Toppers

Full Size

Miniature

SERIES INDEX

Below is a page index of all the series ornaments featrued in this value guide, including their colorways and complements. Final ornaments of a series are designated with an "F" after their series number.

Copyrights and Trademarks

Lost, broken, stolen?
or maybe you just missed it?

How do you find past year Hallmark ornaments?

Each Christmas and throughout the year we receive numerous phone calls from around the world asking about past year ornaments. Many people are unaware that the Hallmark Secondary Market exists and assume that past year ornaments are impossible to find.

NOT true! If you discover that a treasured heirloom is broken or missing it is possible to purchase a replacement. Perhaps looking through this value guide you've made a list of items you wish you had; purchasing these past year Hallmark ornaments is easy at Hooked on Ornaments.

Simply go online to www.hookedonhallmark.com

Hooked on Ornaments offers one of the largest inventories of Hallmark ornaments available anywhere. Our inventory begins with ornaments produced in 1973 and spans the decades to the current year's ornaments.

Our entire inventory is listed online and is continually updated throughout each day as new items come in. Simply follow the easy to use website instructions to make your purchase. Not comfortable ordering online? Call us at (913) 888-4311 we'll be happy to take your order over the phone.

ALSO FROM BANGZOOM

TV Guide: The Official Collectors Guide

The book covers the complete run of this American icon from the first, regional, television listing guides which Walter Annenberg created in order to form the magazine in 1953, to the last issue in guide format on October 9, 2005. The book includes full color reproductions of every *TV Guide* cover ever printed. It is both a collectors guide with a pricing supplement included, as well as a retrospective view of the medium.

List Price: $29.95

The Birth of Christmas
by Clifford F. Boyle

This perfect holiday gift book by author, Clifford Boyle, uses lyrical expression and spiritual imagery to educate readers on the birth of Christ. This book is illustrated with hauntingly beautiful 19th century photographs of little girls posing as angels. At a time when many seek to remove elements of religion from modern-day life, *The Birth of Christmas* helps its readers discover the true meaning of Christmas.

List Price: $19.95

Cyber Screams: Numchuks' Curse
and
Cyber Screams: Numchuks' Revenge

A series of young adult novels set in Salem, Massachusetts, which recount the adventures of teenagers caught inside a video game. *Cyber Screams* is actually a multimedia project including live events featuring screaming competitions, a web site where people can upload their screams and download screaming ring tones for cell phones, and a role playing game.

List Price: $12.95 each

BoydsTracker Plush Guide
and
BoydsTracker Resin Guide

Packed with hundreds of fabulous 4-color photographs, up-to-date secondary market prices, and important news and information. In addition, each *BoydsTracker* Handbook will profile collectors and collections across the country, as well as provide you with websites dedicated to Boyds critters.

List Price: $21.95 each

Ty Beanies Tracker

TyTracker Guides include a year by year account starting with the 1993 introduction, tips and insight for maximum visibility and enjoyment of your collection, great websites for collectors, information and pictures of current releases, and secondary market prices for Beanie Babies. The book is packed with thousands of fabulous 4-color photographs, up-to-date secondary market prices, and important news and information.

List Price: $16.95

Available at www.bangzoom.com or call 1-800-589-7333.

DEC 1 8 2007 7

11/27/07